Morasha Kehillat Yaakov

Essays in Honour of
Chief Rabbi Lord Jonathan Sacks

בית דין צדק לונדון

מגיד
MAGGID

US Living & Learning

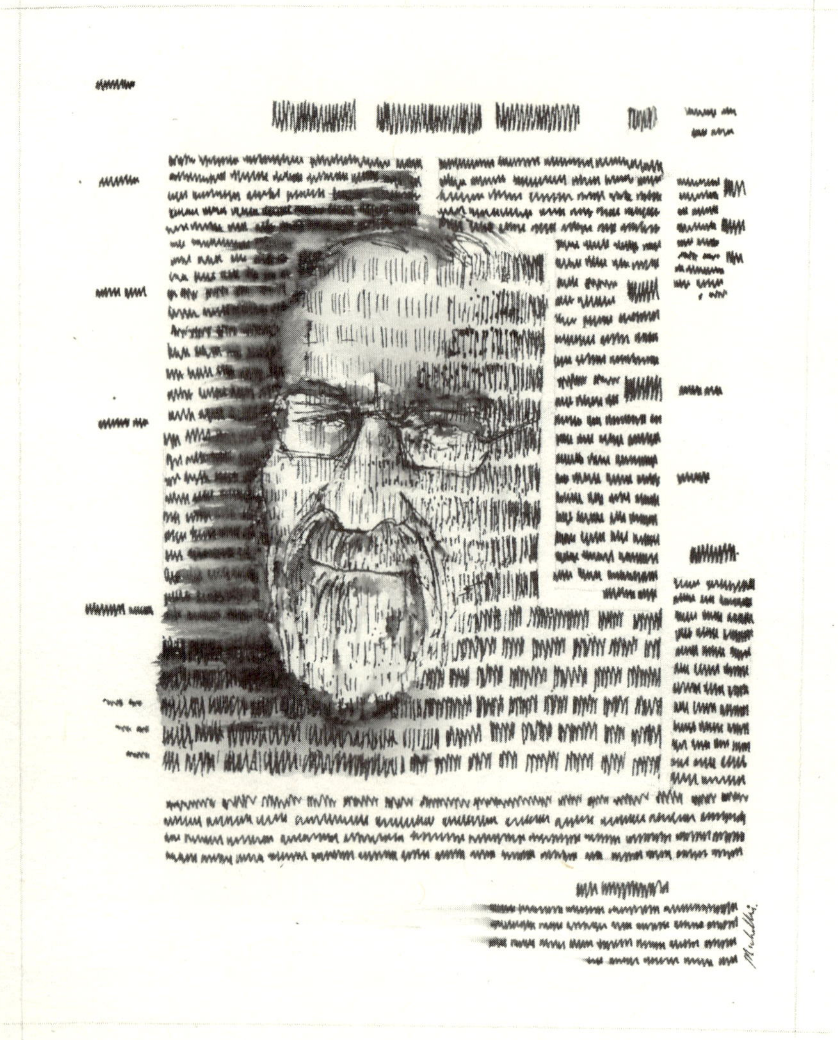

Original sketch by Jac Nicholls

Jacqueline Nicholls is a visual artist and Jewish educator based in London, UK. Her work has been included in significant exhibitions on contemporary Jewish art in Israel, America, and Europe. She is currently drawing the Talmud, a page a day.

MORASHA KEHILLAT YAAKOV

Essays in Honour of Chief Rabbi Lord Jonathan Sacks

Edited by:
Rabbi Michael Pollak
Dayan Shmuel Simons

United Synagogue
London Beth Din
Maggid Books

Morasha Kehillat Yaakov
Essays in Honour of
Chief Rabbi Lord Jonathan Sacks

First Edition, 2014

Maggid Books
An imprint of Koren Publishers Jerusalem Ltd.

POB 8531, New Milford, CT 06776-8531, USA
& POB 4044, Jerusalem 91040, Israel
www.korenpub.com

The publication of this book was made possible
through the generous support of *Torah Education in Israel.*

ISBN 978 1 59264 390 5, *hardcover*

A CIP catalogue record for this title is
available from the British Library

Printed and bound in the United States

Rav Avraham Yisrael Hacohen Kon
(born Lodz 1892–died London 1968)

A great *Talmid Chacham* who led his family through the darkest of nights to put down Jewish roots in a new fertile land.
From his children, grandchildren,
great-grandchildren, and great-great-grandchildren

Contents

Editor's Preface
Rabbi Michael Pollak xi

Introduction
Chief Rabbi Ephraim Mirvis xv

Resurrection of the Dead
Rabbi Joseph B. Soloveitchik 1

The Responsibilities of the Recipient of Charity
Rabbi Aharon Lichtenstein 11

Is There a Talmudic Logic?
Rabbi Adin Steinsaltz 31

Introduction: Rabbi Sacks as 'Chief of Rabbis'
Rabbi Mordechai Ginsbury 45

SECTION I

WORLD JEWRY

An Approach to Dangerous and Terminal Illness
Rabbi Dr Akiva Tatz 51

The Nature of Natural Events
Rabbi Shmuel Goldin 75

The Klal Mensch
Rabbi Warren Goldstein 85

The Emergence of the Written Text of the Talmud
Rabbi Meir Triebitz 93

Halakhic Perspectives on Gun Control
Rabbi Shlomo M. Brody 101

Praying for the Government in the United Kingdom and Elsewhere
Rabbi Dr Barry Freundel 113

Mitzva Observance: The Appropriate Motivation
Rabbi Anthony Knopf 129

Priestly Predicaments: Analysing Sof Tuma Latzet According to Maimonides
Rabbi David Shabtai 139

Lashon HaRa, Democracy, and Social Media
Rabbi Gil Student 163

SECTION II

ANGLO-JEWRY

The Memorial Prayer in Minhag Anglia
Dayan Ivan Binstock 173

A Visit to the Home of a Victorian Chief Rabbi
Rabbi Shlomo Katanka 187

A Scholar in Their Midst: Dayan Jacob Reinowitz
Rabbi Eugene Newman 203

Rashi's Davar Aḥer: Alternatives, Concurrency, and Creative Interpretation
Rabbi Dr Harvey Belovski 223

VeZot HaTorah: The Origin and Objective of the Hagbaha Ritual
Rabbi Dr Jeffrey M. Cohen 239

A Talmudic Discourse on Kevod Habriyot
Rabbi Dr Alan Kimche 253

Should Jews Buy German Products?
Rabbi Mendel Cohen 265

Parallel Thinking: Science, Torah, and Cognitive Dissonance
Rabbi Moshe Freedman 273

'Married to an Angel': The Halakhic Conundrum Concerning Elijah and Other Transcendent Spouses
Rabbi Jonathan Hughes 297

A Brief Study of Responsa Literature
Rabbi Geoffrey Hyman 307

The Blessings over the Torah: Their Meaning and Some Practical Applications
Rabbi Michael Laitner 313

Unfair to Teraḥ?
Rabbi Zorach Meir Salasnik 319

Until Elijah Comes: Two Views of the Messianic Era
Rabbi Rashi Simon 323

"For Zion's Sake I Shall Not Remain Silent": May We Publicly Criticize the State of Israel?
Rabbi Gideon D. Sylvester 331

Ein Mazal LeYisrael: Randomness and Providence in Jewish Destiny
Rabbi Nissan Wilson 343

The Curse of Yoav: The Deadly Challenge of Jewish Education
Rabbi Raphael Zarum 351

Contributors 359

About Rabbi Jonathan Sacks 365

Editor's Preface

There is a longstanding tradition that the London Beth Din presides over the production of a volume of rabbinic essays in honour of an outgoing Chief Rabbi. That the role of Joint Editor should have fallen to me in this instance of celebrating the remarkable years of service of Lord Rabbi Sacks is highly appropriate. I have had the privilege of knowing Rabbi Jonathan Sacks for approximately forty years. During that time a rather introspective genius has gone from rabbi to principal of Jews' College to Chief Rabbi to Knight and then to Lord and now has become a Jewish leader of the highest rank worldwide. Many have confused the nonchalance with which he bears these titles with an ease of progress and effort. Nothing can be further from the truth.

One of our earliest meetings was a gathering of a group of rather pretentious young Orthodox men selected on the basis of an alleged familiarity with both Torah study and academic philosophy. Rabbi Sacks addressed us on the topic of "Wittgenstein and the implications of his later work on Jewish philosophy".

I was puzzled after ten minutes, bamboozled within twenty, and utterly lost by the half-hour mark. I withdrew into a rather non-Wittgenstinian inner world and spent the remaining hour reliving great meals I had eaten over the previous years. Unsure as to whether I was in the majority, I was curious when the host, a graduate of Gateshead and Mir yeshivot, launched into a long and convoluted question in Yiddish. Rabbi Sacks, with excessive politeness and self-deprecation, apologized but said he was unable to reply as he did not understand Yiddish.

"Well now you know how we have felt for the last ninety minutes," trumpeted the questioner triumphantly.

Never again did I ever hear Rabbi Sacks take an audience for granted. Every lecture, every *shiur* was perfectly crafted for the moment, exquisitely constructed to achieve clarity and resonance, and entirely relevant to the audience before him. His output is ever-evolving, ever-improving, pushing at the boundaries of previous achievements to attain the levels which have become his trademark. There is no ease in this progress and whilst many contributors to this volume will rightfully laud Rabbi Sacks for his unusual natural talents, let me remind all those who have admired him that this talent has been carefully nourished through toiling amongst the world of books of every discipline, crowned by his unstinting efforts in the Library of Jewish Learning.

It has been both an education and a delight to act as Joint Editor with Dayan Shmuel Simons of the London Beth Din in bringing *Morasha Kehillat Yaakov* to completion. Working with the *dayanim* of the London Beth Din under Dayan Gelley has been a revelation. There are many aspects of these volumes which were not of their precise choosing but in the name of *aḥdut* they showed that true leadership is not the relentless application of authority but can also involve real partnerships and mutual respect.

The *rabbanim* of the United Synagogue must be commended for the quality of their contributions. We were unable to include them all and I apologize to those that were left out. The professional leadership of the United Synagogue showed enthusiasm and generosity and must also be thanked. Our other contributors are the giants of Torah and halakha from around the globe. The name Jonathan Sacks galvanised some of our greatest thinkers to put pen to paper and we are grateful to them all.

A word for our publishers, Maggid Books, and especially Matthew Miller, Rabbi Reuven Ziegler, and Tomi Mager. Their patience, skill, and enthusiasm for their first-ever venture into a publication of this type would suggest that they are "to the manor born". Similarly, our editorial team of Rav Moshe Gross, Rav Tuvia Freund, Rav Fishel Adler, Eliot Pollak, and Agi Erdos may not have worked on a comparable volume previously but they have produced a text which is both highly accurate and very readable. Rav Tuvia is worthy of special mention for using his rabbinic contacts in soliciting some of the most interesting of our articles. Recognition is due to our US editor Rabbi Gil Student, who procured and reviewed all of the marvellous contributions which came from "over the water". He was ably assisted by Rabbi Sam Taylor.

We have benefited from a superb management team who found sponsors, read articles, kept me on the right track, and at all times offered sound advice. Ashley Rogoff, Louise Brayam, and Dr Brian Berenblut – many thanks.

Personally, I have been helped firstly by my various employers – UJIA, PaJes, LSJS, US, and Ner Yisrael who by never trying to correct my very occasional absences and late arrivals have made a vital contribution to this project's realization. Finally, as is customary, I would like to thank my family – my wife Ruth, children Kara and Aaron, Eli and Abi, and grandchildren Ari, Yoni, Rikki, and Dani. I have been hugely motivated by a desire to show you all that your loyalty and love would raise me to achieve worthwhile results in life. No expression of gratitude could possibly suffice.

Michael Pollak
Sivan 5774/June 2014

Introduction

Chief Rabbi Ephraim Mirvis

A famous passage in the Torah states, "Moses commanded us the Torah. It is an inheritance [*morasha*] for the congregation of Jacob" (Deut. 33:4). A mishna in Avot seems to contradict this: "Rabbi Jose says, 'Prepare yourself to learn Torah, for it is not an inheritance [*yerusha*] for you'" (Avot 2:12). The Maharam of Rothenburg explains that there is a significant difference between the terms *morasha* and *yerusha* and therefore there is no contradiction between these two teachings.

An earlier reference to *morasha* appears in Exodus 6:8: "And I will bring you to the land, concerning which I lifted up My hand to give it to Abraham, to Isaac and to Jacob; and I will give it to you for an inheritance [*morasha*]." The Maharam explains that while *yerusha* is an inheritance received in a passive capacity, where the recipient is not required to do anything in order to attain it, *morasha* is a legacy for which we are required to work hard, not only to obtain it in the first place, but also to retain it. According to the Maharam, Exodus 6:8 teaches that the Land of Israel is the sacred legacy (*morasha*) of the Jewish people. However, it is not an automatic entitlement; we must strive to attain it.

Similarly, the phrase *morasha kehillat Yaakov* implies that we must invest time and energy in our Torah, showing complete dedication and commitment to its study both day and night. It is our calling, as individuals and as a people, to be challenged by it and to grow through it. We are worthy of our inheritance only by virtue of our engagement with its timeless truths.

As spiritual head of the United Hebrew Congregations of the Commonwealth, Rabbi Lord Jonathan Sacks inspired a generation to invest in Torah study, to work hard to internalize the values of our tradition and to keep them at the heart of community life. He strengthened our appreciation of our sacred *morasha* by championing high-quality Jewish education. His many lectures, *shiurim*, broadcasts and writings are testament to this.

It is, therefore, particularly appropriate for *Morasha Kehillat Yaakov* to be produced in tribute to Rabbi Lord Sacks upon his retirement. The quality and depth of the assembled articles is clear to see. A welcome feature of this Festschrift is the broad selection of rabbinic thinkers and personalities who have contributed. Chief Rabbis appear together with *rashei yeshiva*; world famous *poskim* share space with historians, philosophers and scientists; Israeli scholars sit alongside colleagues from the Diaspora.

The breadth of scholarly material in this work is a well-deserved and most fitting tribute to Rabbi Lord Sacks, whose mastery and fusion of our tradition with different fields of academic endeavour have made him a compelling advocate for Jewish values and ideals.

The authors hail from our own communities, showcasing Anglo-Jewry at its finest, and from around the world. Collectively they create a global *kehilla* of open and engaged scholars, partnering in the glorification of God, His Torah and the values and ideals it represents. This is at the very core of the institution of the Chief Rabbinate and is personified by my illustrious predecessors. I greatly value and cherish the inheritance that I have received from the Emeritus Chief Rabbi and through this volume we thank him for all he has done for the Jewish people.

Chief Rabbi Ephraim Mirvis
Adar II 5774/March 2014

Resurrection of the Dead

Adapted from a lecture by Rabbi Joseph B. Soloveitchik *z"l*[1]

In the mid-twentieth century, Rabbi Soloveitchik (1903–93), known by many simply as the Rav, gave a series of lectures on Jewish philosophy and on the fundamental principles of belief. In this, the third lecture of that series, the Rav enlightens us on the essential nature of the resurrection of the dead and why it is so fundamental to our belief system.

While the resurrection of the dead is often thought of as a demonstration of God's supernatural mastery over the world, the Rav points out that such an approach misses the point. Unlike the Greeks, who denied the reality of evil and its expression in death, Judaism accepts evil face on. There is evil, there is death, and they are part of the world, but they are also to be overcome. That is the true meaning of ethics. The resurrection should therefore be understood as the ultimate victory against evil. In its essence, it is the realization of the underlying ethical nature of the world. For now, death

1. The lecture on which this chapter is based was given as part of the Rav's courses in Bernard Revel Graduate School of Yeshiva University between 1948 and 1952. Thanks are owed to OU Press for giving permission to publish these lecture notes and annotations, which will be included in a forthcoming book to be published by OU Press. The notes of the lecture were originally taken by R. Yaakov Homnick and were edited and annotated under the auspices of OU Press by R. Meir Triebitz and Dr. Aaron Segal. Thanks also to R. Stephen Kaye for his introduction above and further editing.

and evil are part of reality, but eventually God will remove them and restore the world to the pristine and inherently good state in which it was first created.

Through this, the Rav explains why the Greeks could not accept resurrection, but instead developed the concept of the immortality of the soul. Whereas resurrection is a victory over death, the immortality of the soul side lines the significance of death and attributes worth only to the soul. The Greeks could not accept that there could be a change in the nature of existence. So either death and evil were to be a part of the unchanging fabric of the world, but that was unfathomable, or the true essence of a person was to be found only in his unchanging, eternal soul.

The Rav continues to explain that this understanding of the resurrection as an ethical act of God can also shed light on the true nature of our belief in God. The Greeks viewed God as a cosmological force. Hermann Cohen claimed that God is an ethical norm. Judaism denies both extremes. God is not an abstract concept; He is more real than anything else, but our belief in Him encompasses the fact that He is also the ethical driver of the world. It is that relationship that the prophets emphasized and re-emphasized throughout their calls to the Jewish people. And it is that relationship on which we focus when we express our belief in Him.

INTRODUCTION

The last of Rambam's thirteen fundamental principles of faith is the belief in the resurrection of the dead. As we will demonstrate, this belief was always part of Jewish thought and, unlike similar beliefs held by other cultures, the Jewish belief in resurrection reflects its unique approach to death, evil, and the ethical nature of the world, and is not limited to a belief in God's ability to effect a supernatural phenomenon.

Seemingly, this principle follows from the twelfth principle, the belief in the advent of the Messiah. However, there is a sharp distinction between them. The belief in the advent of the Messiah is primarily a historical hope. The messianic era represents the historical climax of the Jewish people. Its essence lies in the fact that it will bring about the political redemption of the Jewish people. The Talmud states: "The only difference between this world and the days of the Messiah is with regard to the subjugation to foreign kingdoms" (Berakhot 34a), a statement which Rambam fully embraces in his discussion of the messianic era.[2] This political redemption will provide the context in which the Jewish people

2. See Rambam, *Hilkhot Melakhim* 11:1 and *Hilkhot Teshuva* 9:2, where Rambam emphasizes that the messianic era will not bring about any fundamental change in the nature of man and the world, but only freedom from political oppression.

will be able to fully devote themselves to the love of God.[3] As such, the messianic era should be understood as a development of the Jewish people's status within history. The same forces that determine history are involved in creating the messianic era.

The resurrection of the dead lies in contradistinction to this. The resurrection of the dead is essentially eschatological; it is beyond history and has nothing to do with Jewish history. Indeed, it is something that cannot develop from within history based on the forces that determine it; it is a supernatural phenomenon. Nevertheless, its essence does not reside in that aspect. Rather, as we will explain, the essence of the resurrection of the dead is that it is a reflection of the ethical nature of the creation itself.

LIBERAL JUDAISM'S ATTACK ON THE RESURRECTION

Liberal Judaism attacked the concept of the resurrection of the dead. We will turn to their stated reasons shortly, but first we have to understand the context for this rejection.

In the middle of the nineteenth century, the Reform movement in both Germany and the United States viewed Judaism as essentially theological. The only thing that was real for liberal Judaism was dogmatic theology. This, however, was a mistake. The halakha is not theological. Our scholars only occasionally dabbled in theology. Some even rejected any attempt to reduce Judaism to dogmatic structures. Both Radbaz and Ḥatam Sofer rejected any attempts to formulate fundamental principles of belief.[4] Even those who embraced the principles did not dwell on them. Their main focus was the analysis of halakha, and the basis of halakhic discourse is academic freedom, but in theology there can be no criticism. While the halakha does have a philosophy, it is different from theology. When the liberal movement eliminated halakha from Judaism, it reduced it to a theological religion. The philosophy of Judaism became theology.

Mendelssohn, the father of liberal Judaism, was nonetheless a child of the traditional world, a child of a halakhic home. In his book *Jerusalem* he cast doubt upon the importance of dogmatic principles. For him, Judaism was more concerned with law than with beliefs. All of those who associated themselves with liberalism tried to refute Mendelssohn because they looked to him as a father. As far as they were concerned, the only possible foundation of Judaism is dogma.

3. Ibid.
4. Radbaz (Rabbi David Ibn Zimra), responsum §344; Rabbi Moses Sofer, *Responsa Ḥatam Sofer, Yoreh De'a* §356.

Once they had divorced the foundations of Judaism from halakha, and based it on dogma, they then proceeded to define which dogmas were acceptable to them. They immediately deemed the resurrection of the dead a non-Jewish concept. They did so for various reasons.

The Tanakh does not speak much about the resurrection. Prophecy devoted itself to reward and punishment and to the advent of the Messiah, but there are only a few passages regarding the resurrection of the dead. Bible critics claimed these passages were a later appendage to the prophets that was introduced to Judaism during the time of the Hasmoneans. They claimed that the notion had been developed by zealots who fought and thereby placed themselves in great danger, and who therefore needed an assurance of resurrection. The zealots used this hope as a political instrument in order to cultivate nationalistic passions. Thus the passages in Tanakh that refer to it were viewed as later additions, and the idea was defined as being alien to the prophets of the first Jewish commonwealth. Liberal Judaism therefore eliminated the resurrection from the canon of Jewish beliefs, claiming it was not an authentically Jewish belief.

Furthermore, the belief in the resurrection was viewed as rationally unacceptable, and that provided further reason to dispense with it. This perception was not new, but has a long history. During the Middle Ages, the dogma was perceived as contradicting the fundamental claims of Greek philosophy. As a result of this, even those medieval Jewish thinkers who tried to harmonize Jewish thought with Greek philosophical principles did not attempt to do so with regard to the resurrection. So, for example, Rav Saadya Gaon, who deals with the resurrection towards the end of his philosophical treatise *Emunot VeDe'ot*, cites numerous passages from our sages, but refrains from subjecting the concept to philosophical analysis. Their perception was accurate. From the perspective of Greek philosophy, resurrection is completely absurd, as we will explain below. For this reason, the Greeks don't even mention it. The doctrine was brought to the Occidental world primarily by the Christians, who took the concept from Judaism and used it for their own purposes, as part of the story of salvation, crucifixion, and resurrection.

ANCIENT JEWISH ROOTS OF THE RESURRECTION

However, the claim that the resurrection of the dead is not an authentic Jewish belief is totally unfounded. The concept is found explicitly in the book of Daniel (12:2) and even earlier, in the story of the son of the Shunammite (II Kings 4:8–37), and it was fully accepted by the sages. The resurrection provides the central theme of the second blessing of the *Amida*, which makes numerous references to it and even concludes, "Who resurrects the dead". The content and order of the *Amida* is very ancient. Indeed, the Talmud (Megilla 17b) states that it was composed by the men of the Great Assembly, which included a number of prophets.[5]

The Mishna in the last chapter of Sanhedrin mentions two principles: the divine origin of the Torah and the resurrection of the dead, and brands anyone who denies that these beliefs have a basis in the Torah as a heretic. That chapter continues to cite the heated debates between the Pharisees and the Sadducees with regard to belief in the resurrection. Although their disputes, for the most part, were with regard to matters of halakha, the underlying philosophical debate is clearly sensed. One revealing example of this is cited by the Talmud in Berakhot (54a). In the Temple, at the conclusion of each blessing, the phrase "Blessed is the Lord forever" was inserted. The word "forever" (*ad ha'olam*) literally means "until this world" and was misconstrued by the Sadducees of the time, who claimed there was only one world. To dispel their claims, the sages modified the blessing to state *min ha'olam ve'ad ha'olam* – literally, "from this world to the next world". Changing the formula of a blessing was very uncommon and demonstrates how important the issue was.

ETHICAL NATURE OF THE RESURRECTION

Let us now return to explain the essential nature of the resurrection. As we mentioned, the main theme of the second blessing of the *Amida* is the resurrection of the dead. The blessings and prayers that were instituted by the sages were based on the prophets, both in their structure and their phraseology. Our case is no exception. The template for this blessing is to be found in the prayer of Hanna (I Sam. 2). This is a very old prayer, even as far as the Bible critics are concerned. In her prayer one can identify three themes:

1. God associates Himself with the outcasts of the world.[6]
2. The serenity that derives from wealth or the stress of poverty do not mean anything. God can change a person's situation from one extreme to the other in an instant.[7]
3. Among all this, the theme of resurrection suddenly enters. Hanna declares, "God puts to death and brings to life, takes down to the grave and brings

5. See Rambam (*Mishne Torah, Hilkhot Tefilla* 1:4), who identifies the authors of the *Amida* as the court of Ezra.
6. See verses 4–5, 8.
7. See verses 7–9.

up" (v. 6). This is understood by our sages (Sanhedrin 92b) as a metaphor for the resurrection.

Based on its context here, we can understand the nature of the resurrection. Overall, Hanna's prayer speaks of the suffering of a barren mother who is longing for a child. When she was finally blessed with a child, she saw something that strengthened her hope in the elimination of evil. If she was helped, man will be helped when he is poor or sick. The second blessing in the *Amida* is patterned after this prayer: it speaks of God's strength in the performance of ethical acts, and repeatedly mentions resurrection as one of those acts. We see, then, that resurrection is not being described as a miracle, but rather as an ethical act of God, an expression of God's kindness and benevolence; it is part of the motif of the world's having an ethical order. Indeed, the blessing makes no reference to the cosmic forces: the rising and setting of the sun, the movement of the stars, and so on; it deals only with ethical deeds. The theme of the blessing is not that God acts through cosmic forces, but rather that God is ethical.[8] This means that God decrees and acts upon His decrees; He is faithful to carry out His promises and sanctions. Our faith in God's ethical order is often shaken, but the sages knew that if God has promised something, He will not disappoint us. Resurrection, then, is ultimately an expression of God correcting the ethical order of the world. God grants life even to the dead. It is this aspect that provides the essential nature of the resurrection of the dead. It is not just a belief in the supernatural but rather a belief in the ethical acts of God.

OVERCOMING DEATH

Everything we have said should be contrasted with the origin of the Christian belief in the resurrection. The fear of death is the most acute fear in modern man. All of science is harnessed to combat this fear. In Christianity, the fear of death was what brought about their belief in the resurrection. And it was further used as a political tool. Christians who went to the lions in Antioch did so with happiness because of this belief. But the ancient Jewish belief was neither motivated by a fear of death nor employed as a political tool.

In Judaism there was never any horror or excitement about death. The verses speak about death calmly, as a natural phenomenon: "You will come to your

8. While it is certainly true that the blessing is about God's might, it is not about His might in changing the physical world, but about God's unique ability to perform ethical acts of benevolence and to overcome the presence of evil.

fathers in peace" (Gen. 15:15). However, the fact that death is considered natural should not lead us to believe that it is a part of the *fabric* of the world. Quite the contrary is the case. The basis of ethics in Judaism is that God's creation is *inherently* good. "And God saw everything that He had created and behold it was very good" (Gen. 1:31). Creation is perfect, without any evil, and any deterioration is the product of man: "God saw that man was wicked... and that the thoughts of his heart are only evil all the day" (Gen. 6:6). Kohelet says, "God made man just but they desired to complicate things" (7:29). So while we experience evil, death, absurdity, and other negative forces, these phenomena are not an integral part of reality. They appeared after creation, and they are an appendage to it. The role, then, of the resurrection of the dead is to restore creation to its perfect, inherently good, state. All the prophecies of Isaiah treat the era of the resurrection of the dead as involving changes in cosmic occurrences: "The light of the moon will be like the light of the sun" (Isa. 30:26).[9] His prophecy expresses a real and total restoration and rehabilitation of nature and man. Resurrection of the dead is therefore freedom from the forces of nature as part of the restoration of a deteriorated world. One of the sources for the resurrection is the verse, "You will be gathered to your fathers and rise up" (Deut. 31:16).[10] That is to say, the *natural* phenomenon of death will be overcome and the world restored to the inherent goodness with which it was created.

It is helpful to compare our view to the Greek view. The Greeks did not understand the resurrection – it appeared absurd to them. The possibility of life after death, for Socrates and Plato, could only be realized in the immortality of the soul. Resurrection is Jewish and not Greek. The immortality of the soul is Greek and not so much Jewish. Similarly, the Christians speak of the resurrection and not so much of immortality. They inherited this from us.

Why did the Greeks have such trouble with the resurrection? The answer is that for the Greeks, if evil is real, then by definition it must be an essential and unchanging part of nature and so cannot be eliminated.[11] The solution then was to claim that evil is not real, that death is not true.

The Greeks divided nature into two parts, form and matter: form is perfect; matter is chaos and evil. Matter never undergoes any intrinsic change or

9. See Sanhedrin 91b.

10. See Sanhedrin 90b.

11. This was an essential part of Greek philosophy, especially in the thought of Plato, that at the most fundamental level of reality, there is no change or development in the basic nature of the world. See below.

metamorphosis. There is no cosmic or biological evolution. And so there can never be any change in matter for the better. If matter were real, evil would perforce be a permanent fixture of reality. Moreover, it would make the world incomprehensible because if the world is rooted in matter then it is rooted in chaotic elements, which can neither be analysed nor classified. So the Greeks 'solved' this problem by claiming that in fact matter isn't *real*; and hence neither is evil.[12] This then is the basis of their concept of immortality of the soul. Matter is not real, death is not real, but the soul is real, and the soul doesn't die. As such, evil is not part of the fabric of the world and the world can be understood.

Judaism, on the other hand, was able to solve the problem of evil without denying the truth of its existence.[13] According to Jewish belief, the World to Come is a continuation of the present world. This is evident in the blessing, mentioned above, that the sages formulated for use in the Temple, "From this world to the next world". In addition, the sages say, "This world is the corridor leading to the World to Come" (Avot 4:21). The two worlds are not separate; they are continuous with one another. So all the suffering, affliction, and death in this world, which are brought about by human acts of evil in this world, will be redressed by the ethical God, Who will bring justice to the next world.

To summarize: death did not shock or amaze either the prophets or the sages. It was the Greeks who were baffled by it. The Greek concept of the immortality of the soul was a denial of death and evil; they could conceive of no other way of grappling with it. For the prophets and the sages, on the other hand, death was real, and it challenged man to rectify the world through ethical action. Ultimately, in the resurrection, he would receive his reward in the World to Come.

For the Greeks, there was a longing for a golden age, but that itself has no purpose. Jews do not have a notion of a golden age, but we have eschatology, which means that history has a purpose. There is a guarantee for full realization of an ethical system, but that will only be realized in the Next World. In this world, ethics do not find their final realization. The messianic era is part of the resurrection of the dead insofar as it brings the world closer to its full realization of an ethical existence.

---

12. Plato held that only forms have reality, and matter is a mere shadow of the forms. Admittedly, it was more difficult for Aristotle to maintain such a strong view because of his doctrine of hylomorphism (all natural substances are composites of form and matter).
13. It is true that Rambam in the *Guide* (III:10) appears to deny evil. However, his is a minority opinion in the Jewish tradition.

In Judaism there is no dichotomy between death and life. Death is not metaphysical, but rather a natural part of life. But death also has ethical content. Although it is a natural, biological event, it is brought about through man's sin. Through resurrection man will ultimately be the recipient of God's goodness and the fulfilment of God's ethical personality.

APPLICATION TO OTHER PRINCIPLES

An understanding of the resurrection of the dead also highlights the essential nature of the other principles of belief. Let us take, for example, the existence of God. What concept of God are we employing when we affirm God's existence? For the Greeks, God could be understood only from a cosmological approach. Jewish medieval philosophy, which was based on Greek thought, similarly identified God as the Being who played a certain role in cosmological dynamics. Approaching God from a cosmic or biological viewpoint allows us to gain primary principles that are beyond the cosmos and underlie all cosmic occurrences and phenomena. Many Jewish thinkers also had Platonic influences.

Hermann Cohen claimed that the Jews never had a cosmic approach to God. According to Cohen, such an approach is pagan. There is some truth to this view. Crude pagan ideas place God within, or as continuous with, the world. Seeing God as a continuation of the cosmos is paganism. Therefore, Cohen viewed Spinoza as a pagan philosopher. For Cohen, the Jewish approach to God is rather different. God is not to be discovered through the cosmos but through ethics. He gives man a norm, and this norm dictates certain acts. The norm is independent of man's will; its source is God. This is our approach.

Cohen, however, was too radical because he denied the reality of Jewish history and tradition. This was because he was essentially a Kantian philosopher. He denied a cosmic God and looked only for an ethical one. Moreover, his concepts of God and Judaism were purely abstract; he tried to synthesize Judaism with German philosophy, but this led him to abandon the concrete conceptions of God and Judaism. This type of approach was typical of medieval Christian thinkers such as Aquinas, who accepted an Aristotelian cosmic approach to God.

Protestantism was a reaction to abstract theological reasoning and searched for truth inside man as an ethical being. Its most important figure was Martin Luther, who also brought about the renaissance of the study of the Bible. This was more similar to the approach of the prophets. If one takes a look at the Bible, one can appreciate that while the reality of God is absolute, not just an abstract concept, His relationship to the world is an ethical one, not just a cosmological one. It is this aspect that we focus on when we consider our belief in God.

The Responsibilities of the Recipient of Charity

Rabbi Aharon Lichtenstein[1]

One of the fundamental problems troubling those involved in providing welfare services, whether as individuals or as part of the public system, is the issue of the recipient's participation in and attitude towards the assistance extended to him. There is, of course, no disagreement that it is preferable to involve the recipient in the process of and responsibility for providing for his

1. Translated by David Strauss.
Author's note: The appearance of this essay comes after its initial publication in Hebrew in 1979. Hence, its current republication, addressed in a new language to a different community with its own set of fundamental problems, may be, in some sense, out of step. However, as anyone even vaguely familiar with the basic issues confronted here is fully aware, these remain persistent communal, philosophical, and ethical concerns. מרובים צרכי עמך ודעתם קצרה "Thy people's needs are manifold and their means confined." That encapsulation, excerpted from a major *piyyut*, remains no less relevant today than upon the occasion of its initial formulation. Moreover, in certain respects, through the systole and diastole of the global economy, the situation has only worsened, with entire populations in quest of some amelioration of their lot. This essay is a modest contribution to aid in that quest. The publication of this essay is further motivated by the retirement of Chief Rabbi Jonathan Sacks after more than two decades of service to the Anglo-Jewish community, in recognition of his unflagging efforts to cope with social and moral concerns of the modern world, and in recognition of his desire to share Jewish, Torah values in dealing with both universal and specifically Jewish issues.

own needs. In countless cases, however, the recipient appears not to be working as hard as he can, preferring rather to cast the burden upon others. In such circumstances, a piercing question arises: To what degree and by what means should we press for the increased participation of the recipient of aid, and to what extent is it possible to condition the extension of assistance on his readiness to share the burden? Regarding this point opinions differ, and Judaism's position on the matter must be clarified.

The search for an answer will initially be directed, of course, to the halakhic sources, but it will be quickly discovered – and this fact in itself demands investigation – that the fundamental sources in which an answer might be found, whether in the writings of *Ḥazal* (the early sages) or in the works of the *poskim* (decisors), are exceedingly meagre. There are, indeed, limitations that determine who is fit to receive charity. The Mishna in *Pe'ah* states: "One who has two hundred *zuz* must not take gleanings, forgotten produce, field-corner produce, or poor man's tithe."[2] This standard, which applies to agricultural gifts to the poor, was codified as law with respect to charity as well, and was translated into buying power by several *rishonim* (medieval authorities): "Some [authorities] say that these standards applied only in their [*Ḥazal*'s] day, but today one may take [charity] as long as one does not have capital from which to support oneself and one's household from the profits thereof; and this is a well-reasoned position."[3] This limitation does not, however, resolve our difficulty. First of all, it is restricted to *tzedaka* – that is to say, monetary assistance – and does not relate to assistance falling into the category of *gemilut ḥasadim* (acts of kindness) that must be extended to "both the poor and the rich".[4]

---

2. *Pe'a* 8:8.

3. *Yoreh De'a* 253:62. The Mishna cites the measure of two hundred *zuz* with respect to agricultural gifts for the poor, but not with respect to charity. Logically, there are grounds to distinguish. Gifts for the poor are in limited supply, and so it is necessary to establish priority regarding eligibility. This is not the case regarding charity, which is not limited, in the sense that one can give twice. The *rishonim* discuss this point; see *Or Zarua, Hilkhot Tzedaka*, sec. 14. This measure, however, has been codified as law regarding *tzedaka*.

   It should be noted that the measure mentioned here, which is based on the assumption that the needy person will live on his earnings and not eat away at his capital, seems to be exceedingly far-reaching when applied to modern economic reality. A person with an average-sized family (4-5 people) in the United States, who receives a 10% return on his investments (a very good rate), would be considered a pauper who is entitled to receive charity according to this definition, even if he has capital approaching $150,000! [Ed. note: This was written in 1979, and the figure would now have to be multiplied.] This seems to be very novel, and the matter must be examined in light of the *Tur*'s comment (*Yoreh De'a* 253), "It is all in accordance with the time and the place."

4. Sukka 49b.

Second, while it provides a test of means that excludes the "rich" from receiving charity, it does not offer any guidelines on how to relate to one who qualifies for charity because he is poor.[5]

More directly related to our issue is a tannaitic dispute that appears to reflect different attitudes towards the matter at hand:

> Our rabbis taught: "Lend" [Deut. 15:8] – this [refers to someone] who has nothing and does not wish to be supported [from charity], to whom we give [money] as a loan, and afterwards we give [it] to him as a gift. "Surely lend him" [ibid.] – this [refers to someone] who has [resources of his own] but does not wish to support himself [from them], to whom we give [money] as a gift, and afterwards we collect [it] from him after his death. [These are] the words of Rabbi Judah.
>
> But the sages say: [If] he has [resources of his own] but does not wish to support himself [from them], we are not bound to [help] him. How, then, do I explain "surely lend him"? The Torah spoke in the language of people [and we cannot infer anything from this phrase].[6]

We see that, according to Rabbi Judah, a person who has means that he does not wish to exploit is still defined as a needy person who must be granted aid – and this seems to derive from the mitzva of *tzedaka,* not only from *gemilut ḥasadim* – though he does not acquire the charity money permanently. His situation is similar to that of a person who is stuck on the road without any money, about whom Rabbi Eliezer ruled that "if a property-holder was travelling from place to place and in need of taking gleanings, forgotten produce, field-corner produce, or poor man's tithe, he may take them, but when he returns home he must repay them."[7] According to the sages, however, the fact that a person "has resources of his own" in and of itself exempts others from all responsibility to take care of his needs – at least, in the framework of the mitzva of gifts for the poor.

Despite the striking difference in attitude reflected in this dispute, it does not suffice to resolve our question, for we must define the term "someone who has

5. It seems to me that regarding other laws – e.g. *arakhin* or a *korban oleh veyored* – a person without any money but capable of going out to work should be regarded as a poor person; his liability should be evaluated in terms of his present situation. Our discussion here relates to the realms of charity and *ḥesed* (loving-kindness), regarding which the determining factor is not the poverty in and of itself, but the distress that is suffered. This point requires further examination.
6. Ketubbot 67b.
7. Pe'a 5:4.

resources of his own". Rashi explains: "[This means] someone who has resources of his own, but does not want to support himself from his own resources, but rather from charity, and he afflicts himself with hunger."[8] Maimonides (Rambam) sharpens the point: "A wealthy person who starves himself and is miserly about his assets, not to eat or drink from them – we do not concern ourselves with him."[9] This formulation was codified as law in the *Shulḥan Arukh.*[10] We appear to be dealing with a miser who prefers to save and starve – or to take from charity – rather than use the resources already in his possession. Despite all the criticism that may be levelled against a passive person who takes no steps to help himself, he certainly cannot be compared to a person of means who mortifies himself. Even one who maintains that the latter is responsible for his lot can require the extension of assistance to the former.[11]

A clearer source relates to a mitzva that involves not *tzedaka* but *gemilut ḥasadim* – *perika* and *te'ina* (unloading and loading, the positive commandment to help another person unload an animal that has fallen under its load, or to help the master reload the animal that has fallen): "[If the owner] went and sat down and said: 'Since the commandment is upon you, if it is your wish to unload, unload,' he is exempt, as it is said: 'With him' (Ex. 23:5)."[12] This case parallels our question; but the talmudic passage is unclear as to whether this limitation is unique to the mitzva of *perika* and *te'ina,* based on the scriptural decree "with him", or whether it embodies a principle that is valid regarding the provision of assistance in general.

In his commentary on the Torah, *Keli Yakar,* Rabbi Solomon Ephraim Luntshitz adopted the second position. The verse reads, "If you see the donkey of him that hates you lying under its burden, and would forbear to unload it (*veḥadalta me'azov lo*), you shall surely unload it with him" (Ex. 23:5). As opposed to Rashi, *Keli Yakar* understands that the word *veḥadalta* grants an allowance *not* to offer assistance:

8. Ketubbot 67b, s.v. *yesh lo.*

9. *Hilkhot Matenot Aniyim* 7:9.

10. *Yoreh De'a* 253:10.

11. A similar idea is found in Rambam regarding the restoration of lost property: "If one wilfully causes his property to become lost, we do not concern ourselves with him. How so? If one leaves his cow untied in a shed that has no door and goes away... although a spectator may not take the property for himself, he is not obligated to return it. For Scripture states: 'Which he has lost' (Deut. 22:3), excluding cases where one wilfully causes property to become lost" (*Hilkhot Gezela VeAveda* 11:11). It is, of course, possible to distinguish between one who refrains from earning a living and one who is negligent about his property.

12. Bava Metzia 32a.

> Therefore it says "and would forbear to unload it", because the word "*lo*" does not mean "with him", and [therefore we infer that] you are permitted to forbear helping him when he refuses to join you in the task. This is an answer to some of the poor among our people who cast themselves on the community and refuse to do any work, even if they are able to engage in certain work or in some other endeavour that will bring food to the table, and they complain if they are not given whatever they are lacking. For God did not command this, but rather, "You shall surely unload it *with him*," and "you shall surely *help him* to lift them up again" [Deut. 22:4]. For the needy person must do whatever is in his power to do, and if, despite all his efforts, he fails to earn a living, then every man in Israel is obligated to support and strengthen him, and to provide him with whatever he is lacking, and unload even a hundred times.[13]

As opposed to *Keli Yakar*'s certainty about this issue, we find that one of the *rishonim*, Meiri, was in doubt about the matter. In the course of a discussion regarding a talmudic passage in Tractate Kiddushin, he mentions the two possibilities raised above, without deciding between them. The Gemara there states that if a man says to a woman, "Be betrothed to me with this loaf of bread," and she tells him to give it to a dog, she is betrothed to him only if the dog is hers, for only then is she regarded as having derived benefit from the dog's eating. In the continuation the Gemara raises the following question, which it leaves unresolved: "Rav Mari asked: What if the dog was pursuing her? [Do we say that] in return for the benefit of saving herself from it she resolves and cedes herself to him; or perhaps she can say to him, 'By Torah law you were indeed bound to save me'?"[14] On this Meiri comments:

> If a dog was pursuing her in order to bite her, the validity of her betrothal is in doubt. For perhaps owing to his saving her, she resolved and ceded herself to him; or perhaps, since he too is bound to act in that manner, for the Torah states: "Neither shall you stand idly by the blood of your neighbour" [Lev. 19:16], she does not resolve to cede herself.
>
> Now this applies when she agrees to return the value of the loaf of bread, for if not, he is not obligated to save her, for one is even forbidden to save himself with another person's money. But there are some who say

13. *Keli Yakar*, Ex. 23:5.
14. Kiddushin 8b.

> that, while he himself is forbidden to save himself with another person's money when the owner of that money is not there, nevertheless whenever the owner of the money is present, he is obligated to save [the person in distress] even on condition that he will not recover from him what he spends on saving him, and he cannot collect that sum from him in court. This is what [the sages] said regarding the mitzva of unloading: "[If the owner] went and sat down and said: 'Since the commandment is upon you, if it is your wish to unload, unload,' he is exempt, as it is said: 'With him.'" The reason is that it says "with him", but without that [stipulation] he is obligated.
>
> And if you propose to say that even where it does not state "with him", the same law applies – [I would answer that in the case of unloading an animal one is exempt from helping if the owner refuses to participate] because the injured party can help him, and if he refuses to help, others do not have a greater obligation to save his money than he does. Furthermore, there we are only dealing with the rescue of money, but here we are dealing with the rescue of the person himself, and that person is unable to save himself. [The onlooker] is obligated to rescue him even if it causes him a [financial] loss, and he cannot collect from him what he expended on his rescue.[15]

Meiri's words are instructive in and of themselves, but in light of the silence of the rest of the *rishonim* and *poskim* they do not negate the fact that our problem has

15. *Beit HaBeḥira*, ad loc., s.v. *haya kelev*. Meiri mentions two distinctions connected to separate realms: 1) regarding the nature of the recipient's need – rescuing someone as opposed to saving his property; 2) regarding the degree of possible self-help – the ability of the person in need to rescue himself as opposed to the provision of money. The relationship between the two is unclear. Perhaps, according to Meiri, each factor is a sufficient condition – that is to say, one must rescue his fellow, even if that other person is capable of saving himself; and on the other hand, as long as the person in need cannot help himself, he is not obligated to compensate the rescuer, even if the latter only saves his property. Alternatively Meiri may believe that each factor is a necessary but not sufficient condition, so that there is no obligation to help another unless both factors are present, as in the case in Kiddushin. This question, of course, has halakhic and conceptual ramifications. But in any event, Meiri raises the issue of comparing the *mitzvot* of *perika* and *te'ina* to other realms of assistance.

It should be added that Meiri speaks of an obligation to compensate the rescuer after the fact and not about his obligation to rescue in the first place. But the two are interdependent. If Reuven is obligated to save Shimon, Shimon is not obligated to compensate him, for Reuven was not acting on his behalf, but in God's service, though Shimon was the direct beneficiary. This should be compared to the dispute among the *rishonim* about whether a physician is permitted to receive compensation for his services; see *Kitvei HaRamban* (ed. R. Chavel), ii. 43–5.

not been exhaustively discussed in the primary halakhic sources. This silence has left us room to investigate the matter. Specifically, it has left room for a discussion which is based on the halakhic foundations of *gemilut ḥasadim,* and which by its very nature will bring under consideration the moral and ethical dimension of the issue. It is precisely this dimension which is problematic, for our problem is rooted in a clash of values.

On the one hand, there is the mitzva of *gemilut ḥasadim,* with all the halakhic and social obligations that it involves, which demand of the benefactor maximal assistance. On the other hand, there is a demand, perhaps no less legitimate, to minimize the aid and to share the burden. This demand has at least three components – one related to the limitations of the benefactor, and two connected to the welfare of the recipient.

First of all, since we are talking about dividing up limited resources, generosity towards one person always comes at the expense of his fellow. This consideration is true about every act of benevolence, but it is especially valid with respect to a public system built on the money and efforts of others upon whom are made coercive demands. While its full political weight is felt in trying times, whether because of real political and economic limitations or against the background of a taxpayers' revolt, it is valid at all times as a moral argument.[16]

Second, unqualified giving, even were it possible in a practical and budgetary sense, is liable to clash with the fundamental objective of any relief plan: the rehabilitation of the recipient to the point that he is capable of standing on his own two feet, emotionally and functionally. If Rambam placed at the top of the scale of charity "a person who assists a poor Jew by providing him with a gift or a loan or by accepting him into a business partnership or by helping him find employment – in a word, by putting him where he can dispense with other people's aid",[17] then it is clear that the highest goal in helping a person who has already fallen low is the restoration of his independence. It is precisely abundant aid that is liable to block the attainment of this goal, by intensifying the reality and the feeling of dependence to the point of degeneration and even paralysis of the emotional strengths that are necessary for the rehabilitation process.

---

16. Logically speaking, there is, of course, room to distinguish between *tzedaka* as a mitzva devolving upon the individual, which applies even with respect to those who fail to help themselves, and the distribution of communal charity funds. A similar distinction was proposed by several *rishonim* regarding a person's right to receive charity before he sells all of his expensive belongings; see Ketubbot 68a, and *Tosafot,* s.v. *kan; Rif* (ad loc.); *Tur, Yoreh De'a* 253.
17. *Hilkhot Matenot Aniyim* 10:7.

Lastly, the participation of the recipient is necessary for his moral benefit, no less than for his psychological benefit. One need not adopt the views of Emerson or Carlyle in order to understand that the ability to assume responsibility is a measure not only of a person's emotional health, but also of his spiritual level. Therefore, whenever this ability is impaired by unconditional giving – or by giving to which only minimal conditions are attached – there exists an additional dimension to the clash of values that stands at the centre of our problem.

This clash necessitates a dual approach, in the spirit of the words of Napoleon – that a person should pray as if everything depended upon God and fight as if everything depended upon him. When relating to the needy person, one ought to encourage personal effort and stimulate self-confidence. This point has a universal moral foundation, but it draws special strength from the enormous emphasis that Judaism places on free will. The entire halakhic system is based on one central fact:

> Free will is bestowed on every human being. If one desires to turn towards the good way and be righteous, he has the power to do so. If one wishes to turn towards the evil way and be wicked, he is at liberty to do so. And thus it is written in the Torah: "Behold, the man is become as one of us, to know good and evil" [Gen. 3:22] – which means that the human species had become unique in the world, there being no other species like it in the following respect, namely, that man, of himself and by exercise of his own intelligence and reason, knows what is good and what is evil, and there is none who can prevent him from doing that which is good or that which is evil.[18]

The following conclusion may be drawn from this: "Since every human being, as we have explained, has free will, a man should strive to repent, make verbal expression of his sins, and renounce them, so that he may die penitent and thus be worthy of life in the World to Come."[19] What is true about penitence on the spiritual level is true about rehabilitation on the emotional and physical level. Since every man has free will, he must strive to rehabilitate himself and confront his problems and overcome his difficulties so that he may live and merit life in this world. The Torah asserts that, factually, a person is capable; and therefore, morally, he is obligated. *Pouvoir oblige.* The recognition of free will is a basic

18. Rambam, *Hilkhot Teshuva* 5:1.
19. Ibid. 7:1.

component in the Torah's outlook regarding the provision of support in general, and it is especially important in assessing the recipient's contribution to his own rehabilitation. His personal responsibility stands at the centre of Judaism's ethics and psychological understanding, and its practical expression in treating the needy is strengthening the feeling and reality of his personal strength.

As for our problem, this emphasis does not exhaust itself in encouragement. It seems to me that it expresses itself in criticism as well. The final Mishna in Tractate Pe'a states: "And anyone who is not in need of taking and does take will not die before he will be dependent on others."[20] The Mishna does not clarify – nor does the Gemara here or anywhere else – to whom it refers. But it is difficult to assume that it is talking about someone who has two hundred *zuz* (or fifty with which he conducts business), but nevertheless takes charity. Such a person is a real thief. It may be suggested that we are dealing here with a person who does not have two hundred *zuz*, but is capable of earning such a sum. Formally such a person is entitled to accept gifts for the poor, because he is still defined as a pauper. But since he refuses to develop his abilities, *Ḥazal* do not spare him their criticism. Indeed, when Rambam codifies the Mishna's ruling he adds a source but ignores the element of theft: "He who, having no need of alms, obtains alms by deception will, ere he die of old age, fall into a dependency that is real. Such a person comes under the characterization: 'Cursed is the man that trusts in man' [Jer. 17:5]."[21] It is not clear whether the evil lies in his lack of trust in God and his reliance on man – which belongs, of course, to the realm of the relations between man and God – or in the unnecessary exploitation of people through their deception. In any event, we are certainly not dealing here with real thievery, and it is reasonable to assume that the reference is to someone who is capable of sharing the burden but renounces his responsibility.

When relating to the benefactor, the situation is reversed. His readiness and obligation to extend assistance to another person is in great measure a function of that other person's weakness. The stronger the recipient, the more the inclination to help him dissipates. Here, then, is the essence of our question, and it divides into two. First of all, does there exist, fundamentally, an obligation to offer charity and acts of kindness to a person who is capable of overcoming his

20. Pe'a 8:9.

21. *Hilkhot Matenot Aniyim* 10:19. The Mishna cites the parallel verse "Blessed is the man who trusts in God" (Jer. 17:7) as the source of its ruling regarding "one who is in need of taking and does not do so", but it does not explain itself. Rabbi David Ibn Zimra (Radbaz) (ad loc.) understands that Rambam inferred "that 'blessed' implies 'cursed'".

difficulties but for some reason gives up? Second, if indeed such an obligation exists, what factors determine the circumstances in which it applies?

The answer to the first question is connected to the roots of the obligation of *gemilut ḥasadim*. This mitzva has two different but complementary sources. The first is the foundation of interpersonal *mitzvot*, the great principle of Rabbi Akiva: "And you shall love your neighbour as yourself" (Lev. 19:18). This fact should be understandable by itself, but in any event, Rambam explained it:

> The following positive commands were ordained by the rabbis: visiting the sick, comforting the mourners, joining a funeral procession, dowering a bride, escorting departing guests, performing for the dead the last tender offices, acting as a pallbearer, going before the bier, making lamentation [for the dead], digging a grave and burying the body, causing the bride and the bridegroom to rejoice, providing them with all their needs [for the wedding]. These constitute deeds of kindness performed in person and for which no fixed measure is prescribed. Although all these commands are only on rabbinical authority, they are implied in the precept: "And you shall love your neighbour as yourself," that is: what you would have others do to you, do to him who is your brother in the Law and in the performance of the commandments.[22]

The second source is one of the focal aspects of *mitzvot* between man and God: "You shall walk in His ways" (Deut. 28:9). Some of the actions included in Rambam's list under the heading of "loving your neighbour" are characterized by the Gemara in Sota as part of the obligation of *imitatio Dei*, imitating God:

> Rav Ḥama son of Rav Ḥanina said: What means the text: "You shall walk after the Lord your God" [Deut. 13:5]? Is it possible for a human being to walk after the *Shekhina*; for has it not been said: "For the Lord your God is a devouring fire" [Deut. 4:24]? But [the meaning is] to walk after the attributes of the Holy One, blessed be He. As He clothes the naked, for it is written: "And the Lord God made for Adam and for his wife coats of skin, and clothed them" [Gen. 3:21], so do you also clothe the naked. The Holy One, blessed be He, visited the sick, for it is written: "And the Lord appeared unto him by the oaks of Mamre" [Gen. 18:1], so do you also visit the sick. The Holy One, blessed be He, comforted mourners, for it is

22. *Hilkhot Evel* 14:1.

> written: "And it came to pass after the death of Abraham that God blessed Isaac his son" [Gen. 25:11], so do you also comfort mourners. The Holy One, blessed be He, buried the dead, for it is written: "And He buried him in the valley" [Deut. 34:6], so do you also bury the dead.[23]

On the practical level the two sources of obligation are generally congruent, but from a theoretical perspective they are very different; and with respect to our question, it seems to me that a distinction should be drawn between them. Based on "You shall love your neighbour as yourself," it is unreasonable to obligate a person to do for his neighbour that which he would not make the effort to do for himself. The obligation towards his neighbour and his neighbour's right to receive acts of kindness seem to be conditioned on his neighbour's readiness to do his share. However, the obligation to imitate God does not depend upon any other factor, for God's kindness is unconditional. There is indeed a saying that "God helps those who help themselves," which implies that He does not help those who don't help themselves; and whole generations of people who ignored the unfortunate, and even abused them, soothed their conscience with this idea. This, however, is not the Jewish outlook.

Judaism does, of course, recognize man's obligation to do whatever he can to provide for his own needs, and even forbids reliance on miracles, but it does not condition divine assistance on man's contribution. With all the importance of "earthly stirring" (*itaruta diletata*), "heavenly stirring" (*itaruta dile'eila*) does not depend upon it: "'And I will be gracious to whom I will be gracious' [Ex. 33:19] – although he may not deserve it. 'And I will show mercy to whom I will show mercy' [ibid.] – although he may not deserve it."[24] Loving-kindness is provided even to one who is "undeserving" because he is negligent in his efforts to advance himself. The quantitative and qualitative dimensions of God's mercy – "'Abundant in mercy' – to those who need mercy because they have not sufficient merits [to be saved by them]"[25] – include, without a reckoning, even those who are undeserving. If God did a reckoning, who in fact would be able to stand? The same applies, then, to man's obligation to engage in acts of loving-kindness out of a desire to follow in God's ways. Not with calculated

23. Sota 14a. The Gemara here relates to the verse: "You shall walk after the Lord your God" (Deut. 13:5), whereas Rambam, who speaks about character traits rather than about actions (*Hilkhot De'ot* 1:6), cites the verse, "You shall walk in His ways" (Deut. 28:9). It is necessary to understand the difference between the verses, but this is not the forum to expand upon the matter.

24. Berakhot 7a.

25. Rashi, Ex. 34:6.

and planned steps, and not out of considerations of reciprocity and mutuality, agreement and parallelism, does man walk in the footsteps of his Creator, but precisely with acts of kindness that breach the dams of balance and reckoning; which are given, as formulated by Rambam, even to "one who has no right at all to claim this from you."[26]

It is possible to suggest another difference between the two sources of obligation, as far as our question is concerned, if we examine the nature of the relationship to the other person. *Gemilut ḥasadim* that is based on love of one's fellow has an interpersonal foundation. The recipient is considered a party with standing, a *gavra* (subject), in the framework of mutual, if not equal, relations. Thus it is reasonable to condition the obligation of the one party on the conduct of the other. But *gemilut ḥasadim* that is based on walking in the ways of God is not rooted in a relationship with another person. It constitutes a personal moral and religious challenge in the context of which the other person is merely the field of activity, sort of a *ḥeftza* (object) with which the mitzva is fulfilled – and it applies even to animals, for "the Holy One, blessed be He, sustains [all creatures] from the horns of wild oxen to the eggs of vermin"[27] – but not a party with any standing in the matter. Thus it follows that the negligence of the recipient does not negate the obligation of the benefactor. Is a reckoning done with the horns of wild oxen and the eggs of vermin?

According to the aforementioned understanding, there is indeed an obligation to help the needy who do not do their part to help themselves to the best of their ability. But the fact that this duty is based on only one of the two sources of obligation of *gemilut ḥasadim* dulls its force. While on the one hand, as we have seen, the obligation to imitate God has wider application than the obligation to love one's neighbour, on the other hand, its validity is less clear and obligating. With respect to the nature of the mitzva and its obligation, the love of one's neighbour, as it is applied on the practical level – over and beyond the fulfilment in the heart that it requires – is similar to other *mitzvot*. In specified circumstances the actions that are demanded by this duty are as obligatory as wearing tzitzit and constructing a railing on one's roof, as blowing a shofar and donning tefillin. There is no escaping its demands, and it may not be pushed aside because of other spiritual demands, barring cases in which any mitzva would be pushed aside (because of the rule that one who is already engaged in a mitzva is exempt from performing other *mitzvot*, or the like). For example, one may not neglect

26. *Guide of the Perplexed*, III. 53.
27. Shabbat 107b.

gemilut ḥasadim that is connected to the love of one's fellow only in order to study Torah, just as one may not neglect the mitzva of lulav for that reason. Moreover, it is possible that such actions are not merely means to achieve an emotional relationship, or even the external expression that reflects that relationship, but rather the practical dimension of the mitzva.

For this reason, the mitzva also divides, if only by rabbinic decree, into various branches, each one being defined as a mitzva in its own right, to the point that Rambam discusses the priority given to each one: "It seems to me that the duty of comforting mourners takes precedence over the duty of visiting the sick, because comforting mourners is an act of benevolence towards the living and the dead."[28]

As I heard on various occasions from my revered teacher, Rabbi Joseph B. Soloveitchik, such a discussion is possible only if we assume that, by rabbinic law, the comforting of mourners, the visiting of the sick, and similar obligations each become separate entities and categories. Otherwise it would be necessary to adopt a contextual approach that would judge each case according to its specific circumstances. It seems to me that it is reasonable to add that the basis for this development is the Torah level of the mitzva, which grants *gemilut ḥasadim* and its specific actions the status of fulfilments of the mitzva of "You shall love your neighbour as yourself."

The nature of benevolence that is based on walking in God's ways is entirely different. This mitzva, in all its aspects and with all its offshoots, outlines a direction and a goal, but it lacks absolute and specific content. The moral action that it demands is part of an overall spiritual effort. Thus it competes with parallel efforts for a person's attention to and allocation of his resources – such as expanding Torah study or deepening the fear of heaven; and circumstances are possible in which a person's priorities will demand that preference be given to other objectives at the cost of *gemilut ḥasadim*. In this framework the focus is upon the personality of the benefactor, which is fashioned and expressed through his actions, and not the needs of the recipient. To the extent that his spiritual personality can develop more in other ways, the needs of the other person – inasmuch as they are just a means and not the objective – are liable to be set aside. Therefore, basing a specific act of *ḥesed* exclusively on walking in God's ways narrows the dimensions of the obligation.[29]

---

28. *Hilkhot Evel* 14:7.

29. In light of what has been said here, there is room to discuss whether one who engages in such *ḥesed* is exempt from performing other *mitzvot*. Regarding *ḥesed* based on the love of one's fellow,

To this limitation, which is connected to the circumstances of the benefactor, we can add a second limitation, connected to the situation of the recipient and his capability of rehabilitating himself. It seems to me that it is possible to distinguish between two levels of capability. In one, a person is in distress – there being no halakhic doubt about this fact – but he is capable, through intensive efforts, to contribute to the solution of his problems, and perhaps even to rehabilitate himself. Regarding such a person there is room to discuss, at the very most, whether or not his refusal to exert himself as required exempts others from doing for him what he is not prepared to do for himself. Beyond a certain point, however – and I openly admit that, practically speaking, I don't know where to draw the line – it is so easy for the needy person to help himself that his situation cannot be called one of distress. When his own salvation is easy to achieve, but for some reason he refuses to help himself, it is difficult to view him as in need. In such a case, the allowance to ignore his problems is not an exemption that stems from his refusal, but an absence of obligation that is rooted in the fact that he simply is not included in the parameters of the mitzva. With regard to the commandments of *perika* and *te'ina* or *gemilut ḥesed,* he is like a rich man. A doubt may even be raised whether one who goes out and helps a 'needy' person of this sort fulfils these *mitzvot.* Regarding the obligation, in any event, it is certainly possible to distinguish between these two levels. On the first level the other person is fundamentally obligated to extend assistance, though there might be some practical limitations. On the second, he is entirely out of the picture.

This point brings us to the practical complications of our problem. Reaching a fundamental decision and establishing operative guidelines are two different things. The conclusion that there is room to include in the mitzva of *gemilut ḥasadim* the extension of relief to the negligent does not mean that it should be extended – or extended in the same measure – in every case.

Before concluding we must survey the main factors that must be considered when performing such *ḥesed.* One that has already been mentioned is the needy person's ability to help himself. Even in cases where the indigent person is certainly regarded as being in need – for example where a person can do much

---

there is no doubt that the principle that one who is occupied in a mitzva is exempt from other *mitzvot* is valid, and there is no difference between it and the mitzva of *tzedaka.* Whether there exists a communal obligation of *ḥesed* based exclusively on the obligation to imitate God must also be examined, for it is possible that this obligation applies only to the individual, but not to the community. This, however, is not the forum to discuss these issues at length.

to alleviate his distress, but cannot remove it altogether on his own[30] – it is clear that his ability to help himself must impact upon the obligation to help him. The more possible the mission, the more restricted the obligation – both because the recipient is less needy and because his responsibility, in the double sense of burden and guilt, is greater. It is, of course, impossible to establish precise criteria for this point. Regarding loading and unloading when the owner stands on the side, the Mishna states: "If [the owner] is old or sick, [the passerby] is obligated."[31] But it does not clarify the level of old age or illness, and certainly there is room here for different approaches. I am inclined to a liberal definition, but clearly there is no absolute answer; and the same applies with respect to our general question regarding *gemilut ḥasadim*. If we are talking about finding a job – and that is the primary practical point in our day – there is yet another vague factor: dependency on others. As opposed to the cases of loading and unloading, here efforts in and of themselves are no guarantee of success. Thus it is possible to apply the words of the author of the *Me'il Tzedaka*:

> Children, life, and sustenance do not depend on merit, for it is written: "And I will be gracious to whom I will be gracious" [Ex. 33:19] – although he may not deserve it. We learn from here that whoever extends his hand to take, we give him. And there is no proof that if he is healthy, he is fit to work, for his fate does not help him earn a profit, even if he works all day long.[32]

Nevertheless, there is room to distinguish between one who is looking for a job but fails to find one, and one who sits back doing nothing, if we just adopt the principle – as apparently *Me'il Tzedaka* did – that a person's refusal to take advantage of his own abilities lessens the obligation upon others to act charitably towards him.

30. It may be assumed that the Mishna that exempts a person from the obligation of loading and unloading if the person in need does not help out, based on the scriptural decree "you shall surely unload it with him", relates to a case where the person in need can only help. Were he able to solve the problem entirely on his own, it is possible that even without the verse the other person would be exempt, for in that case the person being helped would not be defined as being in need.
31. Bava Metzia 32a.
32. Rabbi Elijah HaKohen of Izmir, *Me'il Tzedaka*, no. 196. This book, written three hundred years ago, is a treasure trove of almost two thousand essays relating to *tzedaka* and *gemilut ḥasadim*.

On this level, one point requires special emphasis. It may be assumed that the illness mentioned in the Mishna – parallel to old age – is a physical illness, the definition of which is relatively simple. The serious difficulty arises with respect to emotional illnesses or hindrances, both because their scientific definition is less precise and because they are subject to sharp ideological controversy. Psychological disability – fear of responsibility, difficulty in adapting oneself to a steady routine, distaste for authority, dependency on the home – can eat away at the ability to work no less than a lame foot. Without a doubt, however, it is less recognized, in both senses of the word.

The degree of recognition depends in no small measure on the idea of free will. This is why the halakhist will be inclined to adopt an ambivalent attitude towards the struggle over welfare budgets across the Western world today, between conservative politicians who are "stingy" and social workers who are "generous". On the one hand, halakha's excessive valuation of *ḥesed* and of society's responsibility towards the needy brings the decisor to support the expansion of aid. But on the other hand, the more that this demand is based on the argument that aid must be expanded because psycho-social circumstances fetter the needy and prevent them from joining the work force, it clashes with the emphasis that Judaism places upon free will.

Halakha indeed recognizes psychological causality, and our sages even saw such circumstances as a factor that mitigates or even altogether removes responsibility and guilt. For example, we find suffering as a mitigating circumstance: "Rav Sheshet said in the name of Rabbi Elazar ben Azarya: I could exempt the entire world [Rashi: the Jewish world] from judgment from the day of the destruction of the Temple until the present time, for it is said in Scripture: 'Therefore, hear now this, you afflicted and drunken but not of wine' [Isa. 51:1]."[33]

With regard to circumstances of seduction the Gemara states:

> What is "and Di Zahav" [Deut. 1:1]? They said in the school of Rabbi Yannai, Thus spoke Moses before the Holy One, blessed be He: Master of the Universe, the silver and gold (*zahav*) which you showered on Israel until they said, "Enough [*dai*]", that was what led to their making the calf… Rav Ḥiya bar Abba said in the name of Rabbi Yoḥanan: It is like the case of a man who had a son; he bathed him and anointed him and gave him plenty

33. Eruvin 65a.

> to eat and drink and hung a purse around his neck and sat him down at the door of a brothel. How could the boy help sinning?[34]

Generally, however, the heavy emphasis that halakha places on man's freedom and ability and the fundamental trust that it puts in him stand in absolute opposition to the psychological determinism that is prevalent in wide circles of those who support an "enlightened and liberal" welfare policy. Trusting man and emphasizing his responsibility mean believing that he is capable of transformation, if he so desires. Shifting the focus from ability to will narrows the definition of "an old or sick man", and it is also liable to diminish the feelings of obligation and sympathy towards the needy: "Rabbi Elazar said: Any person who has no knowledge – it is forbidden to have mercy upon him, as it is stated: 'For it is a people of no understanding; therefore He that made them will not have compassion upon them, and He that formed them will not be gracious unto them' [Isa. 27:11]."[35]

From a certain perspective it is possible to respond in the manner that Rav Chen reported in the name of his father: "How much mercy [has been shown] to one to whom it is forbidden to show mercy."[36] But with all the sympathy over his lack of understanding, the fact that a person is regarded as one with unused abilities certainly tends to diminish the degree to which one fulfils *gemilut ḥasadim* in his regard.

This point borders on a second important factor: the needy person's motives. A lazy person who sneers at society and expects it to support him certainly cannot be compared to a refined person who prefers to remain within the confines of gentility rather than skin carcasses in the market; and between these two extremes there is a broad spectrum. According to the determinist view, this point is significant only with respect to the treatment: help offered to the "lazy" should be restricted or cancelled because it is liable to encourage an anti-social attitude or undermine his ability to function. From a Jewish perspective, however, this distinction is replete with clear moral content, and as such, it has great weight on the operational plane. In certain situations the needy person's spiritual benefit, irrespective of the benefactor's limitations, demands a cessation of *ḥesed* that is liable to produce corruption; and this should be given priority. However, it falls upon the benefactor or the welfare agency to ascertain, honestly and sincerely, that this consideration, and not the natural inclination to scrimp, is the driving force behind this withholding

34. Berakhot 32a.

35. Sanhedrin 92a.

36. R. Avraham Ḥen, *BeMalkhut HaYahadut* (Jerusalem, 5724), ii. 426.

of assistance. If indeed the move is dictated not by budgetary considerations but rather by conscience, the denial of aid might be absolutely justified.

The third factor is the need of the recipient. The graver his situation – and most importantly, the more dangerous it is – the more difficult it becomes to withhold aid, even when it seems appropriate from other perspectives. In the extreme case where the person in need is in mortal danger, it would be unthinkable to allow him to deteriorate because he is responsible for his troubles. This follows by way of a *kal vaḥomer* argument. If in the case of a person who wishes to commit suicide we are obligated to frustrate his design and save him – and this seems to be obvious[37] – then surely in the case of a person who endangers himself in indirect ways, where his 'guilt' is less clear, all the more so must we come to his rescue. Without a doubt, even Rabbi Simon, who maintains that if a person has resources of his own but does not wish to support himself from them, we are not bound to help him, will concede that we may not ignore a person who mortifies himself to the point that his life is placed in jeopardy. Rabbi Meir (Maharam) of Rothenburg has already written:

> I was asked about a teacher who had entrusted a deposit in the hands of his landlord, and he was arrested on false charges, and he instructed his landlord not to ransom him; I wrote that he must ransom him against his will… Even if he says, "I do not want you to ransom me," we ransom him with his money against his will… For we learn from a verse that one who sees his fellow drowning in a river is obligated to save him and exert himself

37. The author of *Minḥat Ḥinukh*, however, thought otherwise: "It seems that if a person wishes to commit suicide and another person can save him, it is possible that he is not governed by this negative precept [i.e. 'Neither shall you stand idly by the blood of your neighbour' (Lev. 19:16)]. It is unnecessary to say that he is not governed by the positive precept '"And you shall restore" – to include the loss of his body', for the positive precept of restoring lost property does not apply to property that was intentionally lost… But he is not even governed by this negative precept" (mitzva 237; in old editions this appears in *Kometz Minḥa*, printed at the end of *Minḥat Ḥinukh*). He tries to adduce proof for his position from the fact that the Gemara in Sanhedrin 73a does not distinguish between the positive and negative precepts. His position, however, is very astonishing. As for his proof from the Gemara, it seems quite the opposite. Regarding bodily harm, even the positive precept is valid. The exemption regarding intentionally lost property applies to property, whether because of *hefker*, as argued by *Tur* (*Ḥoshen Mishpat* 261; and see Rosh, Bava Kama 2:16, and *Shakh*, *Ḥoshen Mishpat* 261:3); or because we don't burden others when the owners themselves abandon and waive their property, as argued by Rambam. Regarding bodily harm we can certainly not speak of *hefker*, or of waiver, for a person has no proprietary rights over his life. Therefore, one who threatens suicide must be saved both because of the mitzva of restoring lost property, and because of the prohibition of standing idly by the blood of your neighbour.

> and hire rescuers, and it is obvious that even if he commands, "Do not save me," one must save him and later one can collect one's expenses from him.[38]

The severity of the situation – and *Ḥazal* viewed the dangers of captivity as exceedingly great[39] – magnifies the obligation to rescue, the responsibility of the person in danger be as it may. While Maharam's conclusion that expenses may be collected from the ransomed captive differs from the position of Rabbi Simon (which was codified as law regarding the provision of financial support), this difference is clearly attributable to the differing needs in the two cases.

This point is reflected in the words of Meiri cited earlier. As may be remembered, one of the distinctions that he offered between the talmudic passage in Kiddushin, which implies that the obligation of rescue falls entirely on the rescuer, and the Mishna in Bava Metzia, from which he infers that it falls also on the rescued party, was the difference between saving a life and saving property. Meiri does not explain, but it seems to me that at the root of the matter is the assumption that regarding bodily danger there is an absolute obligation that leaves no room for any kind of reckoning. Even the lazy and those who take advantage of others have a right to life. As for property, it is possible to demand, at the very least, the needy person's participation – whether in order not to place too heavy a burden on the benefactor, or in order not to detract from others in need, or in order to teach him a lesson. But as for life, the obligation to rescue stands above all other considerations.[40] From this type of danger, while rather extreme, we may

38. *Responsa Maharam ben Barukh*, Prague edn., no. 39. The gist of the responsum is cited in his name by Mordekhai, Bava Kama, sec. 59.
39. See Bava Batra 8b.
40. This is more persuasive if we understand that, according to Meiri, mortal danger is a sufficient condition to distinguish between the passages in Bava Metzia and Kiddushin. But even if he understands that it is merely a necessary condition (see above, n. 14), and even if we accept the position that he cites at the beginning of the passage, that if the woman does not want to return to the rescuer the value of the bread "he is not obligated to save her", it seems to me that a distinction should be made between a threat to life and a threat to property. Regarding property, it is possible that there is no obligation whatsoever, even *lekhatḥila*. Regarding life, one is certainly obligated to save the person – with or without the possibility of recovering expenses – but, according to this opinion, it is possible to recover expenses after the rescue. The continuation of the words of Meiri, "For he too is forbidden to save himself with another person's money," proves this. For is it conceivable that a person who is faced with two choices, either to die or to cause a financial loss to his fellow, is obligated to sacrifice his life? Surely, *Tosafot* already explained the Gemara's problem (Bava Kama 60b), "What is the law about saving oneself by appropriating another's money?" as follows: "He asks whether he is obligated to pay when he saved himself because of *pikuaḥ nefesh*" (ibid. *Tosafot*, s.v. *mahu*). Rambam also understood the

infer, in the framework of our discussion, the law governing other situations. The principle underlying the words of Meiri is valid regarding assistance in general: the obligation to assist the 'lazy' is a function of the danger threatening them.

In the end, of course, these factors, each one independently or all of them taken together, cannot be translated into precise solutions for the problem of assistance to those who are negligent about helping themselves. While they outline a direction and propose guidelines, the need to deal on both a moral and a practical level with the particular aspects of each individual case and every public framework remains in place. This is rooted in the complex social reality and the outlook of halakha. The effort to encourage sensitivity on the one hand and responsibility on the other, to nurture both a work ethic and an ethic of giving, to hold on to both *tzedek* (justice) and *tzedaka* (charity), reflects halakha's values. It is in this complex of values that our problem lies, and within it are also found the foundations of its solution.

---

problem as a question regarding payment: "One who saves himself by appropriating another's money must repay it" (*Hilkhot Ḥovel uMazik* 8:2). It seems to me that there is no other way to understand the Gemara. The Gemara indeed uses the formulation "a person is forbidden to save himself", but one must not understand this to mean that *lekhatḥila* he must refrain from saving himself, for damages and theft are not included among the prohibitions that are not set aside for *pikuaḥ nefesh*. Rather, "forbidden" here means that his act has ramifications regarding payment. If the act is outright permissible, it means that the Torah permitted the other person's property to the saved party, as if it had pledged it for this purpose and removed the other person's proprietary rights to it. Thus there is no room for compensation, for the rescued party did not make use of property belonging to another person, but rather halakha granted him use of the property from the very outset. If, however, a person is forbidden to save himself by appropriating another's property, the other person's proprietary rights remain in place, and the saved party, when he sets aside this "prohibition" for reasons of *pikuaḥ nefesh*, makes use of money that was not given to him for that purpose, and therefore he is obligated to make compensation. See Meiri, Bava Kama 114b, who writes that a person is permitted to save himself with another's property having in mind to make restitution, but if he has in mind not to make restitution, he is forbidden to do so. Clearly, he means that *lekhatḥila* he must have in mind to make restitution, but not – if no possibility of restitution exists – that he should die rather than make use of the property. (Rabbi Jacob Ettlinger understood, however, that, according to Rashi, following his understanding of his position in Bava Kama 60b, a person must indeed sacrifice his life in such a situation; see *Responsa Binyan Tziyon*, no. 167, and *Responsa Binyan Tziyon HaḤadashot*, no. 173. But his words are very astonishing. This, however, is not the forum to discuss his position.) Thus, the earlier line in Meiri, "he is not obligated to save her", should also be understood to mean that in actual practice he is obligated to save her, but since he is not obligated financially, then the loaf of bread the rescuer gives her for this purpose is his own and not hers by virtue of his obligation to God, and thus there is a transfer of betrothal money.

Is There a Talmudic Logic?

Rabbi Adin Steinsaltz

The question "Is there logic in the Talmud?" or "Is the Talmud logical?"[1] is, of course, not the issue about which I wish to write here. But the very fact that such a question can even be raised is related to the topic of our discussion. The fact is that one could think that the question whether or not there is logic in the Talmud can indeed be raised, and that the two possibilities are equally open to discussion.

Before going into details, let me begin by positing that any subject that can be studied and taught in an orderly fashion is perforce a subject that has logic. This logic can be different or strange, but it must exist, because the very possibility of conveying subject matter and conducting a joint discussion about it dictates the existence of some logical basis.

This is not the case, for example, in the realm of the emotions. When two people love each other, and even utter the exact same words, they are not necessarily talking about the same thing. In contrast, when two people study the same talmudic passage, they are without a doubt considering the very same issue, even if their views differ and they disagree with each other. I wish to emphasize that this need not be true with regard to other Jewish texts, for example, the book of Psalms. The question whether there is logic in the psalms, in poetry, or in

1. The Hebrew original of this essay was edited by Moshe Koppel and Eli Merzbach, and was first published in *Higayon* (Alon Shevut: Machon Tzomet, 1995), 13-21.

prophecy is a question of another kind, which can be answered in different ways. But as for the Talmud, we are undoubtedly dealing with study that can be communicated, and is therefore based on a fixed and fairly rigid set of assumptions that are built one upon the other and one alongside the other, as in any other orderly logical system.

The issue, then, is not whether there is logic in the Talmud, but rather what kind of logic there is in the Talmud. In other words, is talmudic logic identical with logic as we understand it, or does the Talmud have its own particular way of examining issues, built on entirely different principles? For there can exist a logical system, that is, a system that has fixed rules for transferring information from one realm to another, or from one point of departure; but these rules are not necessarily identical with those found in other systems.

I wish to touch upon a subject that, in my opinion, deserves to be clarified separately, and that also focuses the discussion in a different way. A fairly famous saying – one that is attributed to various yeshiva heads of recent generations, but in fact goes back hundreds of years to Rabbi Jacob Weil[2] – states as follows: The Torah's reasoning is the very opposite of the reasoning of ordinary people. This adage is something that must and should be said. What Rabbi Weil calls "the reasoning of ordinary people" is what in many places is referred to as "common sense". Indeed, in all realms that have any kind of rational meaning – and this is just as true of Boolean logic as it is of tailoring or shoemaking – one of the first discoveries to be made is that many things do not follow common sense. Without delving further into the matter, we can merely say that common sense is at best only very rough guidance, valid almost only for issues that do not require precise clarification. In all areas, and not necessarily at the highest levels, observation of reality and thoughtful contemplation lead to conclusions that common sense would declare impossible or the opposite of common sense. This happens all the time, and it is true about Talmud study as well. In other words, common-sense perceptions and understandings are frequently incorrect. Common sense is therefore a very unreliable guide in all matters, abstract or practical, as soon as one reaches the details and pays attention to minutiae.

So much for this subject in brief. The main question that I will address here is whether something that can be called "Torah reasoning" exists as a defined discipline. This may be a discipline which has not yet been well defined and requires further clarification, study, and deeper contemplation; but it is certainly different in its very essence from other disciplines of thought and study. The first

2. Fifteenth-century German rabbi and Talmudist, a disciple of Rabbi Jacob Moellin (Maharil).

book written by Maimonides was a book on logic – *Milot HaHigayon* (Treatise on Logic). But in Maimonides' day the conception of logic was very simple and one-dimensional. The rules of logic were fixed and rested on a single foundation, and with them it was possible to determine what was logical and what was not.

Since that time it has become clear that many things in reality do not necessarily behave according to the laws of logic. This realization may have been due in part to the encounter with the reality of life in the world. It turned out that the world is not built according to Euclidean geometry, which in many ways is the geometry of common sense. Similarly, the entire complicated and ever-growing field of quantum mechanics is the result of observations that required logical transitions in different areas, even in theoretical fields such as set theory, and created several new logical templates that are not radically at variance with their predecessors, but are definitely different and require their own definition. It seems to me, then, that the question regarding the extent to which the Talmud has a different logic is certainly legitimate. Does it have rules that can be defined as different rules of logic, rules that are unique to talmudic literature and characteristic only of it?

A distinction must be made between modes of thinking and logical systems. This distinction is significant because in different fields one can build different systems of thinking which also have different definitions. For example, the validity of proof in the experimental sciences and in mathematics is certainly not the same. That which is termed proof in the natural sciences would seldom be accepted as proof in mathematics. And as for that which is called proof in mathematics, it is not clear whether, and to what extent, it is appropriate for other ways of thinking.

To return to the Talmud, first of all there is no doubt that it deals with 'other' subjects. It does not deal with nature, but with a particular perspective on nature or reality. For example, the ox and the donkey are frequently mentioned in the Talmud. The reference is not to a celestial ox or donkey, but these animals are also not exactly identical to the oxen and donkeys with which we are familiar, for in a certain sense they are abstract concepts or symbolic terms. For this reason the Talmud can create illogical linguistic anomalies, such as a "rolling pit" (Bava Kama 6a). On the face of it, the term "rolling pit" contradicts reality. However, it is a halakhic term with specific and logical meaning, and which also has aspects that can 'roll'. The basic language, the fundamental set of terms, is unique and relates only to matters of a particular type.

Second, what is considered proof in the Talmud need not be accepted as proof elsewhere. This is a particular field that defines its own method of proof.

Were I to bring a proof in the field of biology or mathematics, and then raise an objection: "How can such an argument be proposed? Surely there is an explicit Mishna that says otherwise" – obviously, this objection would be irrelevant. But when I am engaged in Talmud study and I propose a certain argument, I do indeed ask: "But surely it was taught otherwise," or, alternatively, I bring proof from the sources. That is to say, in every field I define for myself what for me is the foundation of truth, what for me is a valid argument. Thus, in the realm of the natural sciences, I look for experimental verification in order to prove a certain assumption, whereas in the world of the Talmud, I search for textual confirmation. For in the world of the Talmud, the Mishna and the *baraitot* themselves are the foundations of truth. They are the reality to which I must relate, and based on which I must build my arguments.

All this certainly creates a different system of thought, for it deals with different material and its foundations of truth are different. Accordingly, the modes of argument, the methods of proof, and the transition from one point to another are also very different. To illustrate this point, I wish to mention the way the Talmud discusses sources (which, as stated, are the basis for the verification of truth) that contradict each other, or cannot coexist. On the one hand, even in the Talmud itself, and certainly in its commentaries, one can find many different opinions and answers, some of which are extreme examples of source criticism. Talmudic interpretation has a vast system that already contains all the essentials of source criticism, ranging from lower criticism – that is, textual emendations and changes – to higher criticism – reviewing texts and explaining them in light of other sources. The Tosafists were particularly fond of higher criticism, and I emphasize the Tosafists precisely because the foreign influence upon them, if at all, was less than minimal. And yet they can take a whole page of talmudic discussion dealing with derivations of laws from biblical verses and say that these expositions fall into the category of *asmakhta*, biblical texts quoted to support rabbinic enactments. Or they can take an entire passage and argue that it falls into the category of *sugyot hafukhot* (inverted passages), parallel passages that are based on opposing assumptions. Even in the Talmud itself we find many questions of the type: "According to whom was this taught? It was taught according to Rabbi So-and-so," which is nothing but textual criticism, at one level or another.

It is clear, however, that the Talmud's basic system of thinking is not the same as that of those who discuss the Talmud or speak about it as a subject of scholarly analysis. This is due in part to the fact that the talmudic approach – as a matter of principle, and not as a conceptual constraint on the grounds of religion or conservatism – is deliberately and consciously harmonistic. It tries to avoid being analytical, not because analysis is an unacceptable method or approach, but because both the Talmud itself and the post-talmudic literature attempt, for theoretical and theological reasons, to reach a maximal degree of harmonization, and they do so knowing that this involves a large number of forced solutions. Indeed, there is not a page of Talmud that is not filled with such solutions, which of course impacts once again on the method of thinking.

Here is another illustration from the field of philology and textual criticism. Contrary to the practice of most medieval textual amenders, the assumption today is that of two alternative manuscript readings it is precisely the more difficult reading that is more likely to be the correct one. From the perspective of the reasoning of ordinary people, this approach seems to be unfounded, and indeed, every philologist knows that it runs counter to common sense; but anyone dealing with the issue will say that it is dictated by reason. (By the way, this premise is not necessarily always true, as there are also ignorant copyists who wittingly or unwittingly create new errors.) This is a particular way of thinking that is based on the desire to establish the original reading. However, this approach is contrary to that of, for example, Rabbi Joel Sirkis, otherwise known as the *Baḥ*.[3] Anyone who reads through the *Baḥ*'s glosses on the Talmud knows that they are not only logical but also always tend towards the easier reading. In other scientific fields as well, the basic premise is that the simplest or shortest explanation of any particular difficulty is the correct explanation, unless proven otherwise. But this scientific approach is not a matter of logical proof: rather, it is a philosophical concept. Whether the *Baḥ*, in his glosses, restores the original reading is, then, a question that requires extensive examination in itself. Corresponding to this is another question: Is it all that important to reconstruct the original, more difficult version?

This problem is closely related to another fundamental philosophical question, which deals not with the Torah's reasoning, but, as it were, with the mind of the Creator. Does God also think in this manner? That is to say, was the world created in a manner which accords with our rules of logic? Does reality match the human mind? This is a problem not only in the field of Torah and science, but is encountered by almost everyone who has dealt with the philosophy of science in recent generations.

This question has no simple solution, and one who grapples with it often faces a choice, whether to prefer the best approach or the easiest one. It

3. Named so after his magnum opus *Bayit Ḥadash*, Rabbi Sirkis (1561–1640) was a prominent halakhist living in central Europe.

is sometimes possible to explain a difficult passage that has been explicated by the Gemara, the medieval commentators, and the modern authorities in hundreds of forced ways by simply running a line through the sources; for example, by distinguishing between the halakhic *midrashim* of Rabbi Akiva and those of Rabbi Ishmael, or by claiming that one is an earlier edition and the other is a later edition – that is to say, that certain tractates underwent further redaction in a different study centre, and therefore their wording is different. This approach, most common among those engaged in the academic study of Talmud, resolves many of the contradictions and difficulties over which the medieval and modern authorities agonized. But it must be kept in mind that this very fact proves that this methodology is based on a different premise, one that is not the way that the Talmud perceived itself, nor the way that its major interpreters understood it across the generations.

Emphasizing the fact that modern academic talmudic research is essentially alien to, and not in accord with, the Talmud's own way of thinking does not fall into the category of war against heresy. All of these observations – including the fact that some tractates, such as Nedarim or Nazir, have linguistic peculiarities (and must be interpreted differently) – were already made by the medieval commentators; we have said nothing novel. Among the medieval commentators we find text-related comments, both regarding alternative readings, whether major or minor, and regarding issues of higher criticism, for example that the first pages of Tractate Kiddushin were redacted not by the *amora'im* but by the *savora'im* or even later authorities. This method of study, various aspects of which are found in the Talmud itself, is therefore not invalid for reasons of tradition or faith. But nevertheless it must be understood that the Talmud's fundamental way of thinking is harmonistic, and therefore it accepts upon itself from the outset a tremendous number of constraints, and the solutions it seeks are not necessarily the simplest ones, but sometimes precisely the most complex and complicated ones.

It is not my present intention to deal with this approach in itself or to try to justify it, though I do believe that it has considerable theoretical justification. I wish merely to state that all of these things, and many other things that can be said about the Talmud's transitions from one matter to the next, are part of a unique mode of thinking, and that it is important to try to define them in a rational manner in order to understand why the *tanna'im* and *amora'im* struggle to find a solution to a problem that to us seems amazingly simple. In this regard it should be noted that sometimes what seems simple turns out to be truly complex and even extremely difficult, and vice versa.

We may cite an example of this from a different field, that of biblical interpretation. Rashbam[4] often speaks about "the depth of the plain sense [*peshat*] of the text", but his *peshat* is sometimes exceedingly problematic, to the extent that internal censorship removed the first chapters of his commentary on the book of Genesis. For example, he himself undoubtedly stopped all weekday work on Friday afternoon prior to the onset of Shabbat. But in his commentary on Genesis he writes that, according to "the depth of the plain sense of the text", the day begins in the morning. Without a doubt he donned tefillin in the proper manner, but in his commentary on Exodus he writes that, according to "the depth of the plain sense of the text", the words "for a sign to you upon your hand" mean that the matter should be a memorial for you at all times, as if it were written on your hand. It is interesting that Rabbi Abraham Ibn Ezra, who was an exceedingly educated man in all fields of science, opposed those interpretations of Rashbam that are "the depth of the plain sense of the text", with which he was apparently familiar, because he perceived them as a danger to halakha. It turns out, then, that Rashbam, a deeply pious man who was wholly immersed in the world of Torah, proposed 'plain' but highly problematic interpretations, whereas Ibn Ezra, who was a very harsh critic, frequently sought more complicated solutions, because "the depth of the plain sense of the text" was perhaps plain and easy, but not at all simple.

Another example: Rabbi Barukh Epstein, author of *Torah Temima,* and son of the author of *Arukh Hashulḥan,* lived in the generation before us and enjoyed great popularity (primarily because of his questions, and sometimes also because of his answers). He too had a sense for simple solutions that were brilliant, plain, and easy to remember. However, after careful examination of the sources, it turns out that often they are incorrect. These are all examples of an approach that leads to simple interpretations that are not necessarily more correct than interpretations that are not so simple. I therefore argue that a comparison between simple analytical construction and more complex harmonistic construction is not easy. On the contrary, it requires much consideration, both from the perspective of general philosophy and from the perspective of Talmud study.

From here we return to the crux of the discussion. Even if we accept the premise that talmudic thinking is a different way of thinking, with different formats and different foundations, there is still room to ask: Does this difference reach as far as the Talmud's logic, or does it stop with its formats? For example,

4. Rabbi Solomon ben Meir (c.1085–c.1158), Rashi's grandson and a leading French biblical commentator and Talmudist.

someone involved in biology must think a little differently from one involved in physics. Their basic models are different, since the physical world operates in accordance with the law of entropy, while the biologist lives in a world that is working against entropy all the time. Therefore, the biologist's templates of thought can be called evolutionary, whereas the physicist's templates are built primarily on the foundation of dissolution. But all this notwithstanding, and despite the differences in their patterns of thought, the same dimensions of logic operate in both fields.

I wish at this time to present a position upon which I cannot fully elaborate in the present framework. On the face of it, the assumption of the existence of a unique talmudic logic cannot stand without proof. And as long as there is no proof for such a distinct logic, we must accept the position that the essence of talmudic logic is a way of thinking that is identical to the ordinary rules of logic. Despite the sophisticated technique of Torah study, and everything that makes it unique, in the final analysis, as stated by Ibn Ezra, "The Torah was not given to one who is bereft of reason". In other words, a person who lacks reason is also void of Torah. This formulation is exceedingly extreme, but it gets to the heart of the matter. Among other things, Ibn Ezra tries to explain why some Bible verses must be understood in a figurative sense, whereas others can be taken literally. He distinguishes between a verse that can be fulfilled in its literal sense and one that cannot, such as circumcision of the flesh as opposed to circumcision of the heart. No commentator suggests that the commandment concerning circumcision of the heart be applied literally, in an operating room; whereas circumcision of the flesh, which can be fulfilled literally, must be done so, and cannot be interpreted symbolically or spiritually. Incidentally, this is also related to the ancient debate – which began in the Jewish–Christian dispute and continues to this very day in the disagreement between the Orthodox and the Reform – concerning the extent to which symbols can be substituted for actions. But this is already another topic.

The position that Torah study requires a different type of reasoning is an assumption that needs proof, and I do not think such proof exists. Nevertheless I wish to touch upon several points that, in my opinion, open the door to greater understanding. For the sake of convenience, and not because of the profundity of the matter, I would distinguish between the rules by which the Torah is interpreted – and especially the rules by which halakha is interpreted – and talmudic study in general. It is clearly evident that the Talmud does not make equal use of all the rules by which the Torah is interpreted; some are used frequently, while others are not. Among those rules (which are not counted among the rules of Rabbi Yishmael, but it can be demonstrated that Rabbi Yishmael accepts them) are several that raise the question that I asked at the outset: Are we dealing here with a logical system, or is it perhaps an arbitrary system (divine or otherwise)?

In the introduction to his commentary on the Mishna, Maimonides establishes almost unequivocally that many halakhic *midrashim* are not actually the sources of the laws supposedly derived from them, but are merely supports (*asmakhtot*) for laws that have no scriptural basis, yet, according to tradition, were orally transmitted by God to Moses together with the written Torah. He offers the *etrog* as an example. We know what an *etrog* is, not on the basis of the five proofs appearing in the Gemara (one of which is based on the Greek), but rather because in truth we have always known, on the basis of an uninterrupted tradition, that an *etrog* is a citron. The proofs recorded in the Gemara are merely a set of supports. In contrast, *Tosafot* maintain (and this seems to be the position of Maimonides in other places) an intermediate position, which accepts both a true halakhic *midrash* and also what may be called a pseudo-halakhic *midrash*, that is, merely a support. But the analyses and distinctions in *Tosafot* are generally not logical but substantive. They come to prove, usually from other sources, that a particular law is rabbinic in origin, and that the halakhic *midrash* is merely a support.

When we examine the rules by which the Torah is interpreted in the halakhic *midrashim*, the least logical rule of all seems to be that of *im eino inyan*, which states that if a law cannot apply to the context in which it was stated, it must be interpreted as referring to a different context. This rule seems to go against all reason. We can talk about a superfluous word or one that is missing, an amplification or a restriction; but the argument of *im eino inyan*, whether one can apply it on one's own or only based on an ancient tradition going back to Moses at Mount Sinai, removes us from any logical system and puts us in an absolutely wild realm, which recognizes the validity of arguments totally void of logic. Many years ago I wrote an article on this topic, in which I tried to prove that the rule of *im eino inyan* – at least according to the examples given in the Babylonian Talmud (as this rule is almost never mentioned in the Jerusalem Talmud, and very little in the various halakhic *midrashim*) – is in fact not arbitrary. Rather, it is a logical or semantic system that is used to prove certain things in places where the matter has a sound halakhic or textual basis, but due to some external reason there is a technical problem in its application, and then this rule serves as a proof by way of a superfluity in order to restore the system – which is actually entirely logical – to the formal framework of halakhic *midrash*.

On the other extreme, there is a rule that is considered the most logical of all, namely, *kal vaḥomer*, or *a fortiori* inference. Several books deal exclusively with *kal vaḥomer*. On the face of it, *kal vaḥomer* is a most simple logical syllogism: A is greater than B, B is greater than C, and therefore A is greater than C. However, if we examine its application in talmudic literature, and not only according to the standards of modern scientific logic, but even according to less precise standards, we will see that the matter is actually much more complicated, and that this apparently simple rule has so many shortcomings and logical difficulties that it can befuddle anyone's mind. And I am not talking now only about the rule of *dayyo*, which states that it is sufficient for the conclusion that emerged from an *a fortiori* inference to be like the source of the inference; that is a subject for discussion in itself. The entire system of *kal vaḥomer* works like a logical syllogism in only a fairly small number of cases, while in all other cases it simply does not work from a logical perspective.

As an example of a faulty *kal vaḥomer* inference, let me cite what my late uncle would use to demonstrate such improper use: if chickens, which have only two legs, are kosher, then a pig, which has four legs, should all the more so be kosher. It is not very difficult to refute this *kal vaḥomer* from a logical perspective, but the problem is that a considerable number of *kal vaḥomer* arguments in the Talmud do follow this format. In an overly simplistic manner, the difficulty can be formulated as follows: in order for a *kal vaḥomer* inference to work as a logical element, all of its components must lie on the same plane. For example, "If you have run with footmen, and they have wearied you, then how can you contend with horses?" (Jer. 12:5) is a *kal vaḥomer* inference which deals with a single plane: speed, and therefore it is an argument that is given to simple logical presentation. But in other cases, for example the argument in Tractate Berakhot which shows how we derive the blessing recited before eating from the blessing recited over the Torah, or how we derive the blessing recited after reading from the Torah from the Grace after Meals: "If a blessing is recited over temporal life, all the more so should one be recited over eternal life" – when the argument is subjected to logical analysis, it turns out that there are indeed two comparisons, between a minor element and a major one, but the premise and the conclusion are not found on the same plane.

This is not all, because alongside the *kal vaḥomer* argument there is also what is called 'a *kal vaḥomer* that is the son of a *kal vaḥomer*' and 'a *kal vaḥomer* that is the grandson of a *kal vaḥomer*'. And if a *kal vaḥomer* inference, which is a rule that one may apply on one's own – that is to say, it is a rule based on human reason, and not on other principles – is not entirely logical, what shall we say about other rules, such as verbal analogy, an analogy based on one verse, or an analogy based on two verses? In Tractate Zevaḥim there is a discussion that is fascinating from a theoretical perspective, and which extends over several pages and deals with the logical aspects of a comparison between the validity of various rules by which the Torah is interpreted. This is a topic which, from a conceptual perspective, is outstanding, complex, complicated, not understandable, and replete with fascinating theoretical challenges.

I would like to reach at least some conclusions through an examination of some of these matters, though I cannot present proofs, for it is impossible for a single person to go over the entire system, as it is immense both quantitatively and qualitatively. Even properly reviewing one small tractate from a logical perspective is a mission that requires a great deal of work. In general we can say that often what appears to be a difficulty, or an illogical argument, is actually the result of improper use of terms that are the same in form but different in meaning, due to the fact that they are assigned to incorrect logical systems. In other words, what initially appears like a system that has an internal failure or is problematic is often the result of incorrect use of a rule, or incorrect correspondences between things; proper connections would lead to entirely different conclusions.

However, making the right connections requires more thorough study, for the terms of talmudic discussion often mislead us into thinking that we are dealing with terminology familiar to us from general logic, when in fact we are in an entirely different realm of terminology – not simply a different logic, but a totally different system of terminology, and therefore a proper system of transformations is necessary. Returning to *kal vaḥomer,* I believe that this argument, as it is used in the Talmud, is not the usual *a fortiori* argument, but rather a type of analogy. By analysing the argument in a different way, we can see that the comparison drawn between the more stringent element and the more lenient one is a comparison drawn between two elements that are similar to each other, and at times almost identical, and therefore can be inferred from each other. This explains, among other things, rules such as *dayyo,* not merely as a formal limitation, but as a more intrinsic element.

There is one additional point that I can present in this framework only by way of assertion without furnishing evidence for it for the time being. The great mass of halakhic *midrash* should be seen not as an attempt to prove certain conclusions, but rather as an attempt to demonstrate that all the conclusions of the oral tradition are consistent. This is a totally different matter from a logical and theoretical perspective. In other words, the entire genre of halakhic *midrash,* with the various models or operations with which it deals, comes to prove that the system as a whole is a single unified system. This, in fact, is what is done with every structure in every realm, even mathematics and logic. An attempt is made to show the extent to which there is compatibility between all the components in the system. Such an assumption calls for a redefinition of what I require from the entire expanse of proof. What I thought was proof of reality is but proof of compatibility. It involves the construction of a system that needs to demonstrate that certain systems or certain arguments are compatible with each other. The question relating to the truth or reality of the system, when it stems from tradition or other sources, is a different problem and requires separate discussion.

To summarize, I have posited here certain assumptions. I assumed that since the Torah was given to us, and because in the end we rule, like Rabbi Joshua, that the Torah "is not in Heaven", this means that God gave us the Torah so that we may discuss it, using the tools that He gave us. One account of the definition of truth from God's perspective is found in a spectacular story recorded in the Jerusalem Talmud, Tractate Rosh Hashana 1:3, which sounds like a hasidic story, but is found explicitly in the Talmud:

> If the court says: Today is Rosh Hashana, the Holy One, blessed be He, says to the ministering angels: Set up the platform, let the defenders rise, and let the prosecutors rise; for My children have said: "Today is Rosh Hashana." If the court changed [its mind] to make the month full [so that Rosh Hashana will fall on the next day], the Holy One, blessed be He, says to the ministering angels: "Remove the platform, remove the defenders, and remove the prosecutors; for My children have decided to make the month full." What is the proof? "For it is a statute for Israel, an ordinance of the God of Jacob" [Ps. 81:5]. If it is not a statute for Israel, it is, as it were, not an ordinance of the God of Jacob.

This and others stories like it essentially say that the true Torah is the Torah that was given over into our hands. The Torah is not just "God's Torah" but also "his Torah" (Ps. 1:2), the Torah of Man. After a person reaches the level of "his delight is in God's Torah", he continues on to the level of "and in his Torah he meditates day and night", that is, to the acquisition of the Torah. This also indicates that the logic of the Torah cannot be an alien logic that is inherently indecipherable. Such a position denies the Torah from humans. One who maintains such a view basically takes all of the Torah, wraps it up in fancy packaging, and sends it back to the Giver of the Torah, to do with it what He pleases. The fact that we do not do that implies that we are meant and commanded to study the Torah with tools that are perhaps faulty, but they are the only ones that we have.

God gave us the Torah knowing the limits of our cognition, and He gave us the authority to occupy ourselves in Torah study, to propose Torah novellae, and to issue halakhic rulings. Therefore, I am inclined to assume that what Rabbi Kook referred to as "holy logic" is not alien territory established on secret foundations, but rather a logic built upon templates that are open to clarification and discussion. Nevertheless, we must be precise and exacting in our clarification of the Torah, so that we not be misled by false delusions. That is to say, God provided us with reason with which to study the Torah, and therefore He also demands of us that we do so properly. We must understand that we are dealing with a different way of thinking and completely different terminology, which require a different approach to all the practical problems that issue from this, so that we may clarify them in true fashion, both according to halakha and according to the Torah.

Introduction: Rabbi Sacks as 'Chief of Rabbis'

Rabbi Mordechai Ginsbury

An observation frequently cited in the yeshiva world is that the Torah genius of Rabbi Ḥaym Soloveitchik obscured in the public eye a tremendous amount of his great righteousness, whilst the greatness of Ḥafetz Ḥayim as a tzaddik obscured a tremendous amount of his own genius in Torah knowledge.

Much is known and acknowledged about the academic brilliance, public oratory, and prolific writing of Chief Rabbi Lord Sacks. However, what has been less documented as a consequence is his love and support for the traditional congregational rabbi. As a communal rabbi under the aegis of Chief Rabbi Sacks throughout his term of office, I have been fortunate to view at firsthand how he is not just a wonderful teaching rabbi, but also a wonderful teacher of rabbis. He has instinctively understood that for Anglo-Jewry to have great communities, it must also have great rabbis, and has set about effecting this.

In this introduction, I would like to try and outline Rabbi Sacks' key principle for successful rabbinic leadership, using direct examples garnered from working with him, or other sources of which I have gained an additional appreciation through his insightful analysis and eager promotion of their central concepts.

From the beginning of his time in office, Chief Rabbi Sacks was keen to emphasize his philosophy of becoming a successful congregational leader. I recall how, in what must have been his first or perhaps second year, he convened a conference for us all to discuss what he described as 'inreach' – making strides within our own congregations. Whilst many participants had prepared complex presentations, the Chief Rabbi's message was simple – to ensure an instant and instinctive sense of welcome in our synagogues. The 'meeters and greeters' were to be key partners in building our communities. It was this quality above all others that he focused on, and accordingly looked for, in his rabbinate.

In an interview with Rabbi Martin van den Bergh – then editor of the journal of the Rabbinical Council of the Provinces, *Hakshiva* – the Chief Rabbi was asked from where he thought the next generation of mainstream Anglo-Jewish communal rabbis was most likely to emerge. Might it be from academia or from the yeshiva world, from the right or from the left wings of the community? Lord Sacks responded by saying that the question didn't seem to be quite the right one to ask. A good rabbi, he suggested, is a person who cares passionately about his fellow beings, about the Jewish people, and about Torah. Where one finds those qualities, he went on to say, one will find an excellent congregational rabbi, almost regardless of his academic background or religious outlook. As both a direct and indirect consequence of the Chief Rabbi's attitude, today's mainstream Anglo-Jewish Orthodox rabbinate embraces a very wide spectrum of backgrounds, views, and, of course, talents.

In his most recent book, *In the Splendor of the Maggid*, Rabbi Paysach Krohn raises a striking question in the name of the late Rabbi Elya Svei (1924–2009), who served as *rosh yeshiva* in Philadelphia. Quoting from a memoir by Rabbi Boruch Levin of Detroit, Rabbi Svei is reported as pointing out a difficulty concerning a passage of the Gemara in Ḥagiga 15b, which states:

> Rabba bar Bar Ḥana said in the name of R. Yoḥanan: What is the meaning of the verse, "For the Priest's lips should keep knowledge, and they should seek Torah from his mouth, for he is the messenger of Hashem" [Malachi 2]? [This means that] if the teacher is like an angel of Hashem, they should seek Torah from his mouth, but if not, they should not seek Torah from his mouth.

How can one identify a teacher who resembles an angel – has anyone seen an angel so as to advise what we are looking for when trying to identify one? What would the job specification state as the key skills? How then can the Gemara suggest such an unusable criterion for selecting a Torah teacher?

The answer is based on a teaching of Naḥmanides (Ramban) relating to Genesis 1:11: "Every blade of grass has an angel in heaven exhorting it to grow."

The angelic capacity to be a great teacher of Torah as presented in the Gemara is not contingent on merely conveying texts or implanting technical knowledge. What a true Torah teacher has to do is learn from the angels mentioned by Ramban (based on the Zohar), and actively elicit growth from those who seek to learn from him. Where one 'angelically' summons a student or congregant to develop and advance as a person in his or her love of Torah, reverence for God, and commitment to others, therein is a true teacher and leader to be found.

It is this deep concern and regard for each of one's congregants that the Chief Rabbi was attempting to instil within his rabbinate. And to do this, he realized that he had to set his rabbis free. He has often reflected on the plaintive cry that he would hear from Anglo-Jewish ministers at conferences in his earliest years in the rabbinate: "We must be regarded as, and given space to be, more than functionaries – we want to be leaders!" Today's Anglo-Jewish rabbinate has more opportunity than ever before to serve as leaders in their own styles. Rabbi Sacks has set a tremendous example in this regard, doing it very much his way. He is a renowned idealist, always happy to ignore supposed practicalities in favour of what actually needs doing, never hesitating to do things out of the box, such as his YouTube videos and similar engagement with social media. Through this, he has inspired us all to engage more intimately with our congregations, and to focus on the needs for their growth, however that may be done. As one of my congregants has put it to me recently, "The Chief Rabbi has provided an attractive portal into Orthodoxy that nobody else can equal."

Section I
World Jewry

An Approach to Dangerous and Terminal Illness

Rabbi Dr Akiva Tatz

It is my privilege to offer this contribution in honour of Rabbi Lord Jonathan Sacks. I would particularly like to acknowledge the personal welcome given to me by Rabbi Sacks when I arrived to work in this community some fifteen years ago.

The following is adapted from my book *Dangerous Disease and Dangerous Therapy in Jewish Medical Ethics – Principles and Practice* (Targum Press, 2010). The subject is timely because we find ourselves in a social and cultural ethos in which the value of life is too often not appreciated in accordance with halakhic standards. Further detail and clinical cases illustrating the principles described here may be found in my book.

The obligation to save life – *pikuaḥ nefesh* – stands close to the pinnacle of the halakhic hierarchy of obligation; it supersedes virtually all other duties. A dangerously ill patient must be aggressively treated, desecrating the Sabbath and transgressing almost all other prohibitions if necessary. Even where there is no known definitive therapy, whatever can be done for the patient must be done both to prolong life and improve its quality; and even where it is clear that no medical therapy will help, the patient must not be abandoned.[1]

1. Even if only in order not to cause the despairing realization that the situation is hopeless – anguish, despair, and pain are halakhically regarded as real dangers to a very ill patient (*Iggerot Moshe,*

From a halakhic perspective, there are two categories of terminal illness: *ḥayei sha'a* and *goses*. Loosely translated, *ḥayei sha'a* refers to a terminal situation, where death is very likely in the near future; *goses* refers to an agonal situation, where death is almost certainly immediately imminent. These must be clearly distinguished as the *halakhot* (laws) pertaining to patients in these two categories differ markedly.

ḤAYEI SHA'A

Terminal illness, *hayei sha'a,* is generally defined in halakha as a medical condition that is clearly expected to be fatal[2] within one year[3] (as opposed to *ḥayei olam,* life that is under no such short-term threat).[4] The derivation of this twelve-month period is not explicit in original sources; the suggestion that it derives from the period of survival associated with the category of *trefa* should be seen as setting up a general parallel more than a strict derivation.[5] Consequently it has been suggested that this period should not be seen as an absolute cut-off and that a more basic element of the definition of *ḥayei sha'a* is the presence of a lethal process

Ḥoshen Mishpat 2:75). Even where a patient *must* be informed of a grim diagnosis (for example where consent and cooperation will be needed for treatment) the information must be conveyed gently and with a very clear message of hope.

2. A lethally dangerous but curable or definitively treatable condition does not render a patient *ḥayei sha'a* where the appropriate treatment is being given – an insulin-dependent diabetic on appropriate insulin therapy is not in the *ḥayei sha'a* category (and of course such patients must be aggressively treated).
3. *Iggerot Moshe, Ḥoshen Mishpat* 2:75 and *Yoreh De'a* 3:36; R. Shlomo Kluger, *Sefer HaḤayim, Haggahot. Ḥokhmat Shlomo* (155: 1) gives a rationale for the period of twelve months; also quoted by *Darkhe Teshuva, Yoreh De'a* 155:1:6.
4. Some secular jurisdictions adopt six months as the relevant period for a definition of terminal illness. A period of six months was chosen for current Israeli law with regard to possible withdrawal of treatment, after deliberations that included rabbinic advisors; it was decided to regard survival of more than six months as outside the terminal category to allow a margin of safety for diagnostic and prognostic uncertainty (Professor A. Steinberg).
5. Rabbi Feinstein (*Iggerot Moshe, Ḥoshen Mishpat* 2: 75) indicates that since a survival of less than twelve months is relevant (although not definitive) in the category of *trefa* (one who is suffering from any of a set of pathologies that will generally not allow survival of twelve months) it can be applied to the category of *ḥayei sha'a* as the period that indicates loss of the normal assumption of life (*ḥezkat ḥayim*). Rabbi Feinstein emphatically states that where the medical consensus is that the patient will not live for *two* years, such a patient has no less claim to treatment than any other, not even where triage decisions must be made. In other words, patients who are expected to live for more than a year must not be regarded as "terminal" in any way that would deprive them of therapy or appropriate treatment priority.

or pathology that is presently inexorably threatening life in the relatively short term; the exact duration of that short term is not necessarily fundamental to the definition. However, expected survival of less than a year has become the generally accepted criterion of *ḥayei sha'a.*

In certain situations of terminal illness, treatment may be withheld (subject to stringent conditions, see below). There is an important distinction, however, between withholding and withdrawing therapy: while withholding therapy may be appropriate (and even obligatory) under certain specific conditions, withdrawing life-sustaining therapy that is already being administered is generally forbidden. More accurately, because 'withholding' and 'withdrawing' do not correspond exactly to the relevant halakhic categories, while withholding therapy may be proper in certain situations, actively shortening life is not allowed. (This is in clear opposition to a number of secular sources which make no distinction.[6] A strict utilitarian approach holds that the only issue of significance in such situations is the outcome: if the outcome is that the patient will not survive there is no real meaning to the distinction between acting to bring about that death or failing to act in such a way that death is allowed to occur. Some go further and assert that there is no moral difference between murder and failure to save;[7] in Judaism there is certainly a difference between these two forms of moral failure, with very different consequences.)

Three categories must be distinguished:

(a) Withholding: not starting a therapy that is not currently being administered. Examples would be withholding chemotherapy (where such therapy has not yet begun) from a patient with widespread metastatic disease, or the decision not to operate on a patient who is a poor surgical risk.

(b) Withdrawing: stopping a current therapy in such a manner that death is a direct consequence. Examples would be withdrawing ventilation from a patient who is currently totally dependent on ventilation, or stopping an infusion of pressor agents that are currently being continuously infused to maintain adequate circulation.

6. See R. Gillon, *Philosophical Medical Ethics* (John Wiley, 1986), esp. ch. 20: "Acts and omissions, killing and letting die", and M. Hauser, *Moral Minds* (Little, Brown, 2006); see e.g. the case on p. xvi of the prologue and the discussion there. Beauchamp and Childress argue against distinguishing between the language of "killing" and "letting die".

7. See Hauser, *Moral Minds*, for exactly this assertion.

(c) Withdrawing a therapy that is being administered intermittently by withdrawing it during an interval between administrations (stopping a therapy by not starting it after a regular break in its use); this may be seen in some sense as 'intermediate' between (a) and (b). Examples would be:

- the decision, implemented between dialysis sessions, to stop intermittent dialysis;
- stopping the long-term administration of a drug that is being given as a once-daily or weekly dose, or as a series of cycles such as chemotherapy;
- withdrawing demand cycle ventilation while the ventilator is inactive but attached ready to ventilate if respiratory function deteriorates below a set standard;
- inactivating cardiac pacing or defibrillation (by an implanted automatic device) during the inactive standby phase.

In general, category (a) is the most lenient of these categories in halakha; there are cases where such withholding may be allowed and even obligatory. Category (b) is forbidden in the context of dangerous illness; stopping a continuously needed life-sustaining therapy amounts to active euthanasia and is forbidden.[8] (Distinctions between 'withholding' and 'withdrawing', or 'active' and 'passive' conduct may not cover all cases unequivocally; mature halakhic judgment is needed.) Each case in category (c) raises the question of whether that particular treatment modality is seen as continuous or intermittent in halakha. Is a course of treatment comprising intermittent administrations deemed to be continuous in essence from a halakhic perspective? That question must be answered specifically in each case independently. The distinction is important because directly stopping a continuous life-sustaining therapy may well constitute a homicidal act; the perpetrator is terminating the patient's life by stopping a needed therapy, directly bringing about death – that is utterly forbidden in halakha. Distinct from that, however, is the withholding of a therapy that has not yet begun: in that case death results from the underlying pathology and the failure to prevent it – and there are situations in halakha where that may be permitted.[9]

8. A life-sustaining therapy such as ventilation may not be stopped on a terminal patient even to save another patient who could be saved for the long term; the general rule is that one person may not be killed to save another.

9. Other relevant distinctions can be drawn here too: is actively *removing* a device that will be needed soon while it is presently inactive worse than passively *failing to give* such a therapy when

Withholding Treatment in *Ḥayei Sha'a* Situations

A number of sources indicate that certain categories of therapy may (and sometimes should) be withheld in some terminal situations. Although healing is a mitzva (commandment), there are conditions under which it does not apply. In certain situations, treatment that is extremely painful or that prolongs severe suffering falls into this category.[10]

Throughout this section, it should be borne in mind that this discussion concerns the parameters governing withholding treatment, as in category (a) above, not actively hastening death, which is never allowed. It must also be specified that withholding therapy does not include withholding staples such as adequate fluids, nutrition, oxygenation, and other basic needs. Therapy that may be withheld in appropriate circumstances includes surgery, chemotherapy and other medical treatments and interventions that will increase or prolong suffering or add risk; basic and staple needs must always be provided. Perhaps more accurately, all modalities[11] must be provided except those that will add significant danger or pain.

When all of the following conditions are satisfied, treatment may be withheld and indeed may be *forbidden*:[12]

(1) The patient is in the category of *ḥayei sha'a*, terminally ill. In such cases, *ḥayei sha'a* means that the consensus of duly qualified opinion is that the patient will not survive a year. This judgment must be made

---

it falls due? Removing an implanted defibrillator may well be more problematic halakhically than not implanting one in the first place (in situations of equal clinical need), or not giving the next dose of chemotherapy when it is due. The latter cases may be discretionary in halakha, the former may not.

10. *Kraina DeIgerta* 190 states that one should not prolong the suffering of a *goses* and probably not that of any terminal patient. *Iggerot Moshe, Ḥoshen Mishpat* 2:75 adds that one should ask the patient: if he prefers to live despite his suffering, one should certainly attempt to prolong his life. R. Eliashiv points out that life is of such inestimable value that one should ideally choose to live despite great suffering; unfortunately this is not universally recognized and that choice cannot be forced on an individual who does not want it. The *Ḥazon Ish* too (quoted by R. Farbstein) stated that one is not required to prolong terminal suffering.

11. The distinction between 'ordinary' and 'extraordinary' or 'natural' and 'artificial' has limited application in halakha; for detailed discussion of this point see R. J. D. Bleich, *Bioethical Dilemmas*, i. 72–4.

12. *Iggerot Moshe, Ḥoshen Mishpat* 2:75 (also in R. M. Hershler, *Halakha and Medicine*, iv. 102); based on Ketubbot 104 and Ran, Nedarim 40: when therapy can neither cure the underlying disease nor prevent extreme suffering in terminal situations but will only prolong that state of suffering, it is appropriate to withhold such therapy. Where this is clearly the case, although one may do nothing actively to shorten life, it may be appropriate to pray for the patient's demise. See also *Tiferet Yisrael* (Yoma 8: 7, 'Boaz' 3) on this.

by fully competent expert opinion based on the best medical information available in terms of the relevant particular disease process and its clinical stage, applied to the particular patient at hand. If it is doubtful whether the patient has *ḥayei sha'a* or *ḥayei olam*, the stringent view must be adopted – that is, the patient is regarded as having *ḥayei olam* until the doubt is resolved. The general principle in *pikuaḥ nefesh* (lifesaving) is that the default approach must be to regard life as potentially salvageable; the burden of proof always falls on the less optimistic opinion.

(2) The patient is either suffering uncontrollably, or is unconscious with no hope of ever recovering consciousness even for a moment. Uncontrollable suffering may be physical or psychological.[13] Suffering should not be regarded as uncontrollable until all appropriate expert therapeutic options have been exhausted. Pain that has been inadequately treated cannot be used as a rationale for justifying the withholding of lifesaving therapy. Psychological suffering, including depression secondary to somatic pain, indicates failure to treat the pain. All possible treatment must be administered competently before intractable psychological suffering is diagnosed. Psychological and psychiatric problems that are not secondary to physical pain need treatment in their own right no less aggressively than somatic problems. The treatment of psychological issues such as depression and the sense of being a burden on family must be dealt with appropriately: treatment should not be limited to drug therapy – if practical arrangements are necessary to relieve suffering those must be made. Again, failure to relieve psychosocial, practical, or financial issues that can be alleviated cannot be used as justification for withholding lifesaving therapy.

Despite the fact that the patient is not obviously suffering,[14] permanent unconciousness, such as an irreversible coma in a terminally

13. Psychological suffering is no less real than physical suffering in the eyes of halakha – see *Tosafot*, Shabbat 50b.

14. This point is the subject of dissension between Rabbi S. Z. Auerbach and Rabbi Y. S. Eliashiv regarding resuscitation (Prof A. Abraham). Rabbi Eliashiv's view is that coma does not represent a state of suffering; Rabbi Auerbach's view is that it may (that is, perhaps a deeply comatose patient suffers but is merely unable to demonstrate that due to inability to respond appropriately – absence of clinical signs in this situation may not represent absence of pain but only absence of the ability to respond to pain in a clinically recognizable way). Rabbi Auerbach held that if the

ill patient, may justify withholding treatment where the patient has clearly indicated such a wish.[15]

(3) Finally, the patient must have expressed the wish not to continue treatment.[16] Such a wish to allow a lethal condition to take its natural course is relevant only when:

- No safe curative therapy exists (that is, therapy that could prolong survival beyond *ḥayei sha'a*). Where safe and painless curative therapy exists it should be administered.[17] Where the effectiveness or safety of a therapy is subject to dispute among experts, the patient is not obliged to undertake it.[18]
- Therapy exists but is risky in its own right and the patient refuses such therapy on account of that risk.
- Therapy exists but is painful or mutilating and the patient refuses it on that account; in some such cases coercion may not be allowed.[19]

---

patient was in pain before becoming comatose it should be assumed that he may continue to suffer while comatose. According to this view, there is no reason to change a decision to withhold resuscitation that was appropriately taken while the patient was conscious; the reason for withholding resuscitation then was to avoid prolonging suffering, and it is no different now. However, according to the view that coma does not involve suffering, perhaps that previous decision should be amended – now that the patient is no longer suffering, that reason for withholding resuscitation no longer applies. (Their respective rulings were made in the context of DNR decisions; presumably their views would apply to treatment decisions as well.) In practice, modern halakhic authorities do not require changing treatment or resuscitation decisions for terminal patients who become comatose.

15. A common error here is to confuse a family's suffering with that of the patient. The family of a comatose patient with no hope of recovery may indeed be suffering greatly, but that is not what is meant by intractable suffering justifying consideration of the withholding of lifesaving treatment; it is the patient's suffering that is relevant here, not the family's.

16. R. Moshe Feinstein states that if a terminally ill patient in extreme suffering requests continued treatment due solely to a conviction that his religious duty requires him to do so, treatment should be withheld – there is no religious duty to prolong terminal life artificially at the cost of extreme suffering. If, however, the patient genuinely wants to continue therapy in the face of severe suffering, that wish should certainly be honoured.

17. Where a more expert physician is expected, treatment should be continued (despite suffering) until that expert has seen the patient. This applies also to a physician who is not necessarily more expert but who may have a helpful opinion (*Iggerot Moshe, Ḥoshen Mishpat* 2:75.)

18. See *Mor uKetzia, Oraḥ Ḥayim* 328 for other limits to obliging acceptance of therapy.

19. The patient is, however, acting incorrectly in refusing safe lifesaving therapy and should be strongly encouraged to consent.

- The patient is a fully informed mentally competent adult.[20]
- The patient is not refusing therapy due to inadequately treated pain, depression, or other ameliorable suffering or any external coercive pressure.

In cases where the patient is unconscious and cannot express the wish to cease therapy, such a patient must have previously unequivocally expressed the personal desire for cessation of therapy in such circumstances and there is no reason to think that that opinion may have subsequently changed. In such cases that opinion would remain valid and may be applied as if given explicitly now.[21] However, where the patient is not known to have expressed a clear personal opinion, the family, knowing the patient well, can testify that the patient would have wished for cessation of therapy. Such testimony can constitute valid proxy. More generally, even if the family does not know what the patient would have wanted they are entitled to decide on his behalf – most people rely on their close family to act in their best interests and this trust tacitly empowers family members as de facto proxies.[22] Of course, this can be accepted only where there is no reason to suspect that the family may be acting from inappropriate motives.

When *all three* of the above conditions are met, treatment should be withheld. However, the details qualifying each of these criteria are critical.

Minors and mentally incompetent patients

Where the patient is a minor[23] or is mentally incompetent, the parents' opinion can substitute for the patient's in such cases. Parents are the usual *apotropos* (guardians) here,[24] and again, this applies only where their motives are not questionable. In general, where it is not possible to ascertain a patient's wishes, it may be assumed that the patient would not want suffering prolonged when that suffering is so great that a clear majority of people would respond thus.[25]

---

20. See below for patients who are unable to express a preference: unconscious, incompetent, or minor patients.
21. This should be established with the family.
22. *Iggerot Moshe, Ḥoshen Mishpat* 2:74.
23. That is, under bar mitzva age: 12 years for a girl and 13 for a boy.
24. Rabbi Y. Zilberstein (*Iggerot Moshe, Ḥoshen Mishpat* 2:74) includes close family (not necessarily only parents) when decisions must be made in a patient's best interest (since most people would rely on family in such situations). Where there is no family, the local *beit din* (halakhic authority) should assume responsibility for such decisions.
25. Professor A. Avraham quoting Rabbi S. Z. Auerbach; *Iggerot Moshe, Ḥoshen Mishpat* 2:73.

Babies with short life expectancies (for example, a baby with Werdnig Hoffman disease) constitute a separate category. Even where there is only a small chance that the child will survive, for example where there is a 5 per cent chance of surviving beyond 18 months, the child must be treated;[26] there is no reason to withhold lifesaving treatment because the patient is a baby. The child who is a *ḥayei sha'a* must receive all the treatment that an adult would receive.[27] The baby must be ventilated if necessary.

If it is clear that the child will not survive and the ventilation or other therapy will be very painful, it should not be administered; oxygen should be given to ease respiratory difficulty. One is not obliged to cause serious suffering to prolong a terminal disease.[28] However, therapy to relieve suffering must be given,[29] even where this may prolong the terminal state.[30]

In cases where ventilation or other lifesaving treatment modalities are limited and there is another child who can be salvaged in the long term who also needs the treatment, that child takes precedence.[31]

When the child is a *goses* do not initiate ventilation; provide oxygen.[32]

The above factors apply regardless of the opinions of the guardians of the child; no guardian is empowered to deprive a child of appropriate therapy. Where relevant decisions must be made, however, it is usually the parents who must make those decisions; but where the parents have abandoned the child and foster parents have stepped in, the foster parents are the proxies; that is, those who have taken upon themselves the mitzva of caring for the child, not those who have abandoned him.[33]

---

26. In general, if the child will survive for at least one year, all treatment should be given (Rabbi Y. Zilberstein). Where survival will be for a few months only and involve suffering, it may be more difficult to decide about therapy such as major surgery. Major surgery with little chance of success which will impose much suffering with no appreciable chance of survival should be withheld.
27. Mishna Yoma 8:6 and Bartenura there; Maimonides, *Hilkhot Shabat* 2:18; *Shulḥan Arukh, Oraḥ Ḥayim* 329:4. See also *Meiri*, Yoma 84b for a rationale behind this ruling where the patient is a conscious adult, and Rabbi Eliyahu Baal Shem Tov, *Sefer HaMitzvot*, where the patient is not conscious. See also *Iggerot Moshe, Ḥoshen Mishpat* 2:71.
28. *Iggerot Moshe, Ḥoshen Mishpat* 2:73.
29. *Iggerot Moshe, Ḥoshen Mishpat* 2:73 discusses the obligation to give therapy to relieve suffering safely.
30. *Tiferet Yisrael*, Mishna Yoma 8:6, 'Boaz' 3, demonstrates that it is preferable to lessen suffering in terminal situations even where such action will prolong the terminal state rather than allow a more rapid demise where that would be more painful.
31. *Iggerot Moshe, Ḥoshen Mishpat* 2:73:2.
32. *Iggerot Moshe, Ḥoshen Mishpat* 2:73:3.
33. Rabbi Y. Zilberstein, based on Maharam Shick and on *Zekher Shlomo, Parashat Lekh Lekha*, regarding a child's obligation to honour parents who abandon the child.

All of the above applies to patients who are mentally incompetent as well as to children.

Analgesia in dangerously or terminally ill patients

In modern medicine, uncontrolled pain should be extremely rare – the modern medical and surgical armamentarium includes modalities capable of relieving even the most severe pain. Traditionally, pain relief was poorly taught and practised (there have been major improvements in this field and pain relief is now a recognized area of specialization and expertise); it has been suggested that one reason for this failure was the fear that liberal administration of narcotics may depress respiration and hasten patients' demise. To be sure, some of the analgesic and palliative modalities that may be needed to relieve severe pain carry significant risk; but such risk is acceptable in the treatment of severe pain in dangerously and terminally ill patients, and in fact such risk *must* be taken, subject to certain principles of care, as detailed below. In life-threatening circumstances risky analgesic interventions may be permitted even if they carry a risk that is more than moderate. This requires explanation: why is an intervention that poses a risk to life acceptable when it is directed at symptoms and not cure? Surely life should not be seriously endangered to deal with symptoms? High-risk interventions are acceptable when they are undertaken in the attempt to cure potentially lethal conditions, but why in situations where the gain will be only symptomatic? Ordinarily, high risk can be undertaken only when life is at stake.

The halakhic rationale is this: unavoidable significant risk accompanying analgesia is acceptable in life-threatening circumstances because in such situations *the pain is not innocuous* – it is an assumption of halakha that severe pain may be a real factor adding to the danger of an underlying primary pathology.[34] In situations of dangerous illness severe pain itself constitutes a real additive risk;[35] it is a burden that increases the present risk to life.[36] A patient's will to live and

34. *Iggerot Moshe, Ḥoshen Mishpat* 2:73. See also "Palliation of Pain" in Rabbi J. D. Bleich, *Bioethical Dilemmas*, vol. ii.

35. Experienced physicians know that adequately addressing severe pain, anguish, despair, loneliness, and depression may be critically important for healing and survival.

36. In life-threatening situations halakha ascribes significance to factors that may be considered minor in other settings. One may desecrate the Sabbath for a critically ill patient to provide for the patient's needs, including needs that may not appear to be directly lifesaving. Where satisfying such needs will help the patient emotionally (though physiologically unnecessary) they are mandated in halakha (*yishuvei daatei*). Such needs are material enough to be considered lifesaving.

battle illness is a real factor in that patient's healing and survival,[37] and relieving severe pain (and alleviating anguish, despair, and depression) is therefore *not only humane but also therapeutic.*

Rabbi Feinstein reasons that since pain (and depression, hopelessness, and mental anguish) are tangible additive lethal elements, a measure of risk is acceptable in the course of treating the pain just as it would be in treating the disease itself. A common clinical application of this principle would be in the case of a terminally ill patient suffering severe pain due to a widespread malignancy. In such circumstances the physician may naturally hesitate to prescribe high doses of narcotic analgesics for fear of suppressing respiration in a very ill patient; however, according to Rabbi Feinstein such medication would be permitted and even obligatory because the patient's pain is part of the clinical problem no less than the underlying pathology.[38]

A number of important limitations apply here, however. For instance, the analgesic must be administered only with the intention of relieving pain, and not to terminate life or compromise it at all. Narcotics must be titrated carefully and expertly against the pain to provide adequate analgesia with minimum danger; any dangerous unwanted effects due to the therapy must be treated appropriately. In addition, only the most qualified and experienced physician available may administer the therapy; this is a general principle in medical halakha, but is particularly relevant in situations of known danger involving very ill patients where therapeutic skill is likely to be critical. Of course, it is the patient's pain that must form the indication for analgesia, not the family's suffering.[39]

---

37. A seriously ill patient must not be given bad news. *Shulḥan Arukh, Yoreh De'a* 337; *Nishmat Avraham* ii. 294; *Iggerot Moshe, Ḥoshen Mishpat* 2:73.
38. Rabbi Feinstein rules that an ordinarily prohibited procedure may be performed for palliation even where there is no registered survival benefit: he allows orchidectomy for palliation of metastatic prostate carcinoma even where research may not have shown a statistically significant survival advantage. Rabbi Feinstein reasons that even if a survival difference is not recognized in terms of statistical significance, since it is known that severe pain may shorten survival in serious illness it stands to reason that alleviation of pain is likely to prolong survival *at least slightly* – and that is enough to allow it (*Iggerot Moshe, Ḥoshen Mishpat* 2:73; also in Rabbi M. Hershler, *Halacha and Medicine*, iv. 114).
39. This error is not unknown. An experienced internist reports: "A terminally ill patient was coherent, lucid and not in pain. His family asked to have him on morphine as they could not deal with relating to him. I refused. During my leave, he was given morphine. On my return I found him heavily sedated. I gave him Narcan, his sedation was reversed and he sat up and hugged his wife (to her distress). Ongoing sedation was requested. There was a standoff and I was removed from his care."

Withholding fluids, nutrition, and other basic needs

Even where therapy may be withheld, basic staple needs must always be provided.[40] A patient may never be starved or dehydrated to death, no matter what the clinical situation. Basics that must be given include adequate fluid and attention to electrolyte balance, adequate nutrition, oxygenation, and anything else that the patient would have ordinarily needed: if the patient is taking insulin, it must be continued. The same applies to thyroid hormone replacement or any other therapy that is a staple ongoing need for that patient. Whatever has been necessary over the long term may not be stopped when the patient becomes terminally ill; those needs are staple and ordinary for that patient, and there is no reason to stop them now. Withholding food or any life-sustaining need for long enough will certainly kill, regardless of the acute clinical situation, and that is never allowed.

In the modern context, in hospices and other settings, it is becoming common practice to withhold food and fluids from terminally ill patients. The undoubted result is that in many such patients the specific cause of death is starvation or dehydration rather than the underlying pathology. This is absolutely unacceptable in Judaism; such action amounts to homicide.[41]

Maintaining fluid and electrolyte balance can be a serious clinical challenge in extremely ill patients; this must be skilfully managed. It is important to understand that the problem here is clinical, not ethical—whatever must be done to maintain fluid balance is obligatory; how that is handled medically may well be a clinical challenge, but that does not in any way allow less than full attention to this basic medical need. This includes intravenous fluid and electrolyte administration if oral intake is inadequate.[42]

Feeding extremely ill patients is recognized as an area of clinical difficulty. Desperately ill and cachectic patients may absorb very poorly no matter what route is chosen for the administration of nutrition. But again, this is a clinical

---

40. *Nishmat Avraham*, ii. 319–25; *Iggerot Moshe, Ḥoshen Mishpat* 2:74. Rabbi Feinstein points out that food, unlike medications, is a constant and universal need for all living creatures; patients must be fed (see there for specific exceptions).

41. For the question of whether causing death by depriving the victim of a life-sustaining need is actionable in Jewish law, see Maimonides, *Hilkhot Rotzeaḥ*.

42. Clinical expertise and experience may be needed. Proper hydration of a clinically unstable patient takes skill; on occasion complications of inadvertent excessive fluid administration such as pulmonary edema can be prevented by the use of a pediatric intravenous administration set – medical and nursing personnel must be adequately expert in all aspects of care when treating terminal patients.

problem; appropriate medical expertise must be applied to the challenge. Despite the fact that it may appear almost impossible to nourish an extremely ill patient adequately, and indeed some forms of nutrition may entail risk and potential harm, withholding all food for long enough will certainly kill the patient.

In an imminently terminal situation where a patient will clearly die from the underlying disease process *sooner* than a lack of nutrition would cause any harm, food may be withheld.[43] Since food is not ordinarily needed from minute to minute or even hourly, where death is inevitable within a very short time there may be no benefit in attempting to feed a patient who is not absorbing and who indeed may be harmed by such efforts. (This is not the case with liquids where fluid balance may be unstable in the very short term.) For the management of a *goses* in general, see below.

Where oral feeding is impossible or dangerous, feeding by nasogastric or other route must be instituted. Where gastrostomy or jejunostomy would be the best clinical solution they must be performed. Where a patient is deemed too ill for such a procedure, some method of feeding must be found (except for situations of imminent demise as outlined in the previous paragraph), no matter how clinically difficult; guaranteeing death by starvation is not a Jewish option.

Breathing is perhaps the most basic of needs, and adequate oxygenation must be provided. Where nasal cannula or facemask administration is inadequate to prevent respiratory failure, mechanical ventilation must be used. Where mechanical ventilation has not been started, the patient is terminal, and is *not suffering from the inability to breathe,* it need not be started (where all the conditions for withholding therapy as discussed above have been satisfied) – not every dying patient needs mechanical ventilation. Where the patient is suffering from acute air hunger that suffering must be relieved;[44] if mechanical ventilation proves necessary for this it must be administered.

---

43. *Nishmat Avraham,* ii. 324 concerning a *goses* who does not want staples, where death will occur sooner than their lack will cause, writes in the name of Rabbi S. Z. Auerbach that these may be withheld.

44. *Iggerot Moshe, Ḥoshen Mishpat* 2:73. Rabbi Feinstein points out that this is a particularly severe form of suffering; it must certainly be treated. Morphine or sedatives must not be used to stop the struggle to breathe; that amounts to active euthanasia and is forbidden. (Where carefully titrated doses of appropriate drugs will allow the patient to relax and breathe more efficiently, however, thus avoiding the need for mechanical ventilation, that may be appropriate; but only where extreme care is exercised to ensure that the patient improves physiologically and remains stable. The goal must be to help the patient breathe; not to facilitate peaceful asphyxia.)

Where mechanical ventilation has been started it may not be stopped while the patient is dependent on it.

Antibiotics, other drugs and blood products must, as a general rule, be given (also as a general rule, intercurrent infection in terminal patients must be treated). This rule applies to blood products and other drugs or agents that would be used if the patient were not terminal. Where a drug or other therapy will itself add a significant new danger, its use may be discretionary. Drugs (such as pressors) need not be given to a patient in the final stages of the dying process where there is no hope of recovery and the drug will not change the overall clinical picture (though a continuous infusion that is already running and that is maintaining life may not be actively stopped).[45]

All standard nursing care must be given to terminal patients including careful attention to movement for the prevention of pressure sores and all related therapy.

Withholding and withdrawing ventilation, dialysis, cardiac pacing

Subject to all the conditions outlined above (terminal illness, intractable suffering, the patient does not want this treatment) ventilation, dialysis, and cardiac pacing may be withheld if they have not been started but may not be stopped if they have.

- Ventilation: see the discussion of oxygenation above.
- Dialysis: a patient in renal failure must be dialysed. A terminal patient who is dying from other (untreatable) causes and whose renal function deteriorates as part of the overall terminal process need not be dialysed (subject to all the provisos governing withholding therapy from terminal patients discussed above). Where renal failure is the specific clinical problem and is reversible it must be treated.
- Cardiac pacing that is sustaining life may not be stopped, whether the pacing is continuous or set to pace only on demand. In the latter case it is protecting life and that protection may not be withdrawn. An implanted defibrillator may not be inactivated; once implanted it is part of the patient's life-protecting functions and may therefore not be withdrawn.[46]

45. *Nishmat Avraham,* ii. 327 quoting Rabbi S. Z. Auerbach.

46. Unless the patient is so distressed by its presence that the distress constitutes more of a threat than the absence of the device.

Risky Treatment in *Ḥayei Sha'a* Situations

Not uncommonly, therapy may be available for the treatment of a *ḥayei sha'a* condition, but only at the risk of worsening that *ḥayei sha'a* situation if it fails. Indeed, such therapy may be curative if successful and lethal if it fails. An example of this type of problem would be a hematological malignancy threatening to terminate life within a year, where long-term remission may be achieved by marrow ablation and rescue grafting, but only with a significant risk of mortality from the procedure. Here, a procedure is available that will result in cure if successful but will foreshorten the patient's *ḥayei sha'a* if not. If successful, the weeks or months of survival that would be expected if the condition were untreated will be extended to years; but if unsuccessful those weeks or months will be sacrificed – the patient will die *sooner* than the natural *ḥayei sha'a* would have lasted. A surgical example would be an enlarging aortic aneurysm that is expected to prove lethal within a year in a patient who is unfit for surgery. Surgery may be curative if successful but on the other hand may result in immediate death during the procedure.

What is the halakha in these situations? Is it preferable to preserve limited *ḥayei sha'a* or to choose a risky attempt to gain *ḥayei olam*? The key source for this area of halakha is Avoda Zara 27b. The discussion there concerns the question of seeking medical attention that may itself prove lethal in a situation of grave danger to life, and offers as a biblical source the case of four lepers who found themselves facing starvation outside the Jewish encampment during an enemy siege.[47] Their options were certain starvation, or entering the enemy camp where they might either be saved or summarily executed. They chose to risk entering the enemy camp (where, as it happened, they survived). This incident suggests that in the equivalent medical dilemma it would be proper to risk immediate death for the chance of long-term survival.

The commentaries engage in extensive analysis of this source, variously construing its constituent parameters particularly with respect to the degree of the risks involved, and a range of halakhic precedents is based on its various understandings. Rabbi Feinstein raises a question that leads him to a principle in this area:[48] these lepers were clearly spiritually negative individuals; why do we base halakhic precedent on them? He concludes that this source demonstrates not necessarily a spiritually correct conduct so much as a logical and acceptable human choice; he therefore rules that in such situations the patient must choose

47. II Kings 7.

48. *Iggerot Moshe, Yoreh De'a* 3:36.

between the immediate risk for long-term survival and the alternative short-term certain demise.[49]

It is thus clear that risk is permissible in these situations,[50] and even high risk according to many authorities.[51] *Shevut Yaakov* deals with a case in which a patient was faced with a disease that, untreated, would prove fatal within days, but had the option of taking a drug which might either cure or kill immediately; he allows taking the drug.[52]

Rabbi Chaim Ozer Grodzensky was presented with the case of a patient in Koenigsberg who was expected to survive for no more than six months without therapy.[53] An operation was however possible that would prove curative if successful but fatal if not (the operation in this particular case had a greater than even chance of proving fatal). Rabbi Grodzensky allows the operation. He goes on to state that this applies even if the operation has only a "distant" chance of success since the language of the Talmud is *leḥayei sha'a lo ḥayshinan* – we are "not concerned" about temporary life in this type of situation and the Talmud makes no distinction between degrees of likelihood of success. In this he explicitly disagrees with *Mishnat Ḥakhamim*, who requires at least an equal chance of success to allow the surgery. (See below for discussion on the permissible limits of this

---

49. The discretionary nature of this acceptance of risk appears to be agreed by the halakhic authorities who deal with this question. Certainly where the risk of losing *ḥayei sha'a* is greater than 50 per cent, those who allow such risk do so subject to the patient's choice.
50. Other sources besides Avoda Zara 27b corroborate the precedence of *ḥayei olam* over *ḥayei sha'a* in allowing such choices. Bava Metzia 62a discusses the case of two stranded individuals one of whom possesses a flask of water sufficient to ensure the survival of only one. Two positions are presented: Ben Petura holds that the water should be shared allowing both to survive temporarily; Rabbi Akiva holds that the owner of the water should drink it and survive. Rabbi Akiva's opinion is halakhically definitive here; *ḥayei olam* takes precedence over *ḥayei sha'a* – at least, one's own *ḥayei olam* takes precedence over another's *ḥayei sha'a*. The *Ḥazon Ish* (*Hilkhot Avodat Kokhavim* 69) states that if a *third party* were the source of the water, that third party would similarly be obliged to give it entirely to one, thereby saving one life in the long term rather than two in the short term (one *ḥayei olam* is preferable to two *ḥayei sha'a*). The *Ḥazon Ish* thus holds that *ḥayei olam* should take precedence over *ḥayei sha'a* quite apart from the obligation to save one's own life first.
51. But not all; see *Meiri* (Avoda Zara 27a–28b), who mentions opinions that would not risk shortening temporary life; presumably this means only that high risk is unacceptable (since the Gemara says explicitly that risks may be taken here). See also *Tosefot Rid* (Mahadura Kama Avoda Zara 28a, para. 10) who distinguishes between expert and non-expert practitioners in this context – his concern appears to be the relative levels of risk that these two confer.
52. *Shevut Yaakov* 3:75 (quoted in *Gilyon Maharsha, Shulḥan Arukh, Yoreh De'a* 155:1).
53. *Aḥi'ezer*, pt. 2, *Yoreh De'a*, 16:6, based on Avoda Zara 27b and referring to *Shevut Yaakov* 75 brought in *Pitḥei Teshuva, Yoreh De'a* 339, *Gilyon HaRashba* 336, *Binyan Tzion* 200, *Tiferet Yisrael* in Yoma (presumably 'Boaz' 3 in Mishna 8:6) and *Mishnat Ḥakhamim* 108.

risk.) He mentions the requirement to have approval of the local halakhic authority in each case and states that the physicians involved must be the most expert.[54]

Rabbi Moshe Feinstein rules similarly that such a risky procedure is allowed,[55] and that when a patient is faced with these options of *ḥayei sha'a* or risky therapy, the patient should be given the choice (as noted above); he agrees that the risky option is allowed even when the chances of its success are less than 50 per cent. Where success is more likely than failure, the patient should choose the therapy (that choice would be halakhically correct and preferable although the patient cannot be coerced);[56] where it is less likely (that is, where the mortality of the therapy is greater than 50 per cent[57]) it is discretionary.[58]

Rabbi Feinstein states that in this context the period to be considered the limit of *ḥayei sha'a* is twelve months[59] – he states that the *Aḥi'ezer* quoted above mentions six months only because that happened to be the period that was relevant in the case at hand; the general rule to be applied should be based on a period of twelve months. Where expected survival is longer than this, one should not undertake such risks; Rabbi Feinstein writes that if a patient has a condition that may allow survival for years although it could prove suddenly fatal at any time, it would be difficult to permit a dangerous procedure to attempt cure.

What choice should be made for a patient who cannot choose (a patient who is unconscious, incompetent, or a minor)? This must be decided in each case by appropriate halakhic consultation. The decision may depend on the degree of risk; if the risk is reasonable, the appropriate choice would be to

---

54. *Shevut Yaakov* stipulates that the doctor must deliberate with particular caution, that he obtain other expert medical opinions, and that they come to a clear majority decision (that is, a proportion of at least 2:1, according to *Melammed LeHo'il*'s understanding of *Shevut Yaakov* here) and in addition that the decision be approved by the local rabbinic authority.
55. *Iggerot Moshe, Yoreh De'a* 3:36.
56. Rabbi Feinstein does not quote a textual source for this obligation; he states that it is "logical" or "reasonable."
57. A risky therapy that has a greater than 50 per cent chance of success is permissible even in *ḥayei olam* situations.
58. Rabbi Feinstein (*Iggerot Moshe, Yoreh De'a* 3:36) allows risky therapy in *ḥayei sha'a* situations only where the therapy will remove the threat to life *completely* if successful; *ḥayei sha'a* should not be risked for longer-term life that is constantly under threat of death. The risky therapy must be *curative* with respect to the threat to life (it may be used where the long-term life gained will be of lower quality than previously, but not where the original pathology will linger, subjecting the patient to ongoing risk of death that could occur at any time).
59. *Iggerot Moshe, Ḥoshen Mishpat* 2:75 and *Yoreh De'a* 3:36; Rabbi Shlomo Kluger in *Sefer HaḤayim*.

attempt cure despite the risk. Some authorities hold that even where the chance of success is under 50 per cent that chance should be taken where the alternative is certain death.[60] Where the mortality is less than 50 per cent (that is, there is a majority chance of saving life for the long term) most would agree with Rabbi Feinstein that the choice to be preferred is the active attempt to save long-term life.[61]

Does halakha empower or indeed oblige parents to choose for a child in this situation? Some authorities hold that only the patient can choose to actively undertake high risk; caregivers cannot impose high risk on incompetent wards. Rabbi Feinstein holds that parents can make this choice for a child.[62]

Limits of risk

In these *ḥayei sha'a* situations, how small must the chance of cure be to render the procedure forbidden? There is a range of opinion on this point: *Mishnat Ḥakhamim* quoted by *Aḥi'ezer* requires a success rate of at least 50 per cent to allow the attempt.[63] *Aḥi'ezer* does not give a figure but holds that even a "distant" chance of success in an otherwise hopeless situation is enough.[64]

---

60. Rabbi M. Sternbuch.

61. Rabbi Feinstein holds that this amounts to an obligation; presumably he would require it for an incompetent or minor patient.

62. *Iggerot Moshe, Ḥoshen Mishpat* 2:74. This is the generally accepted view. See however *Melamed LeHo'il* (104; p. 115) who states that where there is a clear majority of medical opinion (at least 2:1) in favour of a risky operation on a child where the alternative is certain death, parents have no right to refuse and that indeed parents never have a right to endanger their children.

63. The logic behind this figure appears to be that a therapy that has a success rate of over 50 per cent is properly considered a therapy; a procedure with a *mortality* of over 50 per cent cannot be deemed to be "therapy" (Rabbi Moshe Shapira). *Tzitz Eliezer* (10:25) similarly requires a 50 per cent chance of success.

64. The logic behind this opinion (and the others that find a chance of less than 50 per cent acceptable) would seem to be that as long as the therapy is successful in a *significant minority* of cases it is worth attempting in otherwise hopeless circumstances; the Talmud states that the temporary life being risked is "of no concern" here. (The debate among these opinions is on the question of how small a minority should be considered significant in this particular context.) *Tosafot* and others ask how the Talmud can hold that temporary life is "of no concern" when elsewhere (Yoma 85a) it mandates desecrating the Sabbath to excavate a person who is buried under rubble no matter how temporary the life gained will be; the saving of even moments of life obliges this. The answer is that in both cases we act for the patient's good: in the case of excavating a victim, if nothing is done he will certainly die, and in the case of lethal illness too, if nothing is done the patient will die. In both cases we choose the lifesaving attempt (*Tosafot*). Put another way: in the case of excavation where the victim faces certain death or only temporary life, we act to save that temporary life. In the case of lethal illness where the patient faces certain death

Rabbi Feinstein similarly holds that even a distant chance of success is adequate to make the risk permissible.[65] Rabbi Eliashiv requires a chance of success of at least 30 per cent.[66] Others hold[67] that even one in a thousand may be adequate.[68] The *Ḥatam Sofer* would not sanction a "remote" chance but does not stipulate a specific probability.[69]

The range of opinion is thus wide;[70] this is an area for judgment by competent halakhic authority.

Terminal life, therapy safe but efficacy doubtful

Where *ḥayei sha'a* can be treated with a therapy that is safe but of doubtful efficacy (that is, where the therapy may or may not succeed in prolonging *ḥayei sha'a* into *ḥayei olam* but will certainly not shorten the *ḥayei sha'a*) it should be attempted.[71]

Risking terminal life to prolong terminal life

There is a general obligation to prolong temporary life (except in the specific circumstances discussed above). This is so even when the extended period will remain in the temporary category, since any period of life, no matter how short, is of inestimable value,[72] and the patient should be counselled thus. Is there such an obligation in the face of significant risk? If there is no obligation, is it permissible to risk terminal life for its temporary extension?

Where a risky therapy exists that will extend terminal life (but not long enough to constitute long-term life) if successful, but will shorten it if unsuccessful,

---

or the chance of cure, we risk temporary life for that chance of cure (Ritva; *Tosefot R. Elḥanan*). Temporary life is "of no concern" *only* when long-term life is the possible alternative.

65. *Iggerot Moshe, Yoreh De'a* 2:58.

66. R. Y. Zilberstein.

67. Rabbi Y. Zilberstein would be unwilling to allow surgery for a neonate with congenital heart disease where the chances of surviving surgery are given as no more than 5–10 per cent. Even where the prognosis without surgery is dismal (less than one year survival), such surgery is too risky to allow (based on R. Eliashiv; see above).

68. *Beit David* 2:340.

69. *Ḥatam Sofer*, Yoreh De'a 76.

70. It appears that there are two broad issues here: firstly, there is a debate over whether more than 50 per cent chance of success is required; as suggested (nn. 74–5 above) the point at issue here may be whether a therapy that has a mortality of over 50 per cent can properly be regarded as "therapy" or not. Secondly, among those who allow less than 50 per cent chance of success there is a debate over how small the chance must be in order to be reckoned insignificant.

71. *Iggerot Moshe, Ḥoshen Mishpat* 2:74.

72. Rabbi I. Jacobovitz, *Jewish Medical Ethics*, 152.

the therapy should ordinarily not be given;[73] however, some authorities would allow a patient that choice, at least where the risk is low enough.[74] What is the limit to the risk that may be accepted in this circumstance? It seems that less than 50 per cent risk may be acceptable, and that 50 per cent risk or more would make the therapy prohibited.[75] Where patient choice is not an issue, the proper course of action is to avoid adding any significant degree of risk of precipitating death for the possible benefit of prolonging temporary life.[76]

Intercurrent and Secondary Problems in Terminal Illness

Intercurrent or secondary problems (such as an intercurrent pneumonia) in a terminally ill patient must be treated (where treatment will not add risk or suffering, as outlined above).[77]

Acute Intermittent Threats to Life

What is the halakhic status of a patient who has a chronic threat to life due to acute events, or exacerbations of his chronic disease? Where patients typically survive for more than a year but there is an incidence of acute events that may

73. *Iggerot Moshe, Ḥoshen Mishpat* 2:75. Rabbi Feinstein does not offer a primary source for this ruling but states that logic suggests it. In summary: where the dangerous therapy has only a 50 per cent chance of prolonging life beyond 12 months, it is doubtful whether it should be given (but the patient may choose to take it); where the chance is over 50 per cent it is certainly permitted (and should be chosen); where there is no chance of prolonging life beyond twelve months but only extending it somewhat at the cost of risk, this should not be done. Where it is clear that the therapy will extend temporary life with no risk, or at least will do no harm if unsuccessful, it should certainly be given (unless it will add or prolong unbearable suffering and the patient declines for that reason).
74. Rabbi Y. Zilberstein. Rabbi Feinstein appears to disagree; see next note.
75. R. Feinstein states that high risk is acceptable in *ḥayei sha'a* situations only where a successful outcome will remove the threat to life *completely*; that is, where the *ḥayei olam* gained will not be under constant threat of death due to ongoing pathology (see n. 69 above). Thus it follows that Rabbi Feinstein would not allow high risk where the *ḥayei sha'a* status will not be removed at all. In fact, in *Iggerot Moshe, Ḥoshen Mishpat* 2:75 he states clearly that risk is not permissible to prolong *ḥayei sha'a*; there he appears to include any significant level of risk, and he makes no mention of allowing a choice (although it is possible that he does not mean to prohibit such a choice).
76. An example of this type of situation would be a terminally ill cancer patient who develops massive gastro-intestinal bleeding and becomes severely unstable hemodynamically; if transfer to hospital for fluid resuscitation and transfusion is likely to involve significant risk of precipitating death because the patient is too ill to survive the transfer, it should not be attempted (see previous note). A risk of 10–20 per cent is probably sufficient to be considered significant here.
77. *Iggerot Moshe, Ḥoshen Mishpat* 2:75 states that there is no reason to think otherwise.

be life-threatening occurring at any time, is such a patient in the *ḥayei sha'a* or the *ḥayei olam* category?

There are two broad groups of clinical conditions that raise this question. The fist includes chronic conditions with acute exacerbations such as chronic obstructive pulmonary disease, where the patient has an ongoing illness that may worsen gradually over time but tends to be punctuated by acute exacerbations that may be life-threatening. The second group includes conditions in which the patient is typically well but is subject to unpredictable acute events such as cardiac arrhythmias, as in intermittent atrial fibrillation without structural cardiac disease, or the Wolff-Parkinson-White syndrome.

Other conditions may be intermediate between these groups: for example, chronic conditions that smoulder in a low-grade or quiescent manner for long periods but may become active – some hematological malignancies that tend to be indolent but may become acute, such as chronic lymphomas that may undergo unpredictable blastic transformation.

In these categories, statistical survival figures are much less meaningful for the individual patient than in a gradually and uniformly progressive disorder. Actuarial survival for the group may be measured in years, but some individual patients will experience an acute threat to life in any given year, and it may be impossible to predict which individuals will experience such a threat sooner and which will experience it later or never.

Where the group survival is more than a year, these types of conditions are not considered *ḥayei sha'a*. Therefore, despite the fact that the individual with such a condition is under a certain degree of constant threat, it is difficult to allow a high-risk procedure or therapy in an attempt to lessen the risk of an acute episode.[78]

These same general considerations probably apply to patients who have life-threatening allergies triggered by particular antigens (such as foods or insect stings). Here, a statistic is even less meaningful – the danger depends on whether the patient is exposed to the particular trigger or not. Again, where the risk of exposure is low it would be difficult to allow a therapy that carries high risk.

Extreme Old Age

Age has no bearing on the obligation to treat. Even in extreme old age all available therapy must be given. Where an old patient requests no therapy in a dangerous

78. *Iggerot Moshe, Yoreh De'a* 3:36. Rabbi Feinstein states that if a patient can live for years but could die at any moment, it is hard to permit a dangerous procedure.

situation claiming old age as a reason to be allowed to die, that is not a halakhically acceptable reason to abandon the patient. Old age should not be invoked as a reason to give a patient lower priority even in triage decisions.[79]

Risking long-term life for longer-term life

May one risk long-term life for longer term life (risking *ḥayei olam* for longer *ḥayei olam*)? Where the risk is low enough, this may be considered.

Prolonging long-term life with severe suffering

As discussed above, where terminal life can be prolonged only for the short term and at the cost of great suffering, there is no general obligation to do so. However, where a patient's life can be prolonged indefinitely (*ḥayei olam*) but only at the cost of severe permanent pain and suffering, it is more difficult to decide whether an obligation exists. In practice, Rabbi Feinstein rules that the decision should be left to the patient, or the patient's family in the case of a child.[80]

GOSES

It is important to distinguish *ḥayei sha'a* from the situation of a *goses*: a *goses* is agonal, that is, in the throes of death.[81] Understanding the distinction is vital because the halakhot pertaining to a *goses* differ radically from those pertaining to a *ḥayei sha'a* who is not a *goses*.

A *goses* manifests certain signs, among them a characteristic gasping respiratory pattern or inability to clear respiratory secretions; the Talmud states that most *gosesim* do not survive for seventy-two hours (although this is not part of the definition of *goses*; a small majority do survive longer than this).[82]

A patient may become a *goses* in the final stages of disease, or due to injury.[83] At least one authority holds that brain stem death represents a possible *goses* status.[84] A *goses* may not be moved. The reason for this is that the *goses*'s hold

---

79. *Iggerot Moshe, Ḥoshen Mishpat* 2:75.
80. *Iggerot Moshe, Ḥoshen Mishpat* 2:74.
81. Shabbat 151b; *Shakh, Yoreh De'a* 339:5; Semaḥot 1:4; Maimonides, *Hilkhot Avelut* 4:5.
82. Rabbi M. Feinstein suggests that although it is claimed that expertise in diagnosing the state of *gesisa* is rare nowadays, doctors can become familiar with the signs characterizing this condition by observing patients *in extremis* in the clinical setting (in Rabbi M. Hershler, *Halacha and Medicine*, iv. 106).
83. It is clear that Rabbi M. Feinstein (*Ḥoshen Mishpat* 2:73; also in Rabbi M. Hershler, *Halacha and Medicine*, vol. iv) regards an individual in the throes of death due to injury as a *goses* – Rabbi Feinstein is discussing the case of Rabbi Ḥanina ben Tradyon, who was being burned to death.
84. Rabbi S. Z. Auerbach; see brain stem death, pp. 135-8.

on life is so tenuous that any movement may snuff it out – a *goses* is likened to a candle flame at its last ebb; the slightest movement may extinguish it, and to do that would constitute taking life.[85]

Whether injecting fluids or drugs intravenously (into an existing intravenous line – that is, without moving the patient) is considered "movement" that is forbidden for fear of extinguishing life is debatable. There are authorities who hold that it is;[86] such injections should therefore be limited to fluids and drugs that are already being continuously infused, or material injected in an attempt to cure.

Although one may do nothing to shorten the life of a *goses* directly, one may remove an external impediment to the dying process[87] in order to avoid unduly prolonging the last moments of separation of body and soul.[88] If an external stimulus is responsible for maintaining the flickering *gesisa* status (such as a repeated loud noise that stimulates the patient to continue gasping respiration when respiration would otherwise cease), one may remove that stimulus (in this case, stop the noise).

Similarly, medical modalities that merely prolong the state of *gesisa* may be withheld – for example where repeated bolus doses of pressors are being infused to maintain blood pressure in an inevitably terminal *goses* situation these need not be continued indefinitely.[89]

A *goses* is considered alive in all respects. If there is a chance that treatment may reverse the *gesisa* situation and bring about recovery it must be given. Where there is a chance of curing a *goses* but only at the risk of precipitating death, the halakha is no different than for any *ḥayei sha'a*; the treatment may be given (for that purpose the *goses* may be moved – the risk of precipitating death is acceptable where there is a real chance of cure).[90]

---

85. *Avel Rabba*; Semaḥot 1:4; Shabbat 151b; Maimonides, *Hilkhot Avelut* 4:5.
86. Rabbi S. Z. Auerbach was of the opinion that intravenous injection may in fact cause a more significant perturbation than external movement and is therefore more dangerous and hence certainly forbidden (*Nishmat Avraham*, ii. 32).
87. *Sefer Ḥasidim* 723; Rema in *Shulḥan Arukh, Yoreh De'a* 339:1 and also in *Darkhei Moshe* on *Tur, Yoreh De'a* 339:1. From these sources it is clear that only an extrinsic impediment to the dying process may be removed; no action may be done to the *goses* himself, not even mere movement, that may extinguish life. The distinction is this: one may not actively shorten life – that is homicide and utterly forbidden (regardless of the state of health of the victim); however, where a stimulus entirely external to the *goses* is preventing death, thus prolonging his suffering (see next note), one may stop it.
88. This is understood to be a spiritually painful state (*Iggerot Moshe, Ḥoshen Mishpat* 2:74).
89. See *Nishmat Avraham*, ii. 327, in the name of Rabbi S. Z. Auerbach.
90. *Beit Meir, Yoreh De'a* 339; see there for details. See also *Tzitz Eliezer* 17:10.

A *goses* may be moved indirectly – that is, the bed on which he lies may be moved carefully for an essential need, for example, to save another endangered patient.[91] Routine observations such as temperature and blood pressure measurement should generally not be performed where they require directly moving the patient and will not alter what is being done for the patient.[92]

91. See *Nishmat Avraham* ii. 318–19 for details and related extensive discussion regarding *goses*.
92. See exceptions in *ibid.*, ii. 318–19.

The Nature of Natural Events

Rabbi Shmuel Goldin[1]

Rarely does one have the opportunity to pay tribute to a leader of Rabbi Lord Jonathan Sacks' calibre – simply because leaders of such calibre are themselves exceptionally rare. With global reach, Rabbi Sacks eloquently articulates the most detailed nuances of Jewish experience to the broadest of audiences. He possesses an extraordinary capacity to captivate individuals from all walks of life and to faithfully convey essential Jewish ideas and values in contemporary terms. Finally, his capacity to present current affairs through the prism of Jewish tradition enriches the perception of Jewish thought for Jew and non-Jew alike. I extend my best wishes and the best wishes of my rabbinic colleagues to Rabbi Sacks as he marks this life milestone. We look forward, with God's help, to learning with him and from him for years to come.

Following the death of Aaron and the battle against the Canaanites of Arad, the nation rises in complaint over the conditions of their continuing journey. God responds with a punishing attack of poisonous serpents, causing a multitude of deaths among the people. When Moses, hearing the desperate pleas of the nation, prays that this devastating attack be suspended, God commands him, "Make for yourself a fiery serpent and place it upon a high pole and it shall come to pass that

1. This essay is an excerpt from *Unlocking the Torah Text: Bamidbar* (Jerusalem: Gefen Publishing, 2013).

anyone who has been bitten shall see it and live."[2] Moses obeys and the Torah states: "And Moses made a copper serpent and set it on a high pole; and it came to pass that if a serpent bit a man, he would look upon the copper serpent and live."[3]

God's instructions to Moses concerning this incident seem abundantly strange. What is the import of the serpent that Moses is commanded to fashion?

How can the God who commanded at Sinai, "You shall not make for yourself a graven image nor any likeness of that which is in the heavens above or that which is on the earth below or that which is in the water beneath the earth"[4] now instruct Moses to create what seems to be divinely sanctioned idolatry? Why doesn't God simply suspend the attack of the serpents without the introduction of this strange symbol?

APPROACHES

Mishna

Rabbinic recognition of the serious philosophical issues raised by this episode is attested by a dramatic departure from the norm in the Mishna. In the third chapter of the tractate of Rosh Hashana, the Mishna interrupts its halakhic discourse to raise two philosophical questions. The second of these reads as follows: "Does a [copper] serpent cause death; or does a [copper] serpent grant life? Rather, when Israel glanced heavenwards and submitted their hearts to their Father in the heavens they were cured; and if not they perished."[5] Clearly, to the rabbinic mind, no supernatural powers can be attributed to the copper serpent. Any cure granted to the Israelites could only have issued from God Himself.

The rabbis of the Mishna, however, seem to beg the central question. If the Israelites were cured when they "submitted their hearts to their Father in the heavens", why was the copper serpent necessary at all? If this event is simply an example of divine response to mortal prayer, what role does the copper serpent play?

Commentaries

Some commentaries consider the episode of the copper serpent to be beyond the realm of human understanding. Ibn Ezra, for example, connects our questions concerning this event to the shroud of mystery that envelops all divinely ordained miracles. Even during moments of clearest divine revelation, God's ways remain

2. Num. 21:8.
3. Num. 21:9.
4. Ex. 20:4.
5. Mishna Rosh Hashana 3:8.

beyond our ken. We can no more comprehend why God commands Moses to perform a miracle through the medium of a manufactured serpent than we can understand why a tree branch should sweeten the waters of Mara,[6] or why, much later in Jewish history,[7] date honey should cure King Ḥizkiyahu's affliction of boils.[8]

Other scholars, however, unwilling to accept this episode at face value, struggle to find logical meaning in the symbol of the copper serpent. Rabbi Meir ben Barukh of Rothenburg (the Maharam) and Rabbi Jacob ben Asher (the Baal Haturim), for example, maintain that the copper serpent is designed to prevent further sin on the part of the Israelites. Just as a father might leave his disciplining rod in full view to deter his children from further mischief, so too, God commands Moses to display the copper serpent to the Israelites as a clear reminder of the potential ramifications of their actions.[9]

The Sforno, on the other hand, finds reference to the nature of the Israelites' sin in the symbol of the "fiery serpent". Just as a mythical fire-breathing serpent damages through its breath, so too, the Israelites sin through their complaints against God – complaints carried on their breath.[10]

Finally, Naḥmanides (Ramban) argues that the creation of the copper serpent enables God to further demonstrate His power through the performance of a "miracle within a miracle". Usually, this scholar argues, the condition of an afflicted individual will worsen if that individual is openly confronted with the source of his malady. By nature, therefore, the victim of snakebite will suffer a setback if he sees the image of a snake. Miraculously, however, during the episode of the copper serpent, God causes the suffering Israelites to heal upon symbolic confrontation with the source of their illness.[11]

Samson Raphael Hirsch

Most intriguing, perhaps, is the approach to this episode mapped out by Rabbi Samson Raphael Hirsch. Hirsch notes a powerful linguistic detail in the Torah's introduction to the serpents' attack: *Vayeshalaḥ Hashem ba'am et haneḥashim haserafim* ("And God let the fiery serpents loose against the people").[12]

---

6. Ex. 15:22–25.
7. II Kings 20:7.
8. Ibn Ezra on Num. 21:8.
9. Maharam on Num. 21:9; Baal Haturim ad loc.
10. Sforno on Num. 21:9.
11. This point is very similar to the interpretation of Rabbi Ḥezekiah ben Manoaḥ (Ḥizkuni) in his commentary on Num. 21:9.
12. This detail is further elaborated upon by Neḥama Leibowitz in her study on this *parasha*.

There is a significant difference between the words *vayishlaḥ* (conjugated in the Hebrew *kal* form) and *vayeshalaḥ* (conjugated in the *pi'el* form). The former term indicates an act of "sending", while the latter term implies an act of "setting free" or "letting loose". By introducing the attack of the serpents with the term *vayeshalaḥ* as opposed to *vayishlaḥ*, the Torah conveys that God does not "send" a supernatural plague of serpents to attack the Israelites. The nation is, after all, already travelling through a land of "snake, fiery serpent, and scorpion".[13] God simply lifts His divine protection from the people and, by doing so, "lets loose" the dangers that are already there. The copper serpent can therefore be seen, Hirsch boldly suggests, not as a symbol of God's miraculous intervention, but as a reminder of what can occur when God fails to intervene.

As each afflicted Israelite lifts his eyes to the copper serpent, he recognizes anew the hidden dangers that have dogged the heels of his people throughout their wilderness journeys. He realizes that only God's protection has enabled them to reach this point. This new grateful awareness lends fervency to his prayers, granting them the capacity to awaken God's compassion.

The symbol of the copper serpent, Hirsch concludes, speaks with clarity across the ages, reminding us of the unseen dangers that surround us each day: "Nothing is so thoroughly calculated to conciliate us in the everyday disappointments in life which so easily sting us to impatience…than the conviction of the abyss on the narrow edge of which the whole path of our life treads [and] which the loving hand of God veils from our sight."[14]

There but for the grace of God go we…. If the copper serpent is held in view, the petty disappointments that regularly afflict us will be kept in perspective as we realize with gratitude the gifts that God bestows upon us daily.

PROVIDENCE

Hirsch's original approach to the episode of the copper serpent opens the door to a powerfully perplexing philosophical question. God is, after all, the creator of the very dangers from which He potentially protects us. What, then, is the character of God's continued involvement in these "natural" forces that surround us daily? Is every event that occurs in our environment divinely ordained, or do some forces in the natural world proceed on "autopilot", affecting man automatically and arbitrarily unless God steps in? Are the calamities that rock our world, from illness to earthquakes, to be viewed as punishment or, at the least, messages

13. Deut. 8:15.

14. Rabbi Samson Raphael Hirsch on Num. 21:8.

from God? Or can we regard some of these phenomena as arbitrary, deliberately placed by God outside the realm of His own conscious control? And what about the "good things" that happen to us – are they all, in every detail, deliberately divinely sent our way? Or, once again, can we attribute some of these events to good fortune that just happens to cross our path?

While recognizing that a full understanding of God's divine justice can only emerge when we become privy to the whole picture – including the character of the spiritual "World to Come" after death – the question remains: How clearly can we perceive God's hand in this world? To put the question in other words, what is the relationship between the natural order of the world around us and the concept of divine providence (God's direct governance of the world and His active providential care of man)?

Providence in the Bible

A full discussion of the nature of divine providence in Jewish thought is well beyond the scope of this limited study. A brief review of some fundamental issues involved, however, will help us appreciate the intellectual honesty with which these questions have been debated across the ages.

At first glance, one might wonder what the fuss is all about. A faith tradition that, on the one hand, fully believes in God's omniscience and omnipotence, and, on the other hand, considers divine providence an essential philosophical principle, must certainly maintain that God ordains every last detail of our lives. And, without question, this approach of direct divine control is reflected in numerous foundational sources in Jewish tradition. The Torah itself is replete with passages underscoring God's use of natural forces as mediums of reward or punishment. The most familiar of these sections, the second paragraph of the *Shema,* openly speaks of "rain in your land at its proper time" and "grass in the field for your cattle" in response to man's obedience to God's laws and of "restraint of the heavens so that there will be no rain", "failure of the ground to yield its produce", and "banishment from the land" in response to disobedience.[15]

Numerous other biblical sections, including the two *tokhaḥot* (sections of rebuke), feature warnings concerning the various natural and man-made calamities that will befall the nation if they stray from God's mandated path.[16] God's providence on both an individual and a national scale is further attested in the narratives concerning early man, the flood, the patriarchal era, the Exodus, and

15. Deut. 11:13–17.

16. Lev. 26:14–43; Deut. 28:15–68.

more. While the Torah applies no definitive label to the concept of God's ongoing oversight of the world, the Hebrew term for providence, *hashgaḥa,* does emerge from a passage in Psalms that proclaims: "From His lofty throne *hishgiaḥ* [(God) looks down upon] all the inhabitants of the earth."[17] As discussion continues across the ages, God's personal care for His creations becomes more specifically known as *hashgaḥa pratit,* specific providence.

Rabbinic Literature

Moving to rabbinic sources, no systematic analysis is found in the Talmud or Midrash concerning the issue of divine providence (or, for that matter, any other major philosophical issue). Instead, the opinions of the rabbis emerge from disparate statements scattered across various tractates and volumes. The clearest of their observations support the vision of a God who is actively involved in all aspects of the world's functioning, down to the smallest detail. In the talmudic tractate of Ḥullin, for example, the rabbis proclaim, "No man bruises a finger on earth unless it is decreed in heaven";[18] while, in the tractate of Avoda Zara, God is described as sitting and nourishing the entire world, from "the horns of a wild ox to the ova of lice".[19] God is viewed as the arbiter of man's fate and fortune, "creating ladders upon which He casts one individual down while He raises another";[20] and He serves as a divine matchmaker, "sitting and pairing couples: the daughter of so-and-so to so-and-so".[21]

The rabbis are quick to recognize the need to carve out space for man's independent free will within the context of this deterministic world-view. They therefore proclaim: "Everything is in the hands of heaven, except the fear of heaven,"[22] and "All is foreseen, but freedom of choice is given; and the world is judged with goodness, and all is in accordance with the works."[23] Ultimately, even man's mortal character is not an automatic reality, but rather a divinely ordained response to man's actions: "There is no death without sin and there is no suffering without transgression."[24]

17. Ps. 33:14.
18. Ḥullin 7b.
19. Avoda Zara 3b.
20. Genesis Rabba on Gen. 68:4.
21. Ibid.
22. Berakhot 33b.
23. Avot 3:19.
24. Shabbat 55a.

The Concept of *Mazal*

These and other rabbinic statements seem to leave little room for belief in natural events and forces occurring without the benefit of God's active manipulation. Nonetheless, a discordant note is struck by another, less obvious series of talmudic and midrashic observations. Here, the rabbis seem to reflect discomfort with a world in which each and every event is directly and individually attributable to God's direct intervention. No one would argue, of course, God's power to control the forces of nature at will. The question is whether or not He chooses at times to allow the world to follow a natural course, absent His immediate involvement.

Literally dozens of references, for example, are found in the Talmud and Midrash concerning the role of *mazal* (fortune), an arbitrary force associated with the constellations, in determining the world's fate. Even man, some authorities maintain, comes under its sway. The famous talmudic sage Rava proclaims, "The life of my son and my sustenance are not dependent upon merit but upon *mazal*";[25] while in the tractate of Shabbat the Talmud states: "*Mazal* increases wisdom and *mazal* engenders wealth."[26] One opinion in the Zohar goes so far as to claim: "Everything is dependent upon *mazal*, even the Torah scroll in the Sanctuary."[27]

Of particular interest is a talmudic debate concerning the vulnerability of the Jewish nation to the power of *mazal*, with Rabbi Ḥanina maintaining, *Yesh mazal leYisrael*, "The Jewish people are susceptible to *mazal*," and Rabbi Johanan arguing, *Ein mazal leYisrael*, "The Jewish people are not susceptible to *mazal*."[28] While numerous other talmudic authorities support Rabbi Johanan's position, excluding the Jewish nation from the vagaries of fortune,[29] the debate itself is noteworthy, reflective of the rabbinic struggle to balance God's ongoing care for His chosen people with the arbitrary forces that might impinge on their fate.

In addition to the many discussions concerning the impact of *mazal*, talmudic sources reflect recognition of other arbitrary forces that can potentially affect man's destiny. Some scholars, for example, note that when Moses repeats God's instructions to the nation concerning the night before the Exodus, he adds the warning "And, as for you, let no man go out from the entrance to his house until morning."[30] Moses' admonition, these scholars maintain, is motivated by a desire to keep the Israelites safe from the plague of the firstborn and reflects the

25. Moed Katan 28a.
26. Shabbat 156a.
27. Zohar, *Parashat Naso*, 134.
28. Shabbat 196a.
29. Ibid. 196a–b.
30. Ex. 12:22.

recognition that, "Once permission has been given to the 'destroyer' [to act], he does not distinguish between the righteous and the wicked."[31] Even if an individual does not "deserve" death, he should not place himself in potential danger, lest he be caught in the conflagration.

Further in this talmudic passage, the same sentiment is echoed in more pedestrian yet practical fashion by scholars who observe, "If pestilence is in the city, bring your feet in [go indoors to avoid infection]."[32] The rabbis conclude with a series of similar advisories, including the general warning, often found in rabbinic literature, that an individual should travel only during the day in order to avoid nightly dangers.[33] These and other admonitions reflect rabbinic awareness that naturally occurring forces can seriously endanger an individual's safety.

Medieval Sources

By the time we arrive at the medieval period of Jewish history, complex comprehensive theories concerning the parameters of divine providence begin to emerge. Some scholars, such as Ramban, set forward the deterministic position that "an individual does not have a stake in the Torah of Moses, our teacher, until he believes that our affairs and chance occurrences are all miraculous, that there is no 'natural order' or 'routine working' within the universe."[34] Other authorities offer alternative positions.

As a case in point, the approach of Maimonides (Rambam) in his *Guide of the Perplexed* proves particularly instructive. After discussing a series of theories concerning God's governance of the world – from the Epicurean model that perceives the universe as totally governed by chance, to the view of the fatalists that any event in the universe is the direct result of God's intervention – Rambam sets forth what he considers to be the Jewish approach to divine providence. In a lengthy exposition, this scholar remains true to form. A supreme rationalist in all areas of theology, here he posits the view that divine providence is connected with divine intellectual influence, and the same beings which are benefited by the latter so as to become intellectual, and to comprehend things comprehensible to rational beings, are also under the control of divine providence, which examines all their deeds with a view to reward or punish them.[35]

---

31. Bava Kama 60a.
32. Ibid. 60b.
33. Ibid. 60a–b.
34. Naḥmanides on Ex. 13:16.
35. Maimonides, *Moreh Nevukhim* 3:17.

According to Rambam, *hashgaḥa pratit*, God's direct individual care, extends only to human beings, who as creatures of intellect can themselves relate directly to God. Divine care for species other than man, on the other hand, remains in the realm of *hashgaḥa klalit*, general (rather than specific) providence, and is limited to the preservation of the species as a whole. God does not directly determine by specific decree whether "a certain leaf drops from a tree" or "a certain spider catches a certain fly". These events are the result of chance, in a world that continues to follow natural rules set in place by God at Creation.

Even when it comes to His relationship with man, God's gift of providence is not universally applied. Since divine influence reaches man through man's own intellectual strivings, the greater man's intellectual and spiritual perfection, "the greater the effect of divine providence upon him".[36] Man thus plays a direct role in determining the impact of divine providence on his own life. God's care over man will be commensurate with man's own religious search. Those individuals whose lives are unfortunately animalistic and brutish in nature will find themselves largely governed by the forces of chance that rule the non-human species. Those, on the other hand, who aspire to human perfection, will find divine providence playing a much greater role in their lives.[37]

Rav Soloveitchik

Centuries later, in his classic work *Halakhic Man*, Rabbi Joseph Soloveitchik elucidates the full implications of Rambam's approach to divine providence:

> The fundamental of providence is here transformed into a concrete commandment, an obligation incumbent upon man. Man is obliged to broaden the scope and strengthen the intensity of the individual providence that watches over him; it is all in his hands. When a person creates himself, ceases to be a mere species man, and becomes a man of God, then he has fulfilled that commandment which is implicit in the principle of providence.[38]

To Rav Soloveitchik, providence is not only a divinely granted gift but an explicit imperative. Afforded the opportunity to establish an association with God, man is *obliged* to do so. The Man-God relationship, however, is a two-way street. When

36. Ibid. 3:18.
37. Ibid.
38. Joseph B. Soloveitchik, *Halakhic Man*, trans. Lawrence Kaplan (Philadelphia, 1983).

an individual reaches out to God, God reaches out in return, bestowing upon that individual, in ever-increasing measure, the personal gift of divine providence.

Rav Soloveitchik, however, recognizes that this model of personal providence can fall short in the face of the episodes of overwhelming tragedy that periodically engulf mankind. While the phenomenon of individual personal suffering is difficult enough to comprehend in a world governed by divine providence, even more difficult are those national moments, such as the Holocaust, when God's presence seems to disappear entirely. Such moments can best be approached, Rav Soloveitchik maintains, by turning to the difficult biblical concept of *hester panim*, the hiding of God's face. The Torah prophesies that, at particular moments in history, God, in response to sin, will take the radical step of hiding His face from the world.[39]

The phenomenon of *hester panim* connects to the Torah's narrative of creation at the beginning of time, Rav Soloveitchik explains. As described in the Torah, creation emerges as a process by which God, step by step, imposes order upon *tohu vavohu* (primordial chaos). Such chaos, however, never disappears, but continues to course beneath the surface of existence, held at bay only by God's constant renewal of creational order. When God "hides His face", He withdraws from direct maintenance of that order and, as He backs away, the world reverts to its original state of *tohu vavohu*. During such tragic times, divine providence seems to disappear and the violent forces of nature and chance hold sway, engulfing righteous and non-righteous alike.

A myriad of other scholars, from medieval to modern, posit their own theories concerning divine providence. As I have attempted to illustrate, some of the Jewish authorities emphasize God's control over all world events, while others limit such control in various ways. All, however, struggle to find a balance between the care of a thinking God towards man and the arbitrary forces that often seem to govern our lives.

39. Deut. 31:18.

The *Klal Mensch*

Rabbi Warren Goldstein

Chief Rabbi Lord Jonathan Sacks is a towering figure in the Jewish world today. Through his intellectual brilliance and magnificent eloquence he has led Anglo-Jewry for more than two decades and has also inspired Jews across the globe. Over all these years Chief Rabbi Sacks has sanctified God's name worldwide by presenting Torah values and thoughts in a way that reveals the moral and intellectual supremacy of divine wisdom. On behalf of the South African Jewish community, I would like to express our particular grateful thanks to Chief Rabbi Sacks for his visits, writings, and care, which have strengthened and uplifted us all.

On a personal level, I am grateful to Chief Rabbi Sacks for his support and friendship for so many years. This article, which seeks to describe the values and vision of a *klal mensch*, is dedicated as a tribute to Chief Rabbi Lord Jonathan Sacks, who is the living embodiment of what it means to be a *klal mensch*.[1] May God bless Chief Rabbi Lord and Lady Sacks, and their family, with many years of continued success in all their endeavours, and especially in their mission to lead and serve the Jewish people.

Connecting to Klal Yisrael, the community of Jews, is such a fundamental principle that Maimonides, based on the Talmud,[2] writes: "One who separates from

1. This essay is a slightly modified excerpt from Berel Wein and Warren Goldstein, *The Legacy: Teachings for Life from the Great Lithuanian Rabbis* (Jerusalem: Maggid Books, 2013).
2. Rosh Hashana 17a, based on Rif, not Rashi.

the paths of the community – even though he has not transgressed any sins except separating from the Congregation of Israel, and does not do *mitzvot* with them, and does not enter in their troubles and does not fast in their fasts – but rather goes in his path like a member of the nations of the world as if he is not one of them [the Jewish People] – has no portion in the World to Come."[3]

This terrible fate is reserved for transgressors of a few select categories, such as those who do not believe in God or in the divine origin of the Torah. Separation from the *klal* is defined by Rambam as a similarly grave sin. Attachment to the *klal* means, among other things, "entering in their troubles". This includes praying for the welfare of the *klal*, and that is why virtually all our official prayers are phrased in the plural. It includes helping the *klal* and its members with practical acts of giving and kindness. In its broadest sense, it means taking responsibility for the welfare of Klal Yisrael in every respect, from its physical to its spiritual needs.[4]

These values are captured in the term *klal mensch*. This role is part of a broader life mission of every Jew to become a giver and to accept responsibility for the *klal*, to give to and to help others in all areas of life. In his famous essay "*Kuntres HaḤesed*", Rabbi Elijah Dessler explains that there are two kinds of people: givers and takers, and that the ultimate goal of living a Torah life is to become a giver.

The Torah says, "And the boy grew up... and Moses grew up and went out to his brothers and saw their suffering."[5] Rabbi Judah Loew (Maharal) explains the repetition of "grew up": the first time it refers to physical growth and the second time to moral and spiritual growth. The Hebrew word for "grew up" in this passage is *vayigdal*, literally translated as becoming big, or becoming a *gadol*, a great leader. Going out of his way to see the suffering of his brothers was an act of greatness for Moses, who could have remained in the privileged and protected environment of the palace; yet he gave it all up because of his concern for the *klal*.

Many contributions to the *klal* come at the price of personal sacrifice. Conventional wisdom considers commitment to one's own needs and to those of the *klal* to be in conflict. In contrast to this attitude, Rabbi Joseph Horwitz, known as the Alter of Novardok,[6] says that it is *only* through contributing to the community that a person can refine his *middot* (character traits). A person who is

---

3. *Hilkhot Teshuvah* 3:11.
4. One of the central values emphasized by my *rebbi*, Rabbi Goldfein, was that of responsibility, which he said was emphasized by the Telzer *rashei yeshiva*.
5. Ex. 2:10–11.
6. All of the references to the writings of the Alter of Novardok in this chapter come from his essay "*Mezake Harabim*", published in his book *Madregat HaAdam*.

involved only with his own needs has no arena in which to become a great person. When working for the betterment of the *klal,* one must use all of one's character traits for the sake of Heaven; one can achieve what needs to be done only if one has complete mastery over oneself. The Alter writes that doing communal work is complicated, requiring one to refine one's *middot* and to galvanize all of one's potential strength of character and wise discernment:

> Sometimes the matter requires that a person behave with pride, and sometimes with submissiveness, sometimes with cruelty, and sometimes with compassion... sometimes with modesty and sometimes with publicity, sometimes to teach new things, sometimes to protect old things, sometimes to speak close to the natural inclination and sometimes far from it, sometimes with new, sometimes with old, sometimes with someone who wants, and sometimes where it is against that person's will. Sometimes it is spiritual work and sometimes it is physical work. Sometimes to speak and sometimes to be silent, everything for the benefit of the thing that is required.

As many people may protest that they do not have such wisdom, or the stamina to take on *klal* responsibilities, the Alter counters that once a person begins the work, help comes to him or her from Heaven. That help materializes, however, only if the person is truly devoted and carries out his or her task. The more that a person accepts, the easier it becomes, for one merits God's help, which God's help is given "for the sake of the many – to save them from tests, whether physical or in the spirit, whether in strength or in intellect". The very embracing of responsibility brings with it the merit and the support of God sufficient to carry it out. Initially it may well appear that the task is too heavy, but once the responsibility is accepted, great blessing and support come from Hashem. The Alter writes: "One who accepts upon himself responsibility, although in the beginning it will be bitter, in the end it will be sweet; for he will merit to influence others also seeking to perfect their lives. He can rely on help from Heaven at all times and in all places and at all hours."

Rabbi Solomon Wolbe explains that one's soul comes into this world filled with potential greatness that must be actualized by living in accordance with Torah principles through life's events. That potential is actualized in direct proportion to the degree that a person becomes a *klal mensch*. In practical terms, Rabbi Wolbe explains that becoming a *klal mensch* is achieved by taking on more and more responsibilities throughout life. Marriage is an important part of this journey, for one has to expand oneself to make space and be responsible for a spouse. Raising children forces a person to assume even greater responsibility, expanding one's identity to become more of a *klal mensch*. Rabbi Wolbe says that the next stage of expansion is to assume communal responsibility. "A *talmid ḥakham* [Torah scholar] who is in the city – all matters of the city are placed on him,"[7] whether he has an official position or not. Rabbi Wolbe elaborates at length that to be a *klal mensch* means taking responsibility for Klal Yisrael, Eretz Yisrael, and eventually even the entire world.

Rabbi Simon Shkop says that love of self is a natural force in every human being; but the task of every person is to expand the definition of self-identity to include as many other people as possible.[8] A lowly, coarse person sees himself as only a physical body. Someone slightly more elevated includes his soul as part of his self-identity. At a higher level, one includes his or her spouse; and on the next level, one's children are included in the definition of self-identity. And so it goes. The more spiritually elevated a person is, the more people are included in his sense of "I". A greater person will go beyond immediate family to local members of his synagogue, school, or community. A truly great person, says Rabbi Shkop, will include all of Klal Yisrael and even the entire world, in his sense of "I". From such a lofty perspective, there is no conflict between the needs of self and those of the *klal*. It is our task, therefore, to become holy people who harness the natural force of self-love, expand the concept of self to include the *klal*, and use it to benefit others.

In fact, according to Rabbi Shkop, the definition of *kedusha* (holiness) is to give to others. In so doing we emulate God, who does everything for the benefit of His creations. "Our purpose should always be to dedicate our physical and spiritual capabilities for the good of the many… and in my opinion this entire matter is included in God's commandment, 'You shall be holy'.… Included in this mitzva is the foundation and root of the ultimate purpose of our lives – that all of our work and toil should always be dedicated to the good of the *klal*."[9]

The reason we should dedicate all our abilities to the good of the *klal*, Rabbi Shkop continues, is that, in reality, all gifts and blessings given by God to an individual are actually intended for Klal Yisrael. They are given to the individuals in the *klal* as custodians who are duty-bound to share these gifts with the *klal*, in accordance with the needs of others. He says that this applies to material gifts,

7. Moed Katan 6a.
8. Introduction to *Shaarei Yosher*.
9. Ibid.

such as wealth, and spiritual gifts, such as a brilliant intellect. The former must be distributed to the poor and the latter must be properly utilized: one who is so gifted must learn and teach so that Torah can be spread far and wide. When a person who has received gifts from God uses them for the benefit of the *klal,* he is rewarded with more of that gift. This principle is illustrated in the teachings of the Talmud: one who gives *tzedaka* generously will be rewarded with wealth. Rabbi Shkop explains that if a 'custodian' fulfills his mandate well, he will be given more things to look after.

In keeping with this thought, Rabbi Shkop explains a statement in the Talmud that says: "one learns most from one's students." He says that (in addition to the obvious explanation that students add to the insight of their teachers) it means that God rewards the teacher with more insight and knowledge, for he has properly discharged his obligation as a custodian of the knowledge and intellect with which he had been blessed.

The practical application of this principle on a communal level is the obligation to spread Torah through establishing educational institutions, which means the sharing of Torah knowledge on a broad level. All people with sufficient Torah knowledge are required to share it with the *klal,* not to sit and learn merely for their own spiritual benefit in splendid isolation from the world. Of course, different people will make different contributions, depending on their talents and desires. Some become school teachers, others become lecturers at yeshivas, others become community rabbis, and a select few can become *rashei yeshiva, dayanim,* and *poskim.* The common denominator is the burning passion to spread Torah for the good of the *klal.*

It should not be assumed that these obligations fall only upon professional appointees and designated leaders. Every Jew can and should reach out to spread Torah and *mitzvot* in whatever way possible. The Alter of Novardok shows how one private citizen made a major contribution: Elkana lived during the era of the Tanakh, when the Mishkan (the Tabernacle) was in Shilo, and in his time, attendance at the Mishkan during festivals was quite low, as many Jews opted to stay home. The Midrash says that, on their pilgrimage to the Mishkan, Elkana and his family would make it a point to sleep in the streets of the towns they passed through, in order to draw attention. People would ask, "Why are you sleeping here?" They would answer that they were going up to Shilo in order to fulfil the mitzva, and then invite the questioners to join them on the pilgrimage. Slowly but surely they began to build up a following. In the first year, five households joined them; in the second year, ten, increasing all the time. Ultimately, Elkana restored the practice of going to Shilo to the Jewish people. The Midrash concludes: "The Holy One, blessed be He, said to Elkana, 'You have tipped the scales of merit for my people and educated them in *mitzvot,* and you have brought merit to the multitudes. I will therefore bring out a son from you who will bring merit to the multitudes of Israel and educate them in *mitzvot.*'" That son was the prophet Samuel.

The Alter points out that the mitzva of pilgrimage to the Temple at the time of the festivals is one that goes against human nature: it requires families, including those with young children, to move with great effort and trouble. Yet Elkana and his family had dedication and commitment, and through their personal example they were able to inspire so many people to do this. The Alter emphasizes that we must never underestimate the power of a few individuals to influence many people.

The Mishna recounts: "Rabbi Johanan Hasandlar said, 'Any community dedicated to Heaven will endure forever.'"[10] *Avot DeRabbi Natan* explains that the community referred to is Knesset Yisrael, the community of Israel at Sinai. Accordingly, the community "dedicated to Heaven" that will endure forever spans more than 3,300 years – from Mount Sinai to the present. We can term Knesset Yisrael a vertical community, rooted in Sinai. All the generations from Sinai until now form one community. To identify fully with the *klal* means identifying with Jews in the world today as well as with previous generations.

When we learn Torah, we rely on the Oral Tradition and the power of accumulated learning of generations of Torah scholars. This is indicated in the foundational verse: "Torah was commanded to us by Moses; it is the heritage of *kehillat Yaakov.*" The "*kehilla* of Jacob" includes all generations of Jews from the beginning. The *Torah Temima* says that this verse entrenches the fact that the tradition we received from Moses, handed down for generations, is the entirety of what the Torah is about. When we teach a child this verse, we are telling him that the only way to understand what the Torah says is via this community.

To be a *klal mensch* is to identify not only with the history of Klal Yisrael, but also its future and its destiny. The destiny of Klal Yisrael is connected to God's grand vision for the redemption of the Jews and, indeed, of all mankind. As the mishna quoted above states, "Rabbi Johanan Hasandlar said, 'Any community dedicated to Heaven will endure forever.'" Rabbi Johanan Hasandlar, a direct descendant of King David, was a student of the famous Rabbi Akiva, and lived during the Roman military occupation in the immediate aftermath of the destruction of the Second Temple – an era in which calamitous events ultimately

10. Pirkei Avot 4:14.

led to the exile of the Jewish people from the Land of Israel. Sforno points out that, at the time Rabbi Johanan spoke, the future outlook of the Jewish people seemed bleak. His own mentor, Rabbi Akiva, was executed for teaching Torah in defiance of tyrannical Roman decrees; and so to claim that the Jewish people, if they were dedicated to Heaven, would "endure forever" must have seemed quite unrealistic. The mighty Roman Empire with its elaborate civilization must have had a much greater prospect of survival than the small and beleaguered Jewish nation. But the Roman Empire is no more. Its values, its legal system, its political system, and now even its language, have vanished from the daily lives of all humanity. And yet we, the spiritual heirs and descendants of Rabbi Johanan Hasandlar and Rabbi Akiva, are still here today, and we share their values, their ideals, and their laws as contained in our Torah.

To be a *klal mensch* is to believe in the future and the destiny of Klal Yisrael as they are connected to the Torah. This passion drove one of the most courageous eras of recent Jewish history. After the Holocaust, much had been destroyed, yet the many stories of heroism of the rebuilding of yeshivas and Torah communities that emerged during and after the war declared the eternal connection between the Torah and the future of Klal Yisrael. These stories speak of the indestructible fervour for the destiny of the Jewish people rooted in Torah, and symbolize everything there is to say about being a *klal mensch*.

The Emergence of the Written Text of the Talmud

Rabbi Meir Triebitz

The transformation of the Talmud from an oral tradition to a written text is of monumental significance, yet it is a process shrouded in mystery.[1] As Professor Yaacov Sussmann writes in his definitive essay:

> We are therefore forced to conclude that the transition took place during a period about which we have no knowledge, that is, the long hidden era between the classical period of talmudic sages and the classical period of the *geonim*. In another context I have already pointed out the immense historical vacuum between these two periods, that is, the last of the Babylonian amoraic sages and the first great *geonim*. During this long era, between the fifth and eighth centuries, we have almost no information at all on Jewish history in general and on Torah scholars in particular.[2]

1. The common notion that Rabbi Judah HaNasi wrote the Mishna and that Ravina and Rav Ashi wrote the Talmud is rejected by R. Isaac Stein in his commentary on the introduction to the *Sefer Mitzvot Gadol*. For more sources see Y. Sussmann, '*Torah Shebe'al Peh: Peshuta KeMashma'a*', in id. (ed.), *Meḥkerei Talmud* 3 (Jerusalem: Magnes Press, 2005), 320 n. 4, and 369 app. 10.
2. Sussmann, '*Torah Shebe'al Peh*' (above, n. 1), 322–3.

Sussmann dates the inscription of the Talmud to somewhere between the fifth and eighth centuries. He assumes that it cannot have been committed to writing later than the eighth century, based upon his understanding that there is evidence of a written talmudic text by the beginning of the ninth century. This evidence is taken primarily from a responsum by Rabbi Natronai Gaon, which reads:

> *Megillat Setarim*: A scroll which contains halakhic decisions [*halakhot pesukot*], a type of book of *halakhot* that is unlike the Talmud, which everyone has, therefore it is called *Megillat Setarim*.[3]

We note that in the published responsum the editors have inserted commas in such a way that the Gaon seems to be stating that everyone was in possession of a manuscript of the Talmud. This appears to me to be highly unlikely. I believe the proper punctuation is to place a comma before and after the phrase 'unlike the Talmud'. The passage should then read: "A type of book of *halakhot* that is, unlike the Talmud, [the kind of book] which everyone has." In other words, it is books of halakha that everyone has, and not the Talmud. I base this idea upon the fact that the statement is made in the context of Rabbi Natronai's explanation of the word *megilla*. In the Gemara there is a dispute between Rabbi Yoḥanan and Resh Lakish as to whether the Torah was given all at once or piece by piece [*megilla megilla*].[4] The word *megilla* there refers to part of a larger work. It follows then that these scrolls may have been only the halakhic parts of a larger, possibly unwritten text known as Talmud. If so, no evidence can be adduced from here that the Talmud was a complete written text in the time of Rabbi Natronai.

In his introduction to the *Commentary on the Mishna*, Maimonides (Rambam) implies that the Talmud was still unwritten in the time of the *geonim*: "The *geonim* authored many commentaries, but nobody was able to complete a commentary on the entire Talmud as far as we know."[5] Rambam stresses that nobody was able to write a commentary on the *entire* Talmud. This point is crucial. The

3. *The Responsa of Rav Natronai bar Hilai Gaon* (Jerusalem-Cleveland: Ofeq Institute, Friedberg Library, 1993), 566:

   מגלת סתרים (שבת ו ב): מגילה שיש בה הלכות פסוקות כעין ספר הלכות שאינו כתלמוד שמצוי אצל כל אדם, לפיכך ניקרא מגילת סתרים.

4. Gittin 60a.
5. Shilat edn. (Ma'ale Adumim, 1994), 61. It is interesting to note that the common version of Rambam's introduction to his commentary on the Mishna found in the standard Talmud specifically says that Rav Ashi and Ravina wrote the Talmud, but the Shilat edition, which is a new translation from the original Arabic, omits the word "wrote" completely.

most likely reason for this is that there was no written text of the entire Talmud. The main difference between the works of the *geonim* and the works of the *rishonim* (medieval commentators), therefore, is that the latter were able to write commentaries on the Talmud because they had it as a written text, whereas the former were unable to.

Despite the prohibition of committing the Oral Torah to writing, the Talmud itself mentions in several places a dispensation for writing parts of it down, invoking the verse in Psalms: "It is time to act for God; they have made void Your Torah."[6] This is interpreted to mean that in cases of need one may waive the prohibition, as was done in the geonic period, when numerous books of halakha were composed. However, there is no mention of any dispensation for writing down the entire Talmud.

The difference between having only a few parts of the text and the entire Talmud in written form is not only quantitative but qualitative. Fragments of texts do not allow for creative interpretations in the same way that complete texts do. The Tosafists, for example, in effect edited the Talmud through their dialectical synthesis of disparate and seemingly contradictory statements and entire sections. Such an achievement is impossible if the written text is incomplete.

In the first half of the tenth century, R. Sherira Gaon writes in his famous Epistle:[7]

> Concerning that which you asked: "How was the Mishna written and the Talmud written?" The Mishna and Talmud were not written but rather after matters were settled the Rabbis were careful to teach them orally without the use of texts in accordance with the talmudic dictate, 'Matters which were transmitted orally you are forbidden to write down.'"[8]

Though one might interpret Rav Sherira as referring only to an earlier time before he had written his epistle, in its French edition he makes no mention at all of the inscription of either the Mishna or the Talmud.[9] In addition, there is an alternative version of the epistle which reads: "Were the Mishna and Talmud

6. e.g. Gittin 60a.
7. *Iggeret Rav Sherira Gaon*, ed. B. M. Levin (Haifa, 1921), 71.
8. Temura 14b.
9. It is widely agreed that the question of whether the Mishna and Talmud existed in a written form at the time of their redaction is one of the issues dividing the Spanish and French versions of R. Sherira's epistle. The French version, which, since the landmark research of Y. N. Epstein, is acknowledged to be the more authentic one, supports the opinion that neither were written.

written down?" This implies that even as late as the tenth century there was still no written text of the Talmud in existance.[10]

It is clear that Rabbenu Ḥananel,[11] Rabbenu Gershom,[12] and Rashi[13] had access to written texts of the entire Talmud, since they all wrote commentaries on large parts of the text. Therefore, taking into consideration the evidence from Sherira Gaon's epistle, the written text may have emerged sometime in the latter half of the tenth century.

I believe that Ra'avad (Rabbi Abraham ibn Daud, 1110–80) also alludes to this dating in a well-known story in *Sefer HaKabbala*. The "Story of the Four Captives" describes four rabbis who left Babylonia by ship to raise funds for the yeshivas.[14] However, their ship was captured by pirates, and each of the rabbis was sold by the pirates to a different community in North Africa or Europe. The text states:

> Then the commander arrived at Cordoba, where he sold Rabbi Moses along with Rabbi Enoch. He [Rabbi Moses] was redeemed by the people of Cordoba, who were under the impression that he was a man of no education. Now there was in Cordoba a synagogue that was called the College Synagogue, where a judge by the name of Rabbi Nathan the Pious, a man of distinction, used to preside. However, the people of Spain were not thoroughly versed in the words of our Rabbis of blessed memory. Nevertheless, with the little knowledge they did possess they conducted a school and interpreted the traditions more or less accurately. Once Rabbi Nathan explained the "immersion of the finger for each sprinkling", which is found in Tractate Yoma, but was unable to explain it correctly. Thereupon Rabbi Moses, who was seated in the corner like an attendant, arose before

10. It is also clear from Rav Sherira that the Mishna was written down at the same time as the Talmud, and neither existed in written form until the end of the geonic period.

11. *c.*990–1050.

12. *c.*960–1040.

13. 1040–1105.

14. The sages used the allegory of a ship at sea to narrate and interpret Jewish history in the turbulent diaspora. The most well-known example of this is a long aggadic section in chapter 5 of Bava Batra which relates the stories of Rabba bar bar Ḥanna. Rabba bar bar Ḥanna details a sea journey in which he witnesses incredible events. Ritva comments on this: "These events are a metaphor for the kingdom of Arabia, which ruled the Jewish people after having mixed with other nations.... The metaphor is that [the sages] saw that there would come days when the Jewish people would find themselves in a peaceful exile and it would be more difficult to guard over the Torah for it could be more easily lost."

> Rabbi Nathan and said to him: "Rabbi, this would result in an excess of immersions." When he and the students heard his words they marvelled at each other and asked him to explain the law to them. This he did quite properly. Then each shared with him all the difficulties they had, and he replied to them out of the abundance of his wisdom.
>
> The community then assigned to him a large stipend and honoured him with costly garments and a carriage.[15] The [pirate] commander wished to retract his sale. However, the king would not permit him to do so, for he was delighted by the fact that the Jews of his domain no longer had need of the people of Babylonia.
>
> The report spread throughout all of Spain and the Maghreb and students came to study under him. Moreover, all questions which had formerly been addressed to the academies were now directed to him. This affair occurred in the days of Rabbi Sherira in about 4750 (989–90), somewhat more or less.
>
> Rabbi Moses acquired numerous disciples, one of whom was Rabbi Joseph ben Isaac ben Shatmash, also known as Ibn Abitur. He interpreted the whole of the Talmud in Arabic for the Muslim King al-Hakam.[16]

My intention in what follows is not to examine the historical truth of the story itself but to try to understand the message that Ra'avad is conveying. It is my contention that, in this story, he is describing the origins of the written text of the Talmud.

The story states that "He interpreted the whole of the Talmud in Arabic", which appears to be a clear reference to a written text of the Talmud. For it is unlikely that an interpretation of the Talmud into Arabic could have been anything other than a written document, in which case there certainly had to have also been a written text in Aramaic to serve as a basis for the interpretation. Thus Ra'avad dates the writing of the Talmud to the time of Rav Sherira, at the end of the tenth century.

---

15. The literary structure of the story parallels a well-known aggadic passage in the Talmud which also speaks of a revolution in the nature of the halakhic process. Pesaḥim 66a describes the ascension of Hillel to the position of Nasi of the Sanhedrin. The Tosefta (Sanhedrin 7:5) states that Hillel taught seven exegetical principles on that day. In essence what Hillel did was to introduce the rabbis of Jerusalem to the wisdom of Shemaya and Avtalyon and, as a result, revolutionize the methodology of Torah scholarship and halakhic adjudication.
16. The translation of the "Story of the Four Captives" is mostly taken from the article by Gerson D. Cohen in the *Proceedings of the American Academy for Jewish Research*, xxix (1960–1).

It is of interest to note that the same story also mentions in another place that Rabbenu Hushiel "begot his son Rabbenu Ḥananel". As Rabbenu Ḥananel is known to have authored the first complete commentary on the Talmud,[17] we can surmise the existence of a written text at that time.

The emergence of the talmudic text is described as an open challenge to the authority of the *geonim*. Ra'avad states explicitly that "The king would not permit him to do so, for he was delighted by the fact that the Jews of his domain no longer had need of the people of Babylonia." Furthermore, Ra'avad concludes the story by writing:

> Rabbi Enoch passed away in 4775, thirteen years before the passing of Rabbenu Hai, of blessed memory. Nevertheless, the communities of West and East did not resume the sending of gifts to the academies, inasmuch as these scholars raised many disciples and the knowledge of the Talmud spread throughout the world.

The transformation of the Talmud from an oral to a written text, then, undermined the authority of the geonic heads of the Babylonian academies, for now the Talmud could be interpreted by all. Rabbis in the Diaspora were no longer bound to Babylonia for their halakhic rulings. Oral texts serve as a device by which access to the law can be limited to a small and select group, thereby protecting the authority of that group. However, once a text is written down the twin consequences of unlimited interpretation and facilitated dissemination remove the monopoly over the law. A parallel episode is discussed in Tractate Berakhot,[18] where the head of the academy, Rabban Gamliel, is deposed and the doors of the academy are opened up for everyone who wants to come and participate in the debates and discussion.

Nonetheless, the challenge to geonic authority was not random. The phrase "The king would not permit him to do so" may be a reference to the King, that is, divine providence. As believing Jews, we know that revolutions are not planned but they are guided by spiritual factors.

All of the above would seem to support that Ra'avad, through his story, is claiming that the entire Talmud was committed to writing sometime towards the end of the tenth century and not before.

17. His commentary is in fact restricted to the orders of *Mo'ed, Nashim,* and *Nezikin,* i.e. those sections that had practical relevance at the time of its writing.
18. 27b–28a.

This comparatively late date for the emergence of the written text may also be alluded to by Rashi, who writes, "For in their days the Talmud was not written and was not permitted to be written but since the hearts had been lessened the later generations began writing it."[19]

The phrase "later generations" usually indicates a different era. However, there is a variant text which, according to Sussmann,[20] is the more correct and authoritative one. It reads, "They began in our generations to write it." Rashi's usage of the term "began", along with the expression "in our generations", may well indicate that the written text of the Talmud emerged only shortly before his lifetime.

There is a further, equally fundamental question which must be answered. Assuming that we have established the time of the writing of the Talmud, it remains for us to explain why it may have happened then. Why was the "time to act for God" such that it then became permitted to write down the Oral Law in defiance of the talmudic dictum?

Ritva comments with regard to the aggada of Rabba bar bar Ḥanna[21] that these passages are a metaphor for the survival of the Jewish people and the Torah under Islam and Christianity. The Gemara states: "Rabbi Judah says in the name of Rav: Everything in the world that God created He created male and female. Even the Leviathan was created male and female... for if they would not engage in reproduction they would destroy the world."

Ritva explains:

> Leviathan refers to Edom, and the beasts of the great mountains refer to Islam. Some say that the male Leviathan is a metaphor for wisdom... and the female Leviathan is a metaphor for material luxury. If they did not need each other, and man would be drawn exclusively to the material, or exclusively to wisdom, the world would be destroyed.

My understanding of Ritva is that the Jews who found themselves in the throes of the foreign culture of Islam were in danger of losing their tradition despite the fact that they were living in relative quietude and peace. As Ritva himself writes, "Under these conditions they are in need of guarding the Torah for the wind very

---

19. Bava Metzia 33a.
20. See Sussmann, '*Torah Shebe'al Peh*' (above, n. 1), 370 (app. 10).
21. Bava Batra 73a–b.

quickly blows by."[22] It is likely that the situation of the Jews in the cultural and material enticements of their surroundings in North Africa created the need for a change in paradigm so as to ensure their spiritual survival. It could have been for this reason, then, that the Talmud was committed to writing.

It is interesting to note that *Sefer Mitzvot Gadol* also connects the rise of Islam and the strength of Christianity to the inscription of the Talmud. In his introduction, Rabbi Moses of Coucy writes, "In heaven it was not agreed that [the Talmud] should be written down until after the Islamic and Christian empires had arisen, lest the gentiles write it down and use it for evil, as they did with the Written Law."

Rabbi Isaac Stein, in his commentary, learns from this that the Talmud was, in fact, written down after the time of Ravina and Rav Ashi, these sages predated the rise of Islam, and Christianity was not a major threat to them in Babylonia.[23]

Returning to Ra'avad: he relates the story of Rabbi Moses and the allusion to the writing of the Talmud as taking place in Cordoba, located in Andalusia in southern Spain. In the tenth century Cordoba was, according to estimates, the most populous city in the world, and, under the rule of Caliph Al Hakam II, became the intellectual centre of Europe for several centuries. Its predominantly Muslim society was known for its tolerance of the Christian and Jewish minorities. This state of affairs sounds exactly like that described by Ritva which led to the necessity of committing the Talmud to writing.

Ra'avad understood that the establishment of a written text, and the process of creative interpretation it generates, were the best means of ensuring the survival of the Torah and Judaism in an intellectually and materially thriving but spiritually threatening environment. The system of Torah instruction and transmission which had worked so well for the geonic academies, despite the cosmopolitan culture of Baghdad, no longer worked for the Jews of Kairouan and al-Andalus. It was for this reason, to quote the *Sefer Mitzvot Gadol,* that "it was decided in heaven to permit the writing of the entire Talmud".

22. Ritva on Bava Batra 73b (Jerusalem: Mossad HaRav Kook, 2005).
23. Though he claims it was written during the time of the *geonim*.

Halakhic Perspectives on Gun Control

Rabbi Shlomo M. Brody

In his wonderful book *The Home We Build Together*, Rabbi Jonathan Sacks poignantly depicts the roots of the societal descent into violence over the past half century. The loss of civility – as exemplified by picketing miners, rampaging football fans, and road rage – is more than just a breakdown of civility. Rather, it is the result of the breakdown of communal moral consensus in which ethical discourse has lost its meaning and has been replaced by political correctness. One particularly bloody manifestation of this phenomenon, as Rabbi Sacks notes, are shooting rampages that have taken place in the United States, including the killing of thirty-two people in Virginia Tech University in 2007 and twenty-six people (including twenty schoolchildren) in Newtown, Connecticut in 2012. In this book and elsewhere, Rabbi Sacks eloquently argues that the ultimate cure to this violence is to recreate society through a new social covenant.

As society looks to accomplish that goal, one central question will relate to the regulation of weapons, which can both propagate and prevent violence. Particularly in the United States, where the problem of gun control is perceived as most acute, Jews have played a prominent role in debate over gun control. Interestingly, both sides have culled Jewish sources to support their position. Can halakha truly provide guidance in preventing further massacres in America and elsewhere? This essay seeks to establish the principles of gun control found in Jewish law, thought, and history and then determine how these might be implemented within contemporary debates.[1]

GENERAL PERSPECTIVE ON WEAPONRY IN THE TORAH AND HALAKHA

As with warfare in general, the Bible is ambivalent towards weaponry: weapons are necessary but not idealized. The Torah frequently refers to weapons;[2] while some of these references merely describe contemporary instruments of war, many are symbolic. After Adam and Eve's exile, the Garden of Eden is protected by revolving swords, signifying the beginning of an era in which weapons will be needed to protect our most treasured property.[3] Cain's descendant Tubal-Cain invents "instruments of copper and iron", understood by the sages to symbolize weapons of destruction.[4] The transformation of swords into ploughshares represents the end of war and the beginning of the messianic era.[5] The word *keshet* not only describes the violent arrow employed by Ishmael and others but represents God's rainbow, His promise to protect the world from further destruction.[6] The imagery strongly suggests a biblical belief that weaponry, like war, is a reality of life – but that it should not be glorified, since our greatest hope is for an end to its use.

This moral sentiment is expressed in law as well. The Torah forbids the use of certain metal instruments to construct a *mizbe'aḥ* (altar).[7] The reason, in one interpretation, is that those same instruments may be used to shorten life, while worship on the altar intends to extend life. Similarly, the sages forbade entering the Sanctuary with a sword,[8] a restriction later interpreted by medieval Jewish law to forbid bringing sharp knives, apparently used by travelling merchants for protection, into a synagogue.[9] In contemporary Israel, where armed soldiers and citizens regularly enter synagogues to pray, contemporary decisors

1. An earlier version of this essay appeared in two instalments on the *Jewish Ideas Daily* website: http://www.jewishideasdaily.com/5893/features/the-halakhah-of-selling-arms/. I thank the editors for their permission to use this material.
2. See Amotz Cohen, "Weapons and Armament in the Bible", *Maḥana'im*, 69 (2011).
3. Gen. 3:24.
4. Gen. 4:22.
5. Is. 2:4.
6. Gen. 9:13.
7. Ex. 20:21.
8. Sanhedrin 82a.
9. *Oraḥ Ḥayim* 151:6 and *Mishna Berura* 151:22.

(*poskim*) contend that one should, where possible, cover the weapons or remove the ammunition.[10]

The same sentiment informs the conceptual analysis of handling weapons on Shabbat, a day when one generally may not move certain types of objects regularly used for activities forbidden on Shabbat (known in Jewish law as *hilkhot muktze*). One should not handle a hammer, for instance, because building is a category of forbidden labour. What about a gun? It produces a flame and draws blood, both of which are banned Shabbat activities; therefore, many decisors believe that handling a gun is prohibited on Shabbat (under the category of *kli shemelakhto le'issur*, an object primarily used for prohibited purposes) except in limited circumstances and, of course, if necessary for saving lives (*pikuaḥ nefesh*). Yet Rabbi Shlomo Goren, former chief rabbi of the Israel Defense Forces and the State of Israel, has argued that Jewish law perceives the intended goal of guns more broadly: not to produce a flame or draw blood, but rather to deter enemies, prevent danger, or save lives. As such, a gun is intended to be used for morally imperative purposes only, and under these conditions its use is always permissible, whether during the week or on Shabbat. Therefore a gun is not deemed *muktze*.[11]

These sentiments make the notion of using guns for recreation, for example hunting, totally alien to Jewish law. Some say that the use of a gun to earn a living by hunting – or even by operating a recreational hunting facility – may be permitted, especially if other jobs are unavailable. But to use weapons to kill animals for fun, as Rabbi Ezekiel Landau declared in a celebrated responsum,[12] is to imitate biblical villains like Nimrod and Esau, not our forefathers Abraham, Isaac, and Jacob.[13]

---

10. See e.g. Rabbi Obadiah Yosef, *She'elot UTeshuvot Yeḥave Daat* 5:18; Rabbi Eliezer Waldenburg, *She'elot UTeshuvot Tzitz Eliezer* 10:18, and Rabbi Mordecai Eliyahu, *Shabbat BeShabbato*, 1251 (9 Kislev 5768 [2007]).
11. See Rabbi Shlomo Goren, *Meshiv Milkhama* 2:61. A similar conclusion, albeit for different reasons, is reached by Rabbi Shlomo Zalman Auerbach, who argues that the average Jew bearing a pistol or rifle primarily intends to deter attacks (as opposed to actually firing the weapon and drawing blood). Since deterrence is not a prohibited labour (*melakha*) on Shabbat, a gun is not deemed *muktze*. The different positions on this debate are presented in *She'elot UTeshuvot BaMareh HaBazak* 6:37, published by Kollel Eretz Ḥemda.
12. Rabbi Ezekiel Landau, *She'elot UTeshuvot Noda BiYehuda, Tinyana Yoreh De'a* #10. For more on hunting and the notion of *tzaar baalei ḥayim* (cruelty to animals), see chapter 5 of the comprehensive work of Rabbi Isaac Eshkoli, *Tzaar Baalei Ḥayim* (5762/2001). See also my short summary of the topic, "Ask the Rabbi: Not Sporting", *The Jerusalem Post*, 5/15/2008 (accessible online at http://www.jpost.com/JewishWorld/Judaism/Article.aspx?id=101262).
13. Since 1955 Israeli law has, unfortunately, allowed recreational hunting, despite the objection of various religious Knesset members including MK Rabbi Zerach Warhaftig. A recent rise in

In the same way, while it is understood that the use of weaponry is sometimes morally necessary, the glorification of weaponry is foreign to Jewish thought. In a well-known mishna the sages, in line with Isaiah's messianic vision, banned bearing weapons in public on Shabbat, even as an ornament, since "they are merely shameful":

> A man must not go out with a sword, bow, shield, lance, or spear [on the Sabbath]; and if he goes out, he must bring a sin offering. Rabbi Eliezer said: They are ornaments for him. But the sages say, [swords] are but a disgrace, for the verse [Is. 2:4] says, "They will beat their swords into ploughshares and their spears into pruning hooks; nation will not take up sword against nation, nor will they train for war anymore."[14]

Very few historical sources refer to Jews wearing arms as ornaments, except for certain early modern court Jews who thereby signified their social rank.[15] One thirteenth-century scholar, Rabbi Isaac of Vienna, criticized Bohemian Jews for wearing armoury on the Sabbath eve – but defended the practice if it was intended to deter bandits.[16]

IMPLICATIONS FOR PUBLIC POLICY

What do these sentiments imply for public policy? First, society should abhor and boycott cultural media, movies and video games, which glorify guns and violence. Social scientists debate the extent of the impact these media have on behaviour.[17] Irrespective of that debate, however, violent imagery without educational purpose violates the values of our religion, which goes so far as to prohibit even raising one's hand against someone else without cause, let alone actually striking them.[18] The second necessary implication is that guns should be used only for protection, not for recreation.

---

illegal poaching has renewed debate about the practice and may lead to its curtailment. This would be a good initial example of how halakha can impact contemporary Israeli law.

14. Shabbat 63a.
15. F. Battenberg, "Court Jewry and the Bearing of Weapons in Early Modern Times", *Jewish Studies* 41 (2002), 93–104.
16. *Or Zarua* 2:84.
17. For a sample of the research, see Craig Anderson et al., *Violent Video Game Effects on Children and Adolescents: Theory, Research, and Public Policy* (Oxford, 2007).
18. Sanhendrin 58b; Rema on *Ḥoshen Mishpat* 34:4. See also Rabbi Daniel Z. Feldman, *The Right and the Good: Halakha and Human Relations* (Yashar Press, 2005), 159–68.

Yet in many countries, both media violence and recreational use of weapons are difficult to regulate. Take, for example, the case of the United States, where the First Amendment broadly protects the media and freedom of expression while the Second Amendment has been interpreted as protecting weapons use by civilians. Moreover, large numbers of Americans view recreational hunting as morally acceptable. In these areas, alas, specifically Jewish perspectives are outside the contemporary American consensus. In this regard, part of the contribution of Jewish thought to the renewed social contract discussed by Rabbi Sacks would be to counter those trends. At the same time, greater emphasis should be placed on promoting Jewish perspectives within the private spheres of home, school, and synagogue. If we want Jewish principles to impact the broader world, we must provide clarity within our own community concerning these values.[19]

But none of the legal sources contemplate banning weapons – certainly not weapons used for self-defence. As Rabbi Isaac of Vienna's ruling testifies and historians have confirmed, Jews have owned weapons during many historical periods, even when discriminatory laws purported to ban Jewish ownership.[20] Rabbi Isaac Zeev Kahane has documented discussions of Jewish-owned weaponry in everyday legal texts on topics from property disputes to broken contracts for weapons training.[21] Equally significantly, there are numerous halakhic discussions of the issues involved in weapons sales by Jews to their non-Jewish neighbours.[22] Many medieval Christian texts stress the obligation of Jewish citizens to assume their share of the defence of city walls, and this obligation led to a rich halakhic discussion of bearing arms and going to battle on Shabbat. In Spain, one twelfth-century French scholar noted, "it is still common for Jews to go to war with the king,"[23] reflecting the early Hispano-Jewish tradition of warrior leaders like Samuel HaNagid. There is even documentation of Jews' occasional use of weapons to defend themselves against anti-Semitism, like this passage from the so-called

19. This is particularly important within the State of Israel, where a stress on the great mitzva of serving in the army and the constant threat of terrorists must not lead to the glorification of weaponry.

20. See e.g. M. Wenninger, "The Bearing of Weapons by the Jews in the Middle Ages" and C. Magin, "Armed Jews in Legal Sources from the High and Late Middle Ages", both found in *Jewish Studies* 41 (2002), 67–92.

21. Rabbi Professor Yitzḥak Zeev Kahane, *Meḥkarim BaSifrut HaTeshuvot* (Jerusalem, 1973), 163–7.

22. See Avoda Zara 15b and the discussion there in the various medieval commentaries. Regarding the implications of this topic for Israel's army industry, see my "The Halakha of Selling Arms", *Jewish Ideas Daily*, 5 Feb. 2013 (available online at http://www.jewishideasdaily.com/5893/features/the-halakhah-of-selling-arms/).

23. *Sefer Ravyah* 4:900.

Crusade Chronicles: "When the people of the Holy Covenant...saw the great multitude...they clung to their Creator. They donned their armour and their weapons of war, adults and children alike, with Rabbi Kalonymos...at their head...and they all advanced towards the gate to fight against the errant ones and the burghers."[24] None of this discussion, of course, marks Jews as warmongers or even habitual hunters, but it does show that Jews owned weapons and used them to defend themselves. Thus the critical question remains how to best regulate the control of these weapons.

VIOLENCE AND SELF-DEFENCE IN HALAKHA: WEAPONS IN CITIES OF REFUGE

To develop a halakhic perspective on gun control, we must first establish the principles that guide Jewish law on violence and self-defence. The Torah instructs, "Take utmost care and watch yourself scrupulously,"[25] and commands a homeowner to build a railing around his roof "lest you bring bloodguilt on your house if anyone should fall from it".[26] From these verses the sages derived the rules that a person should not keep wild dogs, shoddy ladders, or other dangerous objects in his home lest they cause bloodshed,[27] and one should not sell weapons to anyone who one fears will use them inappropriately.[28] Thus, if a careless gun salesman unintentionally contributes to illicit violence, he is guilty of "placing a stumbling block before the blind".[29] While it may be true that "guns don't kill; people do," the responsible "people" under Jewish law are not only individuals who handle weapons badly but also individuals who provide them with those weapons.

Thus, after John Hinkley shot United States President Ronald Reagan with a handgun in 1982, Rabbi J. David Bleich wrote a powerful open letter to the Jewish pawnshop owner who unknowingly sold Hinkley that handgun:

> Jewish law recognizes that indiscriminate sale of weapons cannot fail to endanger the public... Jews ought to be in the vanguard of those seeking to impress upon our legislators that handguns are indeed stumbling blocks which must not fall into the hands of the blind. Criminals do

24. Shlomo Eidelberg (ed.), *The Jews and the Crusaders: The Hebrew Chronicles of the First and Second Crusades* (University of Wisconsin Press, 1977), 30.
25. Deut. 4:9.
26. Deut. 22:8.
27. Bava Kamma 15b.
28. Avoda Zara 15b.
29. *Ḥoshen Mishpat* 427:7.

> commit crimes and it is precisely because the 'morally blind' criminals are disposed to crime that Judaism teaches that it is forbidden to provide them with the tools of their trade.[30]

Yet only indiscriminate sales of weapons are prohibited; sales to responsible people seeking self-protection remain permissible. Indeed, the Torah not only allows people to kill intruders in their homes[31] but actually mandates that potential victims or even bystanders kill a person seeking to commit murder (*rodef*): "Do not stand by the bloodshed of your fellow."[32] The question facing society is how to regulate weapons so as to balance these rules most effectively and to maximize the single value that underlies them: keeping people safe.[33]

Jewish sources have addressed similar issues of balance in two different contexts: cities of refuge and fierce dogs. As for the first, the Torah mandates the establishment of *arei miklat* (cities of refuge) – communities to which individuals who have killed, but are not fully culpable of murder, may flee for legal protection from a blood avenger, an enraged member of the victim's family.[34] What rules should govern such cities, the Talmud asks, given the backgrounds of some of the inhabitants and the standing threats to their lives?[35] One might argue that the values described above dictate strict gun control laws to prevent any sale of weapons or hunting devices that might fall into the hands of a blood avenger or an unsavoury refugee. This was precisely the position of the sage R. Nehemiah.

Yet the majority of sages disagreed. Instead, they argued that weapons sales should be allowed – but no traps should be laid or nooses knotted, "so that the blood avenger should not have a path there". This statement is cryptic; but in the nineteenth century Rabbi Isaac Chajes offered the most likely explanation: with snares readily available, one can make a death seem accidental. Without

---

30. *Sh'ma: A Journal of Jewish Responsibility*, 11:214 (15 May 1981).
31. On the right to kill intruders and its implications in current Israeli law, see Ex. 22:1–2, Sanhedrin 72a, and my "Ask the Rabbi: The Right to Self-Defense", *The Jerusalem Post*, 12/3/2010 (available online at http://www.jpost.com/JewishWorld/Judaism/Article.aspx?id=197688)
32. Lev. 19:16.
33. One immediate halakhic ramification of whether or not a given society has proper gun regulations relates to the propriety of a Jew owning a gun store. On this question, see *Yoreh De'a* 151:5; Rabbi Jacob Toledano, *She'elot UTeshuvot Yam HaGadol, Yoreh De'a* 57; Rabbi Elijah Abrizal, *Dibrot Eliyahu* 3:13, as well as my article, "Ask the Rabbi: May a Jew Own a Gun Store?", *The Jerusalem Post*, 3/8/2013, available online at http://www.jpost.com/Jewish-World/Judaism/Ask-the-Rabbi-May-a-Jew-own-a-gun-store.
34. Num. 35:11–12.
35. Makkot 10a.

them, a blood avenger must try to kill through more open means – and is more likely to get caught.[36]

Still, why not ban weapons sales anyway? Though the Talmud doesn't elaborate, it appears the sages believed that a ban would not prevent a blood avenger from acquiring weapons – but would prevent law-abiding residents from buying weapons for their own protection in an area prone to violence.[37]

In this debate we see two reasonable positions producing very different policies, even though the sages shared the same goal: preventing violence. Cities of refuge ceased to exist after biblical times, thus this particular debate did not much engage later decisors and does not provide sufficient evidence on how particular weapons control policies actually worked. Yet it does highlight for us the fact that reasonable people may disagree about the appropriate policy for a specific context.

FIERCE DOGS IN HALAKHA: SHARED VALUES, DIFFERENT OPINIONS

Fierce dogs, however, still exist. The talmudic sages did not like dogs, especially dogs that attacked strangers. The aversion might have stemmed partly from the association of dogs with Egyptian paganism but mainly reflected the sages' belief that dogs were dangerous: even their barking and growling could terrorize people to the point of causing miscarriages.[38] They also feared that dogs might deter neighbourly intermingling or keep poor people from seeking assistance.[39] Thus they mandated that a person who owns a fierce dog must keep it leashed.[40]

However, they provided that in dangerous areas such as border cities, one could unleash a dog at night, when most people have gone to sleep.[41] Scholars

36. Rabbi Isaac Chajes, *Siaḥ Yitzḥak al Makkot* 10a, s.v. *veshavin*. See also *Ḥiddushei HaRitva, Makkot* 10a, s.v. *vegirsat Rashi*, and Meiri, *Bet HaBeḥira, Makkot* 10a, s.v. *ve'arim*.
37. After initially publishing this suggestion, I later found this interpretation offered explicitly by Rabbi Feinhandler in *Banai Havivai*, ii. 119.
38. Bava Kamma 15b. There is a discussion in the commentaries whether the prohibition refers to the average dog (Maharshal, *Yam Shel Shlomo, Bava Kamma* 7:45) or just particularly fierce dogs, as indicated by Talmud's use of the term *kelev ra* (*Haggahot Maimuniyot, Hilkhot Rotze'aḥ* 11:3 and *She'elot UTeshuvot HaRama MiPano* #30). Popular practice seems to follow the latter opinion. Various aspects of this law are thoroughly discussed in Rabbi Jacob Navon, "*Gidul Kelavim, Nizkam, VeHaMishar Bahem*", *Teḥumin* 9 (Zomet: Jerusalem, n.d.), 171–90.
39. Shabbat 63a and the commentaries of Rashi and Maharsha.
40. Bava Kamma 79b.
41. Bava Kamma 83a.

have debated the scope of this exception. In medieval Germany some asserted that, since Jews lived among hostile neighbours, any Jew could own a dog for protection – and keep it unchained day and night. In sixteenth-century Poland Rabbi Moses Isserles (Rema) agreed, noting that this was the contemporary practice among Jews – though he added that if the dog might attack innocents, it had to be kept chained.[42]

But Rema's cousin and countryman, Rabbi Solomon Luria (Maharshal), condemned the exception altogether, arguing that the outside threat was not so great and the potential for accidents from keeping a dog around children and others was much greater.[43] In the next century, Rabbi Meir Eisenstadt argued that dogs should not be allowed generally but only when needed to protect large groups of people in specific areas.[44] In the eighteenth century Rabbi Jacob Emden proposed a different compromise: one dog per home – or, since some properties might require greater protection, "One may not possess any more than absolutely necessary."[45] Applying these principles to outlying towns in contemporary Israel, Rabbi Pinḥas Zivḥi ruled as follows: If one fears burglary, the dog should be visibly chained during the day, with a warning sign posted; the dog can be released at night, but only within a closed courtyard. If one fears terrorist attacks, the dog can be kept loose at all times – but only if safeguards can be taken to prevent it from harming innocent bystanders.[46]

Substitute handguns for fierce dogs, and you get something like the following debate:

> "Guns are dangerous; no private citizen should own one." "No, they are necessary for protection at night – but only in violent areas." "Today, every area is violent; so, we need constant protection." "This makes sense and agrees with current practice, but people should properly secure the guns in their homes." "That's a terrible idea: guns in the house are more likely to harm innocents than to protect against attackers." "Let's compromise: let citizens carry weapons, but only in significant locations of concern, such as schools." "Or limit people to one gun, or the absolute minimum

42. Rema, *Ḥoshen Mishpat* 409:3. He is adapting the position found in the first note within *Haggahot Shiltei Giborim* on *Mordekhai*, Bava Kamma 7:74.
43. Maharshal, *Yam Shel Shlomo*, Bava Kamma 7:45.
44. *She'elot UTeshuvot Panim Meirot* 2:133.
45. *She'elot UTeshuvot She'elat Yaavetz* 1:17.
46. *She'elot UTeshuvot Ateret Paz* 1:3, *Ḥoshen Mishpat* #8.

necessary." "No, the problem is more complex; we need differing rules for different types of people, guns, places, and circumstances."

Sounds familiar? Admittedly, guns are not dogs, because guns are controlled by rational beings who can use them cautiously – or more recklessly. Nonetheless, the diversity of rabbinic opinions on the proper regulation of dangerous but protective canines shows that reasonable people, even those sharing Jewish values regarding violence and self-defence, can disagree about gun control.

Another factor complicates the situation still more: the positions of the sages and scholars were not formed in a vacuum but related to their particular circumstances. How should our principles apply in the United States, Britain, Australia, Israel, or any other country today? America, for instance, is no longer building a new society. Instead, its society is marked by deep fear of violent attacks by gangs or deranged individuals; an estimated 300 million firearms in the hands of private citizens, legally or otherwise; a strong culture and history allowing the use of hunting and other recreational weapons; and a constitutional right to bear arms – which, though its meaning is contested, cannot be ignored. And that's just for starters. These types of complicating variables, found in every society, can reasonably change (in both liberal and conservative directions) how a person might implement gun policy in America, even as they might have taken an alternative approach under different circumstances or in a different contemporary culture.[47]

---

47. Occasionally some US gun rights advocates, Jewish and non-Jewish alike, claim that Jewish history makes it morally imperative for Jews to own guns. This argument is not persuasive. Yes, fewer Jews might have been killed in the Holocaust if the Nazis had not barred them from owning guns. But the lesson of that experience is that when a totalitarian antisemitic government tells Jews to give up their guns, Jews should keep those weapons or, better yet, flee. How is that relevant to contemporary American society and its police and armed forces? Those who fear that their culture is approaching that of 1938 Berlin, or more moderately fear rampant antisemitic attacks on unarmed Jews, should move to Israel, with its Jewish army and nuclear bombs.

If we accept the fact that twenty-first-century Washington, DC (and numerous other capitals) is not Nazi-era Berlin, here is a better question: In the previous five years, how many Jews have been injured or killed by random gun violence and how many were killed by antisemites? In all likelihood, more American Jews have fallen victim to hunting accidents and careless gun-handling than to punks with swastika tattoos. In America and many other countries, maximizing Jewish welfare means maximizing safety for all citizens. Does this mean encouraging responsible citizens to own handguns, getting weapons off the streets, or any of the other strategies that have been proposed? That is the question to ask.

CONCLUDING THOUGHTS: HALAKHIC VALUES AND PUBLIC POLICY

The legacy of Jewish perspectives on gun control – as related in law, theology, and history – is that weapons should be regulated in a manner that deters evildoers and protects the innocent. What specific policies will achieve this goal in a given society? Reasonable people can disagree because, in this case, halakha does not provide an authoritative solution.

We should, nevertheless, heed the wise statement once made by the late Rabbi Haim David Halevi, Chief Rabbi of Tel Aviv, about foreign policy: even when halakha cannot provide the answers, it may still serve as a guiding light, promoting the critical values that direct policy-makers towards a better resolution. The same is true for gun control. Jews who take part in this dialogue can draw on critical Jewish values that should frame the debate, even if these values cannot provide all the solutions.[48]

48. In this regard, we should be ever thankful to Rabbi Lord Jonathan Sacks for providing a model of how one can take Jewish values and bring them into contemporary dialogue on public policy. May God give him the strength and fortitude to continue serving the Jewish people and broader society for many years to come.

Praying for the Government in the United Kingdom and Elsewhere

Rabbi Dr Barry Freundel

One of my fondest moments in my career in the rabbinate was when Chief Rabbi Jonathan Sacks introduced the American version of his siddur at the pulpit of my congregation, Kesher Israel, in Washington, DC. From a marvellous Friday night dinner hosted by a member of the community, to Shabbat morning when he and I served as *ḥazanim* leading the service from the new siddur, to Shabbat afternoon when, along with Leon Wieseltier, we engaged in a 'trialogue' about the history of prayer and the structure and commentary in Rabbi Sacks' new siddur and its place in that history, it was a wonderful experience of Torah, prayer, and educating a community in things that really matter. That, of course, is but the smallest piece of what Rabbi Sacks means to the vast world of Jewry and beyond, and to the myriad number of Jews and people of all faiths whose lives he has touched.

In that spirit, I would like to discuss the history and halakha surrounding one element of the prayer service, one that is particularly appropriate for Rabbi Sacks. For reasons that will emerge as we go, I have decided to discuss *Tefilla LiShlom HaMedina* (the prayer for the government) in general, and the special place it has in the liturgy of British Jewry specifically.

More years ago than I care to remember, I spent some eleven months as a student in Israel. Given the vagaries of airplane travel, it was less expensive in those days for me to spend some time in England than to fly directly from the US to Tel Aviv. As a result, I spent Shabbat in London. In shul that Shabbat morning, I heard the British version of the prayer for the government for the first time in my life. I was used to such a prayer from the synagogue of my childhood but was surprised to hear the listing of the members of the royal family as part of that prayer. I did not know then, but do now, that this is part of a special halakhic reality that makes the prayer for the government different in the UK than in other countries. Discussing that difference will be the final point in this essay. To get to that point and to adequately explain it, we first need to explore the history of the prayer and the changing status of its recitation in halakha.

BIBLICAL ATTESTATIONS

It is hard to say where the earliest reference to the prayer for the government appears. Many point to the famous verses from Jeremiah 29, where the prophet gives instruction to the Jews who, after the Babylonian conquest, find themselves in exile for the first time since the Exodus from Egypt. He famously says to them:

> Thus says the Lord of hosts, the God of Israel, to all who are carried away captives, whom I have caused to be carried away from Jerusalem to Babylon: Build houses, and dwell in them; and plant gardens, and eat their fruit; take wives, and father sons and daughters; and take wives for your sons, and give your daughters to husbands, that they may bear sons and daughters; that you may be increased there, and not diminished. And seek the peace of the city where I have caused you to be carried away captives, and *pray to the Lord for it; for in its peace shall you have peace.*[1]

Often cited along with this verse is the mishna in Avot 3:2: "Rabbi Ḥanina the assistant high priest said: 'Pray for the sake of the government for if not for the fear of it each person would swallow his neighbour alive.'" Despite the fact that this mishna does not make reference to the verses in Jeremiah and does not speak of the city and its well-being, it does seem to recommend a similar liturgical requirement – to pray for the government. Since the well-being of the city depends in large measure on the functioning of the government, these two calls

1. Jer. 29:4–7.

for prayer seem to be related. That is certainly how a number of halakhic authorities understood these texts, as we shall see below.

There is, of course, a conceptual difference between Jeremiah, who seems to speak only in purely pragmatic terms about Jewish self-interest, and R. Ḥanina, who makes his appeal using a Hobbesian political formulation that takes all who live in the area controlled by the government into consideration.[2] Nonetheless the desired result seems to be the same: pray for the government because its continued well-being prevents bad things from happening and brings good things to fruition. As a result, it would seem that we should all be praying in this way. However, as we shall see shortly, things are not quite that simple.

Let us compound the problem. In point of fact, these two texts seem not to be the earliest references that we have to such a prayer, whether we look in traditional or in non-traditional sources. While many of the texts that we will now explore appear in the period of time between Jeremiah and the Mishna, at least one may be quite a bit earlier.

In 1 Kings 8:66, as King Solomon concludes the dedication of the First Temple, the verse reads: "On the eighth day he sent the people away; and they blessed the king, and went to their tents joyful and glad of heart for all the goodness that the Lord had done for David His servant, and for Israel His people." The Tosefta (Sukka 4:17) quotes this verse as an indicator that one of the differences between Shemini Atzeret and the other days of Sukkot is *berakha le'atzma* (its own blessing): "And the last holy day of Sukkot has a lot for itself, a time for itself, a pilgrimage festival for itself, a sacrifice for itself, a song for itself, a blessing for itself, as it says: On the eighth day he sent the people away; and they blessed the king."

Notice that the wording in Kings is "they blessed the king". Rashi understands the Tosefta to mean that not only in King Solomon's time but every year, on Shemini Atzeret, a special blessing was said for the king in commemoration of what occurred at the Temple's dedication: "They would bless the king in memory of the dedication of the Temple, as it says: 'On the eighth day he sent the people away; and they blessed the king.' So it is explained in Tosefta Sukka."[3] That would make this the earliest prayer for the government recited at regular intervals that we can find.

---

2. Thomas Hobbes, *Leviathan*.
3. Rosh Hashana 4b, s.v. *berakha le'atzma*, and Yoma 3a, s.v. *berakha le'atzmo*; see also *Malbim* on 1 Kings 8:66.

On the other hand, *Tosafot* and many others understand this text to mean that we refer to Shemini Atzeret and not Sukkot in the Grace after Meals and the *Amida* on this day.[4] That is, of course, our current practice, and for these commentators that is the separate blessing referred to by the Tosefta. Finally, Meiri and others mention both practices[5] (as does Rashi himself in one place in which he discusses this issue[6]). Meiri also says that this blessing for the king was recited on all holidays, not just Shemini Atzeret.

The Tosefta's prayer for the government would seem to have affinities with the contemporary Israeli prayer for the government,[7] as it expresses pride in Jewish sovereignty and not the types of insecurity reflected in the iterations of the prayer for the government recited in the Diaspora or under foreign domination in the Holy Land that I will be discussing in the rest of this essay. Interestingly, Tosafot in one location says that "now we do not recite this blessing" (meaning the prayer described by Rashi), implying that under different circumstances to those in twelfth- or thirteenth-century Franco-Germany such a prayer might be said.[8] Perhaps the contemporary State of Israel represents such a case.

As we move past Kings and Jeremiah in biblical history, we find these verses in Ezra 6:8–10:

> Moreover, I make a decree regarding what you shall do for the elders of these Jews for the building of this House of God; that from the king's goods, from the tribute beyond the river, expenses be given to these men, so that they should not be delayed. And that which they need, young bulls, and rams, and lambs, for the burnt offerings of the God of heaven, wheat, salt, wine, and oil, according to the requirements of the priests who are at Jerusalem, let it be given to them day by day without fail; that they may offer pleasing sacrifices to the God of heaven, and pray for the life of the king, and of his sons.

4. *Tosafot*, Rosh Hashana 4b, s.v. P-Z-R K-SH-V; Yoma 3a, s.v. P-Z-R K-SH-V; Sukka 48a, s.v. *regel bifnei atzma*; Ḥagiga 17a, s.v. P-Z-R K-SH-V; *Rabbenu Behaya, Bamidbar* 29:35; *Ḥidushei HaRamban*, Sukka 48a; *Ḥidushei HaRitva*, Yoma 3a; *Rif*, Sukka 23a; *Rosh*, Sukka 4:5.
5. Meiri, *Beit HaBeḥira*, Sukka 47a; *Ḥiddushei HaRashba*, Rosh Hashana 4b.
6. Sukka 48a, s.v. *berakha le'atzmo*.
7. Rabbi Mordecai Fogelman (1899–1984), *Responsa Beit Mordecai* 1:18, speaks eloquently of the need for such a prayer given the founding of the state after the tragic experiences of Jewish history.
8. Yoma 3a, s.v. P-Z-R K-SH-V.

These lines are described as being part of a scroll containing the decree of Darius, which allowed the Jews to finish rebuilding the Second Temple in Jerusalem so that the offerings for the king mentioned here could be brought to the altar.[9] This part of the scroll actually cites the royal proclamation of Darius' ancestor Cyrus, who, using these words, had permitted the Jews to start this rebuilding only to have the project stopped.[10] That work stoppage occurred because the Samaritans, who had come to occupy Judaea while the Jews were out of the land enduring the Babylonian exile, had hired counsellors and lobbyists who slandered the Jews to the government. This slander succeeded in bringing the work to a screeching halt, as described earlier in the books of Ezra and Nehemiah.[11] With this decree issued by Darius, the work could be finished and the sacrifices for the king would become a reality.

EXTRA-BIBLICAL WITNESSES

Intriguingly, a version of Cyrus' decree that ended the Babylonian exile and began the second Jewish commonwealth and the building of the Second Temple seems to have been discovered in what is known in archaeological circles as the Cyrus Cylinder. It reads in part:

> Akkad, the land of Eshnunna, the city of Zamban, the city of Meturnu, Der, as far as the border of the land of Guti – the sanctuaries across the river Tigris – whose shrines had earlier become dilapidated, the gods who lived therein, and made permanent sanctuaries for them. I collected together all of their people and returned them to their settlements, and the gods of the land of Sumer and Akkad which Nabonidus – to the fury of the lord of the gods – had brought into Shuanna, at the command of Marduk, the great lord, I returned them unharmed to their cells, in the sanctuaries that make them happy. May all the gods that I returned to their sanctuaries, every day before Bel and Nabu, ask for a long life for me, and mention my good deeds, and say to Marduk, my lord, this: "Cyrus, the king who fears you, and Cambyses his son, may they be the provisioners of our shrines until distant [?] days, and the population of Babylon call blessings on my kingship. I have enabled all the lands to live in peace.[12]

9. Ezra 6:1.
10. Ibid. vv. 2–3.
11. Ibid. 4:5–24, and cf. Neh. 1–3.
12. Irving Finkel, translation of the text on the Cyrus Cylinder, on the website of the British Museum at http://www.britishmuseum.org/explore/highlights/articles/c/cyrus_cylinder_-_translation.aspx, vv. 31–6.

All of this tells us, in both biblical and non-biblical texts, that, at least for Cyrus and Darius, the idea of having their subject populations praying for the government was important and that this was a practice that the Jews accepted, if not embraced.

This also appears to be true with other rulers, as reflected in various sources from antiquity. Barukh son of Neriah was Jeremiah's scribe, who wrote down the words of God that Jeremiah prophesied,[13] including, presumably, the letter to the exiles that speaks of praying for the peace of the city in which these exiles live, as mentioned above. After the close of Tanakh, the apocryphal book of I Barukh from the second century BCE, anachronistically ascribed to Jeremiah's scribe, tells of the beginnings of the Babylonian exile.[14] In words that parallel Jeremiah, the text says (1:9-12):

> After Nebuchadnezzar King of Babylon had carried away Jeconiah, and the princes, and the captives, and the mighty men, and the people of the land, from Jerusalem, and brought them unto Babylon. And they said, "Behold, we have sent you money to buy you burnt offerings, and sin offerings, and incense, and prepare you the shew bread, and offer upon the altar of the Lord our God; and pray for the life of Nebuchadnezzar King of Babylon, and for the life of Belshazzar his son, that their days may be upon earth as the days of heaven: And the Lord will give us strength, and lighten our eyes, and we shall live under the shadow of Nebuchadnezzar King of Babylon, and under the shadow of Belshazzar his son, and we shall serve them many days, and find favour in their sight."[15]

Again, ancient kings (this time Nebuchadnezzar), expect and appreciate prayers by Jews and other subject peoples on their behalf, and the Jews would seem to be well advised to comply with this expectation.

I Maccabees may be an eyewitness account of the Hasmonean victory against the forces of Hellenism in the second century BCE, written by a soldier in Judah Maccabee's army who was a traditional Jew. It was certainly authored by a pious Jew with first-hand knowledge of the events and who lived at the time they

13. Jer. 32, 36, 43, and 45.
14. P. J. Berlyn, "Baruch ben-Neriah: The Man Who Was Not a Prophet," *Jewish Bible Quarterly* 25(3) (1997) 150–61; Kenneth M. Craig, Jr., "Baruch and the Letter of Jeremiah," in *Mercer Commentary on the Bible* (1994) 853–8; Jonathan A. Goldstein, "The Apocryphal Book of I Baruch," in *Proceedings: American Academy for Jewish Research* 46–47(1) (1978–9), 179–99.
15. Translation from http://www.kingjamesbibleonline.org, modified by me.

occurred or perhaps shortly thereafter.[16] The Talmud, quoting from *Megillat Taanit*, tells us of Yom Nicanor, which commemorated the defeat of a Greek general of that name who had been sent by Antiochus to end the Maccabean insurrection.[17] I Maccabees fills in the details and includes the following description in 7:26–33:

> Then the king sent Nicanor, one of his honourable princes, a man that bore deadly hate to Israel, with the commandment to destroy the people. So Nicanor came to Jerusalem with a great force; and sent to Judah and his brethren deceitfully with friendly words, saying, "Let there be no battle between me and you; I will come with a few men, that I may see you in peace." He came therefore to Judah, and they saluted one another peaceably. Howbeit the enemies were prepared to take away Judah by violence. Which thing after it was known to Judah, to wit, that he came to him with deceit, he was afraid of him, and would see his face no more. Nicanor also, when he saw that his counsel was discovered, went out to fight against Judah beside Kephar Salama: Where there were slain of Nicanor's side about five thousand men and the rest fled into the city of David. After this Nicanor went up to Mount Zion, and there came out of the sanctuary certain of the priests and certain of the elders of the people, to salute him peaceably, and to show him the burnt sacrifice that was offered for the king. But he mocked them, and laughed at them, and abused them shamefully, and spoke proudly.[18]

I Maccabees tells us a little bit more about these prayers, or in this case sacrifices, for the government. Here we have not just the theoretical statement that this type of worship should occur but an indication that it did occur.

A further example of this type of literature, Josephus in *War of the Jews* (Book 2, ch. 10) describes a confrontation between the Romans and the Jews in Jerusalem concerning an issue of great sensitivity to the Jewish people:

> Now Caius [or Caligula] Caesar[19] did so grossly abuse the fortune he had arrived at, as to take himself to be a god, and to desire to be so called also, and to cut off those of the greatest nobility out of his country. He also extended his impiety as far as the Jews. Accordingly, he sent Petronius with

16. Jonathan A. Goldstein, *I Maccabees* (NY: 1976).
17. Taanit 18b, Y. Taanit 2:12 (66a), Y. Megilla 1:4 (70c).
18. http://www.kingjamesbibleonline.org with modification.
19. See also Philo of Alexandria, *On the Embassy to Gaius* XXX 201–3.

an army to Jerusalem, to place his statues in the Temple, and commanded him that, in case the Jews would not admit of them, he should slay those that opposed it, and carry all the rest of the nation into captivity. But God concerned Himself with these his commands. However, Petronius marched out of Antioch into Judaea, with three legions, and many Syrian auxiliaries. Now as to the Jews, some of them could not believe the stories that spoke of a war; but those that did believe them were in the utmost distress how to defend themselves, and the terror diffused itself presently through them all; for the army was already come to Ptolemais.... But now the Jews got together in great numbers with their wives and children into that plain that was by Ptolemais, and made supplication to Petronius, first for their laws, and, in the next place, for themselves. So he was prevailed upon by the multitude of the supplicants, and by their supplications, and left his army and the statues at Ptolemais, and then went forward into Galilee, and called together the multitude and all the men of note to Tiberias, and showed them the power of the Romans, and the threatenings of Caesar; and, besides this, proved that their petition was unreasonable, because while all the nations in subjection to them had placed the images of Caesar in their several cities, among the rest of their gods, for them alone to oppose it, was almost like the behaviour of rebels, and was injurious to Caesar. And when they insisted on their law, and the custom of their country, and how it was not only not permitted them to make either an image of God, or indeed of a man, and to put it in any despicable part of their country, much less in the Temple itself, Petronius replied, "And am not I also," said he, "bound to keep the law of my own lord? For if I transgress it, and spare you, it is but just that I perish; while he that sent me, and not I, will commence a war against you; for I am under command as well as you." Hereupon the whole multitude cried out that they were ready to suffer for their law. Petronius then quieted them, and said to them, "Will you then make war against Caesar?" The Jews said, "We offer sacrifices twice every day for Caesar, and for the Roman people"; but that if he would place the images among them, he must first sacrifice the whole Jewish nation; and that they were ready to expose themselves, together with their children and wives, to be slain. At this Petronius was astonished, and pitied them, on account of the inexpressible sense of religion the men were under, and that courage of theirs which made them ready to die for it; so they were dismissed without success.[20]

20. http://www.godrules.net/library/flavius/flaviusb22c10.htm with modification.

It seems clear from all the above textual witnesses that the custom of praying (or offering sacrifices) for the government began very early in Jewish history, was taken quite seriously by the Jews and by the rulers they served, and, at least as custom if not as full-fledged Jewish law, it has been an integral part of Jewish liturgy from time immemorial.

To cite a final source for our review of the ancient history of this practice, a similar story from antiquity to those we have seen above appears in the Babylonian Talmud, Yoma 69a. The text reads:

> For we have learned: The twenty-fifth of Tevet is the day of Mount Gerizim, on which no mourning is permitted.[21] It is the day on which the Cutheans demanded the House of our God from Alexander the Macedonian so as to destroy it, and he had given them the permission, whereupon some people came and informed Simeon the Just. What did the latter do? He put on his priestly garments, robed himself in priestly garments, some of the noblemen of Israel went with him carrying fiery torches in their hands. They walked all the night, some walking on one side and others on the other side, until the dawn rose. When the dawn rose he [Alexander] said to them [the Samaritans]: Who are these? They answered: The Jews who rebelled against you. As he reached Antipatris, the sun having shone forth, they met. When he saw Simeon the Just, he descended from his carriage and bowed down before him. They said to him: A great king like yourself should bow down before this Jew? He answered: His image it is which wins for me in all my battles. He said to them: What have you come for? They said: Is it possible that star-worshippers should mislead you to destroy the House wherein prayers are said for you and your kingdom that it be never destroyed! He said to them: Who are these? They said to him: These are Cutheans who stand before you. He said: They are delivered into your hand. At once they perforated their heels, tied them to the tails of their horses and dragged them over thorns and thistles, until they came to Mount Gerizim, which they ploughed and planted with vetch, even as they had planned to do with the House of God. And that day they made a festive day.

Again, the pattern of the prayer for the government being well established and strongly approved by the king appears here. We also get a sense from many

21. This too derives from *Megillat Taanit*.

of these sources that the prayer itself was a witness to a great deal of Jewish insecurity and was frequently used to placate various rulers as to Jewish loyalty and concern for those in power.

MEDIEVAL TESTIMONIES

Turning now to post-talmudic literature, and despite all of the antecedent sources including the verses from Jeremiah and the mishna from Avot, our earliest siddurim, by Rav Amram Gaon[22] and by Simḥa of Vitry,[23] do not describe a formal prayer for the government. Nonetheless, in the early Medieval period we have evidence from the Cairo Geniza that Jews prayed for the government, at least as individuals, particularly when it served their interests to do so.

It was in this spirit that a petitioner opened his request to the Fatimid Caliph Al-Mustansir with a description of himself as "the slave of my lord (blessings of God be upon him), who kisses the ground and humbly beseeches that he be granted a service."[24] Similarly, when Solomon ben Judah al-Fasi, the *gaon* of Fatimid Egypt and Syria in this era, expressed concern that the Caliph was giving some of the *gaon*'s power to a rival, he ended his letter with a blessing that "God bestow glory upon the Caliph's victories".[25] So too, when Daniel ben Azarya was appointed *gaon* of the Jerusalem Yeshiva,[26] his letter of response includes the words "may God prolong his [the Caliph's] days, exalt his fortune, and destroy his enemies, his opponents, and those who wish him evil."[27] All these examples originate from the eleventh century.

From the twelfth century and the era of the Crusades, we find two formal prayers for the government in the Cairo Geniza. The first, from sometime between 1127 and 1131, asks for blessings on the royal family and the second, from a few years later, may actually have been supplied by the government. We can see evidence for this claim in the honorific that appears in the following

22. R. Amram ben Sheshna Gaon (d. 875) of the yeshiva in Sura responded to a request from Spanish Jewry to explain what should be prayed when, throughout the Jewish year. He wrote a work, now called *Seder Rav Amram Gaon,* which serves as one of the important contributing sources for Sephardi custom.

23. *Maḥzor Vitry* by R. Simḥa of Vitry (twelfth century), a student of Rashi, is generally considered the earliest Ashkenazi siddur.

24. Marina Rostow, "Formal and Informal Patronage Among Jews in the Islamic East: Evidence from the Cairo Genizah," *Al-Qantara* 29(2) (2008), 356.

25. Ibid. 357.

26. He served as *gaon* between 1051 and 1062.

27. Ibid. 376.

sentence from the prayer: "His [God's] greetings and call of peace be upon our Lord and Master the Imam al-Hafiz li-din Allah, the Commander of the Faithful." Intriguingly, the Caliph of Baghdad in 1138 concluded his charter with the Nestorian Church with the requirement that the Church "set up prayers and invocations for the Commander of the Faithful as a token of your gratitude and a sign of your allegiance".[28]

Franco-German sources from the same era also provide evidence of prayers for the government, beginning with eleventh-century Worms, where the supplication sought the protection of the government for the Jews. This was presumably to protect them from the Crusaders of that era.[29]

HALAKHIC TEXTS

Moving back to our halakhic sources, the earliest mention I have been able to find of the formal practice of reciting a prayer for the government in the post-talmudic era is in the thirteenth- or fourteenth-century Franco-German work *Kol Bo,* which says: "And on the Sabbath at Shaḥarit after the Haftara, they were accustomed to say a *Mi Sheberakh,* and there are places that bless the king and then the community and it all follows the [local] custom."[30] Intriguingly, from precisely the same era but from a Sephardi source, *Sefer Abudraham* writes:[31]

> And they were accustomed to blessing the king and to praying to God that He should aid him and strengthen him over his enemies, as it says: And seek the peace of the city where I have caused you to be carried away captives, and pray to the Lord for it; for in its peace shall you have peace.[32] And the peace of the city is that he shall pray to God that the king shall defeat his enemies. And we say in the first chapter of Tractate Avoda Zara:[33]

---

28. S. D. Goitein, "Prayers from the Geniza for the Fatamid Caliphate," in *Studies in Judaica, Karaitica and Islamica Presented to Leon Nemoy on his Eightieth Birthday* (Ramat Gan, 1982), 48–55.
29. Michael Laitner, "The Prayer for the Royal Family" (2011), online at http://youandus.theus.org.uk/living-and-learning/jog/the-prayer-for-the-royal-family/; Barry Schwartz, "'*Hanoten Teshua'*: The Origin of the Traditional Jewish Prayer for the Government," in *Hebrew Union College Annual,* 57 (1986) 113–20.
30. Apparently by Rabbi Aaron ben Rabbi Jacob HaKohen of Narbonne, France; *Sefer Kolbo,* no. 20, s.v. *Din Hotzaat HaTorah.*
31. *Sefer Abudraham: Hilkhot Keriyat HaTorah,* by Rabbi David ben Rabbi Joseph Abudraham, who lived in Spain during the thirteenth century. The excerpt is my translation.
32. Jer. 29:7.
33. Avoda Zara 3b.

> Rab Judah says in the name of Samuel: Why is it written: And You make man as the fishes of the sea, and as the creeping things, that have no ruler over them? Why is man here compared to the fishes of the sea?... Just as among fish of the sea the greater swallow up the smaller ones, so with men, were it not for fear of the government, men would swallow each other alive. This is just what we learnt: R. Ḥanina, the Deputy High Priest, said, Pray for the welfare of the government, for were it not for the fear thereof, men would swallow each other alive.[34] And after this he blesses the community, as it says: [And the king turned his face around] and blessed all the congregation of Israel.[35]

Abudraham cites the verse from Jeremiah with which I began my discussion, marking the earliest formal connection between the prophecy and the prayer. He also refers to the mishna of R. Ḥanina, the second classically cited text of origin for the prayer for the government. In addition, he provides nice symmetry for our subject by quoting a verse from King Solomon's dedication of the Temple from earlier in the same chapter that provided the text which led the Tosefta to describe a custom of blessing the king on Shemini Atzeret. In the verse cited by Abudraham the king blesses the people, while in the Tosefta the people bless the king. Like the *Kol Bo,* Abudraham speaks of the prayer for the government as a custom.

Some two hundred years later, what had been the "custom" of praying for the government became a "need" (*tzerikhin*) and a mitzva. In *Sefer Seder Hayom,* written by Rabbi Moses b. Judah ibn Mahir in the sixteenth century, the author writes:

> After [the Haftara], the *ḥazan* shall bless the king who rules over us. Even if he is from the nations of the world, since we stand under his control and his rule, we must [*tzerikhin anu*] pray for him. For in his peace we will find peace. So it is an affirmative commandment from our tradition [rabbinic law], for so it says in Jeremiah: "And seek the peace of the city where etc." and the entire nation shall say Amen.[36]

---

34. The Bavli here cites the mishna from Avot 3:4 discussed above.
35. 1 Kings 8:14.
36. *Sefer Seder HaYom: Seder Keriyat HaTorah BeShabbat* by Rabbi Moses ben Rabbi Judah ibn Mahir, who lived in Safed in the sixteenth century. My translation.

When we come to the eighteenth century, Rabbi Ezekiel Landau writes:

> It is already known and well published in all places where I have been that I warn and remonstrate in most of the Torah expositions that I proffer publicly that we be extremely careful of the honour of the nations of our time, in whose lands and states we find sanctuary. And we are required [*ḥayavim*] to pray for the peace of the kings, the officers, and their soldiers and to pray for the sake of the state and its inhabitants. And God forbid that we be ungrateful since they are good to us and they grant us life and a remnant in the land.[37]

Rabbi Landau's claim that this prayer is required is reiterated at least three times in the twentieth-century responsa of Rabbi Moshe Feinstein. In one place he says:

> We certainly should not speak before non-Jews concerning their faith to which they hold on today to maintain peace in the country because as a result of the kindness of God we dwell in their shade in peace and tranquillity and we are commanded to pray for its [the United States'] peace.[38]

In a second responsum, Rabbi Feinstein addresses a question comparing secular and Jewish landlord/tenant law. He says (again concerning the United States):

> And also so that it not appear, God forbid, that we are diminishing the honour of our nation's government with what we say, because we are required to give gratitude for the kindness that they perform with us and with all our brothers the children of Israel who live in this country. So we bless them and pray to God at all times and moments for the peace of the country, its president and its officers, as we have been commanded. Therefore it is not my desire to write about and adjudicate this.[39]

---

37. Rabbi Ezekiel ben Judah Landau was born in 1713 in Opataw, Poland, and died in 1793. The above quote is from his introduction to *Tzela*, called *Hitnatzlut HaMeḥaber*, and is my own translation.

38. Responsa *Iggerot Moshe: Yoreh De'a* 2:53, my translation. Rabbi Moshe Feinstein was born in Russia in 1895, and died in 1986 in New York.

39. Ibid., *Ḥoshen Mishpat* 1:72.

And in a third place he says (note the title of the responsum):

> *Concerning the prohibition against Torah institutions taking from the government more than [is commensurate with] the conditions it has established*

> Regarding the matters of kindness which our government of the United States of America, which God in His great kindness over the saved remnant of the Jews from all the countries of Europe and over the remnant of the great Torah sages and their students has brought here, where they have established Torah institutions, both older ones from Europe and new ones. Because this government of kindness, whose entire purpose is to do good for all those who dwell in this land, has created a number of financial programmes to help students in all the schools in the country so that they can study and grow in their education, so that also Torah institutions receive great help for their students, certainly all *rashei yeshiva*, principals [of schools], and students feel great gratitude to the state and bless with all blessings for the sake of peace of the state and all those who stand in its leadership.[40]

Here, despite not mentioning the word *ḥiyuv* (requirement) specifically, Rabbi Feinstein seems to imply such an obligation by the requirements of gratitude he describes in this responsa and by his own words in his other two answers.

In short, then, we have moved across the centuries from relatively early biblical times to the twentieth century, and the prayer for the government has moved with us from where it was a fairly widespread practice throughout the ancient world, mentioned in biblical and rabbinic sources, to its being a custom endorsed by a number of medieval European halakhic texts, to pre-modern and modern sources that see the prayer as an obligation or a command.

All of this also applies to the United Kingdom, of course, but British Jewry has another reason to see the prayer for the government as a requirement in that country. Several hundred years after their expulsion from England in 1290, Jews petitioned Oliver Cromwell to be allowed to return. This petition came, in part, in two polemical works by Menasseh ben Israel, leader of the Amsterdam Jewish community. These works, entitled *The Humble Addresses to His Highness the Lord Protector on Behalf of the Jewish Nation* (1655) and *Vindiciae Judaeorum*

40. Ibid. 2:29.

(Vindication of the Jews; 1656), include the promise that, should the Jews be allowed to settle in England again, they would pray for the state and particularly for the royal family. This petition was accepted.[41]

Halakhically, when Jews make a pact with a non-Jewish government, they are bound by the terms of that agreement and all of its details.[42] As a result, on one Shabbat morning many years ago when I was in London, as on every Shabbat for centuries, British Jewry recited its version of the prayer for the peace of the government, which includes specific mention of the members of the royal family. They did so for all the reasons that apply in other countries (at least in those that treat their Jews well), plus the halakhic principle that when Jews promise something to a non-Jewish government or people, they must fulfil that promise. This additional requirement is met by British Jewry every time they recite their version of *Tefilla LiShlom HaMedina*.

41. Schwartz, loc. cit. 116, Lucien Wolf (ed.), *Menasseh ben Israel's Mission to Oliver Cromwell: Being a reprint of the pamphlets published by Menasseh ben Israel to promote the re-admission of the Jews to England, 1649–1656* (London, 1901); California State Library, *Pamphlets relating to the Jews in England during the 17th and 18th centuries*, ed. Ariel Hessayon (1939). *From Expulsion (1290) to Readmission (1656): Jews and England*, online at http://www.gold.ac.uk/media/350th-anniversary.pdf.

42. See Maimonides, *Mishne Torah, Hilkhot Melakhim* 7:3, and Rabbi David ibn Zimra ad loc.

Mitzva Observance: The Appropriate Motivation

Rabbi Anthony Knopf

It is a great privilege to be writing for this publication to show honour to Chief Rabbi Sacks, from whom I have learnt so much and whose writings have played such a major role in my own religious development.

INTRODUCTION

In an article published in September 2011,[1] Rabbi Adin Steinsaltz revealed that he was often asked, especially by non-believers, whether religious practice can actually make us better human beings. Rabbi Steinsaltz indicates that the answer depends on the attitude of the religious person towards observance. For many, observance of the *mitzvot* involves commitment to a ritual practice which has no connection to any overarching ethical or spiritual values. The *mitzvot* are kept out of a sense of obedience with no identification with their underlying ideas and concepts. Rabbi Steinsaltz bemoans this lack of depth and meaning in the ritual observance of so many religious practitioners and indicates that this attitude does not allow for maximum spiritual development.

1. 'Why Doesn't Religion Make Us Better People?', *New Jersey Jewish News* (21 Sep. 2011), http://njjewishnews.com/article/6546/why-doesnt-religion-make-us-better-people.

In this article I discuss a topic that is highly relevant to the importance of ethical and spiritual values in the halakhic life. The specific question that I tackle is that of appropriate motivation for mitzva observance. Should *mitzvot* be performed out of a sense of submission to an inscrutable divine command or is it preferable to be motivated by the values underlying the particular commandment? To take an example, should the proper motivation for giving *tzedaka* be compassion for the recipient or adherence to the Torah obligation?[2]

Whilst the contemporary zeitgeist accepts comfort and self-expression as appropriate litmus tests for choice of lifestyle, Jewish sources emphasize the centrality of obedience and responsibility in submission to divine imperatives. We ignore this underscoring of obedience to God at our peril; but at the same time, there is an equally significant emphasis in Jewish sources on a motivation for observance grounded in a love for the mitzva and the values it represents.

DIVINE COMMAND AS APPROPRIATE MOTIVATION FOR MITZVA OBSERVANCE

As mentioned above, many Torah sources ascribe great importance to the submission of the religious believer to the command of God. Congruous with this approach is the understanding that mitzva observance should be motivated by a commitment to obeying God's command. A classic example supporting this approach is found in the Midrash: "Rabbi Elazar ben Azarya said: ... [A] person should not say, 'I loathe pig's flesh,' or 'I do not desire to wear [a mixture of] wool and linen.' Rather, he should say, 'I do desire it; yet what can I do because my Father in heaven has decreed upon me against it.'"[3] Rabbi Elazar ben Azarya presents adherence to the laws of kashrut and *shatnez* not in terms of a sense for the inherent repugnance of these foods and clothing but through a commitment to the law of God, who has forbidden them.

---

2. The issue of motivation should not be confused with that of *ta'ame hamitzvot*, discerning reasons for particular commandments. It is possible to maintain that there are rational reasons underlying the *mitzvot* but that one should be motivated to observe them solely because they are divine commands. Such is the position of Rabbenu Tam as understood by Rabbi Moshe Feinstein. In his responsa *Iggerot Moshe, Yoreh De'a*, I:6, Rabbi Feinstein explains that Rabbenu Tam applies the talmudic principle that "one who performs a mitzva when commanded to do so is superior to one who performs a mitzva when not commanded to do so" to *mitzvot* which have a reason. Even though Rabbenu Tam accepts that some *mitzvot* have a reason, he emphasizes the importance of performing the mitzva simply because it is a commandment.
3. *Sifra, Vayikra* 20:26; *Midrash Yalkut, Vayikra* 20:26.

Another fundamental source for the desirability of obedience as motivation for mitzva observance makes reference to R. Joseph, a blind rabbi of talmudic times.[4] R. Joseph cites a teaching of R. Ḥanina, who said that one who does a mitzva which he is commanded to do is greater than one who does a mitzva which he is not commanded to do. In the light of this teaching, R. Joseph says that he hopes that the halakha does not follow R. Judah, who opines that blind people are exempt from certain *mitzvot*. If R. Joseph were exempt from the commandments he was performing, then his observance would merely be voluntary. From R. Ḥanina's teaching he understands that performance of *mitzvot* which one is obliged to keep is superior to voluntary observance. Whilst the commentators and philosophers offer several different understandings of this talmudic passage, the plain reading supports the view that obedience to the divine imperative is the proper motivation for mitzva observance.

In Deuteronomy 22:6 there is a commandment to send away the mother bird from her nest before taking her eggs. In Megilla 25a the Mishna teaches that one who says to God that "Your mercies extend to the bird's nest" should be silenced. The objectionable phrase is understood as explaining the mitzva of sending away the mother bird in terms of God's compassion for the bird. There is a dispute among the rabbis of the Gemara as to what exactly is objectionable about such a statement, and one of the rabbis affirms that the problem is that it explains this commandment of God in terms of mercy when, in reality, *mitzvot* are decrees of the King (*gezerot hamelekh*). With reference to this view, Rashi explains that the purpose of *mitzvot* is for us to accept upon ourselves the yoke of Heaven and to demonstrate that we are servants of God. According to this understanding, sending away the mother bird has nothing to do with compassion and everything to do with obedience.[5]

In a similar vein, Rabbi Moses Sofer (*Ḥatam Sofer*) expressed grave concern that people may only observe the *mitzvot* because they identify with them. He felt that it was difficult to say about such a person that he or she was serving God.

> For we observe God's statutes and teachings as statutes without reasons, the Torah being the decree of the King, may His name be blessed. Even if a person observes the entire Torah and all the commandments as he

4. Bava Kama 87a.
5. For a similar orientation advanced by Rashi in a different context, see Rashi, Sanhedrin 76b, s.v. *vehamaḥazir aveida lenokhri*.

> is required, if in his heart he does so for some particular reason, it is not received by God with favour.[6]

The ideological foundations of the preference expressed in the aforementioned sources are explained compellingly by Rabbi Aaron Lichtenstein.[7] He argues that we are called upon to live theocentric rather than anthropocentric lives. As such, God's will, rather than our own preferences, lies at the centre or even at the apex of our spiritual lives. Being called and commanded, Rabbi Lichtenstein states, is what religious existence is all about, and it "certainly applies to Judaism more than to most other religions".[8]

Whilst Rabbi Lichtenstein's explanation seems relevant to the positions advanced in the aforementioned sources, other Torah authorities have argued against an intuitive approach to mitzva observance on different grounds. In his *Ruaḥ Ḥayim* commentary on Pirkei Avot,[9] Rabbi Ḥayim of Volozhin insists that, since the giving of the Torah, loving-kindness and divine service have been meaningless unless they are in accordance with Torah. He cites the example of Rabbi Akiva, who, before he became an accomplished scholar, had come

---

6. *Derashot HaḤatam Sofer* (Klausenberg, 1889), vol. i, 19*b*.
7. *By His Light* (Ktav, 2003), 51–6. It should be noted that Rabbi Lichtenstein recognizes the importance of appreciating the intrinsic goodness of many of the *mitzvot* whilst warning the reader not to lose sight of the element of command.
8. The position that obedience should be the motive for character development was supported by Rabbi Isaac Schmelkes in the introduction to his *Beit Yitzḥak*. Rabbi Schmelkes contends that the Torah says little about the development of good character traits because if they were to be included in the Torah, this would make them attractive. According to Rabbi Schmelkes, character development should not be attractive but should be cultivated only out of deference to the divine will.

   In a similar vein, Rabbi Naftali Tzvi Judah Berlin (Netziv), in his approbation to the book *Ahavat Ḥesed* by Rabbi Israel Meir Kagan (Ḥafetz Ḥayim), praises Ḥafetz Ḥayim for teaching that practising loving-kindness is not just a nice thing to do but an absolute mitzva. Whilst Netziv is certainly not suggesting that positive character traits should seem inherently unattractive, he does underscore the importance of recognizing positive ethical behaviour as a religious duty.

   In more recent times this approach was advanced by Rabbi Feinstein (*Derash Moshe*, i. 196). According to Rabbi Feinstein, "even the commandments that deal with obligations between man and his fellow, such as honouring one's parents and refraining from theft and robbery, must be observed because they are God's command and not because they are proper as the non-Jews understand them. The importance of submission to God in halakhic observance was also emphasized by Rabbi Joseph B. Soloveitchik. In *Uvikashtem MiSham* Rabbi Soloveitchik writes that one is overcome by the presence of God and, as a result, feels constrained to submit to His will. See the discussion by Rabbi Walter Wurzburger in Eliezer L. Jacobs and Shalom Carmy (eds.), *Covenantal Imperatives* (Urim, 2008), 189.
9. *Ruaḥ Ḥayim*, Avot 2:1.

across a dead body. Thinking that he was doing the right thing, he carried the body to the next village for burial. Only later was he informed by his teachers that halakha considers the greatest kindness to bury the body where it is found and that every step that he had taken with the body was in fact a sin.[10] In emphasizing what he saw as the deficiencies of a rational approach to morality, Rabbi Ḥayim demonstrates the danger of observing halakha on the grounds that it conforms to our intuitive understanding. In truth, the human ethical intuitive capacity is imperfect and we are reliant on the authority of the divine Lawmaker.[11]

From our discussion thus far we have seen that several classical sources and Torah authorities have advanced considerations that are in tension with the idea that the motivation for mitzva observance should be an intuitive identification with their underlying ideals. Whereas some sources emphasize the fundamental importance of obedience and submission in the religious life, others stress the limitations of man's ability to understand the rationale of the *mitzvot*.[12] In the next section I will show that there is strong support in Jewish tradition for balancing this sense of being commanded with an identification with the values and goals of the *mitzvot*.

---

10. *Semaḥot* 4. http://www.chabad.org/search/keyword_cdo/kid/17205/jewish/Tractate-Semachot.htm
11. In noting the rational mind's limitations in understanding moral truth without divine revelation, R. Haim was following in the footsteps of Saadya Gaon. Saadya had, centuries earlier, advanced the view that divine revelation was needed in order to define both the parameters of the rational *mitzvot* and their level of severity (*Emunot VeDe'ot* III:3). At the same time, Saadya strongly affirmed the capacity of human beings to recognize the inherent truth of many of the *mitzvot*, at least in broad outline. Rabbi Joseph Albo also stresses the inevitable imperfection of the moral sense such that something may seem desirable when, in fact, it is abhorrent (*Sefer ha'Ikarim* I:8). This position was also represented by R. Soloveitchik in his *Yahrzeit Shiur* on 2 March 1975 at Yeshiva University. A transcript of the talk can be accessed at http://www.heartherav.org/Transcript.htm. For another instance in which Rabbi Soloveitchik affirmed this position, see *Community, Covenant and Commitment* (Ktav, 2005), 333. A final example of an exponent of this position is Rabbi Menachem Mendel Schneerson, who wrote: 'generally, the human intellect ... is not always reliable in judging what is good and what is the reverse. Therefore, God, the Creator of the world and man, knowing the human limitations and difficulties, has given us the Torah.' *Letters by the Lubavitcher Rebbe* (Kehot Publication Society, 1979), 62.
12. A third position which recognizes the value of a non-intuitive approach to mitzva observance is represented by Rabbi Jacob Emden in his commentary on Maimonides' *Shemona Perakim*. Based on classical sources, Rabbi Emden states that greater credit is given to one who has struggled to overcome his aversion to observance of the mitzva than to one who is intuitively inclined towards observance.

INNER IDENTIFICATION AS APPROPRIATE MOTIVATION FOR OBSERVANCE OF *MITZVOT*

Rabbi Ovadia Yosef, one of the great halakhic authorities, discusses whether or not one can perform *mitzvot* in a dirty area which is unfit for making blessings.[13] In the course of his discussion, Rabbi Yosef draws a distinction between *tzedaka* and many other *mitzvot*. He explains that there may be grounds to refrain from the performance of *mitzvot* in an unclean area as it would be improper to think about the Creator in such a place and, hence, one could not have proper intent for the mitzva. In contrast, he argues, when performing *tzedaka* it is unnecessary to think about the Commander of the mitzva. Rather, one should focus on providing benefit to the recipient. Rabbi Yosef notes that the idea that divine command is not the necessary motivation for the mitzva of giving *tzedaka* was articulated by the great eighteenth-century halakhic authority, Rabbi Ezekiel Landau (*Noda BiYehuda*). Rabbi Landau opined that, in general, *mitzvot* are meaningless if not done to fulfil the divine command. When one shakes a lulav or wears tefillin or tzitzit, it is necessary to do so to fulfil the mitzva because it is the commandment itself that lends significance to the act. By contrast, there is significance to giving *tzedaka* independent of its status as a mitzva because through giving to the poor person one brings him benefit. Therefore, the intention to fulfil the mitzva is not necessary when giving *tzedaka*. In the responsum, Rabbi Yosef quotes other sources which seem to express the same idea and apply it to all interpersonal *mitzvot*.

Rabbi Yosef and the authors he quotes in support of his position understand that, in the case of many *mitzvot*, it is *acceptable* to perform the mitzva out of a sense of inner identification with its goals instead of through submission to the divine commandment. Rabbi Judah Loew (Maharal) of Prague goes a step further than this in asserting that, with regard to a few specific *mitzvot*, inner identification with the mitzva is *essential* and fulfilment solely to comply with the commandment is inappropriate. In Exodus 22:24 the Torah uses an unusual phraseology to express the mitzva of providing free loans: "If you provide a loan to My people, to the poor person who is with you, do not act towards him as a creditor; do not lay interest upon him." In his commentary, Rashi notes that the word *im* (if) typically connotes that the activity is optional. He asserts that, in this instance and two others, the activity is obligatory despite the anomalous terminology. In his supercommentary on Rashi, *Gur Arye*, Maharal seeks to explain why the term *im* is used in relation to an obligatory mitzva.

---

13. Responsa *Yabia Omer, Yoreh De'a* 6: 29.

> For if a person would fulfil these dictates because he is obligated to fulfil the decrees of the King, this would not be the desire of God, for God wants man to fulfil the command out of his own desire to do so.... Indeed, if a person would do these three acts out of a sense of being decreed to do so by the King, unwillingly, this would not be something for God to be proud of.

According to Maharal, there are *mitzvot* which must be performed out of one's own desire to do so. He explains that if one provides a loan simply in order to comply with the divine decree (*gezerat hamelekh*), then one does not fulfil the mitzva as one must give out of the desire of a good heart.

The dominant trend in Jewish thought favours observance of interpersonal *mitzvot* out of an appreciation for their goals and underlying values and not solely out of deference to the commandment.[14] Of course, this is not to divorce the observance of interpersonal *mitzvot* from our relationship with God. In the quote above, Maharal writes that it is not God's desire that we observe these laws simply because we are commanded to do so.[15] The genuine concern and love which we are to feel towards others is itself the fulfilment of the will of God. Rabbi Isaac Blau explains this approach with a compelling analogy. Imagine a father asking his oldest son to take care of his younger brother out of love for a family member. If the older brother looks out for his sibling solely because his father told him to do so then he fails to fulfil the parental directive. The father had instructed the son to sense the familial ties with his brother, not merely to perform actions of

---

14. See e.g. Maimonides, *Shemona Perakim*, ch. 6, where he notes that the Greek philosophers considered it more virtuous to have no desire for evil behaviour than to foster such desires but manage to overcome them. He adds that, on the face of it, there is an outright contradiction between the view of the Greek philosophers and the view of the rabbis of the Talmud. However, there is, in fact, no contradiction. The Greek philosophers, Maimonides explains, were referring to activities which are universally considered to be wrong, for example murder, theft, and disrespecting one's mother and father. In relation to such behaviour, the philosophers and our sages would be in agreement: having no desire to commit these actions is preferable to desiring to commit them but abstaining out of deference to the moral or religious prohibition. When the talmudic sages attribute credit to someone who follows the laws through deference to their Commander, Maimonides explains that this was said in relation to *mitzvot hashimiyot*, behaviour which would not be evil at all had it not been prohibited by the Torah, for example cooking milk and meat together, wearing *shatnez*, and forbidden sexual relations. Maimonides' distinction is accepted by Rabbis Menahem HaMeiri, Moses Trani, Ḥayim Halberstam of Sanz, Israel Lipshutz, Barukh Halevi Epstein, Meir Simḥa HaKohen of Dvinsk, and Elijah Lopian, as well as by Yeḥiel Yaakov Weinberg (*Seridei Esh*).
15. The Maharal wrote this about three specific laws. Other authorities we have discussed have applied this more broadly.

kindness.[16] So too, in the case of the interpersonal *mitzvot*, God's expectation of us is that we perform them, not solely to comply with halakhic imperatives, but with sincerity and genuine love.

In his lecture "Jewish Ethics and the *Aseret Hadibrot*", Rabbi Joseph B. Soloveitchik provides a personal example in relation to a different mitzva:

> When I fast on Yom Kippur, I am completely unaware of the precept and commandment '*te'aneh es nefshoseichem*' [the obligation to fast]...I do it [fast] not because of normative pressure or imperativistic coercion. I simply love it: I find delight, joy and happiness in cleansing myself, in being close to the *Ribbono Shel Olam*. I would be the most miserable, the most unhappy person in the world if the great privilege of '*teaneh es nafshseichem*' [*sic*], of offering the small sacrifice, be denied to me.... As I get older, I have an inner fright that *chas veshalom* [God forbid], I will be forced to break the *taanis* [fast] because of reasons of health. Such a traumatic experience would be *rachmana litzlan* [God forbid], as far as I'm concerned, tragic, even fatal. I pray to God that it will never happen.[17]

In this passage Rabbi Soloveitchik speaks movingly about his love for the mitzva of fasting on Yom Kippur. Particularly noteworthy is his assertion that if he became unwell and, hence, halakhically exempt and indeed forbidden from fasting, he would regard it as a tragedy. Of primary relevance for Rabbi Soloveitchik was not the halakhic imperative but the pivotal role this fasting played in his relationship with God.[18]

---

16. *The Implications of a Jewish Virtue Ethic*, p. 24.
17. The lecture was delivered on 22 June 1972. See Internet Parsha Sheet (Shavuot and 'Naso' 5767), www.parsha.net/bamidbar/ShavuosNaso67.doc.
18. A further source for applying the idea of observing the *mitzvot* due to an inner identification of some of the *mitzvot* between man and God is Rabbi Kook, in his explanation of Maimonides, *Mishne Torah, Hilkhot Melakhim*, 8:11. Maimonides is discussing non-Jewish observance of the seven Noahide laws, some of which are clearly in the category of *mitzvot* between man and God (e.g. the prohibitions against blasphemy and idolatry). It is generally agreed that the correct text of this passage reads that non-Jews who observe the Noahide code because they are commanded by God in the Torah are considered amongst 'the pious of the nations' and gain a place in the World to Come. In contrast, if they observe the laws out of an intellectual recognition of their truth, they are considered to be amongst the wise of the nations. The usual understanding of this text is that non-Jews who observe the laws due to intellectual conviction rather than divine command do not merit the World to Come. A different interpretation is advanced by Rabbi Kook in *Iggerot Re'iya*, 100. About one who comes to understand the Noahide commandments

As an extension of what I have written above regarding interpersonal commandments, it would seem that, in the view of several important authorities, God's will is that many of the *mitzvot* relevant to the man–God relationship are to be observed in order to attain their goals and to express their underlying values, and not merely to comply with the command.

CONCLUSION

The teaching that observance of *mitzvot* should be motivated by both deference to divine command and love for the underlying values provides a compelling approach towards halakhic observance. In addition to the priceless *intrinsic* value of the performance of *mitzvot*, this approach nurtures a deep spiritual connection with the beautiful and insightful ideas contained within our tradition. I would venture to suggest that, if everyone adopted this approach to mitzva observance, the question of whether being religious helps one to be a better person would become obsolete. The interpersonal sphere in particular is, for followers of this approach, inspired by a deep natural sense of right and wrong which is only enriched and elevated through intellectual exposure to Jewish wisdom and existential engagement with Jewish spiritual life. In the words of Rabbi Nathan Tzvi Finkel (the Alter of Slabodka):

> All of the good character traits and attributes are included in *derekh eretz*; they were ingrained in human nature and for them there is no need for the giving of the Torah. The giving of the Torah came to build on these and to command him [man] to continue to rise heavenward to ever higher levels, transcending those who are in the realm of *derekh eretz*.[19]

as a result of his or her own thinking, Rabbi Kook writes that "it is superfluous to say that he has a portion in the World to Come". Rabbi Kook understands that the World to Come which Maimonides says is merited by those who observe the *mitzvot* because they were commanded is of a lower level than that which will be experienced by those who keep the laws out of rational conviction.

19. *Or Hatzafun*, I 175.

Priestly Predicaments: Analysing *Sof Tuma Latzet* According to Maimonides

Rabbi David Shabtai

Science takes things apart to see how they work. Religion puts things together to see what they mean.
(JONATHAN SACKS, *THE GREAT PARTNERSHIP*)

The Great Partnership" of science and religion, the challenge this integration presents, and the beauty that emerges from this confluence is what I aspire to explore, ponder, and attempt to understand each day. Rabbi Sacks's vision in championing the necessary integration of the worlds of Jerusalem and Athens by respecting the complementary differences that each provides is a guiding light. With his clear formulations, astute observations, and penetrating insights he has shaped attitudes and crafted an atmosphere where religious thought is not only seriously considered but actively sought out for meaningful guidance. We are fortunate that it is on the shoulders of giants such as Rabbi Sacks that we stand.

Standing in stark contrast to the grandiose and almost magical description of the Kohen Gadol's service on Yom Kippur are the mournful lamentations of the Temple's destruction, immediately following its recitation. Many of the losses described in this part of the Yom Kippur liturgy relate to the Temple and communal activities, but there is at least one aspect that used to permeate the life of every halakhically abiding individual, and for which current Judaism has almost no appreciation – *tuma* and *tahara*. Loosely translated as impurity and purity, the concepts of *tuma* and *tahara* are far richer than their translated counterparts (and the Hebrew terms will therefore be used throughout). Visiting the Temple, eating and even coming into contact with sacrifices, separating and handling *teruma* (priestly tithes) all demand a state of *tahara*. Being cognizant of one's state required sensitivity to a plethora of detailed rules and regulations, many of which may appear somewhat foreign to modern students of halakha. Nonetheless, a full order of the Mishna is devoted to the many details and principles that govern such conduct. This essay explores one facet of these laws still practical in our time, its potential pervasiveness, and an argument for leniency in particular situations.

TUMAT MET

Today, one of the only vestiges of *tuma* and *tahara* relates to kohanim, who are prohibited from becoming *tamei* through *tumat met*. *Tumat met* refers to any type of *tuma* ultimately emanating from a corpse, be it a full corpse, an olive's volume of flesh, a complete skull, a quarter *log* of blood, or a complete *log* of bones, among other manifestations. A person becomes *tamei* from *tumat met* in one of three ways: direct contact (*maga*) such as touching; indirect contact (*masa*) such as carrying *tuma* without touching it directly – both familiar from many other types of *tuma*; as well as *ohel* (lit. tent), unique to *tumat met*.

Contracting *tuma* via *ohel* occurs through one of two mechanisms: *maahil* and *ohel hamshakha*. *Maahil* refers to a person or other object hovering directly above or directly below a source of *tumat met*, while *ohel hamshakha* generally refers to being under the same ceiling or roof as the corpse. The ceiling or roof that a person or other object shares with the *tamei* object is called an *ohel* and the *tuma* spreads throughout the entire area sharing that contiguous roof, making *tamei* anything in that airspace. The requirements for a room to qualify as an *ohel*, the intricacies of defining what it means to share a roof, and the technicalities of how *tuma* practically spreads throughout the *ohel* are vast, explored in exquisite detail in Mishna Ohalot.

From a kohen's perspective, avoiding *maga*, *masa*, and *maahil* with respect to *tumat met* is straightforward. While it necessitates a certain sensitivity to one's surroundings, with appropriate training and awareness it can be practised easily, since becoming *tamei* through *maga, masa,* or *maahil* usually requires a conscious effort. Avoiding *ohel hamshakha,* however, is far more complex and difficult.

Modern architecture and today's multi-story buildings often create convoluted and complicated structures that may qualify as an *ohel.* It is frequently not apparent to somebody standing in the lobby of a building how far the *ohel* that person is under actually extends. Locations that pose the greatest difficulty are often hospitals and museums. Hospital sources of *tuma* include not only recently deceased patients on hospital floors, but frequently also morgues that house the corpses until funeral arrangements can be made, pathology labs with various specimens, surgical suites performing amputations, and many more. Depending on the type of museum, exhibits may house mummies, skeletons, bone-derived tools, and other preserved body parts. All of these may pose problems for kohanim.

Before delving further, it is important to draw attention to an early debate as to the source of the *tuma.* Briefly, Maimonides (Rambam) claims that only Jewish corpses can impart *tumat ohel,*[1] while Rabbenu Tam argues that even non-Jewish corpses do.[2] The *Shulḥan Arukh* quotes the stringent opinion, ruling that "it is appropriate [for kohanim] to be careful" and avoid travelling through non-Jewish cemeteries,[3] while Rabbi Moses Isserles (Rema) notes both opinions and concludes, "it is appropriate to act stringently". Practically, modern halakhists are divided on the matter, some permitting entirely,[4] others opting for a stringent approach,[5] and some advocating the middle path of permitting relying on Rambam's approach only when particularly necessary.[6] This essay will not attempt to adjudicate between these positions.

SOF TUMA LATZET

There is an additional factor to consider when analysing *tumat ohel* that has the potential to significantly transform the pervasiveness of this form of *tuma,* namely, *sof tuma latzet* (the realization that *tuma* will eventually spread beyond its current confines). Under normal conditions *tuma* spreads throughout an *ohel* – meaning any area bound by a contiguous roof or ceiling – until the airspace is no longer contiguous. For example, *tuma* in an apartment will cause all objects and people in that apartment to become *tamei,* but if the door to the apartment is closed, the

1. *Hilkhot Tumat Met* 1:13.
2. *Tosafot* Yevamot 61a, s.v. *mimaga.*
3. *Shulḥan Arukh, Yoreh De'a* 372:2.
4. Rabbi Ovadia Yosef, *Ḥazon Ovadya, Aveilut* ii. 52.
5. Rabbi Moshe Gross, *Taharat HaKohanim KeHilkheta,* 69.
6. Rabbi Aaron Felder, *Yesodei Semaḥot* (New York, 1976): 66.

tuma will not spread into the lobby. Although the lobby and the apartment might share a ceiling, the closed door blocks the contiguity of the airspace beneath the two ceiling areas. The door is described as a *ḥatzitza* (partition), blocking the spread of *tuma*. Broadly speaking, two *ohalim* are considered contiguous if there is as little as a square *tefaḥ* of contiguous airspace between the two. Mishna Ohalot deals extensively with which substances qualify as a *ḥatzitza*, how it must be constructed, and its necessary size and shape, among many other details.

The principle of *sof tuma latzet* states that even though *tuma* is currently blocked from spreading into a second space because of some *ḥatzitza*, if it will eventually travel through that second space, the latter is considered *tamei* as of now. In the example above, although *tuma* cannot spread from the apartment into the building lobby because the door is closed, if it will eventually travel through the lobby (perhaps on the exit of the *tamei* object from the building), the lobby is *tamei* already now (even while the apartment door is still closed) by virtue of *sof tuma latzet*. As *sof tuma latzet* is effectively an expansion of *tumat ohel*, it functions in much the same way. When one area becomes *tamei* through the principle of *sof tuma latzet*, the *tuma* spreads through that area in the same way that 'standard' *tuma* would, causing everything beneath that roof to become *tamei*. It does not go on forever, though, spreading *tuma* throughout any and all buildings that a particular *tamei* object will enter. Rather, it is limited to all adjacent *ohalim* that are only separated from each other by some division that will eventually be moved or removed, so that the *tuma* can pass through.[7] There cannot be any gap, big or small (a small space or the distance between buildings), open to the outside separating the two *ohalim*. Any such break in contiguity will force *sof tuma latzet* to stop at that point.

There is a long-standing disagreement among the medieval commentators as to the status of *sof tuma latzet*, whether it is of Torah or rabbinic origin, and it is extensively discussed elsewhere.[8] Regardless, the general consensus appears to be that kohanim are indeed prohibited from contracting this form of *tuma*.

Taking *sof tuma latzet* into consideration greatly expands the scope of *tumat met* in many contexts. In hospitals, for example, it is not just the room of a recently deceased patient that is *tamei*, but even if the door to the room is closed, the adjacent lobby, waiting areas by the elevators, and perhaps even the elevators themselves[9] and the floors they open up to, as well as any other area

7. Ohalot 11:1; *Shulḥan Arukh*, YD 371:4.
8. *Petaḥ HaOhel*, *kelal* 1:1.
9. See R. Jacob Jaffe and David Shabtai, "Kohanim in Hospitals: Does *Tuma* Enter the Elevator Shafts?" (Heb.), *Assia*, 85–6 (2009), 122–54.

that the deceased will pass through upon exiting the hospital are all *tamei*. The same also applies to museum exhibits containing sources of *tumat met* that will eventually be moved to a different location, whether within the same museum, to storage, or to another facility.[10]

On the face of it, the concept of *sof tuma latzet* is quite novel, inasmuch as it manages to essentially spread *tuma* beyond its otherwise natural boundaries. *Sefer Petaḥ HaOhel*, by Rabbi Hayim Meshulam Kaufman HaKohen – one of the first books dedicated entirely to analysing questions of *tumat met* in essay form – offers two approaches (*kelal* 1:1) to understanding the nature of *sof tuma latzet*. Either it means that we view the *tuma* as already present in all of the locations through which it will eventually travel (bearing in mind the limitations mentioned previously) or that we view all those closed doors and other divisions that currently prevent it from spreading into adjacent areas as being open. Offering a glimpse into the phenomenal scope of his learning, Rabbi Kaufman proceeds to list countless potential proofs and disproofs for both positions, culling from Mishna Ohalot, its commentaries, and well beyond, ultimately concluding that *sof tuma latzet* means viewing the *tuma* as currently present in the *ohalim* into which it will eventually travel.

MAIMONIDES

While prevalent throughout rabbinic literature and assumed to be a normatively halakhic principle, interestingly, nowhere does Rambam ever cite the phrase *sof tuma latzet*, neither in his *Commentary on the Mishna* nor in his *Mishne Torah*. On its own, this is not particularly significant, as the phrase is similarly entirely absent from Mishna Ohalot. It is the commentators who introduce the term to explain various cases and rulings of the Mishna – almost all of the commentators refer to it, except Rambam. Consistently, in both works, in almost each and every case where the other commentators invoke *sof tuma latzet*, Rambam either offers an alternative explanation or describes the case (or makes certain assumptions about it) differently than most of the others. This subtle omission may indeed have wide-ranging practical ramifications.

10. As essentially an expansion of *tumat ohel*, it is interesting to explore whether *sof tuma latzet* applies to *tuma* from non-Jewish sources, for those who believe that *tuma* from a non-Jewish source is also subject to *tumat ohel*. Although this question is not explicitly addressed by the early commentators, several of the later halakhists allow for leniency (*Tiferet Yisrael, Ohalot* 16, *Boaz* 5; *Petaḥ HaOhel, kelal* 1:6), while others take a lenient approach only in the presence of other mitigating factors (Rabbis Yisrael Belsky, Moses Heinemann, Solomon Miller, and Samuel First, cited in Rabbi Mordechai Millunchick, *Midarkei HaKohanim* [Chicago, 2009], Hebrew section, p. 14).

Before continuing, it is important to realize that Rambam's position on non-Jewish sources of *tuma* is independent of his approach to *sof tuma latzet*. These are distinct positions and must be analysed individually. Therefore, even those halakhists who disagree with the first premise and argue that non-Jewish sources of *tuma* do indeed engender *tumat ohel* may very well need to contend with Rambam's positions on various technicalities and particulars regarding the spread of *tumat ohel*. But rejecting Rambam's approach with regard to non-Jewish sources of *tuma* and favouring Rabbenu Tam's in no way necessitates, and should certainly not be taken to mean, a rejection of Rambam's other rulings regarding *tumat met* and its spread through *ohalim*. Therefore, Rambam's positions regarding *sof tuma latzet* are of prime importance, even when not necessarily referring to Jewish corpses or other sources of *tuma*. This caveat is of particular importance because many questions and situations arising from Rambam's (other) rulings may often involve non-Jewish sources of *tuma*.

Addressing this apparent anomaly results in two general approaches. The majority approach looks at each instance where Rambam omits mention of *sof tuma latzet* in isolation, assuming all the while that, like the other halakhists, he agrees to the principles of *sof tuma latzet*. Each case is then analysed individually as to whether Rambam's unique explanation employs the concept or some derivative thereof even though not stating so explicitly, or instead, whether in this particular instance he relies on other principles, although accepting *sof tuma latzet* otherwise.

The second view, advocated by Rabbi Yeḥiel Mikhel Epstein in his *Arukh HaShulḥan HeAtid*, takes a broader view of Rambam's general approach. Although not explaining what led him to differ from the other commentators, he claims – as radical as it may appear – that Rambam simply did not accept the principle of *sof tuma latzet* as normative halakha. Assuming that Rambam endorsed *sof tuma latzet* as halakhically relevant but for some reason chose never to utilize the term requires localized explanations for each instance, resulting in a patchwork that does not evince an underlying theory. A smoother and simpler approach might be to assume that Rambam never cites the phrase because he does not accept the principles of *sof tuma latzet*. The reason that he consistently offers different readings and explanations for these contested cases than the other commentators is that the latter are willing to employ *sof tuma latzet* as halakhically relevant while Rambam is not.

Before analysing the particular representative instances, there is a more general challenge with which to contend. Several times, the Mishna uses the phrase *derekh hatuma latzet ve'ein derekh hatuma lehikanes* – it is the way, manner, or characteristic of *tuma* to exit.[11] Rambam quotes this particular phrase in various contexts.[12]

Some of the commentators assume that *derekh hatuma latzet* is sometimes synonymous with *sof tuma latzet*. However, despite the similarity in formulation, in some other cases almost all admit that this need not be true and use the phrase with that in mind.[13] What this amounts to is a tacit admission that the mere usage of the phrase *derekh hatuma latzet ve'ein derekh hatuma likanes* does not necessarily prove that any particular principle is at play. Therefore, a strong case can be made for completely distinguishing between the terms.

Whereas *sof tuma latzet* looks to the future, *derekh hatuma latzet* deals with the present. Classically understood, *sof tuma latzet* refers to the potential future location of *tuma*, assuming that where it will be in the future has ramifications for the present. *Derekh hatuma latzet* describes the direction in which the *tuma* currently spreads. Depending upon the particular configuration, *derekh hatuma latzet* means that what otherwise appear to be distinct *ohalim* are considered as one *ohel*, since in some circumstances it is the nature (*derekh*) of one *ohel* to be subsumed in the other.[14]

In judiciously avoiding invoking – or at least explicitly mentioning – *sof tuma latzet*, Rambam must still deal with those many rulings and instances in the Mishna which the other commentators explain as dependent upon *sof tuma latzet*. In doing so, he introduces two novel principles: an expanded view of *kever satum* (a sealed grave) and a unique understanding of the relationship between *ohalim* subsumed within one another. Examples of Rambam's substituting these two principles in instances where the other commentators invoke *sof tuma latzet* can be found throughout the *Commentary on the Mishna* and *Hilkhot Tumat Met*.

KEVER SATUM

המת בבית ובו פתחים הרבה, כלן טמאין. נפתח אחד מהן, הוא טמא וכלן טהורין. חישב להוציאו באחד מהן או בחלון שהוא ארבעה על ארבעה טפחים, הציל על הפתחים.

11. Ohalot 3:7, 4:1–3, 9:10.
12. *Hilkhot Tumat Met* 18:4, 19:3, 20:8.
13. Rash on Ohalot 5:1, s.v. *ve'eino*; *Responsa Tashbetz* 3:1; Ramban on Ḥullin 125b, s.v. *hakhi garsinan*; *Kesef Mishne*, *Hilkhot Tumat Met* 6:9, 18:4; *Nimukei Yosef* on Rif's *Hilkhot Tuma* 2a (Rif pagination, s.v. *i hava meta*). However, see *Responsa Ḥatam Sofer*, *Yoreh De'a*, no. 340.
14. *Arukh HaShulḥan HeAtid*, *Hilkhot Tumat Met* 17:9.

> If there is a corpse in a house with numerous entranceways, each of the entranceways becomes *tamei*. If one entrance opened, that entranceway is *tamei* and all the others are *tahor*. If there was intention to remove the corpse through one of the entrances or a window that is four square *tefaḥim* [that entranceway is *tamei* and] it protects the other entranceways [from being *tamei*].[15]

In his commentary on Mishna Ohalot, Rash (Rabbi Samson of Sens) explains that any place from where *tuma* may eventually exit is considered *tamei* already now, since *sofo shel met latzet derekh sham* – the corpse will eventually make that area *tamei*.[16] In a location with multiple exits, all are considered *tamei*, until such time that one is selected for removal of the corpse. Although arguing as to the particular status of this *tuma*, Rabbi Asher ben Yeḥiel (Rosh), in Ohalot 7:3, as well as the later commentators, all invoke *sof tuma latzet* to explain the mechanics of the Mishna.[17]

Deviating from this approach, Rambam interprets the Mishna completely differently.

> אם היו כל הפתחים נעולים נעשה הבית כולו כקבר. ולפיכך מתטמא כל מי שישב בו וכך אמרו בית סתום מטמא מכל סביביו. ואם פתח אחד הפתחים, או חשב להוציא את המת מפתח מסויים ואף על פי שלא פתחו עד כה... הרי זה הציל על הפתחים כולם.
>
> If all the entranceways are locked, the entire house becomes similar to a grave. Therefore, anybody who sits in its entranceways becomes *tamei*. And this is what they said, "A sealed house imparts *tuma* to all of its surroundings." And if he opened one of the entrances or thought about removing the corpse from a particular entrance, even though they have not yet opened that entrance ... this protects all of the other entranceways [from being *tamei*].[18]

Making no mention of *sof tuma latzet*, Rambam arrives at the same practical conclusion as the other commentators, even while utilizing a completely separate set of assumptions. Similar to them, he assumes that the doors to the home in

15. Ohalot 7:3.
16. Ohalot 3:6, cited in Rash on Ohalot 7:3.
17. Rabbi Obadiah Bartenura (ad loc., s.v. *kulan*), *Melekhet Shelomo*, *Tosefot Yom Tov* (ad loc., s.v. *uveit*), and *Tiferet Yisrael* (ad loc., Yakhin 7:34).
18. *Commentary on the Mishna*, Ohalot 7:3.

which the corpse is lying are closed. While the closed doors prevent *tumat ohel* from spreading beyond the confines of the house,[19] the other commentators claim that *sof tuma latzet* causes the rooms behind the doors to be *tamei* as well. Rambam, however, believes that the house in question is similar to the "sealed home" (*bayit satum*) of Bava Batra 12a, which in and of itself is considered a primary source of *tuma*. He explains that the *tuma* of a *bayit satum* is parallel to the Mishna's discussion of mausoleums (*nefesh atuma*).[20]

The Mishna describes two types of structure: the first is closed and built directly above a corpse, with no airspace between the body and the structure, similar to a large coffin. Considering that there is no effective *ohel* above this corpse (an *ohel* requires a cubic *tefaḥ* of space), the rules of *tuma retzutza* (lit. smashed *tuma*) become applicable: only people hovering directly above (or below, if it were physically possible in this case) are rendered *tamei*; merely touching the sides of the structure, however, does not transmit *tuma*.[21]

The second type of mausoleum contains an airspace of at least a cubic *tefaḥ* around the corpse, and the Mishna compares this structure to a *kever satum* – a sealed grave. In contrast to the previous case, the Mishna declares that touching any part of the structure, even the sides and roof not directly above the corpse, transmits *tuma*. Rosh explains the difference in that, although merely containing *tuma*, a *kever satum* is considered itself to be a primary source of *tuma*.[22] Similarly, in codifying the laws of tombs, Rambam also describes a *kever* as transmitting *tuma* via *ohel*.[23]

A standard *kever satum* engenders *tuma* to all of its surroundings because it is completely sealed and the *tuma* is considered to be 'distributed' equally among its outer surfaces; there is no one location that is more likely than another for *tuma* to exit. As such, the *kever* itself becomes an expanded manifestation of the *tuma*. However, a house with doors significantly differs in that the *tuma* will certainly only exit through one of those entranceways; the 'distribution' of the *tuma* is therefore limited to those outer surfaces of the house that provide access to its interior, namely the doorways. A careful reading of *Hilkhot Tumat Met* (7:1–2)

19. Whether or not doors qualify as *ḥatzitzot* is a matter of disagreement between *Taz* (YD 371, sec. 3) and *Shakh* (*Nekudat HaKesef* ad loc., s.v. *rotze*), with the halakhic consensus strongly favouring *Shakh*'s approach that closed doors can block the spread of *tuma*.

20. Ohalot 7:1.

21. The regulations regarding *tuma retzutza* can be found in Rambam's *Hilkhot Tumat Met* (7:5) and are beyond the scope of this essay.

22. Commentary on Ohalot 7:1.

23. *Hilkhot Tumat Met* 2:15.

reveals that a house with closed doors is thus parallel to a *kever satum* only inasmuch as the actual doorways themselves are *tamei*. Just as in a classic *kever satum* the outside surfaces of the structure transmit *tuma* both via direct contact as well as through *ohel*, so too a building with closed doors.

Rambam explains that, when the doors of the house containing the corpse are locked, the house is comparable to a *kever satum*. The Mishna is clear that even the outside surfaces of a *kever satum* are *tamei*, and, based on Rambam's understanding, are also 'primary' sources of *tuma* to transmit *tuma* via *ohel*. Since the outside surfaces of all of the doors transmit *tuma* via *ohel*, all objects in the adjoining hallways – those that are part of the *ohel* of which the doors are vertical components – are *tamei* by virtue of being in the same *ohel* as these doors.[24]

A SUBSUMED *OHEL*

The second substitute principle Rambam appears to utilize is a unique understanding of the relationship of two *ohalim* to each other. Generally, just as an *ohel* allows for the spread of *tuma* (*mevi et hatuma*) within the contiguous airspace beneath it, so too, it prevents the spread of *tuma* (*ḥotzetz bifnei hatuma*) beyond its confines.[25] Rambam codifies this principle in *Hilkhot Tumat Met* 12:1.

However, elsewhere Rambam notes a severe limitation of this idea. Based upon Tosefta Kelim 6:6 (noted in *Kesef Mishne* ad loc.), he lists situations in which objects that share an *ohel* with *tuma* are nonetheless protected from becoming *tamei*: items 'swallowed' (*belu'in*) or absorbed in another object, items contained within a *tzamid patil* (tightly sealed container), and items contained within an inner *ohel*.[26] Elaborating on these categories, Rambam explains that something completely absorbed within another object is considered to be in a separate area. Whereas a quarter *log* of blood from a corpse within a room engenders *tumat ohel*, when the blood is completely absorbed into another object, the room remains *tahor*. Similarly, while liquids located within an *ohel* that contains *tuma* become *tamei*, if the liquids are completely absorbed within another item, they remain *tahor*.

Rambam contrasts these 'swallowed' items with those contained within a tightly sealed container or an *ohel*. Whereas the swallowed items are considered

24. On the apparent contradiction with Bava Batra 12a, see Rash, Commentary on Ohalot 7:3; *Responsa HaRemez* 14; *Responsa Mikhtam LeDavid* 1, *Yoreh De'a* 51; *Mayim Tehorim* on Ohalot 7:3.

25. Ohalot 3:7, 6:1–2, 8:1, 9:3, 10:4–5.

26. *Hilkhot Tumat Met* 20:1.

to be completely separate from the room in which they are found, the container and inner *ohel* are only half as effective. Essentially, these latter two categories function like a 'one-way valve' – they prevent *tuma* from entering (and thereby protect *tahor* items contained therein from becoming *tamei*) but cannot prevent *tuma* from exiting. In other words, when a sealed container or small *ohel* is located within a larger *ohel* that contains *tuma*, they protect any *tahor* objects they are housing from becoming *tamei*. However, *tuma* located within a container or small *ohel* spreads beyond those smaller structures to the larger room (*ohel*) in which they are found.

Rabbi Joseph Karo explains the unidirectional flow of *tuma* by invoking *sof tuma latzet*.[27] Since removing the *tamei* object from the smaller *ohel* requires traversing the airspace of the larger one, *sof tuma latzet* declares the larger *ohel* to be *tamei* even prior to the actual removal.[28] However, Rabbi David Pardo strongly disagrees with this approach and finds it very difficult to read this argument into the text of *Hilkhot Tumat Met*.[29] He also notes that Rabbi Karo's suggestion is actually a restatement of Rabad's position, which explicitly disagrees with Rambam's view of the relationship between smaller and larger *ohalim*.[30] Rabbi Pardo views the suggestion in *Kesef Mishne* as so implausible as to be absolutely incorrect. In fact, Rabbi Karo himself merely offers this approach as a possibility, ending his comment with the ever-present caveat that the matter "still needs further review".

Building upon the analysis in *Shoshanim LeDavid*, Rabbi Gershon Ḥanokh Leiner resolves the contradiction by accepting both premises.[31] He explains that normally *tuma* can only spread within an *ohel*, but not beyond its confines. The relevant question is whether *tuma* contained within a smaller *ohel* is also considered to be within the 'jurisdiction' of the larger *ohel* in which this smaller *ohel* is found, such that the *tuma* should spread throughout the larger *ohel* as well. When located within a larger *ohel*, the inner *ohel* is less significant, inasmuch as anything contained within it can be described as also within the larger *ohel*. The spatial relationship between the two *ohalim* is such that the airspace of the inner one

27. *Kesef Mishne, Hilkhot Tumat Met* 20:6.

28. Conversely, since removing a *tamei* object from the outer *ohel* does not necessarily require traversing the airspace of the smaller one, *tuma* does not spread from the outer *ohel* into the inner one.

29. See *Shoshanim LeDavid* on Mishna Ohalot 15:5.

30. See Rabad's glosses to *Hilkhot Tumat Met* 20:1.

31. *Sidrei Taharot* 87a, s.v. *tzamid*.

can be said to be subsumed within the outer one's space. The opposite, however, is not true and *tuma* does not spread from the outer *ohel* inwards.

In completely rejecting any relationship this notion may have to *sof tuma latzet*, both Rabbi Pardo and Rabbi Leiner agree that Rambam's ruling applies to any smaller *ohel* subsumed within a larger one, even when there is a way to remove the *tuma* from the smaller *ohel* without traversing the larger *ohel*. Such a situation could arise if an exit from the smaller *ohel* was located flush against an exit from the larger one. Since the exits line up, the *tamei* object could be removed from the smaller *ohel* without it ever entering the airspace of the larger one. In light of the rules of *sof tuma latzet*, the *tuma* would not spread into the larger *ohel*, which would thus remain *tahor*. According to this expanded understanding of Rambam's approach, however, the locations of the exits are not relevant to the *tuma* status of the larger *ohel*. So long as the relationship of the two *ohalim* is such that one is subsumed within the other, any *tuma* contained within the inner *ohel* is considered to have spread throughout the outer *ohel* as well.

By introducing this particular approach to the relationship between an inner *ohel* subsumed within a larger one, Rambam may again be read as avoiding the invocation of *sof tuma latzet*.

A SPLIT HOUSE

ד. בית שחצצו בנסרים או ביריעות מן הצדדים או מן הקורות, טומאה בבית, כלים שבחצץ טהורים. טומאה בחצץ, כלים שבבית טמאין...
ה. חצצו מארצו, טומאה בחצץ, כלים שבבית טמאים. טומאה בבית, כלים שבחצץ, אם יש במקומן טפח על טפח על רום טפח, טהורים. ואם לאו, טמאין, שארצו של בית כמוהו עד התהום.

4. A house that has been split [separated into two] with wooden boards or with sheets, whether [suspended] from the sides [i.e. the divider was placed horizontally beneath the roof, such that the two areas are located above one another] or from the roof [i.e. the divider was placed vertically, such that the separated areas are located beside each other]: if there is *tuma* in the house, utensils located in [or behind] the separation are *tahor*; if there is *tuma* in the separation, utensils in the house are *tamei*...

5. If he separated [the house into two] from the ground [i.e. the divider was placed horizontally, such that the separated areas are above one another]: if there is *tuma* in the separation, utensils in the house are *tamei*; if there is *tuma* in the house and utensils in the separation – if the utensils are located in an area of [at least] one cubic *tefaḥ*, they are *tahor*; if not [i.e. they are

> in an area smaller than one cubic *tefaḥ*], they are *tamei* since the ground level of a house and downwards has the same status as the house [under which it is located] [*artzo shel bayit kamohu ad hatehom*].[32]

These two *mishnayot* describe situations in which two parts of a house are separated. The segment located at the rear of the house or nearer to the ceiling (referred to as "in [or behind] the separation") is completely separated from the outer or lower segment (simply referred to as "the house"). The exit of the house is presumed to be found in the outer and lower segments, respectively.[33] While the mishna is ostensibly discussing the status of utensils and *tuma* found within the actual separation itself, *Tosefot Yom Tov* already quotes Maharam of Rothenburg (not found in the standard Vilna edition of Mishna), who interprets the passage as referring to utensils or *tuma* located on either side of the separation.[34] While Rambam initially also refers to utensils or *tuma* located within the actual partition,[35] he subsequently states that, insofar as the conclusion is concerned, there is no practical difference whether they are located within the actual partition or behind it.[36] In fact, in *Hilkhot Tumat Met* he makes no mention of cases in which the utensils or tuma are located within the separation, describing only instances when they are on either side of the barrier.[37]

The simpler case discussed is where the *tuma* is located in the rear or upper section of the house. Following the classic approach, Rabbi Israel Lipschutz explains that, since the only way to remove the *tuma* from the inner segment is by traversing the outer section of the house, utensils in the outer segment are *tamei* by virtue of *sof tuma latzet*.[38] The converse case, where the *tuma* is located within the outer or lower segment, is also easily understood according to this approach. Since the *tuma* can exit the house without traversing the rear or upper segments, there is no reason that they should become *tamei*. Rabad, discussed below, adopted a similar approach, many centuries earlier.

32. Ohalot 15:4–5.
33. *Sidrei Taharot* 185b, s.v. *tuma babayit.*
34. See *Tosefot Yom Tov* on Ohalot 15:4 s.v. *kelim.*
35. *Commentary on the Mishna,* Ohalot 15:4.
36. Ibid. 15:5.
37. 20:6, 24:2.
38. *Tiferet Yisrael,* Yakhin 34.

Rambam, in line with his consistent avoidance of referring to *sof tuma latzet*, explains that, regardless of where the *tuma* is found, the barrier causes the rear and upper areas to qualify as independent *ohalim*. As *ohalim*, they are only effective in preventing *tuma* located in the rest of the house from penetrating the barrier but cannot prevent *tuma* located behind the barrier from spreading beyond its confines. In his *Commentary on the Mishna*, Rambam explicitly quotes Tosefta Kelim 6:6, and even while not making the direct reference, in each of these cases described in *Hilkhot Tumat Met*, he refers to his previous discussion of the relationship between inner and outer *ohalim*.[39]

In several of the instances where Rambam refers to this principle, Rabad strongly disagrees.[40] As noted earlier, Rabad adopts the 'standard' approach that endorses the applicability of *sof tuma latzet* and rejects Rambam's understanding.[41] He interprets each case presented by Rambam in one of two ways: either as referring to instances in which the only possibility for removing the *tuma* from the inner *ohel* is by traversing the larger ohel and invoking *sof tuma latzet*, or by positing that the inner *ohel* containing the *tuma* is constructed from material which itself is liable to becoming *tamei*, invoking the principle that any object that is itself liable to becoming *tamei* cannot prevent the spread of *tuma*.[42] As Rambam makes no explicit reference to Tosefta Kelim 6:6 in *Hilkhot Tumat Met*, Rabad admits to finding no source supporting Rambam's contention, concluding that "a great man erred in this matter [*ve'adam gadol ta'ah bazeh*]".[43]

CHEST WITHIN A HOUSE

א. מגדל שהוא ... עומד בתוך הבית, טומאה בתוכו, הבית טמא. טומאה בבית, מה שבתוכו טהור, שדרך הטמאה לצאת ואין דרכה להכנס ...

39. On the possible discrepancies between Rambam's recording of these *mishnayot* (*Hilkhot Tumat Met* 20:6, 24:2), see *Tiferet Yisrael, Ohalot* 15, Yakhin 40, and *Ḥiddushei Rabbenu Ḥayim HaLevi al HaRambam, Hilkhot Tumat Met* 20:1. A careful reading of these *halakhot* may reveal a further distinction as to whether the barrier is considered to be part of the ceiling (*mikelapei hakorot* in 24:2) or part of the flooring (*mikelapei artzo* in 20:6).

40. *Hilkhot Tumat Met* 20:1, 6; 24:2.

41. Other commentators (Rash, Rosh, R. Obadiah Bartenura, *Ohalot* 15:4) all explain the mishna along similar lines, although invoke language of subsumed *ohalim*. However, as *Mishna Aharona* (ibid.) explains, when these commentators cite the principle of an inner *ohel* being unable to contain *tuma* within its walls or compare an inner *ohel* to a sealed container, they are merely using coded language for *sof tuma latzet*.

42. Bava Batra 19b.

43. Rabad on *Hilkhot Tumat Met* 20:6.

ג. היה עומד בתוך הפתח ונפתח לחוץ, טומאה בתוכו, הבית טהור. טומאה בבית, מה שבתוכו טמא, שדרך הטמאה לצאת ואין דרכה להכנס.

1. A [wooden] chest located in a house: If it contains *tuma*, the house is *tamei* [as well]; if there is *tuma* in the house, that which is in the chest is *tahor*, since it is a property of *tuma* to exit and not to enter [*shederekh hatuma latzet ve'ein darkah lehikanes*]...

3. If [the wooden chest] is located in the entranceway [*betokh hapetaḥ*] with its opening facing outwards and is open to the outdoors: If it contains *tuma*, the house is *tahor*; if there is *tuma* in the house, that which is in the chest is *tamei*, since it is a property of *tuma* to exit and not to enter [*shederekh hatuma latzet ve'ein darkah lehikanes*].[44]

As an apparent prime example of *sof tuma latzet*, many commentators explain these *mishnayot* according to that principle.[45] Completely omitting any mention of *sof tuma latzet*, Rambam interprets these *mishnayot* somewhat differently. He describes the chest located within the house as an "*ohel* within an *ohel*", repeating his oft-quoted explanation, "it is a principle by us that if one *ohel* is subsumed within another [*ohel betokh ohel*] and *tuma* is located within the inner *ohel*, the outer *ohel* is *tamei*," referring the reader to Tosefta Kelim 6:6.[46] When the *tuma* is located within the chest, the house is considered the outer *ohel* and is *tamei*. Conversely, when the *tuma* is located in the house, the inner *ohel* – the wooden chest – can prevent the spread of *tuma* into its space. Rambam seems to find this notion so pervasively important that he exhorts the reader to "pay attention to this [*sim lev lazeh*] since it is an important fundamental principle [*yesod gadol*]." He codifies the Mishna's ruling in *Hilkhot Tumat Met* 18:4 without much elaboration.

The third mishna, though, appears to present difficulties for Rambam's approach. Interestingly, in the *Commentary on the Mishna*, he makes no comment on this section but instead focuses exclusively on a later section. In *Hilkhot Tumat Met* 18:4, he cites the Mishna faithfully without any explanation. Reflecting on his interpretation of the first mishna, it is somewhat perplexing why this mishna records that when *tuma* is found within the chest the house is not *tamei*. Regardless of where the chest is located within the house, it should appropriately be

44. Ohalot 4:1–3.

45. Rash and Rosh on Ohalot 4:1, s.v. *shederekh*; Maharam ibid., s.v. *hava*; Obadiah Bartenura, ibid., s.v. *habayit*; *Tiferet Yisrael*, Yakhin 8.

46. *Commentary on the Mishna*, Ohalot 4:1.

identified as the inner *ohel* with the house proper as the outer *ohel*. One might have in fact expected the opposite conclusion – when *tuma* is in the chest, the house is *tamei* and when the *tuma* is in the house, objects within the chest are *tahor*.

Rabbi Ḥaym Soloveitchik admits difficulty with resolving this mishna according to his own particular approach and suggests an important limitation on the rules regulating the relationship between inner and outer *ohalim*.[47] Normally, *tuma* contained within the inner *ohel* spreads to the outer *ohel* because the inner *ohel* is considered to be subsumed within the larger one or otherwise insignificant as a meaningful partition, given its location within the larger structure. Rabbi Soloveitchik proposes that, were the inner *ohel* to somehow attain increased significance and no longer be considered subsumed within the larger *ohel*, it would function differently and indeed prevent *tuma* contained within it from spreading beyond its walls. It is only because it is subordinate to the larger *ohel* that *tuma* contained within it is also considered to be present within the outer *ohel*. When that is no longer the case, however, the *tuma* should be limited to the confines of the inner *ohel* and not spread any further.

He suggests that, if removing the inner *ohel* from the house would bring the *tuma* along with it – meaning that the inner *ohel* is a box surrounding and not just covering the *tuma* – then perhaps it should be considered independent of the outer *ohel*. The *tuma* within such an inner *ohel* no longer relates to its immediate covering as a subsumed *ohel* – of presumably lesser status – but rather as an independent *ohel* in which the tuma will eventually travel even when no longer found within the larger *ohel*. Therefore, *tuma* located within the wooden chest will not cause the house to become *tamei* and *tuma* within the house will not cause objects in the chest to become *tamei*.

There are several difficulties with this approach, however, which may be why Rabbi Soloveitchik ends off with a caveat that the matter still requires further review. On the most basic level, we need to posit two different scenarios for the two *mishnayot*. The first mishna must refer to a situation in which removing the inner *ohel* will not necessarily cause the *tuma* to travel with it – which would be the case if the chest were merely covering the *tuma* but not housing it within the chest proper – whereas the latter mishna must refer to a situation where removing the chest carries the *tuma* along with it. While not an unheard-of methodology for interpreting the Mishna, it does question the strength of this proposal. Additionally, Rabbi Soloveitchik's assumption that a difference in status

47. *Ḥiddushei Rabbenu Ḥayim HaLevi al HaRambam, Hilkhot Tumat Met* 20:1.

exists between an inner *ohel* whose removal brings the *tuma* along with it and one that does not can itself be challenged, as it is certainly not universally agreed upon,[48] although this discussion is beyond the scope of the current endeavour.

A second approach to explaining this mishna according to Rambam's view builds on Rabbi Soloveitchik's suggestion that mishna 3 is discussing a case in which the inner *ohel* is not considered to be subsumed within the outer *ohel*, albeit for more structural reasons. A number of later commentators argue that an inner *ohel* located specifically and exclusively within the doorway of a larger *ohel* differs significantly from one located completely within the larger *ohel*.[49] In *Sidrei Taharot*, Rabbi Leiner explains that when the chest – the inner *ohel* – is located in the doorway, it may or may not be considered subsumed within the house (the outer *ohel*). When the opening faces inwards, towards the house, and the chest shares contiguous airspace with the house, it is still considered part of, and therefore subsumed within, the house. As *Darkei Shemuel* makes clear, however, when located in the doorway with its opening facing outwards, the chest is considered a distinct space from the house and no longer subsumed within it; it is not located within, nor does it share any contiguous airspace with, the house.

In fact, a careful reading of the mishna bolsters this approach. According to those who explain this mishna through the mechanism of *sof tuma latzet*, it should make little difference in which direction the chest opens. When it is located in the entranceway, removing *tuma* from the house necessitates traversing the airspace currently occupied by the wooden chest, regardless of where its opening is facing.

Perhaps, instead, the Mishna emphasized this detail in order to draw attention to the fact that, when all of these factors are taken together – located exclusively within the doorway (and, according to *Kesef Mishne*,[50] encompassing the entire space of the doorway) and with its opening facing outdoors – the chest takes on an independent identity, no longer considered to be subsumed within the larger *ohel*. Highlighting this factor even more strongly, Rambam ends his short explanation not only with "because it is the way [*derekh*] of *tuma* to exit and not enter" – a direct quotation from the Mishna – but introduces that comment with "since [the chest] is open and located in the doorway".[51] It appears that from Rambam's perspective, the fact that "the manner of *tuma* is to exit and

48. Cf. *Tiferet Yisrael*, Ohalot 4, Yakhin 8.

49. *Ḥasdei David, Ahilot, Kuntres Torat HaOhel*, no. 14; *Mayim Tehorim*, Ohalot 4:2, *Ḥarifuta DeNahara* 3, 4:3; *Nahara Upashta*, s.v. *baRam*; *Sidrei Taharot* 88b, s.v. *haya*, and *Darkei Shemuel*, Ohalot 4:16.

50. *Hilkhot Tumat Met* 18:4, s.v. *migdal*.

51. *Hilkhot Tumat Met* 18:4.

not enter" is insufficient to explain these *mishnayot*. Only because of the two additional factors – the location and the direction of its opening – does the chest assume the status of an independent *ohel* and is no longer subject to the rules regulating an inner *ohel* subsumed within an outer *ohel*.

Thus, when *tuma* is located within the chest, it does not spread to the house. So too, at least in theory, when *tuma* is located within the house, the wooden chest should prevent it from entering its airspace, since it is not considered to be subsumed within the larger *ohel*. However, the 'standard' text of the Mishna, which is the version that Rambam quotes, rules that, under these conditions, objects located within the wooden chest, in fact, are *tamei*. If the chest is considered to be an independent *ohel*, separate and distinct from the house – the outer *ohel* – why then does *tuma* from the house spread into the chest? According to the previous analysis, the chest should be able to prevent *tuma* from entering its airspace.

Answering this question, Rabbi Epstein takes the view of the wooden chest as an independent entity one step further.[52] He argues that not only is the wooden chest an independent *ohel*, but since it is standing in the entranceway to the house and, as stipulated in *Kesef Mishne*, encompassing the entire airspace of the doorway,[53] it qualifies as the outer *ohel* with the house proper identified as the inner *ohel*. Understood in this light, the standard rules of an inner *ohel* subsumed within an outer *ohel* work quite nicely. When the *tuma* is in the house proper – the inner *ohel*, according to the understanding of *Arukh HaShulḥan HeAtid* – the wooden chest (the outer *ohel*) is *tamei*. However, when the *tuma* is in the wooden chest – the outer *ohel* – the house proper is *tahor*, since as the inner *ohel*, it prevents the spread of outside *tuma* into its airspace.

While certainly novel, Rabbi Epstein's proposal does not address the fundamental question of how to determine when one *ohel* is considered subsumed within another and when the two are merely adjacent. Since it is the particular relationship of one *ohel* subsumed within another that causes the *tuma* contained within the inner compartment to spread to the outer section, accurately identifying those sections is of prime importance. As Rabbi Leiner aptly notes, Mishna Ohalot

52. *Arukh HaShulḥan HeAtid, Hilkhot Tumat Met* 37:16.

53. See Rabbi Meshulam Horowitz of Kremnitz, *Mishnat Ḥakhamim* (Ohalot 4:3), who disagrees with Rabbi Karo's contention as being without basis, although this claim is effectively refuted by Rabbi Yehuda Leib Edel in *Mayim Tehorim*, Ohalot 4:3, *Ḥarifuta DeNahara* 3. See also *Ḥiddushei Rabbenu Ḥayim HaLevi al HaRambam, Hilkhot Tumat Met* (11:5), where Rabbi Soloveitchik presents an alternative understanding of Rambam's approach that does not necessitate Rabbi Karo's assumption.

describes numerous cases (6:4, 10:4–5, 17:5) of two- (or more) story houses, assuming all along that when properly divided, *tuma* cannot spread from one floor to the other; the same is true of adjacent *ohalim* separated by a wall.[54] Only when the inner *ohel* is subsumed within the outer *ohel* can the *tuma* physically contained within the inner *ohel* be considered to also be located within the purview of the outer *ohel.* As such, it is very difficult to accept Rabbi Epstein's suggestion.

Accordingly, from the perspective of the relationship between *ohalim,* the wooden chest should prevent the spread of *tuma* from the house into the chest. However, taking into consideration Rabbi Karo's suggestion that the chest is big enough to take up virtually the entire doorway, objects within the chest may become *tamei* for a completely separate reason. If this is the house's only doorway and the chest is completely blocking the exit, then the chest should rightfully be viewed as a physical barrier blocking passage to and from the house, otherwise known as a door. As such, Rabbi Leiner compares this case to the house with sealed doors of Mishna Ohalot 7:3.[55] Based upon the earlier analysis of Rambam's approach to this mishna, the comparison is all the more appropriate, since Mishna Ohalot 4:3 is describing a house with a sealed entranceway. Therefore, even if *tahor* by virtue of being an independent *ohel,* the chest becomes *tamei* since it is effectively the door of a sealed house. Once the chest is *tamei* (or at the very least the surface of the chest that faces the house) and, as argued previously, engenders *tumat ohel,* the contents of the chest also become *tamei.*

PRACTICAL RAMIFICATIONS

Taking Rambam's broader view of the relationship between an inner and outer *ohel* and his expansive approach to *kever satum* into consideration, there are significant practical differences between his approach and that of the other commentators. The differences diverge even more when we approach the matter through the lens of the *Arukh HaShulḥan,* where Rabbi Epstein argues that Rambam fundamentally denies the principle of *sof tuma latzet.*

- Situations in which a small *ohel* is located flush against the wall of a larger *ohel* and the inner *ohel* has an exit leading directly outside, without needing to traverse the outside *ohel,* will result in divergent rulings. Since removing the source of *tuma* will never cause the outer *ohel* to become *tamei* by virtue of *sof tuma latzet* alone, the outer *ohel* will remain *tahor.*

54. *Sidrei Taharot* 87a, s.v. *tzamid.*
55. *Sidrei Taharot* 88b, *Kuntres,* s.v. *tuma babayit.*

However, since the inner *ohel* is subsumed within the outer *ohel,* according to Rambam, the outer *ohel* will become *tamei.*

- Rambam's expansive view of *kever satum* may also create significant differences. Understanding the case of a corpse within a house with closed doors as in the analysis above, he would declare the outside surfaces of any of those doors to be *tamei* (and spread *tuma* via *ohel,* should there be a roof above them), while through *sof tuma latzet* alone, the outside surfaces of the doors should remain *tahor,* so long as there is no overhang or roof extending above the outside surfaces of those doorways.
- Assuming that Rambam in fact denies *sof tuma latzet* as halakhically relevant, the extent to which *tuma* spreads when housed in an inner room is also a matter of debate. According to Rambam's understanding of *kever satum,* so long as the doors to the room containing the *tuma* are closed (perhaps they must be locked), the outside surface of those doors becomes *tamei* and causes *tuma* to spread via *ohel* into an adjacent room; the spread of *tuma* stops at the next closed door. However, for those who endorse and apply the *sof tuma latzet* principle, *tuma* spreads through all closed doors through which the source of *tuma* will ultimately pass so long as they share a contiguous roof. Practically speaking, an example of this discrepancy would exist in a situation where there are three connected rooms, and the only way to remove the *tamei* object from the third room is by traversing first the middle and then the outer room. According to Rambam, only the innermost room and the immediately adjacent rooms are *tamei,* whereas according to the *sof tuma latzet* approach, all three rooms are.
- Another difference may emerge, as suggested by Rabbi Epstein, in cases where the *tuma* will never actually traverse the outer *ohel.*[56] This might occur when the source of *tuma* will be buried or otherwise destroyed in its current location or dissected into sections so small that when traversing the outer *ohel* individually they will not engender the spread of *tuma.* These limitations effectively nullify *sof tuma latzet* and its ability to render the outer *ohel tamei.* According to Rambam, however, these limitations are irrelevant. So long as the inner *ohel* contains *tuma* and is subsumed within the outer *ohel,* the outer *ohel* is *tamei,* regardless of what the future holds for this particular *tuma.*[57]

---

56. *Arukh HaShulḥan HeAtid, Hilkhot Tumat Met* 37:7.

57. The *Arukh HaShulḥan* notes, however, that these examples represent R. Yossi's opinion (Ohalot 4:2), who argues that, when a *tamei* object located in an inner *ohel* can be dissected into

From a practical halakhic perspective, almost all codifications of *hilkhot tuma* endorse the principle of *sof tuma latzet*.[58] Typically, though, Rambam's opinion plays an instrumental and significant role in arriving at normative practice in these areas, if not simply for his sheer brilliance then perhaps by virtue of the massive scope of his work, certainly superseding any other medieval or early modern halakhist's works on the topic.

If we accept Rabbi Epstein's thesis that Rambam rejected the principle of *sof tuma latzet*, then relying on Rambam's approach results in significant leniencies. For example, because of various fire safety codes, hospitals frequently have many sets of doors throughout their hallways, intended to contain the spread of a fire. When a patient dies, the corpse can frequently be separated from any visitor areas by several sets of doors. Although the lobby area and visitor waiting areas may become *tamei* via *sof tuma latzet* according to Rambam's perspective, only the room containing the corpse and the immediately adjacent room will be *tamei*. This can have potentially far-reaching consequences for kohanim wishing to visit sick patients, depending upon the architecture and structure of the particular hospital.

Nonetheless, despite Rambam's stature, if we accept the thesis that he rejected the principle of *sof tuma latzet*, it would still appear inappropriate to follow this notion normatively, given not only the presence of strong disagreement with Rabbi Epstein's thesis but also the overwhelming acceptance of *sof tuma latzet* as normative halakha by virtually all other commentators and halakhists.

At the same time, the question may be relevant in the opposite direction. In light of the normative acceptance of *sof tuma latzet*, must one be stringent and relate to areas and objects deemed *tamei* through Rambam's approach as well? One potential area of stringency may be display cases containing human remains in museums.

As noted previously, museums often exhibit various objects that engender *tuma*. This can present problems for kohanim desiring to visit, especially with regard to objects that engender *tumat ohel*, since avoiding *maga* and *masa* is easily accomplished. Each museum needs to be individually investigated as body

---

small pieces such that the individual pieces cannot engender *tumat ohel*, the outer *ohel* is *tahor*. Normative halakha rejects R. Yossi's opinion (Rambam, *Hilkhot Tumat Met* 18:4; *Tiferet Yisrael*, Ohalot, *Hilkheta Gevirta* 4:2) and therefore it cannot serve as a differentiating case between the various approaches. There may still be room to find differences if there were some other reason that *sof tuma latzet* would not apply in a particular instance.

58. Rosh, *Hilkhot Tuma* 9; *Orḥot Ḥayim, Hilkhot Tuma* 5; Rabbenu Yeruḥam, *Toledot Adam VeḤava, netiv* 28, *ḥelek* 4; *Sefer Kolbo* 114; *Hokhmat Adam, Shaar HaSimḥa, kelal* 159:8.

parts can be present in diverse venues and in multiple areas. In many instances, certain types of *tuma* are contained within display cases and not out in the open. Assuming that these are the only potential sources of *tuma* (something that needs investigation), the permissibility of a kohen visiting the museum may depend on the disagreement between Rambam and the other halakhists.

Display cases present several issues that require analysis, aside from the question of the *tuma*'s origin (mentioned earlier). The composition of the case is of prime importance, since if the case itself is susceptible to *tuma*, then it does not qualify as an *ohel* to prevent *tuma* from exiting under most circumstances, unless permanently affixed to the ground or if it is very large (*haba bemidda*, i.e. larger than 40 *se'ah*).[59] Display glass materials may include plastic, Plexiglas, glass, with parts sometimes made of fiberglass, and other similar materials.

Plastic is a synthetic compound and the general consensus is that only the seven enumerated materials (clothing, sack cloth, leather, bone, metal, wood, and ceramic) are liable to becoming *tamei*, effectively eliminating all synthetic compounds.[60] Plexiglas is similarly a synthetically derived compound.[61]

For the display case to qualify as an *ohel*, it must contain a cubic *tefaḥ* (Ohalot 3:7). Rambam and Rabad disagree, however, as to how to measure the cubic *tefaḥ*.[62] Rambam requires a cubic *tefaḥ* between the source of *tuma* and the roof of the *ohel*, while Rabad allows for including the source of *tuma* in the cubic *tefaḥ*. If there were less than a *tefaḥ* space, either above the *tamei* object for Rambam or even including it, then the *tuma* would qualify as *tuma retzutza*, which penetrates any roof immediately above and enters the room in which the structure is located.

---

59. Bava Batra 19b.

60. *Mishne Torah, Hilkhot Kelim* 1:1.

61. While from a Torah perspective glass cannot become *tamei*, the rabbis added stringency to the matter because of the similarity of origin between glass and ceramic, the latter being subject to *tuma* as stated in the Torah. The generally accepted opinion is that any object that is not susceptible to *tuma* on a Torah level can indeed prevent the spread of *tuma*, including glass (*Tosafot*, Bava Batra 20a, s.v. *ve'oved*; Ran ad loc., s.v. *vegoy*; Ramban ad loc., s.v. *ve'akum*; Rash Ohalot 13:5, s.v. *ufaḥot*; *Responsa Noda BiYehuda, mahadura kama, Yoreh De'a*, no. 96; *Mishne LaMelekh, Hilkhot Tumat Met* 12:2). Fiberglass is also called glass-reinforced plastic, as it is made from a plastic matrix reinforced by small glass fibres. Rabbi Levi Isaac Halperin argues that since the bulk of the material is in fact synthetic and the minute glass fibres may not even qualify as *kelim* to be subject to the rabbinic regulation, fiberglass should be considered unable to become *tamei* (*Sefer Taharat Petaḥim*, sec. 2, ch. 4).

62. *Hilkhot Tumat Met* 7:4.

Assuming that a cubic *tefaḥ* of space is present and the material itself is not susceptible to becoming *tamei,* the display case takes on the status of an *ohel.* As such, there are three avenues of potential spreading of *tuma* to explore: *kever satum, sof tuma latzet,* and an inner *ohel* subsumed within a larger *ohel.*

Although clearly not intended as a burial spot, a display case may in fact be a long-term resting place for some human remains. Most halakhists require a *kever satum* not only to be a final resting place but also to be constructed in such a way that the entrances to the room containing the source of *tuma* have their doorways removed and those spaces completely sealed off.[63] Assuming such a parallel could exist in a display case, it would seemingly require affixing the transparent sections of the case to its base in a permanent manner. It is hard to know if such a display case would qualify under these rigorous criteria. Rambam's approach, however, as argued previously, allows for laxer requirements for an object to qualify as a *kever satum.* If the exits to the room containing the *tuma* are merely closed, the room may attain such a status, leading to a more easily described parallel by display cases. If this analysis is accurate, the outside surfaces of the display case are *tamei* and will cause *tuma* to spread throughout the room housing that particular display.

The second relevant aspect is that of *sof tuma latzet* and this may depend on the particular nature of the exhibit in question. Often museums will have certain exhibits on permanent display, while others may be more temporary. It is possible that the museum's curator has particular plans as to when a given display case containing *tuma* will be removed. Even if not immediate, this may certainly be sufficient for the *tuma* to qualify as *sof tuma latzet.* However, there are those who argue that even if there are definite plans to move *tuma* at some future point, but it will certainly not happen before a particular time, then *sof tuma latzet* is inapplicable until the point in time when the *tuma* might actually be moved.[64] This suggestion would also certainly help in the case of permanent exhibits. Practically speaking, even those halakhists who are generally stringent about *sof tuma latzet* concerning *tuma* from a non-Jew are cited as being lenient with regard to display cases housing *tuma* in permanent exhibitions.

Although, as argued throughout, Rambam rejects *sof tuma latzet* as halakhically normative, the third concern is uniquely relevant. Even if the *tuma* is completely contained within the display case, with the requisite airspace for the

63. Rash, Mishna Ohalot 7:3, s.v. *kulan;* Rosh, Mishna Bava Batra 1:43; *Ḥokhmat Adam, Shaar HaSimḥa, kelal* 159:4.

64. *Responsa Maharit,* no. 98.

case to qualify as an *ohel,* since it is situated within the museum, it should rightfully be described as an inner *ohel* subsumed within the larger outer *ohel* of the museum proper. Therefore, as discussed extensively earlier, the *tuma* within the inner *ohel* should spread throughout the museum, prohibiting kohanim from visiting the vicinity.

Out of all of these issues, the classical commentators and halakhists are generally only concerned with *sof tuma latzet,* which, in this case, may very well be inapplicable. It is only Rambam's expanded view of *kever satum* and particular approach to the relationship between inner and outer *ohalim* that result in *tuma* spreading throughout the particular room in the museum. However, even if it is normally appropriate to act stringently in accordance with Rambam's opinion, particularly in areas of *tuma* and *tahara,* there might be significant room to make an exception in this case.

While the *Arukh HaShulḥan's* thesis that Rambam rejected *sof tuma latzet* as practically relevant may at first blush seem radical, the preceding analysis has shown significant basis for this conclusion. Accordingly, Rambam introduced his two principles of an expanded understanding of *kever satum* and novel approach to the relationship between inner and outer *ohalim* to interpret those cases in the Mishna that would otherwise be easily explained through *sof tuma latzet.* It is only because he rejected the latter concept that Rambam utilized these novel principles. Therefore, since, as a matter of normative halakha, we do employ *sof tuma latzet,* perhaps we need not concern ourselves with the practical consequences of Rambam's approach and may disregard them as halakhically irrelevant.

It is possible, therefore, that under the circumstances described, even those normally stringent in their approach to questions of *tuma* and *tahara,* and take into account Rambam's often novel perspectives, can assume that *tuma* in display cases does not spread beyond the case itself, allowing kohanim to enter rooms containing such exhibits.

Lashon HaRa, Democracy, and Social Media

Rabbi Gil Student

Chief Rabbi Lord Jonathan Sacks has served for me, through his writings and speeches, as a personal source of inspiration and intellectual guidance. I profoundly thank him for his role in sustaining a world of sophisticated Torah discussion, in which a confident faith merges effortlessly with a seeking mind. Torah, science, Tanakh, philosophy... I have learned all of these from Rabbi Sacks but most of all, *menschlichkeit*. May he continue to study and teach in good health for many years to come.

LASHON HARA IN MODERN SOCIETY

To function properly, a modern society requires a relatively free flow of important information. A government with uninformed citizens will quickly turn corrupt and businesses with ignorant customers will inevitably engage in fraud. Alas, such is human nature. If sunlight is the best disinfectant, as the metaphor goes, it must have a window through which society may enjoy its benefit.

However, Judaism prohibits repetition of damaging information, even if it is true, condemning it as *lashon hara*. In *Future Tense*, Chief Rabbi Sacks takes the first steps in articulating a theology of conversation.[1] As he states, "how we

1. London, 2010, p. 184.

relate to other people shapes and is shaped by how we relate to God." The laws of *lashon hara* are important not only to facilitate communal harmony but also to frame our interaction with God. When we judge others favourably, protect the innocent from harm, and avoid prematurely reaching conclusions, we can expect similar treatment from above.[2]

Truth is no justification for verbal harm. If so, the *lashon hara* regulations, when understood simply, potentially undermine a modern society. How can a political candidate campaign for office if he is unable to say, for example, that his opponent is underqualified? How can a newspaper report on a politician's misdeeds, relevant as they may be? Who will warn consumers of malicious merchants? While we intuitively see the importance of responsible negative speech in such circumstances, of voters' and consumers' 'right to know', we need to frame such an attitude within halakhic parameters. Common sense is a crucial life skill but cannot trump halakha. We must instead find realistic halakhic guidance, sensitive to societal needs yet faithful to tradition.

Two avenues of Jewish law offer promise. The first is that of *to'elet* (benefit). Within certain conditions, *lashon hara* is permitted when there is a clear benefit to its recipients.[3] While this category of permission requires further refinement before broad application, it is certainly an important and relevant qualification to the laws of *lashon hara*. Another avenue is that of *nitparsem hadavar* (the information has already been publicized). Recent responsa and articles in Israel have advanced the thesis that once negative information has been widely disseminated, there is room to allow further publicization since, more or less, 'everyone knows it'.[4]

Maimonides permits repeating negative information that is disclosed in front of three people (*be'apei telata*) because, presumably, the information is no longer private and will eventually become widely publicized.[5] Others disagree with this leniency and interpret the underlying proof-text (Arakhin 17a) differently.[6] However, some recent authorities suggest that this debate only revolves around a matter that will inevitably become publicized but has not yet. At this

2. See Rosh Hashana 17a; Sota 8b.
3. See *Ḥafetz Ḥayim*, 1:10:2.
4. American law also adopts this standard regarding invasion of privacy. *The Associated Press Stylebook and Handbook on Media Law 2011* (New York, 2011), 419, states that "facts that are already known to the general public cannot be the basis of a public disclosure claim". However, it adopts a stricter standard for libel. "[A] republisher of libel is generally considered just as responsible for the libel as the original speaker" (ibid. 400).
5. *Mishne Torah, Hilkhot De'ot* 7:5.
6. See *Ḥafetz Ḥayim*, 1:2:3.

time, only three people know. An already widely known fact falls under a different category and is not considered *lashon hara* at all.

In an article about *lashon hara* and newspapers, Rabbi Ari Chwat advances this approach.[7] Rabbi Azriel Ariel quotes Rabbi Chwat approvingly in an article about democracy and *lashon hara*, and reports the apparent agreement of Rabbis Abraham Shapira and Dov Lior.[8] In determining the halakhic propriety of including negative information in a historical archive, a responsum published by Kollel Eretz Ḥemda also advances this approach.[9] Rabbi Eliezer Melamed contends that one is forbidden to publicize in a newspaper information that is widely known but only because of the dictum "Do not do to others what you would not want done to you" (Shabbat 31a) and not because of *lashon hara*.[10] Rabbi Shlomo Aviner cites six places in *Ḥafetz Ḥayim* that seem to justify this view that well-publicized information does not fall under the category of *lashon hara*.[11] Many of these scholars quote Rabbi Moshe Kaufman,[12] who lists a number of examples, discussed below, to defend this approach.

However, with a good deal of trepidation, I respectfully dissent from this view for the reasons I explain below.

ALREADY PUBLICIZED

As mentioned above, there are strong arguments to permit repetition of damaging information that is already well known. Rabbi Yisrael Meir Kagan, in his classic work on the laws of forbidden speech, *Ḥafetz Ḥayim*, states this leniency explicitly several times:

- In explaining the talmudic statement that you may call someone a sinner if he violates a rabbinic prohibition (Shabbat 40a), *Ḥafetz Ḥaim* asks how we can permit such a blatant violation of *lashon hara*.[13] He answers that this must refer to someone who violates the rabbinic prohibition publicly. Because such a violation is well known, the prohibition of *lashon hara* does not apply at all to the information.

7. "Newspapers and News Programmes in Halakha: Mitzvah or Forbidden?", *Yesha Yemino*, 45 (Tammuz 5755/1995), 39–41.
8. "*Lashon HaRa* in a Public Democratic Context", *Tzohar*, 5 (Shevat 5761/2001).
9. *Responsa BeMareh HaBazak* (Jerusalem, 2012), vol. vi, no. 96, n. 1.
10. *Revivim: Am, Eretz, Tzava* [*Droplets: Nation, Country, Army*] (Israel, 2008), 100 n. 20.
11. *Responsa She'elat Shelomo* (Beit El, 2006), vol. iii, no. 485.
12. *Netivot Ḥayim*, commentary on *Ḥafetz Ḥayim* (Bnei Brak: 1990), in *Zera Ḥayim* appendix, p. 313.
13. 1:4 n. 7.

- Similarly, the Talmud (Pesaḥim 112b) relates how R. Judah HaNasi referred to residents of one town as "scoffers". How, *Ḥafetz Ḥayim* asks, can such a negative declaration be permitted?[14] He answers that since the townspeople's behaviour was well known, one was entirely permitted to discuss it.
- In explaining the view of *Tosafot* (Bava Batra 39a, s.v. *leit beih)* on the same passage, *Ḥafetz Ḥayim* states that when one person publicly berates another, you are allowed to relay that information because *lashon hara* does not apply to it.[15]
- Turning to the view of Rabbenu Jonah, *Ḥafetz Ḥayim* suggests that the case in which he permits repeating negative information is one in which the action was done publicly, so the information is already publicized.[16]
- The Gemara (Gittin 31b) mentions that either Rav Huna or Rav Ḥisda refused to rise when the Torah scholar Geniva passed, failing to show him respect. He explained to his colleague that Geniva caused fights among scholars and therefore was unworthy of such respect. *Ḥafetz Ḥayim,*[17] troubled by the negative speech, explains that Geniva's trouble-making actions were widely known and therefore the criticism was permitted.

The conclusion jumps off the page that repeating widely known information does not fall under the prohibition of *lashon hara*. However, the issue is not as simple as may seem.

IN FRONT OF THREE

The *Ḥafetz Ḥayim* contains contradictory statements that complicate the matter:

- It discusses the aforementioned leniency, according to Maimonides and some others, of repeating negative information that is stated in front of three people (*be'apei telata*).[18] However, one may only repeat such information under specific conditions (detailed in his subsequent paragraphs), including that one only mention it incidentally and does not intend to spread the information. How can that be, if public information does not fall under the

14. Ibid. n. 41.
15. Ibid. ch. 2 n. 1 in parentheses.
16. Ibid. ch. 3 n. 12.
17. Ibid. ch. 8 n. 16 in asterisk.
18. Ibid. ch. 2 §3.

prohibition of *lashon hara*? While we can easily distinguish between the cases, further statements reveal that the issue is more complicated.

- In paragraph 4 of the same chapter, *Ḥafetz Ḥayim* states that if the information one heard in front of three people becomes well publicized, one may reveal the name of the person from whom it originated. The wording implies that one may only set aside the condition against repeating the name of the source but not the other conditions. This means that one may still only mention the information in passing and without the intent to spread it. Well-publicized information, then, still falls under the guidelines of *apei telata*.
- In discussing *lashon hara* about a child, *Ḥafetz Ḥayim* states that guidelines on well-publicized information can be found in chapter 2 paragraph 3, the section about *apei telata*.[19] He does not say that *lashon hara* does not apply at all but, implicitly, that the above conditions must be met before the information can be repeated.
- Concerning, furthermore, the issue of a persistent rumour (*yatza kol*), *Ḥafetz Ḥayim* again does not say that the laws of *lashon hara* do not apply.[20] Rather, readers are directed to the above section of *apei telata* and its attendant conditions.
- Lastly, one may not state that someone violates Jewish law, including that he does not learn Torah.[21] Even though it is generally public information that a person does not learn Torah, one may still only repeat such information under the conditions of *apei telata*.[22]

R. Binyamin Cohen, in his *Ḥelkat Binyamin* commentary on the *Ḥafetz Ḥayim*, compiles this list of contradictory rulings and leaves the matter unresolved.[23] I suggest the following explanation, which, I believe, accounts for every case listed above.

GRANTING PERMISSION

Rabbenu Jonah explains that there are two interpersonal elements to *lashon hara*: damaging the person about whom it is told (i.e. causing negative consequences) and embarrassing him (*nezek* and *boshet*).[24] Why is information told to three

19. Ibid. ch. 8 §3.
20. Ibid. ch. 7 §4.
21. *Ḥafetz Ḥayim*, ibid. ch. 4 §2.
22. Ibid. n. 6.
23. *Ḥelkat Binyamin* (New York, 1993), 1:2 n. 10.
24. *Shaarei Teshuva* 3:216.

people treated differently than totally private information? The commentators explain that since here the information will quickly become public knowledge, one's passing it on does not harm the individual. The process of inflicting damage has already been set in motion. But if that is the case, why can't one freely repeat the information? Because, I suggest, one is still insulting and embarrassing him. Even if everyone in the world knows about a politician's marital problems, he will still be hurt when people discuss them. As the Gemara (Bava Metzia 58b) says and Rashi explains, one is forbidden to call someone an insulting nickname even if everyone else commits the offense and the victim has grown accustomed to it (*dash beih*); frequency does not remove pain but only dulls it through surrender. Therefore, one is only allowed to repeat *lashon hara* that was told to three people under specific circumstances in which one does not intend to hurt the subject. However, if a person indicates that he does not object to the insult, if he forgives and permits the shame, then others may freely discuss the information. Absent damage and pain, the information no longer falls under the prohibition of *lashon hara* in any way.

I suggest that the leniency of publicized information (*nitparsem hadavar*) only applies to an act knowingly committed in public. By intentionally sinning in front of others, the actor declares that he does not care whether other people know of his infractions. He does not consider discussion of his actions insulting. He gives others permission to speak of his deeds, thereby removing the prohibition of *lashon hara*. However, when information about a private act is publicized, the prohibition still applies, albeit under the category of *apei telata*.

If we review the first list above, we may see that all the cases where the prohibition no longer applies involve public actions: a public sinner, a city that is publicly full of scoffers, someone who publicly berates others, and a scholar who causes fights among and in front of his colleagues. The second list involves acts in general, presumably only private in contrast to those in the prior list (refraining from studying Torah is not an act committed in public).

APPLICATIONS AND IMPLICATIONS

If all this is correct, then the leniency of publicized information cannot always be used in the public arena. A candidate campaigning for election may freely discuss his opponent's public actions – that is, those committed intentionally in public – but may not mention those committed in private, even if widely reported in the media. Similarly, a newspaper may only report on intentional public, and not private, actions, barring some other avenue of leniency.

Additionally, according to the initial understanding of this subject, one may repeat any information that is well known. Therefore, once the information has left the public arena and has been generally forgotten, one may no longer repeat it. Rabbi Azriel Ariel quotes Rabbi Dov Lior as suggesting, based on Bava Metzia 24a and Berakhot 58b, one year as the time limit on permissibly discussing well-publicized information.[25] My proposed understanding is that the subject has given permission to others to reveal the information. Presumably, this permission has no time limit. Can someone revoke his permission? Certainly a penitent may regain his privacy. Regardless of whether one violates *lashon hara* rules, one may not remind someone who repents of his past misdeeds because of the prohibition of *onaat devarim*.[26] However, the chasm between regret and repentance is wide enough to hold most people in the world.[27] May one discuss the knowing public sin of someone who feels bad about it but may succumb to temptation again? I suspect that one may not and that the other person's implicit permission has been revoked. However, I cannot currently prove either side.

This discussion impacts how we use social media. A common use of Twitter, Facebook, and similar tools is sharing links to interesting news articles. Can one share a link to an article that contains *lashon hara*? *Lashon hara* is forbidden even when communicated non-verbally.[28] Not all articles are widely read, so we cannot assume that every link contains already well-publicized information. Our discussion would not allow bringing a small local story to a national or global audience, absent other permissive factors. However, we can assume that articles in popular national media are well publicized. Can we circulate them? Can we retweet a *New York Times* article about our neighbour's tax evasion? According to the approach I am criticizing, yes we may but only if the issue has remained in the news within the past year. According to my proposed explanation, furthermore, we may only do so if our neighbour committed his misdeeds in public.

The theological implications of this insight deserve consideration. Privacy is a Torah right: someone who reveals another's secret is condemned by Scripture.[29] "How goodly are your tents, Jacob" (Num. 24:5) praises the Jewish

25. Ibid.

26. Bava Metzia 58b.

27. See *Mishne Torah, Hilkhot Teshuvah* 2:2 that regret is only part of the repentance process.

28. *Ḥafetz Ḥayim* 1:1:8.

29. Prov. 11:13; *Shaarei Teshuva* 3:225. See also the exchange between Rabbis Shaul Yisraeli and Shlomo Goren regarding the prohibition against publicizing someone else's words without permission in *Teḥumin*, vol. 4 (5743/1983), reprinted partly in R. Shaul Yisraeli, *Ḥavot Binyamin* (Jerusalem, 1992), ii, no. 75.

concern for privacy. We establish our houses, and our lives, to protect the privacy of others. This right to, or drive for, privacy is an element of our mandate to act in a godly manner. The prophet Isaiah (45:15) proclaims, "Truly you are a God who hides Himself." We, too, are bidden to hide ourselves in modesty, to protect our privacy.[30]

However, the lesson of our analysis is that one cannot abandon one's right to privacy and then later attempt to reclaim it. Once one brings one's reputation into the public domain, one cannot carry it back into the private by invoking Jewish law. Surely, about situations such as this Kohelet (1:15) laments, "That which is crooked cannot be made straight." In a world of overexposure online, of blogging innermost thoughts, tweeting every fleeting idea, posting videos and pictures of personal moments, this message could not be timelier. If we fail to safeguard our own privacy, we lose part of our godliness, which we can only struggle to reclaim.

I began by discussing two avenues of leniency that allow for public discussion within the parameters of the *lashon hara* laws. The permission of publicized information is more limited than we initially thought, even if it provides some public leeway. The leniency of public benefit offers another area with rich potential for contemporary application and requires separate treatment.

30. See Rabbi Hershel Schachter, "On the Matter of Masorah" online at http://www.torahweb.org/torah/special/2003/rsch_masorah.html; id., *Nefesh HaRav*, p. 281, in the name of Rabbi Joseph B. Soloveitchik.

Section II
Anglo-Jewry

The Memorial Prayer in *Minhag Anglia*

Dayan Ivan Binstock

It is an honour to offer this essay as part of a volume of tribute to Chief Rabbi Lord Jonathan Sacks. I have had the privilege to be a member of the rabbinate and a member of the Beth Din throughout the tenure of Chief Rabbi Sacks and I have benefited enormously form his friendship and advice. The Chief Rabbi invited me to assist in the adaptation of the Koren *maḥzor* project for Anglo-Jewry. It has been a privilege to work alongside the Chief Rabbi and the Koren team. As well as illuminating so many areas of Jewish thought and Jewish life with his scholarship and leadership, the Chief Rabbi has made a vital contribution to revitalizing the prayer experience for many, worldwide, with his translations of and commentary on the siddur and the *maḥzor*.

A distinctive feature of Minhag Anglia is its use of memorial prayer. Two forms of prayer are recited that are not found in other communities. The first is the abbreviated prayer "*Adon HaOlamim*":

> Master of the universe; remember the soul of… who has gone to his eternal home. We beseech you, Father of mercy and compassion, may his soul be bound up in the bond of life and may his rest be glorious and let us say Amen.[1]

1. *Authorised Daily Prayer Book*, 4th edn. (London 2006), 840.
אדון העולמים זכור את נשמת פלוני בן פלוני שהלך לעולמו. אנא אב הרחמים והסליחות, תהי נפשו צרורה בצרור החיים ותהי מנוחתו כבוד ונאמר אמן.

It is recited in place of the more widely known prayer, "*El Male Raḥamim*": "God, full of mercy, who dwells on high". This is coupled with an alternative, longer form of memorial prayer, said in the *shiva* house and at the cemetery:

> O Lord and King, full of compassion, God of the spirits of all flesh, in whose hands are the souls of the living and the dead, receive, we pray You, in Your great love, the soul of... who has been gathered to his people.[2]

The purpose of this essay is to explore the background to these prayers and their usage in the Anglo-Jewish community.

BACKGROUND

Whilst there are no explicit prayers for the dead in the Bible, the Talmud interprets David's lament for Absalom (II Sam. 19:1) as a prayer for the elevation of the latter's soul: "And the king trembled, and he went up to the upper chamber of the gate, and wept; and thus he said, as he went, 'O my son Absalom, my son, my son Absalom! Would I had died in your stead, O Absalom my son, my son!'"[3]

The earliest explicit reference to praying on behalf of the dead is found in the Greek apocryphal work II Maccabees, where Judah organizes sacrifices and prayers on behalf of those of his soldiers slain in battle:

> Turning to supplication, they prayed that the sinful deed might be fully blotted out. The noble Judah warned the soldiers to keep themselves free from sin, for they had seen with their own eyes what had happened because of the sin of those who had fallen. He then took up a collection among all his soldiers, amounting to two thousand silver drachmas, which he sent to Jerusalem to provide for an expiatory sacrifice. In doing this he acted in a very excellent and noble way, inasmuch as he had the resurrection of the dead in view; for if he were not expecting the fallen to rise again, it would

---

It is curious that whereas this prayer is found in all editions of the *Singer's Prayer Book*, "*Adon HaOlamim*", though recited in nearly all United Synagogues, is not included in any other edition of the siddur. For the introduction to this prayer, see below. Recent works that contain the prayer include the *Philip Goldberg Memorial Book: A Miscellany of Prayers for Occasional Use in The Synagogue Service*, ed. J. Rabbinowitz (London, 1962) and Geoffrey Shisler, *Tenu Kavod LaTorah: The Call-Up Book* (London, 2006), 35.

2. אנא ה׳ מלך מלא רחמים, אלקי הרוחות לכל בשר, אשר בידך נפשות החיים והמתים, קבל בחסדך הגדול את נשמת פלוני בן פלוני אשר נאסף לעמו.

3. Sota 10b.

> have been useless and foolish to pray for them in death. But if he did this with a view to the splendid reward that awaits those who had gone to rest in godliness, it was a holy and pious thought.[4]

COMMEMORATING THE DEAD ON SHABBAT AND YOM KIPPUR

The earliest midrashic sources refer to remembering the dead on Shabbat and Yom Kippur.

> Therefore we remember the dead on Shabbat so that they should not return to Gehinom. As the verse is expounded in *Torat Kohanim* [Leviticus]: "Atone for your people, Israel" [Deut. 21] – this refers to the living; "Whom you have redeemed" – this refers to the dead. From here we learn that the living can redeem the dead. Therefore it is our practice to remember the dead on Yom Kippur and to pledge charity on their behalf. [5]

Shabbat is a time when the dead have rest from Gehinom and so it is appropriate to pray that they should not return. Yom Kippur is a time when the living, through their charity and prayer, can enable the dead to ascend even further.

Yom Kippur was established early on as a day for remembering the dead – indeed, in twelfth-century Germany this was the only day for doing so.[6] In the thirteenth century, *Hazkarat Neshamot* (lit. commemoration of the souls) occasionally took place on Rosh Hashana as well.[7] In thirteenth-century France[8] and Italy[9] the practice of remembering the dead every Shabbat became well established. No distinction was made between the Shabbatot of the year. Indeed, the reference in *Maḥzor Vitri* follows on immediately after the blessing of the New Month.

HAZKARAT NESHAMOT ON FESTIVALS

The festival Torah potion *Kol HaBekhor* culminates in the phrase *ish kematnat yado*, referring to the offering a person would make in the Temple according to

---

4. II Macc. 12:42–4.
5. *Midrash Tanḥuma* (Warsaw edition), *Parashat Haazinu*, 1.
6. *Siddur Rashi, Seder Yom Kippur*, 214:
פוסקין צדקה ברבים על המתים ועל החיים, אין פוסקין צדקה למתים בכל ארץ אשכנז רק היום לבדו.
7. *Or Zarua I, Hilkhot Tzedaka*, 10:
הלכך אותם בני הישובים שבאים לקהלה בר״ה ויוה״כ ומזכירין נשמות ונודרים צדקה.
8. *Maḥzor Vitri*, 190:
וזוכר את המתים שרבו תורה ותקנות בישראל ואותם שהניחו שום דבר בקהל ושהניחו אחרים בשבילם.
9. *Shibbolei Haleket, Inyan Shabbat*, 81.

his means. It became the practice in medieval Europe that after the conclusion of the Torah reading a blessing was given to the community that would make a pledge to charity. This became known as the ceremony of *matnat yad*. The charity was for the benefit of the living:[10] the *Maḥzor Vitri* emphasizes that the *tzedaka* pledged on a festival (*yom tov*) is not for the dead.[11] To invoke the memory of the dead would cause pain, which is inappropriate on *yom tov*. Yet *Shibbolei Haleket* mentions the practice of remembering the dead on the three pilgrimage festivals as well,[12] when the Torah portion *Kol HaBekhor* is read.

Professor Eric Zimmer has shown that *matnat yad* and *Hazkarat Neshamot* on festivals were instituted independently in medieval Europe.[13] Different communities performed one or the other, or both. The division lay largely along geographical lines, with communities in Western Europe favouring *matnat yad* and communities in Eastern Europe favouring *Hazkarat Neshamot*. Rabbi Jacob Moelin (Maharil) refers, unequivocally, to the recital of both *Hazkarat Neshamot* and *matnat yad*,[14] yet regional variations persisted for some centuries.

With the establishment of *Hazkarat Neshamot* for *yom tov*, other reasons were offered to support its recital. The seventeenth-century Italian rabbi Aaron Berakhia of Modena, in his classic work *Maavar Yabok* (first published in Mantua in 1626), speaks about how the dead can pray for the living and how the living can pray for the dead.[15] He mentions the importance of prayers for the dead on Shabbat and that the mere utterance with devotion of the names of the dead

10. The recipients of this charity were either the local poor or the needy of Jerusalem. See I. Yuval, "Alms from Nuremberg to Jerusalem" (Heb.), *Zion*, 46 (1981), 182–97.

11. *Maḥzor Vitri*, 312:

ופוסקים צדקה ברבים על החיים לבדם: ת׳: מפני שקראו היום (דברים טז) איש כמתנת ידו. וגו׳. וכן מנהג בכל יום אחרון של רגלים שקורין פרשה זו לפסוק צדקה על החיים לבדם ולא על מתים שלא להצטער עליהם. דכת׳ בהו ברגלים (דברים טז) (והייתם) [והיית] אך שמח. וכן מנהג בארץ אשכנז שאין פוסקין צדקה על המתים בג׳ רגלים אלא ביום הכיפורים בלבד.

12. *Shibbolei Haleket, Seder Atzeret*, 239:

וביום שקורין כל הבכור נהגו לפסוק נדבתן לשלש פעמים על שם שלש פעמים בשנה יראה כל זכורך וגו׳... הלכך כשפוסקין צדקה ברבים ומברך החזן אותם בלשון נדבה... ומה שנהגו לפסוק צדקה גם בעבור המתים להזכיר נשמות למנוחה.

13. Yitzḥak (Eric) Zimmer, "The Custom of *Matnat Yad* and *Hazkarat Neshamot*" (Heb.), in *Lo Yisor Shevet MiYehuda: Hanhagah, Rabbanut Ukehillah BeToledot Yisrael. Meḥkarim Mukdashim LiProfessor Shimon Schwarzfuchs* (Jerusalem, 2011), 71–88.

14. Maharil, *Minhagim, Seder Tefillat Ḥag HaSukkot*:

כללא הוא כל יו״ט שקורין בו איש כמתנת ידו מזכירין נשמות ואומר אב הרחמים.

15. *Siftei Renanot* 23–4.

can achieve great spiritual results.[16] He underlines the particular significance of saying *Yizkor* on the second day of festivals. The observance of second-day *yom tov* in the Diaspora causes the *Shekhina* to dwell in our midst. We have, in effect, expanded the boundaries of holiness by creating an extra day of *yom tov*, and recalling the dead on this day generates additional spiritual light, he argues.[17]

Eliya Rabba (Prague, seventeenth century) offers a completely contrasting reason. If the dead did not keep Shabbat or *yom tov*, they need extra prayers on these days to ameliorate their punishment.[18]

OCCASIONS ON WHICH *HAZKARAT NESHAMOT* IS OMITTED

Whilst the suspension of *Taḥanun* in the month of Nisan is already found in Tractate Soferim (21) and is cited as halakha by many medieval commentators (*rishonim*), it is in the fifteenth century that both Rabbi Isaac of Tirnau (Mahari)[19] in Austria and Maharil in Germany extend this to omitting *Hazkarat Neshamot* as well, though in the case of Maharil it is only on Shabbatot in Nisan that *Hazkarat Neshamot* is to be omitted. He also excludes the four Shabbatot of special *parashot* leading up to Pesaḥ and any Shabbat preceding the New Moon, unless the commemorative prayer (*azkara*) is for someone who had been buried during the previous week.[20] In *Hilkhot Pesaḥ*, Maharil

---

16. *Maavar Yabok, Siftei Renanot* 23, p. 284:
מנהג זכירת המתים בשבת אין ספק שזכירתם ביום המנוחה מועיל להם מאד מפני שהם נחים וע״י הזכירה נשמתם מתחדשת שיש תלייה לשם עם הנשמה... והנה בהזכרת שמו במנוחה מתחדשת שם מנוחתו ויהיה עתה במנוחה ודיוקן נשמתו מאירה

17. Ibid. 285:
ברגלים מנהג לעשות זכרון נשמות ונדבות ביום טוב שני כי היום טוב שני אנו עושים אותו לכבוד שכינה שעמנו חוצה לארץ כדי שתתעכב בעבורנו ההארה הנוספת ביום טוב שני כי להיותנו חוץ מארצנו אנחנו צריכים הארה יתירה וכמו שהאבות קיימו התורה קודם שנתנה להשכין שכינה עמם כל נהגנו אנחנו ביום טוב שני להשכין שכינה עמנו וזהו דשלחו מתם הזהרו במנהג אבותיכם ביצה ד ע״ב והנדבות והזכרת נשמות זוכרים עמהם גם נפש אברהם יצחק ויעקב שהרחיבו גבול השכינה וכן נעשה אנחנו ביום טוב שני והזכרת הנשמות מוסיף אור למעלה.

18. *Eliya Zuta* 284:3:
עוד טעם מפני שמהפכין אש של גיהנם לפניהם ולאחריהם אותן שלא שמרו שבת ויום טוב שנאמר והיה מידי חודש בחדשו וכוי לכך צריכין להתפלל עליהם.

19. *Sefer Minhagim* (Tirnau), *Ḥodesh Nisan*:
כל (נט) החדש (ס) אין נופלין [בתחנון], לפי שבאחד בניסן הוקם המשכן. והקריבו י״ב נשיאים קרבנם כל איש ביומו, זהו י״ב יום. ויום י״ג אסרו חג שלהם. ויום י״ד ערב פסח. וח׳ ימי פסח ואסרו חג [הרי כ״ג ימים], ומתוך שאין נופלין ברובו אין נופלין בכולו. ואין אומרים בו צדקתך צדק וצידוק הדין. כי והוא רחום ותחנון וצדקתך צדק (סא) וצידוק הדין לעולם שוין [הם]. ואין מזכירין בו נשמות.

20. *Maharil (Minhagim), Hilkhot Tevet, Shevat, Adar*:
כל ארבע פרשיות אין מזכירין נשמות ואומרים צו״צ. כל ימי ניסן א״א תחינה, אך אומרים אא״א. ובשבת אין מזכירין נשמות ואין אומרים צו״צ.

offers a reason for these omissions,[21] based on a verse in Ecclesiastes (7:14): "on a good day, be pleased".[22] He further extends the heightened festivity of the anticipation of a new month to any Shabbat where *yotzerot* (special festive hymns) are added.[23] The (knowledgeable) worshipper, whose mood is presumably lifted by the poetic embellishment of the *yotzerot*, is not to be saddened by the recital of *Hazkarat Neshamot*, Maharil suggests.[24]

Yet he does not consider the festivity of *yom tov* to be in conflict with *Hazkarat Neshamot* on the second day of a festival. The practice of *matnat yad* would seem to be sufficient to justify saying *Hazkarat Neshamot*. *Levush* in the sixteenth century makes this point explicitly:

> The reason why we remember the dead on the last day of Pesaḥ is that we want to pledge charity, since we read then the portion of *Kol HaBekhor*, in which it is mentioned, *ish kematnat yado* etc. Since we are dedicating charity anyway, it has become the practice to pledge on behalf of the dead when remembering them, that God should remember them, and through them, He should remember us with them, for good. Therefore we remember the dead on all the festivals on the day that we read *Kol HaBekhor*. On Yom Kippur we remember the dead since it is a day of judgment, even though we do not read *Kol HaBekhor*.[25]

---

21. Maharil (*Minhagim*), *Dinei Hayamim SheVein Pesaḥ LeShavuot*:
שבת שמברכין בו ראש חודש אין מזכירין בו נשמות ואין מזכירין בו התענית של בה״ב, משום שנ׳ בו ביום טובה היה בטוב (קהלת ז, יד).

22. Rabbi Mordechai Jaffe, in his *Levush*, cites an alternative passage to justify the positive mood: "While you can be good, do not call yourself bad" (*Levush, Oraḥ Ḥayim* 284:7).
בשבת שיש בו חתונה או מילה, או ביום שמברכין בו את החדש, אין מזכירין נשמות ואין אומרים אב הרחמים, משום בהיות טוב אל תקרא רע (בבא קמא פא ע״ב) חוץ מבימי הספירה שאומרים אותו אפילו בימים הללו.
The choice of this phrase by *Levush* is not without its difficulties. In the context of the Talmud's use of the phrase (Bava Kama 81b and Berakhot 30a) it refers to someone who does not lose out if he does a favour to others or joins them in their manner of performance of a mitzva. Here, *Levush* is citing this phrase to justify the omission of *Hazkarat Neshamot* on certain Shabbatot.

23. Maharil (*Minhagim*), *Hilkhot Aseret Yemei HaTeshuvah*:
וכללא הוא כל יום שאומר בו יוצר אין מזכירין בו נשמות.

24. A similar principle is given by the contemporary of the Mahari Tirnau, Rabbi Zalman Yent, in his *Minhagei Harav Zalman Yent*:
וזה הכלל בכל שבת שיש בו יוצר אין מזכירין נשמות, וכן בשבת שמברכין בו ראש חדש אין מזכירין.

25. *Levush, Oraḥ Ḥayim* 490:9.

The *Mishna Berura* rules that, apart from the days that *Yizkor* is said, *Hazkarat Neshamot* takes place every Shabbat, except if it is one of the four weeks of the special *parashot*,[26] the Shabbat preceding the New Moon, or during the month of Nisan.[27]

The permissibility of saying *Hazkarat Neshamot* on *yom tov* emerges from a different perspective in a passage in Tractate Moed Katan (8a). The Gemara mentions a disagreement between Rav and Samuel concerning the reasons for not holding a eulogy (*hesped*) within thirty days of *yom tov*. Rav is of the view that a person may spend his money on a professional eulogizer and be short of money to celebrate *yom tov*. Samuel argues that the eulogizer will arouse such grief in his listeners that they will enter *yom tov* in a state of sadness.

The *rishonim* differ as to whether we follow Rav or Samuel, but *Beit Yosef* points out that this dispute was relevant at a time when the eulogizer would generate such emotion that it would remain with people for thirty days.[28] Nowadays the *hesped* that is made at the conclusion of a term of mourning would be permitted within thirty days of *yom tov*, even according to Samuel, since its purpose is not to create a lasting mood of mourning but, on the contrary, to conclude the mourning period.

Rabbi Hillel ben Naftali Hertz, in his commentary on *Shulḥan Arukh*, points out:

> The reference that [Rabbi Joseph Karo] has made to "remembering the dead" – this is not what we are now accustomed to call "*El Male Raḥamim*", for we have the practice to say *El Male Raḥamim* on every festival. If so, since we say it on *yom tov*, this is not a *hesped* but rather a prayer on behalf of the dead, as the *Beit Yosef* has written in *Oraḥ Ḥayim* 284 in the name of *Shibbolei Haleket*: "after the Torah reading it is customary to remember the dead etc."[29]

In fact, Rabbi Shabbatai HaKohen (*Shakh*) points out in the name of *Levush* that memorial prayers can be made, even for the first time, during a festival.[30] In

26. *Mishna Berura* 685:18.
27. Ibid. 284:17.
28. *Oraḥ Ḥayim* 547:5.
29. *Beit Hillel*, 347 on *Yoreh De'a* (Dyhernfurth, 1691).
30. *Siftei Kohen, Yoreh De'a* 337: "The *Ateret Zekenim* (*Levush*) writes 'and our custom is to recite the memorial prayer on festivals even if it is for the first time.'"
וכ׳ העט״ז ואנו נוהגין להזכיר אפילו פעם הראשון אפילו בתוך הרגל.

the following century, Rabbi Eliya Shapira of Prague (1660–1712), in his commentary on *Levush*, cites *Beit Hillel* and *Shakh* verbatim.[31] Rabbi Joseph Teomim (1727–1792) further clarifies that the *El Male Raḥamim* that is recited, permissibly, in the synagogue even on *yom tov* differs in status from the same prayer recited at the cemetery, which would be regarded as *hesped*.[32] This distinction is cited by the *Mishna Berura*,[33] reinforcing the view that *El Male Raḥamim* recited in the synagogue is to be regarded as a prayer for the dead that can be said on *yom tov*, not as a *hesped*.

The anomalies that exist in the current practice in many communities concerning when *Hazkarat Neshamot* is omitted is already noted by Rabbi Ephraim Zalman Margaliot (1762–1828) in his authoritative work, *Shaarei Efrayim*:

> If so [i.e. if the reason the sages prescribed remembering the dead on Shabbat is that on that day the dead are also resting], what justification is there to distinguish between Shabbatot? Why should there be any difference if the New Moon is being blessed or it is a day that during the week would not have *Taḥanun* said? *Levush* writes that on the days that *Tzidkatekha Tzedek* is omitted we do not make *Hazkarat Neshamot*, nor do we say *Av Haraḥamim*, based on [the passage] "While you can be good, do not call yourself bad." I do not understand, according to the reason for saying *Hazkarat Neshamot*, if the dead are also resting on Shabbat, what 'bad' can there be! To the contrary, there is additional rest and sanctity on these days. Moreover, on *yom tov* we remember the dead, and there is no sense not to say *Yizkor* when *yom tov* falls on Shabbat, since on Shabbat itself we say *Hazkarat Neshamot*! Nevertheless, one should not question or object to the customs of the Jewish people, and each person should conduct himself according the practices in the Jewish dispersion.[34]

The reason the *Shakh* does not refer to *El Male Raḥamim* by name is that in his time (1622–1663) it was only beginning to become established as the form of memorial prayer. See below.

31. *Eliya Rabba, Oraḥ Ḥayim* 547:2.

32. *Pri Megadim, Oraḥ Ḥayim, Eshel Avraham* 547:2:
והמה מה שמזכירים נשמות אף ברגל בבית הכנסת אף פעם ראשון ברגל אין זה למה שהולכין על הקבר ומזכירים נשמות ואומר אל מלא רחמים שזה הוה בכלל הספד שאסור.

33. *Mishna Berura, Oraḥ Ḥayim* 597:8; *Shaar Hatziyun* 6.

34. *Shaarei Efrayim, Shaar* 10, *Pitḥei She'arim* 28, 29.

THE FORM OF MEMORIAL PRAYER

We have no record of the explicit form of memorial prayer said in talmudic or geonic times. The oldest memorial prayer in the siddur is the communal prayer for martyrs, *Av HaRaḥamim,* introduced after the First Crusade of 1096, though its exact time and authorship remain unknown.[35]

One of the creations of medieval Germany was the *Memorbuch,* where the names of the martyrs of the community were listed. It seems likely that earlier forms of memorial prayer would follow the formula presented in the *Memorbuch.* For example, in the Frankfurt *Memorbuch,* after *Av HaRaḥamim,* before mentioning the names of the various places and the long list of individuals starting in 1628, we find the prayer: "May God remember the martyrs of ... and the outlying settlements, who died for the Sanctification of the Name; therefore may their souls be bound up in the bond of life with other righteous men and women. Amen!"[36]

Rabbi Aaron Berakhia of Modena, in his *Maavar Yabok,*[37] gives an elaborate *seder hashkava,* or order of prayers that are said at the burial, for seven days at the house of the deceased, and when visiting the grave thereafter:[38]

> Proper rest in the heavenly abode, under the wings of the Divine Presence on the exalted level of the holy and pure ones, who illuminate and shine like the glow of heaven, with the upright and pure, with powers that are strengthened and transgressions that are pardoned, sins kept far and salvation brought near, with compassion and grace from Him who sits enthroned above, with a goodly portion in the World to Come – in that place may there be the share of the abode of the soul and goodly name of our brother (sister) who has departed this world according to the will of God, the Lord of Heaven and Earth.

---

35. Y. (E.) Zimmer, "*Gezerot Tatnu* in Medieval and Modern *Minhag* Books" (Heb.), in Y. T. Assis et al. (eds.), *Yehudim mul HaTselav: Gezerot Tatnu BaHistoryah UvaHistoriografyah* (Jerusalem, 2000), 162–4.

36. http://jnul.huji.ac.il/dl/mss/heb1092/djvu/index.djvu?djvuopts&thumbnails=yes&zoom=page&page=2.

37. This work was to become highly influential as a basis for *ḥevra kadisha* practice in many communities. See Sylvie-Anne Goldberg, *Crossing the Jabbok: Illness and Death in Ashkenazi Judaism in Sixteenth- through Nineteenth-Century Prague* (Berkeley, Los Angeles, London, 1996).

38. *Maavar Yabok,* Ahavat Shalom edn. (Jerusalem, 1996), 129.
מנוחה נכונה בישיבה העיליונה תחת כנפי השכינה במעלת טהורים וקדושים כזוהר הרקיע מאירים ומזהירים עם ישרים וברים בחלוץ עצמות וכפרת אשמות והרחקת פשע והקרבת ישע וחמלה וחנינה ולפני שוכן מעונה וחולקא טבא לחיי העולם הבא שם תהא מנת מחיצת נפש ושם הטוב כמ״ר פלוני בן פלונית או פלונית בת... דאתפטר מן עלמא הדין (או דאתפטרת) ברעות אלהא מרי שמיא וארעא.

This lengthy text is the basis of the briefer prayer currently used in many Sephardi communities.[39]

The form of the *El Male Raḥamim* memorial prayer that is used in the Ashkenazi world would seem to have its origins in the period after the Chmielnicki massacres of 1648. Rabbi Nathan Hanover, in his account of the tragedy, *Yaven Metzula*, refers to a cantor, Rabbi Hirsch of Zhitov, who sang *El Male Raḥamim* at the tragic loss of life.[40] This would indicate that the prayer was already well known by this time. The twentieth of Sivan was adopted as a fast day for commemoration of the tragedy. The first edition of *seliḥot* for that day, published in 1650, contains the long *El Male Raḥamim* composed by Rabbi Yom Tov Lipman Heller to commemorate the martyrs. An elaborate adaptation lamenting the killing of Rabbi Yeḥiel Miḥel of Nemerov, incorporating a stanza of elegy for each letter of the *alef-bet*, is included in subsequent editions.[41] The current version[42] of the prayer is excerpted from these versions.[43]

It therefore emerges that the standard form of memorial prayer is based on a text that was composed for those who had been martyred in pogroms. In light of this fact it is not surprising that some have questioned the appropriateness of this language for those who have died in other circumstances. Rabbi Elijah Henkin says that one may be doing more harm than good in referring to a deceased[44] "in the heights of the holy and pure ones who shine as the brightness of the firmament", and proposes an alternative version:

> God, full of mercy, who dwells on high, grant pardon, forgiveness and atonement to the soul of.... And to this...has pledged charity for the

39. *Order of Service for Burial and the Setting of a Tombstone*, published by the Spanish and Portuguese Jews' Congregation (London, n.d.), 28.
40. R. Nathan Hanover, *Yaven Metzula* (Berlin, 1923), 16.
והיה ביניהם חזן א' ושמו ר' הירש מ"זיואטוב, כשבאו אל הקדרים התחיל לקונן ולשורר "אל מלא רחמים", על הריגת אחינו בית ישראל בקול גדול.
41. *Siddur Otzar Hatefilot, Seliḥot Lekaf Sivan.*
42. Israel Davidson, in his *Thesaurus of Hebrew Poetry*, cites more than twenty examples of *El Male Raḥamim.*
43. There is discussion as to whether one should say *taḥat kanfei haShekhina* or *al kanfei haShekhina*. The *Siddur Shelah* changed the text to the latter and many newer siddurim reflect this. However, many of the early forms of *El Male Raḥamim* cited by Davidson have *taḥat kanfei haShekhina* and this version is justified by other halakhists; see e.g. *Responsa Peulat Tzeddek* 2:221.
44. R. Joseph Elijah Henkin, *Edut LeYisrael* (New York, 1936), 116.
במעלות קדושים וטהורים כזוהר הרקיע מזהירים.

> atonement of his soul. May his repose be in the Garden of Eden and may he rest in peace and let us say Amen.[45]

His suggestion was not taken up and siddurim continue to print the *El Male Raḥamim* without change.[46]

HAZKARAT NESHAMOT IN ENGLAND

Issues of a different kind were being raised in England in the nineteenth century. As mentioned above, *El Male Raḥamim* was being omitted in communities on many occasions during the year. By contrast, the Sephardi community allowed the recital of a memorial prayer on any day of the year.[47] Moreover, among Ashkenazim *El Male Raḥamim* was only recited in the synagogue.[48] It is apparent from the practice of Maharil, mentioned above, that when the *azkara* was to be made on a Shabbat preceding the new month for someone who had died the previous week, this would be the first time a memorial prayer was being made for the deceased. Unlike in *Maavar Yabok*, there was no memorial prayer made at the cemetery.[49] Furthermore, as opposed to

45. Ibid.:

אל מלא רחמים שוכן במרומים המצא מחילה וסליחה וכפרה לנשמת פב״פ בעבור ש... נדב צדקה בעד כפרת נשמתו בגן עדן תהא מנוחתו וינוח בשלום על משכבו ונאמר אמן.

46. It should be noted that the memorial prayers composed by Chief Rabbi Adler (see below) avoid the phrases that Rabbi Henkin found problematic.

47. See e.g. Y. Ratzabi, *Shulḥan Arukh Hamekutzar, Oraḥ Ḥayim* 2, p. 86 n. 38:

אעפ״י שהמשנה ברורה סימן רפ״ד ס״ק י״ז, ועוד אחרונים מרבני אשכנז, הביאו בשם המג״א מנהגם שלא להזכיר נשמות (דהיינו מה שאנו קוראים השכבות) בשבת שמברכין את החודש, זולת למי שנקבר באותו שבוע וכו׳ יעו״ש, ובגשר החיים פרק ל״ג אות ג׳ רשם כל הימים שמנהגם לא להזכיר בהם נשמות. אבל מנהגינו ידוע שלעולם אומרים השכבות, ולמעשה אין שום יום שנמנעים מלומר בו השכבות.

48. R. Ḥizkiya Medini (1833–1904) was once asked by an Ashkenazi Jew about saying *El Male Raḥamim* at night at the cemetery, and he replied that he couldn't see any problem (*Sedei Hemed, Maarekhet Avelut*, 212):

ולומר השכבה בלילה נראה דאין שום חשש ולא ראיתי כעת מי שמפקפק באמירת השכבה בלילה וכן הוא מנהג פשוט בינינו ופעם אחת הייתי בלויית מת איש נכבד מאשכנזים ושאלוני אם לומר עליו אל מלא רחמים (שהוא נוסח ההשכבה שלהם) ואמרתי כי לומר צדו״ה בלילה תלוי במנהג ועל אמירת השכבה איני יודע שינוי מנהגים ואין נראה שום חשש באמירתו ואיה״ש אשאל מפי רבני האשכנזים יצ״ו לדעת מנהגם.

49. Whilst there is no record of the *El Male Raḥamim* prayer being said at the cemetery, it is important to note that the *Sefer HaḤayim*, a classic work on the laws and prayers for sickness and death (1st edn. Sulzbach, 1667; ed. Simon Frankfurt, Amsterdam, 1703), contains a prayer to be said after the interment. This prayer is included in Rev. B. H. Ascher's translated edition of *Sefer HaḤayim* together with the *Kitzur Maanei Lashon*, a further collection of prayers at

Sephardi practice based on *Maavar Yabok*, no memorial prayer was recited in a house of mourning.[50]

In 1879 a ritual revision committee was set up at the Central Synagogue with the aim of presenting to the Chief Rabbi, Dr Nathan Marcus Adler, a number of changes in the ritual. This committee was the latest in a series of attempts during the nineteenth century to propose changes in the service. All the United Synagogues except the Hambro Synagogue sent delegates to the conference. The committee debated over a number of months the changes they wanted to see in the service.[51]

It is very likely that the practice of the Spanish and Portuguese community led the committee to request of the Chief Rabbi that he compose a modified form of *azkara* which could be said all the time, and a prayer to be recited in the house of mourning.[52] In his reply, the Chief Rabbi stated that he would

---

the cemetery. It is not clear whether this prayer was regularly used, and if so, when it lapsed. Nevertheless, it is more of a *Tefilat HaDerekh* for the soul than a memorial prayer:

יהי רצון מלפניך ה׳ אלקי הנשמות שתקבל נשמת (פלוני) לפניך באהבה ובחבה ותשלח לו מלאכים טובים לשמרו מחבוט הקבר ולהוליך נשמתו בגן עדן כאשר שלחת מלאכים ליעקב כדכתיב ויעקב הלך לדרכו ויפגעו בו מלאכי אלקים ויאמר יעקב כאשר ראם מחנה אלקים זה ויקרא שם המקום ההוא מחנים ותקיים בו מקרא זה וקוי ה׳ יחליפו כח יעלו אבר כנשרים ירוצו ולא ייגעו ילכו ולא ייעפו ותנהג עמו בחסדך המרובים ותתענג מדשן נפשו ומרב טוב הצפון לצדיקים ותהי נשמתו צרורה בצרור החיים עם כל שוכני עפר השוכבים פה עם כל צדיקים וצדקניות שבגן עדן אמן.

50. It should be noted that the Rev. B. H. Ascher's *Sefer Haḥayim* (2nd edn. London, 1861), which is the basis for many English *ḥevra kadisha* practices, contains no memorial prayer for the house of mourning, despite an extensive list of *teḥinot* on visiting the cemetery. The social make-up of English Jewry at that time is reflected in a halakha recorded on p. 214: "Servants in mourning are allowed to do any kind of work; but it is just and equitable that their employers should allow them an hour or an hour and a half daily, in which they might sit on the ground, and observe the customary ceremonies."
51. Interestingly, some of their proposals were contrary to halakha, such as sounding the *shofar* on the first day of Rosh Hashana even if it is Shabbat, or replacing the Yom Kippur afternoon Torah reading with the Torah reading for other fast days.
52. There existed a prayer to be said after learning in a house of mourning. It is recorded in the siddur of Chief Rabbi Solomon Hirschell (4th edn., London, 1842), 244. Rabbi Dr S. Schonfeld includes it in his *Standard Siddur – Prayer Book* (London 1973), 308:

אנא ה׳ מלך מלא רחמים אשר בידך נפש כל חי ורוח כל בשר איש יהיה נא לרצון לפניך תורתנו ותפילתנו בעבור נשמת (פלוני או פלונית) וגמול נא עמה בחסדך הגדול לפתוח לה שערי רחמים וחסד ושערי גן עדן ותקבל אותה באהבה ובחבה ושלח לה מלאכיך הקדושים והטהורים להוליכה ולהושיבה תחת עץ החיים אצל נשמת הצדיקים והצדקניות חסידים וחסידות להנות מזיו שכינתך להשביעה מטובך הצפון לצדיקים. והגוף ינוח בקבר במנוחה נכונה בחדוה בשמחה ובשלום. כדכתיב יבוא שלום ינוחו על משכבותם הולך נכוחו. וכתיב יעלזו חסידים בכבוד ירננו על משכבותם. וכתיב אם תשכב לא תפחד ושכבת וערבה שנתך. ותשמור [אותו] (אותה) מחיבוט הקבר ומרמה ותולעה. ותסלח ותמחול [לו] (לה) על כל [פשעיו] (פשעיה) כי אדם אין צדיק בארץ אשר יעשה טוב ולא יחטא. וזכור [לו זכיותיו

sanction "those modifications which do not impair the integrity of our Book of Daily Prayers ... and which do not infringe upon [the statutes] prescribed in the [*Shulḥan Arukh*]".[53]

Dr Adler composed the prayer for the house of mourning, which in due course found its way into the siddur,[54] and the modified *azkara*, which, as mentioned above, was never included in any edition of the siddur. However, its early adoption in the synagogue is attested by its inclusion in the St John's Wood Synagogue 'Bima Book', a hand-written collection of prayers, compiled in 1885.

Thus synagogues had a form of memorial prayer they could use any day of the year. Some shuls continued to use *El Male Raḥamim*. Dayan Isaac Lerner writes that when he came to London to take up his position as rabbi of the New Synagogue, Egerton Road, he was surprised to discover that they were saying memorial prayers every day of the year, but he was able to justify the practice on the basis of the *Mishna Berura* and other authorities cited above.[55] Other synagogues adopted the briefer form, suggested by Chief Rabbi Adler, reserving the longer *El Male Raḥamim* for the occasions when *Yizkor* is said.

וצדקותיו] (לה זכיותיה וצדקותיה) אשר [עשה] (עשתה) ותשפיע [לו מנשמתו] (לה מנשמתה) לדשן [עצמותיו] (עצמותיה) בקבר מרב טוב הצפון לצדיקים. כדכתיב מה רב טובך אשר צפנת ליראיך. וכתיב שומר כל עצמותיו אחת מהנה לא נשברה. [וישכון] (ותשכון) בטח בדד ושאנן מפחד רעה. ואל [יראה] (תראה) פני גיהנם [ונשמתו] (ונשמתה) תהא צרורה בצרור החיים [ולהחיותו] (ולהחיותה) בתחיית המתים עם כל מתי עמך ישראל ברחמים. אמן.

The prayer composed by Chief Rabbi Adler clearly draws on the older prayer.

53. Reply of the Chief Rabbi to the Conference of Delegates (London, 1880).

54. It should be noted that the prayer composed by Dr Adler began with the words:

אנא ה׳ מלך מלא רחמים, אלקי הרוחות לכל בשר, אשר בידך נפש כל חי ורוח כל בשר איש, ממית ומחיה מוריד שאול ויעל, אנא קבל בחסדך הגדול את נשמת...

Chief Rabbi Dr J. H. Hertz revised this prayer (and the Prayer for the Royal Family.) The revised prayer, which is the one currently in use, is first included in the 15th edn. of the *Singer's Prayer Book* (1939).

55. Torat HaMinhagim: *Studies of the* Nusach HaTefillah *and Other* Minhagim *of the United Synagogue*, 2nd edn. (London, n.d.), 36.

A Visit to the Home of a Victorian Chief Rabbi

With notes by Rabbi Shlomo Katanka

THE HISTORY OF THIS ARTICLE

What follows below is an anonymously published article, originally printed in the 27 November 1889 edition of *The World – A Journal for Men and Women,*[1] under the column entitled "Celebrities at Home". It was entitled "Dr Nathan Marcus Adler (Chief Rabbi of the Jews) in the First Avenue, Brighton"; the author would seem to be the founder and editor-in-chief Edmund Hodgson Yates (1831–94). The piece reappeared in an abridged form in the *Jewish Chronicle* of 29 November 1889.

We live in an age when interviews with "the good and the great" are published and broadcast on a near-daily basis. But in the nineteenth century such journalism was in its infancy. Let us go back nearly 120 years and revisit the life of one of the greatest builders and spiritual leaders who have ever lived on these Isles.

My father, Rabbi David Katanka (Rabbi of St Annes and Blackpool Hebrew Congregation), came across a reference to this article and mentioned it to me. My interest in Anglo-Jewish history and the chief rabbinate in particular drove my curiosity into visiting the Colindale Newspaper Library, reading and copying it. It was not disappointing; in fact, it was even more telling than anticipated! This piece captured my imagination as I hope it will capture yours, covering the period of emancipation of British Jewry,

1. First issued in London in July 1874.

the daily routine of the Chief Rabbi, and his many achievements. The homeliness and intimacy of this article is very heart-warming: even the decor of his home is discussed. Many of the historical figures and events mentioned have been obscured over the years so annotation is necessary to fully comprehend the subject matter.

It is my pleasant duty to thank Rabbi Meir Salasnik, who took time out of his busy schedule to clarify, correct, and comment on many of the historical points in the article.

INTRODUCTION

Chief Rabbi Dr Nathan Marcus Adler (*Moreh Moreinu HaRav Natan ben Moreh Moreinu HaRav Mordekhai HaKohen*) was born, a subject of King George III, in Hanover on 15 January 1803 (21 Tevet 5563) and died in Hove on 21 January 1890 (29 Tevet 5650).[2] He studied Torah first under his father and then later at the Würzburg yeshiva under its head, *av beit din* and *rosh yeshiva* Rabbi Abraham Bing (1752–1851), from whom he received ordination (*semikha*) on 28 June 1828. In the same year he graduated with a PhD from Erlangen University. In addition, he studied in Würzburg, Göttingen, and Heidelberg Universities. He served as *Landrabbiner* (District Rabbi) of the Grand Duchy of Oldenburg between 1829 and 1830, being immediately followed by Rabbi Samson Rafael Hirsch. In 1830 his father, Rabbi Marcus Baer Adler (1757–1834), was disqualified midterm from his Hanover chief rabbinate, due to new government legislation requiring the rabbi to have a greater German education. Rabbi Nathan Marcus stepped in until he moved to London in 1845 to become Chief Rabbi of the United Hebrew Congregations of the British Empire.

In an unpretending house on the right-hand side of the modest thoroughfare lying between Queen's Gardens and the Western Road,[3] the venerable ecclesiastic whose jurisdiction is more extensive than that of her Britannic Majesty (for the spiritual authority of the Chief Rabbi is still acknowledged by the Hebrews of the Transvaal[4]) is passing the peaceful evening of an eventful life which began [in 1803] two years before Trafalgar was fought, in the days when Colonel Despard's long-since forgotten conspiracy was still the universal subject

---

2. See n. 62 below.
3. Rabbi Adler moved to 36 First Avenue, Hove BN3 from London in late 1880.
4. Due to the Anglo-Boer War, the London Convention of 27 February 1884 gave the Transvaal complete independence from Britain.

of discussion.[5] There is nothing save a clump of neatly-clipped shrubs to distinguish Dr. Adler's dwelling from those of his neighbours; but the reminiscences of the hale octogenarian who welcomes you presently with the dignified courtesy of a bygone age to his plainly furnished oratory, overlooking a tiny grassplot fringed with evergreens, begin with the march of Napoleon through Hanover on his way to Moscow, and the departure of Baer Adler, Rabbi of Frankfort,[6] for Paris to take his seat as one of the delegates in the Great Sanhedrin of 1807.[7] It is almost impossible to believe that it is the younger brother of this same Baer Adler who rises briskly from the table at which he is working without spectacles on his Biblical Commentary, to tell you that, thanks to the invigorating air of "his best friend Dr. Brighton", he could fast for twenty-five hours on the Day of Atonement, and was once more able to observe the Feast of Tabernacles by taking his meals in an *al fresco* bower [i.e. in a *sukka*], according to the time-honoured tradition of his faith. The carpet which covers the floor is worn by the feet of many worshippers for Nathan Adler's chapel-study has been regarded for some years past as a place of pilgrimage, and it is considered a high privilege to take part in the service which he celebrates there every Saturday. On a bracket-desk close to the window are placed the *Tefilla*, the *Tehillim*, and the *Mischnajoth* – the three devotional volumes always used by the Chief Rabbi, and just opposite, on the other side of his writing-desk, is a curtained cupboard of walnut-wood, surmounted by the Tablets of the Covenant, which serves as the *Aron Hakkodesh* or "Sacred Ark," and contains a number of ancient "Scrolls of the Law" carefully wrapped up in gold brocade,

5. Colonel Edward Marcus Despard (1751–1803) led a plot to assassinate King George III.
6. Dayan Baer Adler (1785–1866), eldest brother of Nathan Marcus Adler, a member of the Frankfurt Beit Din under the leadership of Rabbi Shlomo Zalman Trier (1785–1846). Noted was their unrelenting fight to preserve the right to perform circumcision. Some of his novella on the Talmud were printed at the end of the second volume of *Lashon Zahav* (Offenbach 1826) under the title *Kanfei Nesharim*. He married Esther (1790–1860), daughter of Hirsch Moses Worms, whose sister Henrietta married his brother Chief Rabbi Nathan Marcus Adler. He was not *the* Rabbi of Frankfurt, but rather *a* rabbi and a businessman living in Frankfurt.
7. The Grand Sanhedrin of Paris was convened by Napoleon I (1769–1821) and was made up of 71 members, both rabbis and lay leaders of Jewish communities under French rule (chiefly from the Bordeaux, Alsace, and Lorraine regions). Their task was to answer twelve questions, mainly relating to Jewish attitudes towards non-Jews and secular courts. In actual fact Dayan Baer Adler was not a *delegate* to the Paris Sanhedrin, but rather an assistant to the Frankfurt delegate, Rabbi Solomon Zalman Trier. The other delegate from Frankfurt was the wealthy businessman Isaac Hildesheim (who later adopted the name Justus Hiller).

with chased [engraved] "*yad*" or "pointers" attached to them by silver chains. Many of these valuable "Scrolls" were presented to Dr. Adler by prominent members of his flock in London; but he especially values one written at Wilna, given him by his old friend Sir Moses Montefiore,[8] who was the first to grasp his hand when he set foot on English soil five-and-forty years ago,[9] and who never started on an expedition in aid of his oppressed co-religionists without going to Hanover to seek Rebecca Adler's blessing.[10] The Chief Rabbi's pious mother lived almost long enough to see her son attain his seventieth year, for

8. Sir Moses Chaim Montefiore (b. Leghorn 1784, d. Ramsgate 1885), son of Joseph Elias Eliyahu Montefiore and Rachel Mocatta. In 1812 he married Judith Barent Cohen (1784–1862), the daughter of Levi Barent (Barukh Behrend) Cohen and his second wife Lydia née Diamantschleifer; Montefiore and his wife were childless. After his first visit to the Land of Israel in 1827 he became fully observant and built his own synagogue in Ramsgate (1833). In 1862 he founded the Ramsgate yeshiva, Ohel Moshe VeYehudit. He served as president of the Board of Deputies 1835–74 (with a brief exception) and president of the London Board of Shechita 1842–80. He was Sheriff of London and Middlesex 1837–8, was the second Jew ever to be knighted in 1837, and received a baronetcy in 1846. Sir Moses and Lady Judith Montefiore are buried in a solitary domed mausoleum next to the Ramsgate Synagogue. Montefiore was particularly fond of the mitzva of commencing and completing the first and last words of the Torah and employed Rabbi Tzvi Hirsch Volozhin of Vilna (along with one other scribe) to write twenty Torah scrolls and donated them to congregations, especially in far-flung communities. I acknowledge the input of Miriam Rodrigues-Pereira, Honorary Archivist of the Spanish and Portuguese Jews' Congregation, in the writing of this note.
9. In the first week of July 1845, the Chief Rabbi was welcomed at Dover by a group of prominent members of Anglo-Jewry led by Sir Moses in his capacity as president of the Board of Deputies. His installation into office was held at the Great Synagogue, Dukes Place, on Wednesday 9 July 1845 (4 Tammuz 5605): "the *Rav* was then conducted into the Synagogue, having a splendid canopy of blue damask satin, embroidered with gold, borne over him.... On the entrance of the Chief Rabbi *Baruch Habah* was chanted. Sir Moses Montefiore and the honorary officers then conducted him to his seat near the Ark whilst the choir chanted the verses 'Who shall ascend the Mount of the Lord' etc.... After the reading of the usual *Mincha* service, the Ark was again opened and the *Sepher* taken out and the Reader (the late *Ḥazan* [Simon] Asher [1789–1872]) read other appropriate verses from the Psalms, a *Mi Sheberach* and a special prayer. Dr. Adler then delivered his Inaugural Sermon, previously offering up an appropriate prayer in Hebrew.... After the prayer for the Royal Family and some Psalms had been chanted by the efficient choir, the memorable service concluded" (*Jewish Chronicle*, 24 Jan. 1890).
10. Rebecca Adler died in Hanover (in 1858), still active and alert aged 94, and was buried in the old Jewish cemetery on Am Judenkirchhof. Daughter of the chief rabbi of Hanau, Rabbi Jacob Benjamin Fränkel and Esther née Wronke, she was a scion of the famous rabbinical Katzenellenbogen family and a descendent of Rabbi Moses Isserles, author of the glosses on the *Shulḥan Arukh*. She was the wife of Rabbi and *av beit din* of Hanover Rabbi Marcus (Mordecai) Baer Adler (1757–1834); see n. 40 below.

length of days has for many generations been granted to the family which claims direct decent from Aaron the High Priest, and owns the Hebrew device, "As the eagle stirreth up her nest".[11]

Dr. Adler's theological labours necessitate the constant use of many works of reference. *The Speaker's Commentary*[12] and Mr. W. H. Lowe's *Mishnah*[13] are within easy reach of his hand, and he regards them with quite as much reverence as the more ponderous volumes of rabbinical literature spread out before him. He takes you to his bookcase to see the Wilna edition of *The Talmud,* the gift of his children, and Sir Moses Montefiore's *Portuguese Forms of Prayer,*[14] and calls his faithful Dutch servant, Joseph van Gelder,[15] who officiates at once as valet, librarian, and private chaplain, to bring Sir Anthony de Rothschild's silver tureen; the cup made out of the first gold discovered in Victoria,[16] sent to him in 1852 by his brethren in the Colony as a "token of the high esteem in which he is held, and to mark their sense of his indefatigable exertions in the holy cause of religion and education"; the tallit or prayer-scarf woven for his special use

---

11. "Like an eagle arousing its nest, hovering over its young, He spread His wings and took them, carrying them on His pinions. God alone led them" (Deut. 32:11–12).
12. 1871–88. A thirteen-volume commentary on the entire Bible and apocrypha, written to refute its critics, commissioned by the Speaker of the House of Commons, John Evelyn Denson. It was the work of thirty Church of England scholars in nearly 8,000 pages.
13. *The Mishna on Which the Palestinian Talmud Rests: From the Unique Manuscript Preserved in the University Library of Cambridge Add. 470.1 – HaMishna Asher Nosad HaTalmud HaYerushalmi MiReshitah Ad Sofah* (Cambridge University Press 1883), ed. Rev. William Henry Lowe MA, Christian Hebraist and Lecturer of Hebrew at Cambridge.
14. *Seder HaTefilot Kefi Minhag K. K. Sepharadim – Forms of Prayer According to the Custom of the Spanish and Portuguese Jews with an English translation* by Rev. David Aaron de Sola (1796–1860), minister at Bevis Marks Synagogue, London 1836–8; dedicated to Moses Montefiore.
15. Personal attendant of the Chief Rabbi for twenty years. Born in 1831 in Leeuwarden (Netherlands), son of David and Bertha (née Loewnstamm) van Gelder.
16. Sir Anthony Nathan de Rothschild (1810–76), a Baron of the Austrian Empire, third child and second son of Nathan Mayer Rothschild (1777–1836) and Hannah Barent Cohen (1783–1850). In 1840 he married his cousin Louise Montefiore (1821–1910), a niece of Sir Moses. In 1847 he was awarded an English baronetcy. He served as warden of the Great Synagogue from 1855 to 1870 and then was the first president of the United Synagogue from 1870 until his death. He also served as president of the Jews' Hospital and many other communal bodies. He is buried at Willesden United Synagogue Cemetery.

    The beautiful eighteen-carat gold cup mentioned in the text was presented to the Chief Rabbi on behalf of the Jews of Victoria on 1 August 1853 by the Melbourne Hebrew Congregation, and is now held at the V&A Museum in Kensington.

under the direction of his son-in-law Jacob Israel, Commerzienrath in Berlin;[17] the curious silver ornaments known as *Klei Kodesh*; and the three-centuries-old missal of the *Hagadah* used on the evening of the Passover. Your host is expecting a visit from his son and assistant, Dr. Hermann Adler,[18] who has during the past ten years discharged his public duties in Finsbury Square.[19] Although the Coadjutor Chief Rabbi has crossed swords polemically with Dr. Colenso,[20] Mr. Goldwin Smith,[21] and Professor Max Müller,[22] he always consults his father on important points of business; and when he arrives Dr. Adler will be able to illustrate the comprehensive character of their high office, which has a social

17. Jacob Israel (1823–94), son of Nathan and Edel née Levy. His family owned one of the largest department stores in Berlin and were much involved in communal affairs. Israel was commercial advisor to the emperor.
18. Chief Rabbi Dr Hermann (Naftali) Adler (b. Hanover 1839, d. London 1911), fifth and youngest child of Chief Rabbi N. M. Adler and Henrietta née Worms. In 1867 he married Rachel Joseph (1838–1912) and they had three children: Henrietta (Nettie) CBE (1870–1950), Ruth (1872–1952), and Rev. Solomon Alfred Adler (1876–1910), rabbi of the New Synagogue, Hope Place, Liverpool, and then at Hammersmith United Synagogue (see n. 59). He studied under his father, then at the Prague yeshiva, where he received *semikha* in February 1862 from *av beit din* of Prague Rabbi Samuel Freund, Dayan of Prague Rabbi Simon Ausch, and *rosh yeshiva* and Chief Rabbi of Prague Rabbi Solomon Judah Leib Rapoport. Between 1864 and 1891 he served as rabbi of Bayswater United Synagogue; in November 1879 as Delegate Chief Rabbi due to his father's ill-health, and as Chief Rabbi from 1891 until his death. He prepared parts of *Etz Ḥayim* of Rabbi Jacob Ḥazan MiLondon for publication; the entire manuscript was eventually published with notes by Chief Rabbi Israel Brodie in three volumes (1962–7). He is buried at the Willesden United Synagogue Cemetery. This note and the subsequent notes regarding Hermann Adler are based on the research of Benjamin Elton, *Britain's Chief Rabbis and the Religious Character of Anglo-Jewry, 1880–1970* (Manchester University Press, 2009).
19. 16 Finsbury Square, Islington, City of London EC2.
20. Bishop Dr John William Colenso (1814–83) was a South African missionary. In *The Pentateuch and the Book of Joshua Critically Examined* (1862), he argued against the divine origin of the Torah; in response, Rabbi Hermann Adler produced a book in collaboration with Dr Abraham Benisch (1811–78), entitled *A Jewish Reply to Dr. Colenso's Criticism on the Pentateuch* (London, 1865).
21. Professor Goldwin Smith (1823–1910) was a historian who claimed Jews were enemies of civilization. When Smith claimed that Jews lacked a feeling of brotherhood with members of other faiths, Rabbi Hermann Adler wrote in the journal *Nineteenth Century* (1878) "Jews and Judaism: A Rejoinder", which argued that both righteous non-Jews and Jews have a share in the World to Come. He compared this to the exclusiveness of Christianity, which claims that only those who believe will be saved. Similarly he later rebutted the antisemitic arguments of Goldwin Smith in his article "Can Jews be Patriots?" (*Nineteenth Century*, May 1878), and in "Some Recent Phases of Judaeophobia" (*Nineteenth Century*, Dec. 1881).
22. Professor Friedrich Maximillian Müller (1823–1900), a founder of the field of comparative religion and Indology. Amongst other heresies, he denied divine revelation.

and judicial aspect quite distinct from its purely religious attributes. Meanwhile, Joseph is directed to show you Mr. B. S. Marks's striking portrait of the Chief Rabbi,[23] executed many years before he painted Lord Rothschild taking oath in the Upper House with his hat on;[24] the faded portrait of Sir Moses Montefiore gazing at his wife's portrait, while he holds in his hand the Sultan's firman granting protection to the Jews at Jerusalem;[25] and the embroidered trophy containing portraits of Dr. Adler's children, grandchildren, and fourteen great-grandchildren, arranged by his daughter, Mrs. Stern,[26] the widow of the Chief Rabbi of Hamburg. When you return to the oratory on the first-floor, the Chief Rabbi has put away his MS. book filled with "Rashi" characters as distinctly written as if he were a student of twenty.[27] When he was transferred from Hanover to London in 1845, the "restrictions" born of ignorance and superstition were in full force, and he has many stories to tell of the great emancipation battle,

23. Barnett Samuel Marks RCA (1827–1916) moved to London from Cardiff in 1867. In his illustrious career as an artist he drew many distinguished people. He also served as president of the Cardiff Hebrew Congregation and was honorary art teacher at both the Bayswater Jewish School and the Jews' Free School, and was involved in the running of the latter. This portrait is currently in the library of the London School of Jewish Studies, Hendon. He is buried in Willesden United Synagogue Cemetery. I acknowledge the input of Mrs Erla Zimmels, librarian of LSJS, in the writing of this footnote.

24. Lord Nathaniel (Natty) Mayer Rothschild (1840–1915), president of the United Synagogue (1876–1915) and of the Jews' Free School, served as senior warden of the Great Synagogue London from 1876 until his death. On 16 April 1867 he married Emma Louisa (1844–1935), a second cousin, daughter of Mayer Karl von Rothschild and Louisa Rothschild. He served as a Liberal MP from 1865 to 1885, was the first British Jew to be elevated to peerage, and is depicted taking his oath while holding a Hebrew Bible. He is buried in Willesden United Synagogue Cemetery.

25. In February 1840, in Damascus, Father Tommesco and his Muslim servant Ibrahim disappeared, which led to a blood libel. Seven Jewish leaders were arrested, sixty-three children were imprisoned, and many Jewish homes were destroyed. Sir Moses intervened and travelled to Constantinople, managing to obtain a *firman* (royal decree) on 6 November 1840 from the young sultan of the Ottoman Empire, Abdul Mejid I (1823–61), denouncing the charge as baseless. In addition he promised humane, equal treatment for Jews. Copies of this portrait are held at the Jewish Museum London (dated 1880), but I have been unable to track down the whereabouts of the original.

26. Jeanette (Yentta), his second eldest daughter, married Rabbi Anschel (Asher Jacob) Stern (1820–88) in 1855, who was chief rabbi of Hamburg. They had two sons and seven daughters and are buried in Hamburg Jewish Cemetery in Stellingen-Langenfelde on Fösterweg.

27. Rabbi Adler was preparing a commentary on *Targum Yonatan* (an Aramaic translation of the prophets), which he never completed. The manuscript is part of the Adler Collection at JTS, New York. This was to be a sister volume to his published work on *Targum Onkelos – Netina LeGer* (Vilna, 1874).

quorum pars magna fuit.[28] He saw Sir David Salomons take his seat at Westminster "by force;"[29] he listened to the judicial decision which won for Baron Martin the name of the "Good Samaritan,"[30] and when he sought an interview with an Anglican Bishop, to put the case of his much-persecuted race before him, he was met by many profuse apologies for the inability to converse in Hebrew! Times have changed since then, and the position of the Jews in 1889 is very different from what it was in 1845. When his daily portion of the Commentary on Jonathan ben Usiel's *Targum* is accomplished,[31] Dr. Adler falls back on lighter forms of literature. He even pleads guilty to an occasional novel, but just now he is busily engaged with the *Jewish Quarterly* and its English prototype.[32] He expresses the strongest dissent from Professor Sayce's views concerning "Polytheism in Primitive Israel" as set forth in the former, but points with undisguised

---

28. In which he played a great part.
29. Sir David Salomons (1797–1873), son of Levy Salomon and Matilda née de Metz, grandson of Salomon Salomons (1727–1807) a leader of the Hambro' Synagogue. He married twice: first in 1825, to Jeanette née Cohen (1803–67), granddaughter of Levi Barent Cohen, and a second time in 1872, to Cecilia (Tzila) (1811–92), widow of Phillip Joseph Salomons, a distant cousin of his first wife. He was the first Jewish Sheriff of London and Middlesex (1835–6), after successfully lobbying Parliament to pass a Sheriff's Declaration Act, which enabled him to take the oath without compromising his faith. After a change in law, the 1845 Jewish Disabilities Removal Act, he was finally elected to the Court of Alderman for the ward of Aldgate. In 1855 he became the first Jewish Lord Mayor of London; later he was created a baronet in 1869. He was president of the Board of Deputies in 1838 and 1846, served as president of the Jews' Hospital, and also led other communal organizations.

    In 1851 Salomons stood as a Liberal candidate in Greenwich, and was elected on 28 June. He refused to take the oath as prescribed due to its reference to Christianity ("upon the true faith of a Christian"), instead making his own version. Three days later he took his seat amid cries of "withdraw!" and "divide!". The House adjourned for a vote to confirm his right as an MP, and it was during this debate that he courageously gave his maiden speech, although he lost the vote by a majority of 192. The law was eventually changed in 1858 and Lionel de Rothschild became the first legally appointed Jewish MP, followed by Sir David being elected for Greenwich in 1859. He is buried in West Ham United Synagogue Cemetery.
30. In December 1868 Chief Rabbi Adler declared the meat and poultry from a kosher butcher as *trefa*. This butcher sued, and the case was heard by Baron Martin (1801–83). The Judge decided in the Chief Rabbi's favour. The principle witness for Schott was Rev. Prof. David Woolf Marks (1811–1909), Senior Minister of the West London Reform Synagogue. The judge decided in favour of the Chief Rabbi and he stated that "it was the bounden duty of the Chief Rabbi to tell any Jew that such meat was *t'refah*".
31. See n. 27 above.
32. First published in 1888 by Israel Abrahams (1858–1925) and Claude Joseph Goldsmid Montefiore (1858–1938).

satisfaction to the presence of three Hebrew articles in the latter.[33] Forty-five years ago such topics as Heinrich Heine,[34] the accession of a Jewess to throne on Monaco,[35] and the wrongs of the Israelite inhabitants of East London would have excited far less interest than they do at present, nor could the editor of the *Quarterly* have been induced in the "forties" to devote more than a third of his available space to purely Jewish subjects.

The Adlers of Frankfort-on-the-Maine regard Rabbi Simeon [HaDarshan],[36] the famous preacher of the eleventh century, as their common ancestor, and his *Yalkut* is still the standard authority in Medrashic literature. One of Nathan Adler's forefathers carried the Roman eagle at the head of his compatriots when the Emperor Matthias brought back the Jews to that city after their expulsion by the demagogue Fettmilch, and hence the name they have borne ever since.[37] Their *Stammhaus* [ancestral home] in the *Judengasse* has succumbed to modern

33. Professor Archibald Henry Sayce, Deputy Professor of Philology at Oxford. Printed in October 1889, in the second volume of *Jewish Quarterly Review*, pp. 25–36. The two versions mentioned here possibly refer to the Hebrew and English sections of *JQR*.

34. German poet (1797–1856), born a Jew but converted to Protestantism in 1825. He held radical political views, which led to him moving into exile to Paris in 1831. In 1845 he was deported to Belgium, after writing satirical attacks on the kings of Bavaria and Prussia.

35. Born in America as Alice Heine, HSH the Princess of Monaco (1858–1925) married Prince Albert I of Monaco (1848–1922) in 1889. Her father was a cousin of Henrich Heine.

36. Rabbi Simeon the Darshan (preacher) of Frankfurt am Main, a scion of Rashi (1040–1105). *Yalkut Shimoni* is a major compilation of talmudic and midrashic literature arranged according to biblical verses. It was most probably written during the years 1190–1226 and was first printed in Salonika in 1521–6. For a fuller discussion of its authorship and the period of its writing see Rabbi Prof. Dov (Arthur B.) Hyman's introduction to *Yalkut Shimoni on the Former Prophets* (Jerusalem, 1972), 7–10.

37. Vincent Fettmilch was the leader of an anti-Jewish riot on 22 Aug. 1614. The rioters attacked for thirteen hours the Frankfurt ghetto and the Judengasse, plundering the synagogue, its Sifrei Torah, the Jewish cemetery, and private houses. About 1,380 Jews managed to escape – including their rabbi, Yeshayah Horowitz, author of *Shenei Luḥot HaBrit* (*Shelah*) – some on a ship, others to safe houses in Frankfurt and other neighbouring towns. The town council advised them not to return. The Holy Roman Emperor Matthias (crowned in Frankfurt 23 June 1612) took up the Jewish cause, punished the ringleaders and captured Fettmilch ('the Frankfurt Haman') and his cohorts. They were executed on 28 February 1616 in the Rossmarkt (horse market) and their heads were displayed on iron pikes. On 10 March 1616 (20 Adar 5376) the Jews were escorted triumphantly back into Frankfurt and the Judengasse, accompanied by imperial soldiers and a military band. The community was, from now on, protected by the emperor. Family tradition has it that at the head of the procession marched an ancestor of the Chief Rabbi, bearing a banner with the imperial black eagle (*Reichs-Adler*). This banner led the family to assume the surname Adler. The local rabbinate instituted the day as a local Jewish festival, Purim Vinz. The tune of "The March of Pavia" played by the military band was used in the synagogue service for *Adon*

improvements,[38] although that of their old neighbours the Rothschilds has been preserved. Nathan Adler the elder was one of the most famous Talmudists of the last century; another member of the same family received Lord George Gordon into the Synagogue[39]; and Marcus Adler (the father of Nathan Adler the younger) was Chief Rabbi of Hanover,[40] transmitting the post in 1830 to his son, who had won high degrees at the Universities of Würzburg and Erlangen, and had already held a similar position during twelve months in Oldenburg. Fifteen years later he was installed in London as Dr. Hirschell's successor,[41] and, with Mr. Alfred

---

Olam and part of the *Kaddish* after Torah-reading (if it fell on a Monday or Shabbat), and no *Taḥanun* was said.

38. The corner house at the entrance to the Judengasse *an der Pfort* (by the gate) seems to have been the site of the home of Rabbi Simeon, the Adler family's patriarch. The Frankfurt Judengasse was created in 1462. Originally occupied by about fifteen families, by the sixteenth century it had approximately 3,000 inhabitants. A 1:50-scale walk-through model of the Judengasse is exhibited at the Frankfurt Jewish Museum in 14-15 Untermainkai.

39. Lord George Gordon (1751–93) led a protest on 2 June 1780 in support of the repeal of the Catholic Relief Act of 1778 (which gave partial rights to Catholics). Four days later riots ensued, and 20,000 troops were employed to quell the violence. Lord Gordon later converted to Judaism, taking on the name Israel. Upon his death his non-Jewish family used their powerful social position to claim his body for burial, and there was little the Jewish community could do to prevent the inevitable. He was buried in a vault at the former St James' Chapel in Camden behind the disused National Temperance Hospital.

    Lord Gordon had asked, in a letter to Chief Rabbi David Tevele Schiff (see n. 62), to convert, but was refused. It seems that he finally managed to convert to Judaism through Rabbi Jacob of Birmingham in 1787. The Blasphemy Act of 1698 deemed conversion to Judaism illegal, which would lead us to suspect that his actual conversion was performed in Rotterdam (as suggested by some sources), although the courts often turned a blind eye to its contravention. See Hermann Adler, "A Survey of Anglo-Jewish History", in *Transactions of the Jewish Historical Society of England 1896–8* (London, 1899), iii. 13.

    I am unsure what reception is being referred to in the text here – perhaps Lord Gordon's famous Shabbat visit to the Hambro' Synagogue, when he offered £100 to the synagogue in his *Mi Sheberakh*, after being called to the Torah.

40. Rabbi Mordechai (Marcus) Baer Adler (1757–1834). His father was first cousin of the famed kabbalist Rabbi Nathan Adler (1741–1800), *rebbe* of the Ḥatam Sofer, after whom his son was named. He served as a *dayan* in Frankfurt, then in 1778 as *Landrabbiner* of Hanover. He married Rebecca Fränkel (1764–1858). They had three sons: Baer Adler (1786-1866), *dayan* in Frankfurt (see n. 6 above); Gabriel Adler (1788–1859), Rabbi and *rosh yeshiva* of Mühringen, Württemberg, Chief Rabbi of Schwarzwald at Oberdorf, Württemberg; and Chief Rabbi Nathan Marcus Adler (1803–90).

41. Rabbi Solomon Hirschell (1761–1842), great-grandson of Rabbi Tzvi Ashkenazi (known as Ḥakham Tzvi, 1658–1718), was born in London. Son of Rabbi Hart Lyon or Tzvi Hirsch Lewin Berlin (1721–1800), rabbi of the Great Synagogue London (1756–64), he served as Rabbi of: Halberstadt 1764–71, Mannheim 1771–3, and Berlin 1773–1800. His notes on the Talmud, Mishna,

Wigan's assistance,[42] acquired so complete a mastery over the English language that his sermon on the Crimean War Fast Day was described as "instinct with the fire of an ancient prophet".[43] Dr. Adler has compiled many learned theological treatises;[44] but the poetic eloquence of his prayers on public events, from the birth of the Princess Christian in 1846[45] down to the joint thanksgiving for victory in Abyssinia[46] and the escape of the Duke of Edinburgh from assassination,[47] may possibly have taken a firmer hold on the minds of the general public. His father was in his youth the intimate friend of Amschel Rothschild, and it has been the lot of Nathan Adler since he arrived in England to congratulate Baron Lionel Rothschild and his son Nathaniel on becoming the first Jewish members of either

and *Shulḥan Arukh* were published under the title *Tzava Rav* (Piotrków, 1908), reprinted with additions by Maḥon Yerushalayim in 2002. He first was Rabbi of Prenzlau (Brandenburg, Germany) from 1793, then served as chief rabbi from 1802 until his death. He is buried in Brady Street United Synagogue Cemetery in London. Some of the transactions of his London Beth Din sittings have been published in *Sefer HaYovel Tiferet Tzevi LiKhvod HaRav HaGaon R. Yisrael Brodie* (London, 1967) under the title "Pesakim UTeshuvot MiBeit Dino shel R. Shelomo ben R. Tzevi", ed. Hirsch Jacob Zimmels.

42. Alfred Sydney Wigan (1814-78), a successful actor. The Chief Rabbi was preaching in English (as promised in his inauguration sermon) from about a year after he arrived.

43. On 26 April 1854 a "National Day of Fasting and Humiliation" was held in support of the war.

44. See Ruth P. Goldschmidt Lehmann, "Nathan Marcus Adler: A Bibliography", in *Studies in Judaica, Karaitica and Islamica Presented to Leon Nemoy* (Ramat Gan, 1982), 207–61. This incomplete listing of printed material, from contemporary newspapers and specially printed pamphlets, includes over two hundred sermons, addresses, and lectures, nearly fifty prayers and orders of service, over eighty public notices and letters, seven memorial orations, seven responsa, four approbations, notes to three books, his *Netina LeGer,* and his will. Additionally, various manuscripts survive as part of the Adler Collection held at the JTS Library in New York, including a German translation of Judah HaLevi's *Kuzari* with notes, novellae on the Talmud, *Tur, Shulḥan Arukh,* and its commentaries, additional responsa, and *Ahavat Yonatan* described in n. 27 above.

45. Princess Helena Augusta Victoria, later known as Princess Christian of Schleswig-Holstein by marriage (1846–1923), the fifth child of Queen Victoria and Prince Albert. The Chief Rabbi composed an Order of Service to be "recited in the Synagogues throughout Great Britain on Sabbath the 5th day of Sivan, A.M. 5606" (30 May 1846).

46. The Chief Rabbi composed "*Tefilah Lethodah,* a form of prayer and thanksgiving for the preservation of the life of H.R.H. the Duke of Edinburgh for the success and safety of the Abyssinian Expedition, to be used in all Synagogues of the United Congregations of the British Empire, on Sabbath July 4th 5628".

47. Prince Alfred (1844–1900), the second son and fourth child of Queen Victoria and Prince Albert. Whilst visiting Australia in March 1868, he was shot with a revolver, but made a speedy recovery.

House of Parliament.[48] He has also had the supreme satisfaction of seeing a Jew become Master of the Rolls,[49] while other members of his creed have achieved distinction as politicians, writers, speakers, painters, and men of science. While living in Hanover he enjoyed the friendship of the late Duke of Cambridge,[50] who in after years presided so often at Jewish charity-dinners. His Royal Highness had a standing joke about not caring for the length of the Hebrew grace after meat as long as that before meat was short, and he once startled the Chief Rabbi by asking him abruptly if he kept a "he-cook" or a "she-cook." When Dr. Adler first settled in England he took up his abode in one of the fine "Crosby Place" houses mentioned by Shakespeare,[51] but he afterwards moved to Finsbury Square, which is still the Chief Rabbi's official residence. It was here that Sir Moses Montefiore paid him his last visit when well advanced in the "nineties," and, turning the key on his juvenile host, then nearing the "eighties," tripped lightly down the stairs in order to prevent his old friend escorting him to the door. In 1830 only thirty Jewish weddings were permitted to take place during a twelvemonth at Frankfort, and Nathan Adler had to patiently wait his turn before he could marry the

48. Baron Amschel Meyer Rothschild (1773–1855) of Frankfurt, second child and eldest son of Meyer Amschel Rothschild (1744–1812). He was a staunch supporter of Rabbi Samson Rafael Hirsch's community. When the Reform Minister Leopold Stein was appointed Rabbi of Frankfurt in 1844, he retracted his large donation of 250,000 gulden to the new Temple.

Baron Lionel Nathan de Rothschild (1808–79) was the eldest son and second child of Nathan Mayer Rothschild and Hanna Barent Cohen. After a long struggle, which began when he won a seat for the City of London in August 1847 for the Liberal Party, he eventually became the first professing Jewish MP. He took the amended Oath of Allegiance, omitting the words "on the true faith of a Christian", whilst holding a Hebrew Bible with his head covered, on 26 July 1858 (see n. 29). He sat in the Commons from 1858 to 1868 and 1869–74. He also served as senior warden of the Great Synagogue in London from 1841 to 1876 and is buried in Willesden United Synagogue Cemetery. For Nathaniel Rothschild see n. 24 above.

49. Sir George (Judah) Jessel (1824–83), son of Zadok Aaron Jessel (one-time president of the Western Synagogue) and Mary (Perela) née Harris. He married in 1856 Amelia née Moses (1836–71) and served as Master of the Rolls (second most senior judge in the country) from 1873 to 1881. He also served as Liberal MP for Dover from 1868 to 1873. Jessel was the first practising Jew to hold government office, serving as Solicitor-General from 1871 to 1873. In August 1873 he was sworn in as the first openly Jewish Privy Councillor. He was knighted in 1872, and was Judge of the High Court 1875–81. He was also the first Jew to take a seat on the judicial bench. Sir George was president of the Great Synagogue 1854–6 and is buried in Willesden United Synagogue Cemetery.

50. Prince Adolphus the Duke of Cambridge (1774–1850) was an uncle of Queen Victoria. From 1816 he served as viceroy of the Kingdom of Hanover, which was then under British rule.

51. 4 Crosby Square, Bishopsgate, City of London EC2, mentioned thrice in his play *The Tragedy of King Richard the Third* (I.2, I.3, III.1).

daughter of Hirsch Worms,[52] a great-uncle of the present Under-Secretary for the Colonies.[53] His second wife[54] is a sister-in-law of Dr. Sachs, who was a popular German poet as well as an eminent preacher in Berlin.[55]

The Chief Rabbi is explaining to you the exact functions of the "Beth Din,"[56] or ecclesiastical court, over which he presided for so many years, when the arrival of his son with the week's letters puts an end to his narrative. A dozen abstruse points of ritual must now be discussed in detail; the wants of a congregation in the backwoods of British Colombia have to be duly considered;

52. Rachel Hitzel (Henrietta) Worms (1800–53), daughter of Hirsch Moses Worms and Sorle Worms. They had five children: Sarah Solomon (1831–1907), wife of Henry Solomon; Jeanette Stern (see n. 26); Minna Israel (see n. 17); Marcus Nathan Adler (1837–1911), who married Fanny Myers in 1867, and remarried to Emma Kisch in 1892; and Chief Rabbi Dr Hermann (Naphtali) Adler (1839–1911) (see n. 18). She was the last person to be interred at Alderney Road United Synagogue Cemetery (Mile End, E1), the oldest Ashkenazi cemetery in the English-speaking world (opened in 1697).

53. Baron Henry de Worms (1840–1903), a great-grandson of Mayer Amschel Rothschild. He served as the Under-Secretary of State for the Colonies 1888–92. In 1889 he was appointed a member of the Privy Council and in 1895 was elevated to Lord Pirbright. His communal roles included treasurer (1872) and later vice-president of the United Synagogue (1880–2). It was an unexpected shock when he posthumously severed his ties with Judaism, asking to be buried in a churchyard, despite having reserved a plot at the Willesden United Synagogue Cemetery!

54. Celestine (Tziporah) Lehfeldt or Lehrfeld (b. Berlin 1821, d. London 1891), daughter of Immanuel Nathan Lehfeldt (also known as Elkan Levy) and Ida née Riess; she married the Chief Rabbi in 1857. They had three children: Elkan (1861–1946); Rebecca Heilbut (1862–90), wife of Harry Heilbut of Amsterdam; and Ida Schaap (later Sharp) (1865–1933), wife of Magnus Schaap. She is buried next to her husband at Willesden United Synagogue Cemetery.

55. Rabbi Dr Yechiel Michael Sachs (1808–64). Married Henriette Lehfeldt (b. 1816) in 1837, sister of the Chief Rabbi's second wife. He served as rabbi of the Prague Tempelgemeinde (the *Altschul*) on Dusni Street from 1836, and as a *dayan* on the Berlin Beit Din. He resigned the rabbinate when an organ was introduced in the new synagogue; see his responsum of 13 Nov. 1861: *Gutachten des Dr. Michael Sachs Gegen die Orgel* (published by Abraham Berliner, Berlin, 1904). He is particularly remembered for his German translations of the siddur *Tefilath Yisrael – Gebetbuch der Israeliten* (1858) and *Machzor Lechol Moadei HaShanah – Festgebete der Israeliten* (9 vols., 1855–6), sold in two versions: according to *minhag* Ashkenaz and *minhag* Polin. This was in addition to his works on liturgy and Hebrew poetry. His sermons were published posthumously in two volumes, entitled *Predigten* (Berlin, 1867–9). He is buried in the Schönhauser Allee Jewish Cemetery in Berlin.

56. The *Jewish Chronicle* wrote in the Chief Rabbi's obituary (24 Jan. 1890): "He was perhaps, seen at his best when presiding as *Av Beth Din* at the sittings of the *Beth Din*. . . . His exhortations, admonitions, and efforts at Peace-making were weighted with a remarkable power of persuasiveness which few could resist." The *dayanim* of the Beth Din who served under the Chief Rabbi were Azriel (Israel) Levy, Aaron Levy, Aryeh Leib Barnett, Dov Baer (Bernard) Spiers, Jacob Reinowitz, and his son Rabbi Herman Adler.

an earnest inquirer is most anxious to learn the precise rendering of that most perplexing text about a deceased wife's sister in the eighteenth chapter of Leviticus according to the new German version of the Pentateuch;[57] Lord Salisbury[58] has referred to the Chief Rabbi a petition addressed to the Queen by a Bessarabian Jew to send back his son-in-law, who is supposed to be in Montreal; and the questions concerning succession are scarcely less intricate than those relating to ceremonial. When the reports about the new synagogues at Hammersmith, Hampstead, Nottingham, and Northampton, and the Jews' College,[59] have been gone through there will be still several decisions of the Hebrew Courts of Arches to revise;[60] several epitaphs on deceased worthies have also to be drafted, and there are equally large bundles of correspondence relating to the propriety of Lord Mayor Isaacs using his state-coach on a Saturday,[61] and the progress of the Russian refugee students at Geneva. Dr. Adler and his son have a great deal to settle before nightfall, and he must of necessity postpone till another occasion the continuation of his interesting narrative. The Chief Rabbi of to-day is something more than the head of the Hebrew faith

57. Lev. 18:16.
58. Robert Arthur Talbot Gascoyne-Cecil, Third Marquess of Sailsbury (1830–1903), served as Conservative Prime Minister (1885–6, 1886–92, and 1895–1902).
59. Hammersmith and West Kensington United Synagogue, 71 Brook Green, W6 (1890–2001). In 1895 the male membership was 117. The Ark from this synagogue is now at the Machzikei Hadass Synagogue, Edgware.

Hampstead United Synagogue, 1 Dennington Park Road, NW6 (1892–). In 1895 the male membership was 213. Today, it has a membership of 460 families.

Nottingham Hebrew Congregation, Chaucer Street, NG1 (1890–1954). In 1895 the male membership was 80. The Ark from this synagogue is now at the "new" Nottingham Synagogue, Shakespeare Villas, NG1 (1954–).

Northampton Hebrew Congregation, 95–97 Overstone Road, NN1 (1890–1964). In 1895 the male membership was 15. The current synagogue was rebuilt on that site and was opened in 1965.

Jews' College (10 Finsbury Square, Islington, City of London EC2) was the brainchild of Chief Rabbi Nathan Adler. Thirty-three pupils were originally enrolled.
60. The Beth Din.
61. Sir Henry Aaron Isaacs (1830–1909), Lord Mayor of London between 1889 and 1890, was the driving force behind the erection of Tower Bridge. He was a member of the London Corporation from 1862, an alderman from 1883 and in 1887 was knighted and became Sheriff of London and Middlesex. Sir Henry was also a warden of the Hambro' Synagogue and is buried in the Willesden United Synagogue Cemetery.

The Lord Mayor's Show, the official inauguration of Sir Henry as Lord Mayor, was scheduled for Saturday 9 November 1889, so he asked for it to be postponed until the Monday. His request was refused. See *Jewish Chronicle* (27 Oct. 1889), p. 7 for copies of the official correspondence.

throughout the British Empire. The extent of his dominions gives him a power very much akin to that of the Pope, and Rabbis in all parts of the world have come to regard the offices in Finsbury Square as their Vatican, with the little house at Brighton as its annexe and *sanctum sanctorum*. Dr. Adler's manifold occupations necessitate his rising at an early hour, and his only luxuries are the *Times*, a brief siesta, and an occasional game of chess. The air of Brighton is his principal medicine, and on fine days strangers turn to gaze at the venerable old man, in the garb of a country clergyman, enjoying the sunshine on one of the Queen's Gardens seats, or walking leisurely towards the pier, accompanied by a joyous group of great-grandchildren. On the 26th March 1790 his great-uncle, Dr. Daniel Solomon Schiff consecrated the Duke's Place Synagogue in Aldgate.[62] If all is well on the 26th March 1890, it is not impossible that Dr. Nathan Adler may leave his beloved Brighton for a few hours to participate in a solemn festival which will commemorate something more than the mere centenary of a particular edifice.[63] The era of legal emancipation has also been

---

62. Daniel was mistakenly printed instead of David, meaning Chief Rabbi David Tevele Schiff HaKohen (b. Frankfurt, 1722, d. London, 1791). Son of Rabbi Solomon Zalman and Roesche, daughter of Rabbi Moses Abraham Aberle Hamberger-London, autocrat of the London Ashkenazim – president of the *kehilla*, an accomplished a scholar, and a tycoon in the international gem trade. Chief Rabbi David Tevele Schiff was a pupil of *Shev Yaakov*, Rabbi Jacob Poppers Katz, and *Penei Yehoshua*, Rabbi Jacob Yehoshua Falk. He was the *rosh yeshiva* in Worms (*c.*1748–62) and for a short period served as a *maggid* (preacher) in Vienna (1758–9). From Worms he returned to Frankfurt to serve as *dayan*, assisting Rabbi Abraham of Lissa (1700–68). He was elected as rabbi of the Great Synagogue on 24 February 1765. Rabbi Israel Meshullem Zalman Solomon (1723–94), rabbi of the Hambro' Synagogue, son of Rabbi Jacob Emden, left London in 1780, leaving Rabbi Schiff as the undisputed rabbi of, and the only *av beit din* in, Great Britain. He is buried in Alderney Road United Synagogue Cemetery, London. His *ḥidushim* (novellae) on the Mishna were published posthumously under the title *Lashon Zahav* (Offenbach 1822–6) and were later included in the standard Romm *mishnayot* (Vilna 1905–9). Recently, in an expanded volume of *Lashon Zahav* (London, 1997), his sermons and responsa were published for the first time, culled from his manuscripts at the JTS Adler Collection. His grave in Alderney Road United Synagogue Cemetery, E1 has become a place of pilgrimage.

The Great Synagogue (*Beit HaKeneset HaGedola*) in Dukes Place, City of London, was rebuilt on its original site and opened in March 1790. This building was destroyed by the Luftwaffe on 11 May 1941. A temporary structure on the site was built in 1943, which was used until 1958. The congregation then moved to Adler Street, E1, until its eventual closure in April 1977.

63. Unfortunately, he did not live to be present at that centenary. He passed away in his 87th year on 21 January 1890 at his home in Hove. He was buried at Willesden United Synagogue Cemetery.

The "edifice" referred to here is "One of the world's most famous Jewish congregations – the Great Synagogue in London. The special place the Great Synagogue holds in Anglo-Jewish history cannot be accounted for simply in terms of the two and a half centuries of its life, nor that it

one of material prosperity and progress, and no living man has contributed more to all that has been achieved for the well-being of those whom he always calls his "brethren" than the patriarch who now affectionately bids you farewell. You have scarcely quitted the oratory when Nathan Adler commences to peruse, with eyes undimmed by age, the first of the papers carefully arranged before him by his son, who has inherited so large a share of his characteristic energy, strength of purpose, and administrative ability.[64]

was the first synagogue for the Ashkenazim in England after the Resettlement. Its importance lies rather in its having become the centre of a community that extended throughout the metropolis and beyond.... Its special position as Mother Synagogue came about gradually from its early days until the height of its power and influence towards the end of the nineteenth century" (Paul Lindsay, *The Synagogues of London* [London 1993]).

64. This article omits arguably his greatest accomplishment, masterminding the union of the three pre-eminent congregations in London into the United Synagogue, or Kehilla Kedosha Keneset Yisrael, established in 1870 through an Act of Parliament. The first steps to this goal were taken in a meeting in the Chief Rabbi's *sukka* four years earlier. In 1870 the total number of male seat-holders stood at 1,387. The rest is history...

A Scholar in Their Midst: Dayan Jacob Reinowitz

Rabbi Eugene Newman

Dayan Jacob Reinowitz was one of the foremost scholars and halakhic authorities of late nineteenth-century England. His writing and responsa have served as a model and influence for rabbis and students following in his footsteps. It is unfortunate that Rabbi Reinowitz is not better known in this century, as his erudition and wisdom may serve as a source of inspiration for future students of halakha. It is my hope that this study may introduce the reader to this noteworthy scholar and allow his memory to be a blessing for future generations. The essay below is based on the responsa, halakhic and aggadic works, and letters of Jacob Reinowitz (1818–1893).[1]

Jacob Reinowitz was born in 1818 in Valkovisk, in Russia. Descended from a long line of rabbis and scholars,[2] he had a phenomenal memory, an analytical mind, and a wide knowledge of the Talmud, the codes, and their commentaries. At the age of twenty-six, he was appointed *moreh horaah, dayan* cum *maggid*, of his home town, a position he occupied for thirty years. This appointment was a tribute to his talmudic and halakhic knowledge and a recognition of his qualities of heart, sincerity, humility, and compassion.

1. Paper delivered to the Jewish Historical Society of England, 11 December 1968.
2. Among the manuscripts are novellae on the Talmud by his great-grandfather.

Rabbi Reinowitz was married to Esther Liba Binion,[3] with whom he had three daughters, Bertha, Leah, and Rebecca. Bertha married Susman Cohen, who became a rabbi in Manchester in 1875 and succeeded Jacob Reinowitz as *dayan* of the London Beth Din in 1893. Leah married S. Glucksohn, of Berlin, and Rebecca married a Mr Saul, of Berlin.

LONDON APPOINTMENT

The Chevra Shass (Talmud Society) Synagogue, situated in Old Montague Street, London, England, was founded on 3 Adar 1875.[4] Its primary aim, apart from congregational prayer, was to study the Talmud daily in order to raise the very low standards of such learning in England.[5] Its members, recently settled in that country, were trained in the yeshivas of Poland and Russia. A year after its opening, the Chevra Shass decided to appoint an eminent east European rabbi. Having heard that Rabbi Jacob Reinowitz was visiting Manchester, the Chevra Shass asked him to pay them a visit in London. Rabbi Reinowitz agreed and gave a series of *shiurim* in Talmud and delivered *derashot*. He made a great impression on the members, who believed that "a messenger from above" had been sent to them, and they unanimously decided to appoint him as their rabbi on Sunday, 3 Tamuz 1876:[6]

> All of us, originally from Poland and Russia, gathered here to consider our position regarding heavenly matters, sec that we form a large congregation. We know that every small congregation has a spiritual leader at its head, and why should we be like sheep without a shepherd? Therefore we said to one another, "Let us arise and strengthen one another and the

3. Esther Liba was a sister of Professor S. A. Binion, the Egyptologist. The name Binion is a corruption of Nunez. The family came from Holland, originally from Spain. Letter by Prof. Binion's niece to Mrs H. M. Lazarus on 17 Aug 1948.
4. Pinkas of Chevra Shass, London, 1875. I am indebted to the honorary officers of the Federation of Synagogues and its secretary, Mr Michael Goldman, for permitting me to use it. The Chevra Shass had the following rules: (a) Every member must attend the Talmud *shiur* at least once a week. (b) If a member does not attend even once a month, he is fined by the honorary officers as they think fit according to his means. (c) If a member does not attend for three months consecutively without a valid reason he loses his membership. (d) No one can become a member without the consent of the honorary officers. (e) No honorary officer can be appointed unless he is able to learn a page of the Talmud. (f) Only a member is permitted to conduct the Talmud *shiur*.
5. Ibid. 11a.
6. Ibid. 5a.

> Lord will be with us. Let us appoint a spiritual head who will teach us of his ways, the ways of the Torah, and we will walk in his ways." As this great and honourable man happens to pass by, the distinguished Rabbi, the great light crowned with the ways of the Torah, who acted as *moreh horaah* for many years, our teacher Rabbi Jacob son of Rabbi David, may his light shine, we decided unanimously that he is the man whom we wish to honour. He shall be our spiritual guide. He will instruct us in the laws which are forbidden and which are permitted, and he will teach Talmud, Rashi, and Tosafot every day in the Chevra Shass, which we founded with God's help. We, the undersigned, undertake to pay him a salary of £3 sterling per week. The agreement shall have the force of any other agreement made by Jewish law. As proof, we have signed it on Sunday 1st day of Rosh Ḥodesh Ellul 5636 – 1876, here in London.[7]

The letter was signed by thirteen members. On the day he received his agreement, Reinowitz delivered the *siyum* (conclusion) on the Tractate Rosh Hashana.[8] Soon afterwards Reinowitz, then 56, brought his wife, Esther Liba, and youngest daughter, Rebecca, from Valkovisk to take up residence at 18 Tenter Street East, Goodman's Fields, E1.

SALARY £3 A WEEK

The promise of a salary of £3 a week, which in those days was a good one (a *dayan* of the United Synagogue did not get more), was obviously not fulfilled. The Chevra Shass paid him perhaps £1 a week, the United Synagogue gave him a small annual gratuity,[9] which at the end of his life (1893) did not amount to more than £1. Through the recommendation of Dr Asher Asher, the physician and secretary of the United Synagogue, Reinowitz received £20 from Lord Rothschild on his *yahrzeit*.[10]

Reinowitz's wife, Esther Liba, who was a wise woman, managed on her husband's meagre salary, a fair share of which was given to charity. When

---

7. As this may be the first contract between an east European rabbi and his congregation in England, I quote it in full.
8. It is among the manuscripts.
9. In a letter, 5 Hanukah 1878, to Reinowitz, Dr Nathan Adler, the Chief Rabbi, was pleased to learn that through the recommendation of his son, Hermann, the United Synagogue had granted Reinowitz a gift of £10.
10. Letter by Dr Hermann Adler to Rabbi Susman Cohen, of Manchester (Reinowitz's son-in-law), in 1893.

their youngest daughter became engaged in 1882 to Mr Saul of Berlin, who asked for a large dowry, Dr Hermann Adler, the Delegate to the Chief Rabbi, helped to raise it.[11] The Chief Rabbi, Dr Nathan Adler, in a letter, congratulated Reinowitz on the engagement of 'his wise daughter', which, coming from one who was so sparing in praise, was praise indeed. Rebecca was not only beautiful but also accomplished. She wrote rabbinic Hebrew perfectly, and she copied some of her father's responsa and other writings which are among the manuscripts.

Several Jewish historians have written about the social and political life of Anglo-Jewry in the nineteenth century. I shall therefore confine myself to some social and religious problems as reflected in the responsa, writings, and letters of Jacob Reinowitz which have some bearing on Anglo-Jewish life.

When Reinowitz became the rabbi of the Chevra Shass in 1876, the London Beth Din consisted of the Chief Rabbi Dr Nathan Adler, B. Spiers, who was appointed in that year as *dayan* and librarian of the Beth Hamedrash, which was the seat of the Beth Din,[12] and Dr Hermann Adler. Reinowitz's house in Tenter Street was a humble dwelling, but it was full of activity from morning till late at night: rabbis, scholars, ministers, students of the ministry, emissaries of yeshivas, eminent visitors to London, and the new immigrants who needed help, advice, and guidance on social, economic, and religious problems knew that "the good, wise, and gentle" Rabbi Yankov, or Yankele, and his wife would help them solve their problems. The older settlers of Dutch and German Jewish origin looked down on the new immigrants from Poland and Russia and regarded them as foreigners. At first the Chief Rabbi, Dr Nathan Adler, did not take any notice of the east European rabbi, Jacob Reinowitz, but having heard such glowing reports about his erudition, character, and benevolent activities among the new immigrants who were increasing daily, he decided to invite him for a brief meeting. In the end, the meeting lasted for two hours. The Chief Rabbi was so impressed by Rabbi Reinowitz's personality, his wide and deep talmudic and halakhic knowledge, that he asked him there and then to act as one of his *dayanim*. Although Reinowitz was not appointed as *dayan* by the United Synagogue, its council annually voted him a small gratuity.[13] From that day

11. Letter by Simeon Singer in 1882.
12. P. Orenstein, *Historical Sketch of the Beth Hamedrash* (London, 1905).
13. Minute of the United Synagogue, 4 November 1890: "The Gentleman who acts as second Dayan, the Rev. Jacob Reinowitz, was not appointed by the United Synagogue but a small gratuity is voted to him yearly by the Council for his services. It is but just to point out that this gentleman who is now far advanced in years wields powerful influence over the foreign element in the East

on friendship and mutual regard existed between them, as evidenced by their responsa and correspondence, which could fill more than one stout volume.

Owing to his advanced age, the Chief Rabbi retired to Brighton in 1879 and his son, Dr Hermann Adler, became the Delegate to the Chief Rabbi. Though unable to attend the Beth Din, the Chief Rabbi remained in firm control of Jewish ecclesiastical matters in the country and empire. Any major decision had to have his sanction.

MEMBER OF THE BETH DIN

Though Reinowitz occasionally acted as *dayan* when the Chief Rabbi was unwell,[14] it was only in 1879 that he became a permanent member of the Beth Din. From then on the Beth Din consisted of Dr Hermann Adler, B. Spiers, and Reinowitz, who was its halakhic authority, recognized as such in this country and abroad.

Reinowitz was the original of Reb Shemuel in Israel Zangwill's *Children of the Ghetto*.[15] Zangwill describes Reb Shemuel as

> an official of heterogeneous duties, he preached, he taught and lectured. He married people and divorced them. He released bachelors from the duty of marrying their deceased brothers' wives. He superintended a slaughtering department; licensed men as competent killers of animals; examined the sharpness of their knives, so that the victims might be put to as little pain as possible. But his greatest function was *paskening* or answering enquiries ranging from the simplest to the most complicated problems of ceremonial ethics and civil law. He had added a volume of *she'elot uteshuvot*, questions and answers, to the colossal casuistic literature of his race. His aid was also invoked as *shadchan*, though he forgot to take his commissions. In fine, he was a witty old fellow and everybody loved him. He and his wife spoke English with a strong foreign accent.[16]

End of London, an influence which has been invariably exercised in the interests of peace and of union. It is highly desirable that this connection with the Beth Din should be continued." I am grateful to the secretary of the United Synagogue, Mr Nathan Rubin, for supplying me with a copy of this.

14. Reinowitz arranged a *get*, with Dayan B. Spiers and Dr H. Adler, on 18 Marcheshvan 1878.
15. p. 93. Wayfarer's Library issue, published by dent, 1914 [?].
16. Although he was about fifty-six years old when he arrived in London, Reinowitz began to learn English. I found among his manuscripts the English alphabet transcribed in his fine Hebrew handwriting with the correct English pronunciation of each letter.

The number of *she'elot* submitted to Reinowitz was exceedingly great. One Erev Pesaḥ alone, when Dr Michael Friedlander (the principal of Jews' College) paid him a visit, he dealt with ninety-five cases.[17] By all accounts, Reinowitz had a keen sense of humour. Some *she'elot* were ludicrous and caused amusement. On a Shabbat afternoon, the *dayan* returned from the Minḥa service and a middle-aged woman appeared before him and said, "I have a *she'ela* to ask you, Rabbi." "Let me hear it, please," said the rabbi. The lady took out a pin which had been neatly wrapped up in several pieces of paper and said, "In preparing a fowl yesterday for the Sabbath I found this pin in its stomach." "And why", asked the rabbi, "did you not bring the fowl for me to examine, for the decision solely depends upon the position of the pin in the body of the fowl?" "Oh," exclaimed the woman, with much astonishment, "the fowl we had for dinner today." "Then the pin is quite kosher," said the *dayan* gently.[18]

As to the *she'elot uteshuvot*, I shall mention only some with which he dealt in this country and some which were sent to him from abroad. A rabbinic scholar knows that one of the most difficult problems to solve is that of an *aguna*. An *aguna* is a wife whose husband has left her or disappeared without trace and she is unable to provide evidence of his death and is thus unable to remarry. The rabbi who undertakes to solve the problem prepares a responsum in which he suggests halakhic reasons for freeing her from the state of *aguna*. Then he submits his responsum to two or three halakhic authorities for their approval, and if they agree, a *heter*, permission, can then be given to the woman so that she is no longer an *aguna* and is free to marry again. As a rule, more than three years have to elapse before permission is given.

RABBI REINOWITZ'S RESPONSUM

Unusual *Aguna* Cases

The *aguna* cases are called *Kuntres Aguna* or *Agunot*. I shall mention four special cases of *aguna* which Reinowitz solved. All four cases underline his compassion and are of great halakhic value.

In the first, the year is 1878 and the *aguna* is Zirel Levinsky, of Suvalk. Zirel married Moshe Levinsky in Suvalk thirteen years ago. They had one daughter, who was now twelve years old. They lived first in Suvalk and then in Warsaw. About nine years ago the husband left her and she has not heard from him since. Her father had travelled to many lands, including America, to try to trace him

17. *Jewish Chronicle*, 16 June 1893. *Jewish World*, 16 June 1893.
18. Ibid.

but without success. Zirel came to London to look for her husband. She was a dressmaker and found it difficult to make a living. She was God-fearing and very modest and did not have the courage to consult a rabbi about her problem. But eventually neighbours persuaded her to approach Jacob Reinowitz. When she came to see him, Reinowitz asked her whether she had heard anything of her husband since he left her. Zirel said, "About three years ago my father wrote to me that he had heard that my husband was in Berlin. As soon as I heard this I travelled to Berlin and went to see a German [Christian] couple who had been our neighbours when we lived in Suvalk. As soon as I entered their house the German woman said to me, 'Zirka, it is over three years since your husband died.' When I asked her how she knew this she said that her husband, Lutz, told her. 'If you wait a little while', she said, 'he is due to arrive any minute and he will tell you so personally.' Lutz soon arrived and said, 'Your husband lived in a public-house which I also used to frequent and he used to drink with me and other Germans. When I saw him there for the first time I enquired after you. At first he denied that he had a wife, but when I said to him that I remembered you from Suvalk, saying that you had made me the shirt which I was now wearing, he admitted that he had a wife.' Then I asked Lutz, 'How do you know that my husband is dead?' He said that the publican told him that he died in Berlin in the measles epidemic during the Franco-German War (1870–1). So I went to see the publican, who told me that my husband used to live there but after a time he moved out and a German who used to drink with him told him that he had died of measles. I went to see that German and he told me that it happened a long time ago, and since then he had met many Jews."

It is over three years since Zirel Levinsky returned from Berlin. She is imploring me, wrote Reinowitz, to help her in her tragic plight. In his responsum, Reinowitz suggested halakhic reasons for freeing her from the chains of *aguna*, and submitted his opinion for approval to leading halakhic authorities. Rabbis Naphtali Tzvi Yehuda Berlin of Volozhin (5 Ellul 1877),[19] Tzvi Orenstein of Lemberg (28 Tevet 1878), Israel HaKohen Rapeport, of Tarnow (5 Tezaveh 1878), *Rishon LeTzion* Abraham Ashkenazi (18 Kislev 1878), and Barukh Pinto of Jerusalem, and Ezriel Hildesheimer of Berlin (Bo, 1878) agreed with Reinowitz's solution. Chief Rabbi Nathan Adler, B. Spiers, and Susman Cohen of Manchester also agreed. It is interesting that Reinowitz consulted both Ashkenazi and Sephardi halakhic authorities; it was the first *aguna* problem he solved favourably.

19. *Responsa Meshiv Davar, Even HaEzer* (1894), no. 25.

The second case is that of a mentally ill woman. A young man, Nehemiah ben Shimshon, of Saki, Poland, married Henah, daughter of Leib from England. They lived in Manchester and had two very young daughters. About four years before, the woman had become mentally ill and was now in a mental hospital. The husband was a poor man who had to go out to work and had no one to look after the two young daughters, who needed special care and attention. "My son-in-law, Rabbi Susman Cohen, of Manchester, went with the husband to the mental hospital and he saw that the woman was insane. The doctors say that she will never be well again. The husband implores us", wrote Reinowitz, "to give him permission, according to Jewish law, to marry another woman who will look after his two young daughters."

In presenting the case to the leading halakhic authorities, Reinowitz states (1) that a *get* has never been written in Manchester; (2) that in England only the London Beth Din is authorized to issue a *get*; (3) that as for this case the permission of 100 rabbis (or scholars) is required, and that number cannot be found in England; and (4) that in this country people have queer ideas and often marry out of the Jewish faith, "may God forgive our iniquity, take us out from foreign lands and bring us speedily into our land".

Rabbis Naphtali Z. Y. Berlin of Volozhin, Raphael Spiro, Judah Leib Melzer, and eleven scholars of the Volozhin Yeshiva (10 Sivan 1880), Pinhas Michael of Antipoli, Russia (23 Heshvan 1880), and Samuel Salant of Jerusalem agreed with Reinowitz's solution of the problem.

The third case is that of two *agunot* in London whose husbands were drowned on Tuesday evening, 30 August 1881, in the ship *Titan,* which struck a rock on its way from Cape Town to Port Elizabeth, South Africa. The only survivors out of about two hundred people were eleven passengers and twenty-six officers and men of the crew. In the London Mansion House an appeal was launched on behalf of the widows and orphans of those who perished in the disaster and it raised a large sum of money. Each widow received £40 and they were also informed that each orphan on reaching the age of fourteen would receive £10.

The *aguna* Faiga bat Joseph, the wife of Moshe ben Simḥa, was thirty years old. She had been married for ten years and had three children, the eldest of them nine years old. The *aguna* Pesha bat Ḥanan, the wife of Moshe Naḥum, was twenty-six. She had been married for six years and had a four-year-old daughter. Both of the women had been *agunot* for four years. "They keep on coming to me", Reinowitz wrote, "and implore me to have pity on them and their young children and to find a way of permitting them to marry again."

In presenting the case to the halakhic authorities, Reinowitz stated that in this country people had erroneous views. Some people derided these two women for being *agunot* and scoffed at the prohibition of the sages, "and I heard that there are men who want to marry them as they are".

On the basis of the official version of the disaster from the Royal Navy, Reinowitz suggested a favourable solution to the problem, which was approved by Rabbis Isaac Elḥanan Spektor of Kovno (27 Tishri 1885), and Naphtali Z. Y. Berlin of Volozhin (undated). Berlin in his responsum remarked, "As this is an entirely new case, which will be used as a precedent for similar cases, it is my strong desire that you should copy this responsum and send it to some other *geonim* of our time."

In our final case, we find an *aguna* whose husband was found drowned near London Bridge in May 1884. Before burying the man in a non-Jewish cemetery, the police took a photograph of him. When the woman called at the police station to enquire after her husband, the police showed her a photograph of the drowned man, which she recognized as that of her husband. The police returned to her the diamond ring which was on his finger when he drowned, the latch-key of the door, and a small penknife which he had in his pocket and which she recognized as belonging to her husband. She appeared at the Beth Din on Monday, the day after Sukkot 1884, when she was asked to bring a written statement from the police about the accident. She brought this on the Thursday. On her evidence, as well as the written statement by the police, Reinowitz suggested halakhic reasons for permission and submitted them for approval to Rabbis Isaac Elḥanan Spektor of Kovno (16 Tevet 1886),[20] and Naphtali Tzvi Yehuda Berlin of Volozhin.[21] The former addressed him as *HaRav HaGaon Hamefursam*, and the latter as *HaRav HaGaon HaMubhak*, very high titles indeed, which prove how highly they thought of Jacob Reinowitz as a halakhic authority.

Kuntres Sefeka Deyoma

Jacob Reinowitz was also an authority on the Jewish calendar. After studying the calendar in England, he discovered that the calculations on the times of the day – dawn, sunrise, sunset, and twilight – on which the commencement and ending of the Sabbaths, festivals, and fasts depended, were in accordance with the astronomical tables of the eighteenth-century astronomer, Raphael Levi Hanover (1685–1779), which are based on the Berlin-Hanover-Amsterdam

20. *Responsa Ein Yitzḥak, Even HaEzer* (Vilna, 1888), no. 31.
21. *Responsa Meshiv Davar*, pt. IV (Warsaw, 1894), no. 23.

horizon. The chief rabbis of England from Hart Lyon (1756–64) onwards accepted Hanover's calculations. Reinowitz maintained that, as London has a different horizon, the times should be different. He submitted his treatise of forty-one folios, *Kuntres Sefeka DeYoma*, in 1883 to Dr Nathan Adler, who consulted Dr Michael Friedlander, an authority in the field. They agreed that Reinowitz's times were right and accordingly adjusted the beginning of the fast of Yom Kippur and the beginning of the Sabbath, but the other times they left as before, because that was the *minhag*, custom, of this country. The calculation of the times of the day according to different horizons is quite topical. Leo Levin of New York,[22] and M. Posen of London,[23] with the help of the computer, suggest various times for various horizons, which fundamentally was Reinowitz's thesis.

Problems of Circumcision

Dr Asher Asher, who, besides being a physician, was a distinguished *mohel*,[24] consulted Reinowitz on problems of circumcision. Reinowitz published the results of their discussions in a treatise of sixty-four folios, *Kuntres Atarot Hatanim*, which he divided into three parts:

1. *Katan Hanolad Mahul* (A Babe Born Circumcised);
2. *Ger SheNitgayer KesheHu Mahul* (A Non-Jew Circumcised Before He Became a Proselyte);
3. *Alim Latrufa* (Leaves for Healing [on *metzitza*]).

The problem of *metzitza* particularly had been discussed by halakhists for some time.[25] Since his arrival in London, Reinowitz had observed that the *mohelim* did not practise the traditional *metzitza*, but used other means, which had the same effect. Based on his belief that this practice was sanctioned by the Chief Rabbi, he justified it halakhically as well as on medical grounds.[26] He suggested, however, that those who practised the traditional method of *metzitza* should not do it on a Sabbath for halakhic reasons.

A *mohel*, a newcomer to London, complained to Dr Hermann Adler that Reinowitz was advocating the abolition of the traditional *metzitza*.

22. *Jewish Chrononomy* (New York, 1967).
23. *Kuntres HaNefesh* (London, 1968).
24. Dr Asher Asher, *The Jewish Rite of Circumcision* (London, 1873).
25. *Responsa Maharatz Hayot*, 1. 60; see also *Mezizah* by Dr B. Homa (London, 1960).
26. Ibid. 27.

Adler mentioned this to his father, who wrote to Reinowitz, "with open rebuke and hidden love", to withdraw his view on *metzitza*. In response, Reinowitz sent the Chief Rabbi his *Alim LaTrufa* on *metzitza,* from which it was obvious that the *mohel* had not grasped Reinowitz's view. The Chief Rabbi, in his reply, uses the phrase *shalom al dayanei Yisrael* (peace upon the judges of Israel), implying that he agreed with Reinowitz's view of *metzitza* on the Sabbath.

Machine-Made *Matzot*

In the previous generation halakhists had discussed whether machine-made *matzot* were *kasher lePesah.*[27] By Rabbi Reinowitz's time it was almost generally agreed that they were indeed kosher. However, the kashrut of machine-made *matzot mitzva* used for Seder nights was still an open topic. In 1882, the Chief Rabbi requested that Reinowitz prepare a responsum on the subject. Rabbi Reinowitz ruled that the *matzot* were kosher for use at Seder.

Cremation

During the latter years of the nineteenth century, the subject of cremation was introduced in certain Jewish circles. In his responsum on the subject, Rabbi Reinowitz definitively forbade this practice.

Levy – Kohn-Zedek Controversy

Rabbi Reinowitz was asked to mediate in the controversy between Naphtali Levy (1840–94)[28] and Joseph Kohn-Zedek (d. 1903). Levy was a *shoḥet* of the London Board of Shechita. He was a rabbinic scholar and Hebrew writer and author. In his essay *Toledot HaAdam,* Levy was the first rabbinic scholar to expound in Hebrew Darwin's *Theory of Evolution.* He also refers to Darwinism in his *Shenei HaMatot,* published by Peretz Smolenskin in Vienna in 1880.

In 1883, Joseph Kohn-Zedek, a preacher at the Sandy's Row Synagogue, author of Hebrew books on homiletics,[29] and a fierce critic of Naphtali Levy, asked Rabbi Reinowitz to write to the rabbis of Poland and Russia, with whom he exchanged responsa, asking them to withdraw their approbation of Levy's books. Levy appealed to Reinowitz to plead with Kohn-Zedek not to attack him in his speeches and articles. To clear up the issue, Reinowitz wrote to Rabbi

27. H. H. Medini, *Sedei Ḥemed* (Warsaw, 1903). *Ḥametz UMatza,* pp. 93–5; see also S. B. Freehof, *The Responsa Literature* (Philadelphia, 1959), 183–8.

28. *Jewish Chronicle,* 1 June 1894 and 8 June 1894.

29. *Jewish Chronicle,* Dec. 1903.

Samuel Mohilewer, of Bialystok, who had known Levy from his yeshiva days. Rabbi Mohilewer replied that he had never given Levy an approbation.[30] Moreover, he regarded Levy as an *apikores,* because he had not listened to his advice to alter some statements in his book *Shenei HaMatot,* which implied a denial of Jewish beliefs, e.g. creation of the universe, the existence of a soul, and *Torah min hashamayim.*

Hobebey Eretz Society

Rabbi Abraham Eber Hirschowitz of Kovno came to England in 1884 on behalf of the rabbis and leaders of Poland and Russia. His visit, perhaps in light of the Ḥovevei Tziyon Conference in Katowice that year, aimed to establish an organization for the settlement of Jews in the Holy Land, where they would make their living from the land. After interviewing him in Brighton, the Chief Rabbi and Dr Asher Asher introduced Rabbi Hirschowitz to MP Mr Samuel Montagu, Jacob Reinowitz, and others in London and the provinces. Each one encouraged Rabbi Hirschowitz to set up an organization for this purpose. As a result, the Hobebey Eretz Society was founded in London on 15 Av 5648 – 23 July 1888, with its office at 84 Leman Street. The Trustees were Messrs. M. Cohen, H. Goodman, and M. Goldstein, and A. E. Hirschowitz served as Hon. Secretary. A copy of the constitution, distributed to members, was found among Rabbi Reinowitz's correspondence, leading me to believe that he too was a member. Reinowitz instructed Hirschowitz in matters of practical halakha relating to the colonization of Palestine among other, more general matters.[31] The latter left England in 1892 for Australia, where he became the rabbi of the Shomrei Emunim Beth Hamedrash in Melbourne.

Machzikei Hadass Controversy

The Machzikei Hadass controversy, in which a group of Eastern European rabbis recently arrived in England questioned the halakhic standards of Anglo-Jewry, began not long after Dr Hermann Adler (1839–1911) succeeded his father as Chief Rabbi. It is described in detail in Dr Bernard Homa's book *A Fortress in Anglo-Jewry* (1953), and I therefore do not need to deal with it in detail. Reinowitz received many letters from famous rabbis in Poland and Russia in support of the Chief Rabbi, and even the Machzikei Hadass could not find fault with Reinowitz himself, except that he was old, and they said that he was the only *dayan* whom they could trust.

30. Letter by S. Mohilewer in 1888.
31. In his correspondence he refers to Reinowitz as "my master and my teacher".

Ministers' Conference 1892

In May 1892, the Chief Rabbi convened a ministers' conference, where it was decided, among other things, that the repetition of the Musaf *Amida* was no longer necessary. In a letter to Dr Michael Friedlander, Rabbi Reinowitz strongly objected to this decision. Friedlander replied in Hebrew:

> I too am displeased with the young who wish to break down the fence and destroy the vineyard of the Lord. I have no share in them. But this I must say before my Master. We have to investigate and examine each problem and question which they submit to the Chief Rabbi. We have to listen to their questions and arguments and rule according to the *Din*.

After stating his view of the repetition of the *Amida*, Friedlander continues:

> In this age, and especially in this country, it is impossible to insist and say, "this is my will and this you shall do". If we do this, we shall, God forbid, drive many away from us and put to shame the Torah and men of Torah. This, everyone who fears the Lord should understand and especially those who call themselves Machzikei Hadass, who lie in wait to attack the Chief Rabbi with all kinds of false charges. It is better to walk in the middle way. I do not wish to help those who transgress but only to help them to return to the fold.

WIDESPREAD INFLUENCE

Over the years, Rabbi Reinowitz issued many responsa to questions put to him in various cities in this country and abroad. I quote a number of instances:

Manchester: His son-in-law, Rabbi Susman Cohen, submitted many *she'elot* to him, and their halakhic correspondence, too, could fill more than one volume. One day I hope to discuss the content of the responsa of Susman Cohen, in which I shall show his contribution to responsa literature in this country. Had L. P. Gartner known of Reinowitz's, Chief Rabbi Adler's, and Susman Cohen's responsa, he would not have written, "There is no sizeable body of responsa ... issued in England".[32] The correspondence between Reinowitz and Cohen is, of course, in Hebrew, but Esther Liba Reinowitz often added a few lines in Yiddish about family and domestic matters, to which their daughter Bertha replied.

32. *The Jewish Immigrant in England 1850–1950* (London, 1960), 245.

Bradford: The *shoḥet*, Z. T. Jaffe of Bradford, in 1884, asked Reinowitz a *she'ela* about menstruation, and described the poor religious conditions in the city.

Coventry: The Rev. Jacob Bonner submitted to Reinowitz *she'elot* on *sheḥita* (no date).

Hull: *She'ela* by H. Horowitz, Ellul 1878, on *ḥuppa* (marriage) which was not held in the local synagogue but privately.

Ramsgate: Rabbi Saul of Ramsgate, in 1877, submitted talmudic problems.

South Africa, Cape Town: No date. One of the questions was whether a woman who suffers much pain during childbirth may prevent her pregnancy with her husband's consent.

Berkeley East: Three *she'elot* from E. Rosenberg, two about *sheḥita* and one (March 1888) about kashering, referring to animal ribs.

Australia, Melbourne: As mentioned, after taking up the position of Rabbi of Shomerey Emunim Beth Hamedrash in Melbourne, Australia in 1892, Rabbi Hirschowitz submitted several *she'elot* to Rabbi Reinowitz in 1892 and 1893, addressing him as "my teacher, my master". Among them:

1. Is Jamaica rum *kasher lePesah*?
2. As there is no *mikve* in Melbourne, may a Jewish woman supervise the immersion of a female proselyte which is performed in the open sea?
3. In Melbourne the prayer for rain, *mashiv haruaḥ umorid hatal* and *veten tal umatar* was not read.
   Hirschowitz submitted the problem to Rabbi Isaac Elhanan Spektor, who ruled that the prayer should be read in the place in the prayer book where all Jews read it. Rabbi Samuel Salant, of Jerusalem, was of the opinion that it should be read in the sixteenth blessing of the *Amida* after "turn us not empty-handed away".[33] Asked for his ruling, Reinowitz agreed with Spektor. Hirschowitz then asked Reinowitz to ask the Chief Rabbi to instruct the Jewish congregations in Australia to read the prayer for rain.
4. In 1892 the Chief Rabbi, Dr Hermann Adler, asked Reinowitz to prepare a responsum for an *aguna* in Australia whose husband was drowned on a sea journey.

China, Hong Kong: No date. Israel Weinberg enquired about *ḥalitza*.

America, New York: Reinowitz instructed Rabbi Abraham Joseph Ash, in New York, on spelling the words 'New York' and the names of its two rivers

33. S. Singer, *Authorised Daily Prayer Book* (London, 1962), 51.

correctly in a *get*. Rabbi S. M. Suskind of New York also submitted a *she'ela* about a *get* in 1880.

Denver, Colorado: The rabbi of Colorado asked Reinowitz (no date) how to spell 'Denver' in a *get*, and also how to build a *mikve*.

France, Paris: Rabbi Judah Lubetzki arrived in London in 1880 as an emissary of the Mir Yeshiva. The head of the yeshiva wrote to ask Reinowitz to hand over to Rabbi Lubetzki the *pinkas*, the list of subscribers, which the last emissary had deposited with him, and to assist him in raising funds for the yeshiva. From England, Lubetzki went to Paris, where the Polish-Russian community was seeking a rabbi. Lubetzki was keen to obtain the position but Israel Salanter (1818–1883), the founder of the Musar movement, who happened to be in Paris at that time, thought that the community should appoint an older, more experienced rabbi. Lubetzki wrote asking Reinowitz to recommend him as being fit for the position, because he knew that Salanter valued Reinowitz's opinion more highly than that of the rabbis in Poland and Russia. Salanter came to Paris in 1882, most probably to straighten out certain irregularities regarding *gittin* (divorce). He sent a telegram to Reinowitz to come to Paris immediately. Reinowitz went and discussed several problems with Salanter and, no doubt, recommended Lubetzki for the rabbinical position there. He went on to Berlin for the engagement of his daughter, Rebecca, to Mr Saul in 1882.[34] Subsequently, Lubetzki submitted *she'elot* continually to Reinowitz in London.

I would like to mention the case of an *aguna* which is of special interest. It concerns the wife of a man, Metchick, who was imprisoned in London for seven years for selling forged bonds. After serving his prison sentence Metchick went to Switzerland, where he was sentenced to four years' imprisonment. His wife, who came from Warsaw, spent some time in London and then in Paris. Concerning the case, Lubetzki wrote:

> I promised her, if her husband sent her a *get* I would hand it over to her according to Jewish Law. But the rabbi of Baden, who is also the rabbi of Zurich, where Metchick is imprisoned, is very strict. He is a disciple of Rabbi Samson Raphael Hirsch, of Frankfurt-on-Main. He will not permit the *get* to be handed over through a messenger in any circumstances. Metchick's wife travelled to Zurich and the rabbi asked me to come there to assist him in arranging the *get*. He had already obtained permission from the governor to write the *get* in prison and there is a kosher scribe and

34. Letters by J. Abraham, Berlin, 1882; M. Rosenblatt, Paris, 1882.

> witnesses. I promised to go to Zurich Monday next, provided you agree, as you know the ease and you are a great man in our midst and we can rely on you. As a *get* has not been written before in Zurich, and in order to write it the permission of a great man is required, I ask you, therefore, to grant me permission, as it is a case of emergency.

Reinowitz granted Lubetzki permission by return of post and also advised him how to spell 'Zurich' and the name of its two rivers in Hebrew. Thus, Reinowitz was instrumental in getting a *get* written for the first time in Zurich.

In 1884 Lubetzki asked Reinowitz to advise him on how to build a *mikve*, as "I know that you put right the London *mikve*; perhaps you could send me a plan of it, which I will return to you."[35]

In 1892 the London Beth Din sent a *get* to Rabbi Lubetzki in Paris through Harris Cohen, Lubetzki's son-in-law.

Germany, Berlin: Reinowitz corresponded in 1877 with Rabbi Barukh Yitzhak Lipshutz of Berlin, informing him of his appointment as rabbi of the Chevra Shass and enquiring the meaning of a passage in Tractate Shabbat in *Tiferet Yisrael*, a commentary on the Mishna by Lipshutz's father.

In 1886 Reinowitz informed Rabbi Benjamin Ze'ev Eger, son of Rabbi Akiba Eger, that the father's name of a woman whose *get* he had arranged was incorrect. Eger replied on 3 Menaḥem Av 1886 that the woman should not live with the man whom she had married after she received her *get*.

Konigsberg: In 1881 Rabbi Israel Lipkin (1810–1883) submitted a *she'ela* to Reinowitz on whether a Jew may instruct a non-Jew on Friday to act on his behalf on the Sabbath on the stock exchange.

Russia, Volozhin: As already mentioned, Reinowitz exchanged responsa with the head of the yeshiva, Rabbi Naphtali Tzvi Yehuda Berlin (1817–93). From 1876 onwards, Rabbi Berlin wrote continually to Reinowitz asking him to assist in obtaining funds for the yeshiva, which he did.[36] Two letters are of particular interest. In 1879 Rabbi Berlin informed Reinowitz that officials of the Russian Government had searched the documents and correspondence of the yeshiva and taken away "all my correspondence with you" – the reason being that "a vile person forged a letter of a secret nature which I am supposed to have sent to you". In his next letter Rabbi Berlin said that the correspondence had been returned after a few hours and that nothing untoward had resulted.

---

35. Letter by Dayan B. Spiers to Reinowitz on *mikva*, 22 July 1880.
36. Rabbi Berlin wrote to Reinowitz about forty letters.

In a letter of 1889 Rabbi Berlin told Reinowitz that he would make an exception and accept a *baḥur*, student, from London who desired to study in Volozhin. The cost per week would be two roubles: one rouble for board and lodging, and one for a teacher. That student was Judah Kyanski, later Rabbi Kyanski (the father of Judge Bernard B. Gillis), who was Reinowitz's great-nephew. He was perhaps the first and only student from this country to study in the famous Volozhin Yeshiva.

Kovno: As mentioned above, Reinowitz exchanged responsa with the rabbi of Kovno, Isaac Elhanan Spektor (1819–96). Spektor wrote in 1886 to Reinowitz for financial aid for his *kollel*, for a poor student who was an *illui* (prodigy), and for families who had suffered in the pogroms.

Brest-Litovsk: Rabbi Moshe Yehudah Leib Diskin (1818–98), a talmudic authority, wrote to Reinowitz on 4 Adar 1877 asking him whether tea was *kasher lePesah*; if so, would he send 2 lb., together with 2 lb. of *kasher lePesah* sugar, by express so that it should arrive in time. This letter is of interest because it is in Diskin's own handwriting.

ROYAL VISITORS TO JERUSALEM

Reinowitz was deeply attached to the Holy Land. Not only did he hope for the return of the Jewish people but he also encouraged every activity towards the fulfilment of that hope. In 1880 he provided financial aid to two of the original settlers of Petaḥ Tikva, Ḥayim Shimoni and Moshe Tzvi Levinson. They repeatedly thanked him for his donations, which he sent through Rabbi Samuel Salant, the Rabbi of Jerusalem. Shimoni asked Reinowitz to continue supporting him financially and thus be counted "among the founders of the Yishuv".

Rabbi Moshe Y. L. Diskin, mentioned above, settled in Jerusalem, where he founded the Diskin Orphanage. On 14 Shevat 1881 he wrote to Reinowitz that the orphanage was functioning and appealed to him for financial aid, which Reinowitz provided continually.

Of special importance is a letter written by Moshe Tzvi Levinson on 7 Iyar 1882, on Diskin's behalf. After thanking him for his financial aid and telling him that Rabbi Diskin read his responsum three times, to which he would reply as soon as his secretary returned, he informed Reinowitz that the sons of the Prince of Wales spent Seder night at Rabbi Diskin's home. The rabbi explained the Haggada to them, putting special emphasis on the prayer *Vehi SheAmda*, which described how God delivered the Jewish people in every generation from their persecutors throughout the ages. The princes were deeply moved and wept. They drank the first two glasses of wine and ate matza and bitter herbs. They enjoyed themselves and departed with deep affection and respect. I am, however, unable to verify this story.

In 1882 was a Year of Release (*shemitta*). Some halakhists maintained that it was not obligatory on Jewish colonists to observe the law of *shemitta*, but Rabbi Diskin ruled that it was obligatory to observe it in the Holy Land. He wrote requesting that Reinowitz speak to the Chief Rabbi and ask him to write to Baron Edmond de Rothschild of Paris, telling him not to seek permission, a *heter*, to disregard the *shemitta* law, but to enable the colonists to observe it.

In Ḥeshvan 1881 the Ḥevra Shomerei Emunim in Jerusalem wrote to Reinowitz to exert his influence against the proposed opening of a day school in Jerusalem, claiming it would be a great danger to Judaism.

REINOWITZ'S OTHER WORKS

Rabbi Reinowitz left a complete volume, *Tolaat Yaakov*, as well as *ḥiddushim*, novellae, on the Talmud, and a large collection of *siyumim* which he delivered at Valkovisk and London.

In addition, he completed one volume of *derashot* (sermons), *She'erit Yaakov*, and numerous individual *derashot*. In 1869 he delivered a *derasha* in Valkovisk in which he admonished the people to observe the Sabbath, not to commit acts of immorality, and urged women not to wear immodest dress.

In addition to his own writing, Reinowitz edited the talmudic commentary of Rabbenu Ḥananel ben Hushiel (990–1050), printed in the Vilna edition of the Talmud. Among the correspondence, I found a letter dated 13 Ellul 1880 in which the famous publishing firm of Romm thanked Reinowitz for editing the Rabbenu Ḥananel text and expressed the hope that he would edit other works for them.

RABBINIC LIFE IN LONDON

The United Synagogue arranged special Minḥa services on the Sabbath for immigrants at the Duke's Place Synagogue, at which rabbis and *maggidim* delivered *derashot* in Yiddish. In 1889 Reinowitz addressed the congregation on the subject '*Dina Demalkhuta Dina*', the law of the country is the law, admonishing them to observe the laws of England, which offered them hospitality and freedom. In 1890 he appealed to his listeners to observe the Sabbath in spite of the many difficulties. He reminded them that the Chevra Shomrei Shabbat Society, whose aim was to find work for those who wished to keep the Sabbath, had been formed recently. He also appealed to them to be honest and upright in their business dealings and to observe the laws of the country. They should thank God that He had brought them to this country, where the Queen and her princes were good to them, granting them equal rights with the other citizens.

Reinowitz had several disciples in London. Among them, Dr Hermann Adler, whom he taught *Ḥoshen Mishpat*,[37] and the Rev. Simeon Singer (1848–1906), who began his rabbinic studies with Reinowitz in 1879.[38]

Jacob Reinowitz died on 2 Sivan 1893, and was buried at the West Ham Cemetery. The *Jewish Chronicle*, in its leader, wrote:

> The Jewish community of London will learn too late that in the deceased Dayan, the Rev. Jacob Reinowitz, it harboured a true messenger of Heaven, one whose worth and learning were enshrined in a singularly modest character. To his intimate associates he was known as a man of profound talmudic attainments and in that branch of Jewish lore which deals with the legal aspect, with the manifold questions of everyday life, he was in England, at least, without compeer. Many Jews of the East End of London will unfeignedly mourn his loss, not only because they have been bereaved of a trustworthy religious guide but because he wielded no inconsiderable, if unseen, influence in reconciling them to their environment. His efforts always tended in pacific directions. Unfortunately, his work, which was really useful and beneficial, much more so than that of self-advertising individuals, was but little understood and appreciated by the community and he was allowed to subsist on a miserable pittance grudgingly given by the United Synagogue.[39]

37. Letter by Chief Rabbi Dr N. Adler to Reinowitz, stating how pleased he was to know that his son was learning *Ḥoshen Mishpat* with him. It is dated 5 Hanukah 1879.
38. Letter by S. Singer, Dec. 1879, that he would commence his rabbinic studies on the following Monday.
39. *Jewish Chronicle*, 19 May, 1893.

Rashi's *Davar Aḥer*: Alternatives, Concurrency, and Creative Interpretation

Rabbi Dr Harvey Belovski

INTRODUCTION

Rashi (Rabbi Solomon ben Isaac, 1040–1105) is considered to be the greatest Jewish textual interpreter of all time and is "universally regarded as one of the most creative figures in medieval Jewish society".[1] He wrote commentaries "on the Bible and the Talmud, responsa, liturgical poetry, and, perhaps, legal documents related to community affairs".[2] His commentary on the Torah is known for its minimalism, accuracy, and consistency; as a result, over the centuries, hundreds of supercommentaries and academic studies have explored his interpretative objectives and hermeneutic methodology.

Rashi comments on most verses in the Torah. It is clear that each of his comments is offered in response to a specific problem that he has identified within the text. His interpretative methodology is based on the assumption that the Torah is a multi-layered divine text replete with hints, linguistic nuances, and even ambiguities, which invite and require explanation.[3]

1. Avraham Grossman, *Rashi*, trans. Joel Linsider (Oxford: Littman Library, 2012), 73.
2. Ibid.
3. See Rashi's commentary on Gen. 1:1, s.v. *bereshit bara*, where he claims that the phrase 'says' "interpret me!"

In the great majority of places in his Torah commentary, Rashi offers one reading of a problematic word or phrase, in accordance with his stated approach of supplying the plainest meaning of the text.[4] Yet sometimes he offers more than one reading of a difficult passage: in some cases, he provides multiple plain readings and in others, a combination of plain and midrashic readings; the latter generally deviates from the plain reading of the text. In many cases, he separates these multiple readings with the phrase *davar aḥer* – another thing. This essay is a study of Rashi's use of *davar aḥer* and whether, and if so how, his multiple explanations are related to each other.

I am privileged to dedicate this study to Rabbi Lord Sacks, a remarkable teacher, inspirational leader and visionary for our community.

THE APPROACH OF THE *MASKIL LEDAVID* TO MULTIPLICITY IN RASHI'S COMMENTARY

I will initially examine Rashi's use of *davar aḥer* with reference to Rabbi David Pardo's supercommentary on Rashi, *Maskil LeDavid*.[5] Given that Rashi seldom offers any meta-interpretation within his commentary – indeed, he rarely even states the difficulty with the verse that prompted him to comment in the first place – supercommentaries seek to reconstruct Rashi's thinking in formulating his comment and, in some cases, either challenge his reading or defend it against its detractors. They frequently try to list the problems he may have identified, explain how his reading deals with those problems, and, where appropriate, why

4. See his commentary on Gen. 3:8, where he states, "I have come only to [explain] the simple meaning of Scripture and to [present] aggada that resolves the words of Scripture." The key phrase in this comment is *peshuto shel mikra*, which I have translated here as "simple reading of Scripture". Benjamin J. Gelles, *Peshat and Derash in the Exegesis of Rashi* (Leiden: Brill Academic Publishers, 1981), 10–12 provides helpful tables of places in Rashi's commentary where he refers to his desire to pursue a programme of interpretation according to *peshuto shel mikra*. Given that Rashi frequently deploys midrashic interpretations, it is unlikely that by "simple reading" he means the literal meaning of the words. I understand Rashi to mean the "simplest reading of a word or phrase that justifies its existence in context". This suggestion is supported by Raphael Loewe, "The 'Plain' Meaning of Scripture in Early Jewish Exegesis", in J. G. Weiss (ed.), *Papers of the Institute of Jewish Studies London*, i (Jerusalem: Magnes Press, 1964), 140–85 (esp. 155–62), who points out that the fundamental meaning of the word is to "strip", "flatten", or "extend"; this "can obviously develop semantically into such meanings as *flat, straight, simple, uncompounded, innocent, unlearned*". See also "On the Meaning and History of the Noun *Peshat*" in David Weiss Halivni, *Peshat and Derash: Plain and Applied Meaning in Rabbinic Exegesis* (New York: Oxford University Press, 1991), 52–88 (esp. 54–63), where the author asserts that the correct reading of *peshat* is 'context'.
5. David Pardo, *Maskil LeDavid* (Venice, 1761, repr. Jerusalem: Even Yisrael, 1986).

he may have been dissatisfied with a single interpretation. The *Maskil LeDavid* offers an especially thorough treatment of Rashi's use of *davar aḥer*.[6] Major objectives of this work include reconstructing the thought processes that led Rashi to offer more than one reading of a given verse, and explaining the benefits and deficiencies of each.

Examples of Rashi's Use of *Davar Aḥer* as Explained in the *Maskil LeDavid*

A. *Other gods*

לא יהיה לך אלהים אחרים על פני.

> You shall not have other gods before Me. (Ex. 20:3)

> אלהים אחרים - שאינן אלהות אלא אחרים עשאום אלהים עליהם ולא יתכן לפרש אלהים אחרים זולתי שגנאי הוא כלפי מעלה לקרותם אלהות אצלו.
> דבר אחר אלהים אחרים שהם אחרים לעובדיהם צועקים אליהם ואינן עונין אותם ודומה כאלו הוא אחר שאינו מכירו מעולם.

> [Rashi's first reading:] Other gods – which are not divine, yet others have adopted them as divinities over themselves. It is not possible to explain (the text as referring to) gods other than Me (God), since it would be shameful to Heaven to (even) refer to them as other gods next to Him.
> [Rashi's second reading:] Another explanation: other gods – they are 'other' to those who worship them: [the worshippers] cry out to them, but [the gods] do not answer them, as though [the god] is 'other', who has never known [the worshipper].[7]

Rashi is clearly troubled by the phrase "other gods", which appears, inconceivably, to suggest the existence of deities other than the one God. Indeed, *Maskil LeDavid* explains that Rashi's comment is motivated by the concern for those who might think that other gods actually exist, although it is forbidden to worship them.[8] As such, Rashi's theological objection to the most literal meaning precludes the 'plainest' reading of the phrase. In his first reading, he reassures his reader that

6. See Yehudah Cooperman, *The Plain Sense of Scripture: On the Place of the Plain Sense of Scripture in the Perfection of the Torah and Its Sanctity* (Heb.), 2 vols. (Jerusalem: Irving Cymberknopf Publication Foundation, 2001), ii. 32 n. 7, who notes that *Maskil LeDavid* explains "the necessity in every place where Rashi mentions 'another explanation'".
7. Rashi, commentary on Ex. 20:3.
8. *Maskil LeDavid*, 198.

'other gods' means gods *according* to others – that is, they are only considered 'gods' by idolaters, but they are not actually gods. Yet, as *Maskil LeDavid* explains, this reading is not faithful to the text's grammar, which actually reads *elohim aḥerim* (other gods), not *elohei aḥerim* (gods of others).[9] Rashi addresses this difficulty in his second reading: idols are 'other gods' not because they possess divinity, but because they fail to answer those who call out to them – in this respect they are 'other': distant from their worshippers. This is more remote from the plain meaning, yet makes it easier to read the phrase *elohim aḥerim*.

B. *The murder of Abel*

ויאמר מה עשית קול דמי אחיך צעקים אלי מן האדמה.

> He said: what have you done? The sound of your brother's bloods is calling to Me from the ground. (Gen. 4:10)

דמי אחיך - דמו ודם זרעיותיו.
ד"א שעשה בו פצעים הרבה שלא היה יודע מהיכן נפשו יוצאה.

> [Rashi's first reading:] Your brother's bloods – his blood and the blood of his descendants.
> [Rashi's second reading:] Another explanation: [Cain] wounded [Abel] in many places, so that it was not known from where his soul departed.[10]

Rashi is troubled by the unexpected plural usage: *demei* (bloods), which is difficult to read literally. In his first reading he assumes that God criticized Cain for having killed Abel and for 'murdering' any hypothetical unborn descendants. This is not a literal reading, but is as close to one as Rashi can offer. But *Maskil LeDavid* points out that this reading is problematic, as this usage of 'blood' always refers to murdering someone living, but never to preventing someone from being born.[11] Furthermore, *Maskil LeDavid* notes that "since the two 'acts' [killing Abel and preventing his descendants from being born] are dissimilar, they cannot be circumscribed by a single verb" (calling).[12] Rashi offers a second reading, in which the plural form of *demei* is explained solely in reference to Abel, who bleeds from many wounds. Yet *Maskil LeDavid* notes that this

9. Ibid.
10. Rashi, commentary on Gen. 4:10.
11. *Maskil LeDavid*, p. 23.
12. Ibid.

explanation is also problematic – there may indeed have been several wounds, but Abel still only had one 'blood', which flowed from many places, making Rashi's reading of the plural *demei* questionable.[13] According to *Maskil LeDavid*, then, Rashi's first interpretation deals with the plural *demei* but neglects its correct meaning; his second reading preserves its meaning, but only partially explains the plural usage.

It is clear that Rashi offers the plainest or most literal reading of a problematic word or phrase that he can identify. In most cases, this approach resolves his difficulties. However, as *Maskil LeDavid* explains, in some cases his reading is either inherently problematic or creates new difficulties: in case A it neglects the grammar of the phrase and in case B it misuses the word *demei*. In such instances Rashi offers a second, usually 'less plain' (i.e. more midrashic) interpretation, which deals with the issue raised by the first reading. Yet this reading is itself deficient in some way, usually in that it distorts the plain meaning of the word, disqualifying it from being the sole explanation.

Based on *Maskil LeDavid*'s approach to *davar aḥer*, there emerge two scenarios: in the first, Rashi identifies a simple problem with the word or phrase under scrutiny; his first reading resolves the problem but in so doing creates a new one; his second reading resolves the new problem but does not fully address the original one. In the second scenario, Rashi identifies a complex problem of which each reading addresses only one part but leaves other parts unresolved.

IS THERE A RELATIONSHIP BETWEEN RASHI'S READINGS?

While Rashi commonly offers more than one reading of a word or phrase, he does not discuss the relationship between them. As Sarah Kamin notes, "Rashi never explains the appearance of multiple readings, nor is it clear what relationship exists between the two readings he cites".[14] Indeed, there is scant internal evidence from the wording and structure of his commentary in the above examples, or, indeed, from elsewhere, that he believes there to be any relationship between his proposed interpretations; he simply lists them, dividing them with the phrase "another explanation" or similar.

The most obvious explanation of this phenomenon is that Rashi's multiple readings ought to be treated as simple alternatives. By this I mean that just one of his readings reflects the original intention of the divine Author (the

13. Ibid.

14. Sarah Kamin, *Rashi's Exegetical Categorization: In Respect to the Distinction Between Peshat and Derash* (Heb.) (Jerusalem: Magnes Press, 1986), 180, 183.

'correct' reading); however, Rashi is uncertain which it is. As such, he offers two or more alternatives: each of these is a possible *sole* correct reading, yet since neither completely resolves his issues with the text, it is not possible to definitively identify which of them it is. Rabbi Amnon Shapira helpfully styles these "weak alternatives",[15] since neither is "strong" enough to fully deal with Rashi's problem. The identification of the correct reading would automatically disqualify the other.[16] There is no connection whatever between these alternatives. This is clearly the approach of *Maskil LeDavid*. The same is true for a number of other classic supercommentaries on Rashi, who either do not comment where he offers multiple readings, or, where they do, make no attempt to connect them.[17]

An alternative approach is advocated by Rabbi Pinḥas Doron, who suggests that Rashi's two readings "*together* answer all of the questions on the verse, or at least most of them" (my italics).[18] I think that Rabbi Doron is mistaken: read as *alternatives*, only one of Rashi's explanations is correct and, obviously, therefore, the other is incorrect. Either his first reading resolves a problem but generates another, or his second reading deals with the new problem but fails to fully solve the original one, or each reading addresses one part, but not the other, of a complex problem. The two readings do not achieve anything "together", as Rabbi Doron claims. What, perhaps, he should have said is that each of Rashi's readings addresses different aspects of his problem, and, as such, a solution is known to all parts of it. But even this is not strictly true: since one of the readings is incorrect (since it is not the 'correct'

15. Amnon Shapira, "Whether 'Another Explanation' in Rashi Indicates Two Interpretations that are Alternatives or Simultaneous" (Heb.), in Moshe Arnon, Ruth Ben-Meir, and Gavriel Hayyim Cohen (eds.), *Pirkei Nehama: Memorial Volume for Nehama Leibowitz* (Jerusalem: The Jewish Agency of the Land of Israel, 2001), 279.

16. Of course, it is possible that neither is correct. Perhaps a solution exists to the outstanding difficulty with the correct reading, but it is not known to Rashi.

17. Examples are Shemuel Almosnino, *Rabbi Shemuel Almosnino on the Commentary of Rashi* (Heb.) (Petaḥ Tikva: Phillips, 1998); Jacob Kenizal, *Rabbi Jacob Kenizal on the Commentary of Rashi* (Heb.) (Petaḥ Tikvah: Phillips, 1998), first published together as part of *Commentaries on Rashi of Almosnino, Kenizal, Rabbi Aaron and el-Bilada* (Constantinople, 1524). See also Shapira, 277, who notes that Rabbi Charles Chavel, author of an important critical edition of Rashi's Torah commentary (*The Commentaries of Rashi on the Torah* (Heb.) (Jerusalem: Mosad HaRav Kook, 1982)), follows the same approach. Rabbi Shapira points out that "in every place, without exception, when *davar aḥer* appears in the words of Rashi", Chavel "explains which problem Rashi found with his first reading, such that he wrote the 'other explanation' in the course of his second reading".

18. Pinhas Doron, *Interpretation of Difficult Passages in Rashi (Genesis)* (Heb.) (No place given: no publisher given, 1985), 17.

reading), it follows that the solution that it offers to its part of Rashi's problem is also incomplete. As such, the true position is that two partial solutions exist; for each, it is unknown how the remaining difficulty could be resolved. Alternative readings are not just unconnected; each, in fact, excludes the other.

Treating Rashi's readings as simple alternatives is certainly the most obvious way to understand them, especially given the lack of internal support from his commentary for any other approach. Yet it is common for Rashi to offer two readings, one of which is generally more 'midrashic' – more distant from the plainest reading of the text – than the other. For Sarah Kamin this suggests that the more 'midrashic' of the two readings "resolves problems in the text that [Rashi's] plain reading does not interpret".[19] This approach, she continues, "sharpens" the problem, rather than resolves it, since it implies that the "midrashic reading provides a fuller reading of the verse than the plain reading" – in other words, the second reading is 'better' than the first. Yet if this is true, then the two readings are not really alternatives, since one effectively supersedes the other. Kamin is correct about this: for example, in A, the second, more midrashic reading of *elohim aḥerim* (gods that are 'other' to their worshippers) may be more distant from the plain meaning of the text than the first reading (gods according to others), but it explains better than the first reading why they are 'other'. As such, it is hard to see how the two readings can be considered legitimate alternatives: it is true that the second reading is still imperfect, but it is less imperfect than the first, ostensibly eliminating the need for the first altogether. And since the second reading is also 'weak' (albeit not as weak as the first), in that it fails to entirely resolve Rashi's original problem, then, in Rabbi Shapira's words, "Why isn't Rashi inclined to offer a second *davar aḥer*, a third, a fourth, a fifth? Do not we ourselves do so when we are stymied by a problem, whether in a biblical verse or in a unit of Talmud?"[20] Rabbi Shapira means that the lack of additional readings strongly indicates that Rashi assumes that the second, more midrashic reading *fully* answers the original problems. This questions the role of the first, less midrashic reading, which can no longer be considered an equal alternative to the second.

Yet it is not necessary to understand Rashi's multiple readings as alternatives; perhaps this complexity can be avoided by treating them instead as *concurrently* correct. By this I mean that the ambiguity or difficulty in a particular biblical phrase allows it to hold more than one meaning, in which case both of

19. Kamin, *Rashi's Exegetical Categorization*, 185.
20. Shapira, 292.

Rashi's readings reflect the divine Author's original intention. In the above examples, this would mean: In A, the 'other gods' are *both* gods of others *and* distant from those who worship them; in B, 'blood' refers *both* to the blood of Abel and his descendants, as well as to Abel's multiple wounds.

The distinction between reading Rashi's interpretations as concurrent or alternative is illustrated by the following example. At the burning bush, Moses asked God to select someone other than him as leader, but without identifying whom:

ויאמר בי אדני שלח נא ביד תשלח.

> [Moses] said: Oh Lord! Please send by the hand of the one whom You will send. (Ex. 4:13)

ביד מי שאתה רגיל לשלוח והוא אהרן.
ד"א ביד אחר שתרצה לשלוח שאין סופי להכניסם לארץ ולהיות גואלם לעתיד יש לך שלוחים הרבה.

> [Rashi's first reading:] By the hand of one whom You are accustomed to send – this is Aaron.
> [Rashi's second reading:] Another explanation: by the hand of another whom You will wish to send; I am not destined to take [the Israelites] into the Land and to be their redeemer; You have many agents.[21]

Alternative readings: Moses meant either Aaron or some other, unidentified leader, but not both. This is the interpretation adopted by *Maskil LeDavid*,[22] who notes that for Rashi's first reading to be correct, the text should have said "by the hand of one You have sent" (past tense), rather than "by the hand of one You will send", because Aaron had already been selected as a leader. However, the second reading, which preserves the future tense of *tishlaḥ*, is also problematic: even had Moses already been aware that he was not destined to lead the Israelites into the Land, it is unlikely that he would have sealed his fate by mentioning it in such an overt way. Neither reading completely fits the verse. Read as *alternatives*, Moses meant either Aaron *or* a future leader, *but not both*.

Concurrent readings: Moses meant both Aaron and another leader. It is as if Moses had said to God: instead of me, please choose Aaron, or another person;

21. Rashi, commentary ad loc.
22. *Maskil LeDavid*, 147.

both options were in his mind. The ambiguity allows a single phrase to convey both meanings. Alternatively, a looser concurrency may allow for the possibility that Moses said more than he consciously intended; with hindsight, both interpretations are true – that is, an unconscious and unintended second meaning of his words was played out as the story unfolded: while consciously he referred exclusively to Aaron, his words unconsciously also accommodated the possibility of any other divinely chosen leader. Read as concurrent options, Moses meant both Aaron and a future leader, either consciously or unconsciously.

Kamin asserts that Rashi's multiple readings are concurrently true: both are related to the content of the verse and are, in most cases, based on an unusual usage in the text.[23] She finds further support for a concurrent approach[24] in the supercommentaries on Rashi of Rabbi Simon Oshenberg (*Devek Tov*)[25] and Rabbi Isaac Jacob Horowitz (*Be'er Yitzḥak*).[26]

Kamin clarifies her position in the course of examining Rashi's multiple readings of the problematic phrase *ve'et ha nefesh asher asu beḤaran* – the souls that (Avram and Sarai) 'made' in Ḥaran.[27] She points out that, "according to our proposal, the two readings do not spring from *a problem* with the

---

23. Kamin, *Rashi's Exegetical Categorization*, 183.

24. Ibid. 198 n. 141.

25. Simon Oshenberg, *Devek Tov* (Venice, 1558, repr. Warsaw: Walden, 1914).

26. Isaac Jacob Horowitz, *Be'er Yitzḥak* (Lemberg: Ziss, 1873).

27. Gen. 12:5 and Rashi, commentary ad loc. The full verse reads:

> ויקח אברם את שרי אשתו ואת לוט בן אחיו ואת כל רכושם אשר רכשו ואת הנפש אשר עשו בחרן ויצאו ללכת ארצה כנען ויבאו ארצה כנען.
>
> Avram took Sarah his wife and Lot his brother's son and all their possessions that they had amassed and the souls that they had made in Ḥaran. They left to travel towards the land of Canaan; and they came to the land of Canaan.

Rashi comments on the phrase "the souls that they had made in Ḥaran":

> שהכניסן תחת כנפי השכינה אברהם מגייר את האנשים ושרה מגיירת הנשים ומעלה עליהם הכתוב כאלו עשאום... ופשוטו של מקרא עבדים ושפחות שקנו להם... לשון קונה וכונס.
>
> Whom they had brought beneath the shelter of the Divine Presence – Abraham converted the men and Sarah converted the women. Scripture considers it as though [Abraham and Sarah] had made them .... But the plain reading of Scripture is – slaves and maidservants that they had acquired for themselves ... a phrase of acquisition and bringing in.

Rashi is clearly troubled by the unusual usage of the verb *asu* (made) used with reference to souls. Furthermore, while, as he says, the simplest reading is as a reference to the acquisition of slaves, it is likely that slaves are actually included in the phrase *kol rekhusham* – all their possessions – requiring a different explanation for the 'making of souls' to avoid redundancy.

expression 'making souls', rather from *its selection*... Scripture's selection of a particular usage is not random, and the two readings together function to explain this selection" (my italics).[28] For Kamin, Rashi's question is, "Why was this unusual phrase chosen?" He answers with two readings of the phrase, as if to say, "The phrase is polysemic and was chosen by the divine Author in order to convey meanings A *and* B". The second reading neither supplants the first nor resolves problems that it created or leaves unresolved, as *Maskil LeDavid* claims; instead, it *adds* to the first reading. The second reading is required because the first does not offer enough information to justify the unusual phrase – this justification is only achieved by including the second reading. In this sense, the readings function together, as only when the two are taken together is the anomalous phrase justified. Kamin has, then, methodologically distinguished the two modes of reading Rashi: if alternatives, his comments are motivated by a problem with an unusual phrase; if concurrent, his motivation is to explain the very selection of that phrase. However, I think that this distinction is questionable: within either approach, there is a problem with the choice of phrase, which is either entirely redundant at a plain-text level, or could have been written in simpler language. What differs is not the problem, but the nature of the solution.

TWO CREATIVE ALTERNATIVE WAYS TO UNDERSTAND *DAVAR AḤER*

Thus far, I have considered two ways of understanding the relationship between Rashi's explanations – treating them as either concurrent or alternative readings. In this section I will briefly consider two further creative alternatives – simultaneous and explanatory organization.

Rabbi Amnon Shapira offers a fascinating variation on the concurrency model, in which he refers to Rashi's readings as simultaneous. While Kamin and her supporting supercommentaries make no attempt to connect the readings, Shapira insists that Rashi's multiple interpretations, particularly those in which he uses the phrase *davar aḥer,* exhibit what he calls a dualistic inclination.[29] He summarizes his view: "There exists underlying Rashi's 'double readings' an 'organic' perception within which there is an internal tension, which expresses a

28. Kamin, *Rashi's Exegetical Categorization*, 185.

29. Shapira, "Whether", 279; see also id., "Rashi's Multiple Readings: An Inclination to Dualism?" in Sarah Yefet (ed.), *Scripture Reflected in Its Commentators* (Jerusalem: Magnes Press, 1994), 288-311 (esp. 290).

general conceptual position, already found in *Ḥazal* (such as the opposite pairs of heaven and earth, holy and mundane, upper and lower)."[30]

Rabbi Shapira further clarifies that Rashi's double readings express an idea that "reflects a conceptual tension that is already found in Midrash and which is based on dual meanings in Scripture".[31] In short, his curious position is that Rashi offers two readings of a verse in order to teach the existence of "complementary or contradictory" pairs of ideas.[32] Because of this, Rabbi Shapira correctly points out that, in contrast to alternatives, concurrent readings are not 'weak' at all.[33] He is so convinced of this novel reading of Rashi that he suggests that, at least in some cases, "it is possible that Rashi doesn't see a real problem (in the text), but exploits the opportunity to articulate his fundamental dualistic perception".[34] Rabbi Shapira's suggestion is far-reaching (and far-fetched): while for Kamin, Rashi's readings at least respond to the selection of an anomalous phrase, Rashi himself may not have identified a problem in the text at all. In turn this means that, according to him, Rashi's interpretative goal is to find opportunities to teach dualistic ideas. This conflicts with all 'normative' readings of Rashi, which insist that he always seeks to identify and interpret a textual anomaly.

However, apart from the complete lack of internal evidence from Rashi for Rabbi Shapira's position, it is also imperilled by numerous examples of *davar aḥer* which do not support a dualistic reading.[35] It is further weakened by the existence of comments by Rashi that include three or more interpretations, despite Shapira's claim that there are always only two alternatives proposed by Rashi. To support his theory, Rabbi Shapira refers to double rather than multiple readings, and he explains away each additional reading in Rashi as "merely a variant of a previous [reading] or one that completes it".[36] This is artificial: there are clear cases where Rashi offers three *different* readings;[37] these problems seriously undermine Shapira's position.

Another distinctive approach to reading Rashi's *davar aḥer* appears in Rabbi Samuel Bornstein's *Shem MiShemuel*. Rabbi Bornstein's method is to

---

30. Shapira, "Whether", 280.
31. Ibid. 281.
32. Ibid.
33. Ibid. 285.
34. Ibid. 282. Oddly, Rabbi Shapira (ibid. 296) also says that he doesn't know the answer to the question, "When is Rashi satisfied with one reading of some problem in the verse and when does he resort to *davar aḥer*."
35. Examples are Rashi's commentary on Gen. 2:4 and Ex. 32:4.
36. Shapira, "Whether", 280.
37. Examples are Rashi's commentary on Gen 21:9 and Deut. 25:18.

explanatorily organize Rashi's readings. In this context organization (the arrangement of interpretations in some way that connects them) is a further subcategory of concurrency, since two of Rashi's readings that have been organized are obviously concurrently correct. However, while concurrently true interpretations need not be linked, Rabbi Bornstein asserts that they are connected: indeed for him it is an important objective to show that the views are related and to explain how. Two examples of his approach to Rashi follow.

A. *Pharaoh's attack*

> ופרעה הקריב וישאו בני ישראל את עיניהם והנה מצרים נסע אחריהם וייראו מאד ויצעקו בני ישראל אל ה׳.
>
> Pharaoh drew near. The Children of Israel lifted their eyes and behold – Egypt was journeying after them. They were very afraid and the Children of Israel cried to the Lord. (Ex. 14:10)
>
> נוסע אחריהם – בלב א׳ כאיש אחד.
> ד״א והנה מצרים נוסע אחריהם ראו שר של מצרים נוסע מן השמים לעזור למצרים.
>
> [Rashi's first reading:] Egypt was journeying after them – with one heart, like one man.
> [Rashi's second reading:] Another explanation: they saw that the guardian angel of Egypt was journeying from the heavens to help Egypt.[38]

Rashi is troubled by the anomalous singular verb *nasa* (journeying): in context, given that *ufaro hikriv* – Pharaoh drew near – appears in the singular, and all the verbs referring to the Israelites appear in the plural, the expected usage would have been the plural form: *nose'im*. Rashi's first reading preserves the narrative voice of the text: the Egyptians were single-minded in their pursuit of the Israelites; however, this forces the need for the words *nasa* and *Mitzrim* to concur by treating the latter as singular. His second reading preserves the grammatical agreement between the words, yet it warps the simple meaning of *Mitzrim* – Egyptians (plural) – into a reference to the guardian angel of Egypt (singular). Alternatively, *Maskil LeDavid* notes that, for Rashi's first reading to be correct, instead of "the Children of Israel lifted their eyes", the text should have said that they "turned their faces". However, in Rashi's second reading, for "Egypt" to refer to the "guardian angel of Egypt", the text should have read "journeying *upon* them"

38. Rashi, commentary on Ex. 14:10.

rather than "journeying *after* them".[39] As expected, *Maskil LeDavid* suggests no link between Rashi's two readings.

Shem MiShemuel attempts to organize Rashi's readings thus:

> It writes: and behold – Egypt was journeying after them, explained by Rashi as: with one heart, like one man. Ostensibly, this is incomprehensible, for were [the Egyptians] not discreet entities? From where did this capacity to unify come? It seems that this was due to the fact that the guardian angel of Egypt was journeying after them, as in Rashi's [second] explanation: they saw that the guardian angel of Egypt was journeying from the heavens to help Egypt. The two explanations need each other.[40]

In distinction to *Maskil LeDavid,* the understanding of *Shem MiShemuel* is that Rashi's readings explain one another: the Egyptians were able to unify (first reading) *because* their guardian angel was journeying to help them (second reading) – that is, *Shem MiShemuel* organizes the views explanatorily. This is what he means by saying that "the two explanations *need* each other" – they are interdependent in an explanatory way. That Rashi offers his second interpretation *in order to explain* the first is the hallmark of *Shem Mishemuel*'s interpretative approach.

---

39. *Maskil LeDavid,* 179. An alternative reconstruction of Rashi's thought-process is offered by the supercommentary on Rashi by Rabbi Meir Benjamin Menaḥem Danun, *Be'er BaSadeh* (Jerusalem: no publisher given, 1846), a disciple of Rabbi Pardo. Rabbi Danun suggests that Rashi's first reading – the Egyptians pursued the Israelites single-mindedly – is difficult to reconcile with the verb *nose'a* (journey): the text should have used *rodef* (pursue), which actually appears in the previous verse. According to Danun, Rashi responds to this difficulty with a second reading – the guardian angel of Egypt journeyed from the heavens to help the Egyptians. This explains the verb *nose'a* and also cleverly reinterprets the word *aḥareihem* (after them) to refer not to the Israelites but to the Egyptians – the angel of Egypt journeyed after the Egyptians to help them. However, Rabbi Danun points out that this second reading has two flaws: (1) the word Egyptians, as opposed to Egypt, does not appear in the verse, and (2) the claim that *aḥareihem* refers to Egyptians, rather than Israelites, is a distortion of the meaning of the text, something avoided by Rashi's first reading (Danun, *Be'er BaSadeh*, 91a).

40. *Shem MiShemuel* Ex. i. 231:

ונראה דהנה כתיב והנה מצרים נוסע אחריהם, וברש"י בלב אחד כאיש אחד. ולכאורה בלתי מובן הלוא הם ענפין מתפרדין מאין באה להם ההתאחדות. ונראה שזה הי' מפני שהשר של מצרים נסע אחריהם, כברש"י ד"א והנה מצרים נוסע אחריהם זה שר של מצרים נוסע מן השמים לעזור למצרים, ושני הפירושים צריכין זה לזה.

B. *Jacob's message to Esau*

> ויצו אתם לאמר כה תאמרון לאדני לעשו כה אמר עבדך יעקב עם לבן גרתי ואחר עד עתה.
>
> [Jacob] instructed them [the messengers] as follows: so shall you say to Esau my brother – thus says your servant Jacob: I have sojourned with Laban and I have delayed until now. (Gen. 32:5)

According to *Maskil LeDavid,*[41] Rashi is troubled by the appearance of these apparently redundant details in Jacob's communiqué to Esau – why did he find it necessary to mention his sojourn with Laban, which was extraneous to his attempt to make peace with Esau? Furthermore, the word *garti* – I have sojourned – is anomalous: it usually indicates temporary residency, something hardly reflected by the many years that Jacob lived with Laban:

> גרתי – לא נעשיתי שר וחשוב אלא גר אינך כדאי לשנוא אותי על ברכות אביך שברכני הוה גביר לאחיך שהרי לא נתקיימה בי.
> ד"א גרתי בגימטריא תרי"ג כלומר עם לבן הרשע גרתי ותרי"ג מצות שמרתי ולא למדתי ממעשיו הרעים.
>
> [Rashi's first reading:] I have sojourned – I have not become a prince or dignitary, rather [I remained] an alien. It is not appropriate for you to hate me regarding the blessings of your father, since I have not fulfilled his blessing: be more successful than your brother.[42]
> [Rashi's second reading:] Another explanation: *garti* has a numerical value of 613, as if to say, "I have sojourned with the wicked Laban, yet I observed the 613 commandments and I did not learn from his wicked deeds."[43]

Maskil LeDavid observes that Rashi's first explanation leaves the reader wondering about the relevance of the blessing to Esau's hatred for Jacob. Since the fulfilment of the blessing remained in God's gift in any case, and Jacob had tried everything, including trickery, to obtain it, Esau had sufficient reason to hate his brother, even if the blessing had not been fulfilled. As such, Rashi offers a second reading: Jacob informed Esau that he was not frightened of him because he was

41. *Maskil LeDavid,* 88.
42. Gen. 27:29.
43. Rashi, commentary ad loc.

confident that his personal righteousness would protect him.[44] However, this is refuted by the continuation of the biblical narrative, in which Jacob humbles himself before Esau. Once more, *Maskil LeDavid* views these readings as unconnected alternatives.

Again, *Shem MiShemuel* attempts to organize Rashi's readings:

> Rashi [comments]: I have sojourned with Laban – I have not become a prince or dignitary, rather [I remained] an alien, etc. Another explanation: I have observed the 613 commandments. It seems that the two explanations are dependent on each other and arise from one origin. The holy Zohar states that the souls of the righteous sojourn in this world; presumably this is because they constantly recall that [this world] is not their permanent place, rather [they are] like guests who pass from one place to another. As the sages say: prepare yourself in the anteroom so that you can enter the banqueting hall:[45] an anteroom is not a place of permanence and restfulness; rather, one passes through it en route to the banqueting hall. This is the meaning of "I have not become a prince or dignitary"; rather, I have remained an alien in my own eyes. This is synonymous with "I have observed the 613 commandments". It is certain that one whose ultimate objective is to experience the pleasures of this world will find the commandments to be a burden and he will collapse beneath his burden. In contrast, since I [Jacob] am like an alien in this world, as the ultimate objective is the next world, perforce it is simple for me to observe the 613 commandments.[46]

Shem Mishemuel asserts that Rashi's two readings are explanatorily linked – Jacob was able to observe the 613 commandments with ease (second reading) *because* he viewed life in this world as temporary (first reading): one is able to observe the *mitzvot* because one considers oneself to be an alien in this world.

---

44. *Maskil LeDavid,* loc. cit.

45. Mishna Avot 4:16.

46. *Shem MiShemuel,* Gen. ii. 37:

ברש״י עם לבן גרתי לא נעשיתי שר וחשוב אלא גר וכו׳, ד״א ותרי״ג מצוות שמרתי. נראה דשני הפירושים תלויים זה בזה ובקנה אחד עולים, כי איתא בספה״ק כי נשמות הצדיקים הם גרים בעוה״ז, ובפשיטות מפני שהם זוכרים תמיד שאין כאן מקום קביעותם אלא כאורח העובר ממקום למקום, וכאמרם ז״ל (אבות פ״ד) התקן עצמך בפרוזדור כדי שתכנס לטרקלין, שאין הפרוזדור מקום קבוע ומנוחה אלא שעוברין דרכו לטרקלין. וזהו לא נעשיתי שר וחשוב אלא גר בעיני עצמי, וזהו עצמו הוא שתרי״ג מצוות שמרתי, שבודאי מי שתכלית כוונתו להתענג בתענוגי עוה״ז המצוות הן עליו למשא ורובץ תחת משאו, אלא מחמת שהייתי כגר בעוה״ז ותכלית הכוונה היא עוה״ב, ע״כ נקל הי׳ בעיני לשמור תרי״ג המצוות.

While this is an attractive alternative to standard ways of understanding Rashi's multiple readings, there is no internal evidence whatever from Rashi's commentary to support it. In fact, Rabbi Bornstein himself offers only two other examples of this methodology.[47]

SUMMARY

I have shown that there is a range of ways to understand the relationship, if any, between Rashi's multiple readings of a biblical phrase. What I have termed alternative and concurrent approaches attribute to Rashi quite different interpretative agendas. The alternative approach assumes that he believed there to be a single correct reading of every scriptural phrase; where he cannot certainly identify that reading, he provides two or more mutually exclusive alternatives. In this model, uncertainty of meaning is a result of human interpretative deficiency or loss of tradition. The concurrent approach, on the other hand, assumes that he accepted that, while some scriptural phrases are monosemic, others are polysemic. Where he provides a single reading, he understood the phrase to be monosemic; where he provides more than one reading, he understood it to be polysemic – indeed, in the concurrency model, distinguishing between monosemic and polysemic phrases constitutes a core interpretative objective. In this model, uncertainty of meaning is a result of divine intent. I have shown that Rabbi Amnon Shapira's simultaneous model and the process of organizational explanation in *Shem MiShemuel* are variants on the concurrent approach.

Although Sarah Kamin adduces proof for concurrency from other works by Rashi, and Rabbi Shapira claims that it is the only logical option, it remains difficult to muster internal evidence from Rashi's Torah commentary for the concurrent approach. Indeed, as Rabbi Shapira indicates, the approach that treats the two readings as 'weak' alternatives, not concurrency, is the "accepted position in [interpreting] Rashi".[48]

47. Ibid. Deut., p. 23, commenting on Gen. 44:22; Ibid. Deut., p. 119, commenting on Deut. 18:3–8.
48. Shapira, "Whether", 279. Indeed, Rashi's use of *davar aḥer* to introduce his second interpretation strongly suggests that Rashi himself understands his readings to be simple alternatives.

VeZot HaTorah: The Origin and Objective of the *Hagbaha* Ritual

Rabbi Dr Jeffrey M. Cohen

It is a great privilege to have been invited to contribute to this volume, dedicated to the unique spiritual, communal, national, and academic contribution of Chief Rabbi Lord Sacks. Although the scope of his theological writing encompasses the entirety of our heritage, it is known that liturgy is particularly close to his heart, and that the acclaimed siddurim and *maḥzorim* that he has edited and annotated have brought him a considerable measure of fulfilment. In tribute to that particular aspect of his prolific contribution, and in appreciation of all his encouragement to me both in my rabbinate and in my own literary endeavours, I have chosen to present an analysis of the liturgical theme of the *hagbaha* ritual and its attendant "*VeZot HaTorah*" verse(s).

The origin and objective of the *hagbaha* ritual remain shrouded in mystery.[1] Daniel Sperber,[2] quoting the view first propounded by R. Nathan b. Judah

1. I wish to place on record my thanks to my friend Professor Stefan Reif, former director of the Taylor-Schechter Genizah Unit in Cambridge and authority on Jewish liturgy, for having read the draft of this article and for several most pertinent observations. I was especially encouraged by his belief that this article has "uncovered traces of an important liturgical development and raised valid questions as to its origins, its usage and its adjustment".
2. See D. Sperber, *Minhagei Yisra'el* (Jerusalem: Mosad HaRav Kuk, 1991), i. 78–81.

(fourteenth century) in his *Sefer HaMaḥkim*,[3] takes the view that, 'without doubt the *hagbaha* ritual goes back to the period of Ezra and Nehemiah'.[4] I do not accept, however, that the biblical event to which he refers provides any such precedence. That event was a festive, national convocation that took place 'on the first day of the seventh month' (Neh. 8:2), namely, Rosh Hashanah, to inaugurate the rededicated Temple. Ezra stood on a high platform (v. 5) to enable the vast crowd that had assembled for that unique occasion to see him, and, more importantly, to view the Torah from which he was reading. Considering that most of the Judaeans, who had long since defected from religious practice and intermarried – thus necessitating Ezra and Nehemiah's missions – might never have seen a Sefer Torah, it is not surprising that he felt obliged to raise up the scroll and exhibit it to the throng. It is also not surprising, therefore, that 'all the people stood up' to catch a view of it. To suggest that, in doing this, Ezra was enacting an already well-established *hagbaha* practice, associated with the reading of the Law in his own country of Babylon, would require evidence that we do not possess.

To view that special convocation as having created the precedent for our regular *hagbaha* practice would also beg the question of why the first reference to that ritual occurs only in the late talmudic Tractate Soferim, written over a thousand years later, having leapfrogged in silence over all the preceding talmudic literature. The fact that a talmudic tradition views the wooden platform upon which Ezra stood as symbolic of the Temple Mount is also indicative that he was not introducing to the Judaeans an established prayer-house ritual, as practised by the Babylonian community from which he hailed, but was merely adopting a practical method of addressing the assembled masses.[5] It thus provides no evidence for a pre-existent *hagbaha* ritual.

The custom of raising the Torah aloft, and displaying it to all sides of the synagogue while the congregation declaims the affirmation *vezot haTorah asher sam Moshe lifnei benei Yisrael* (Deut. 4:44), is problematic in several respects. I have dealt elsewhere with some of the problems raised by the second half of that declamation: *al pi Adonai beyad Moshe*.[6] That part-verse occurs in both Numbers 4:37 and Numbers 4:45, and, when grafted on to Deuteronomy 4:44, it serves to create a rather infelicitous and hybrid biblical verse. The appended part-verse

3. See *Sefer HaMaḥkim*, ed. Y. Freimann (Cracow, 1889), 127.
4. The precise dates of Ezra and Nehemiah's missions in Judaea remain in doubt. The present scholarly view places the date of the arrival of Ezra "in the seventh year of Artaxerxes" as around 458 BCE if the king is Artaxerxes I. The mission of Nehemiah is placed between 445 and 433 BCE.
5. See Sota 40b–41a; Yoma 69b.
6. See Jeffrey M. Cohen, "*Ve'zot ha-Torah*: A Liturgical Reassurance", *Judaism* (Fall 1991), 407–18.

is also devoid of contextual significance in that it derives from a section dealing exclusively with the census of the Levitical families conducted "according to the commandment of the Lord by the hand of Moses". This has absolutely no bearing upon the subject of the Torah to which the first part of the verse – a complete biblical verse – relates. Even more problematic, the new, composite version creates a superfluous repetition (*asher sam Moshe... beyad Moshe*) of the theme of Moses as agent of God's Law.

These problems were already raised by R. Yeḥiel Michael ben Aaron HaLevi Epstein (1829–1908), who dubbed them *kashe tuva*, "most problematic".[7] His son, R. Barukh HaLevi (1860–1942), goes further and notes the halakhic impropriety of creating such a hybrid verse which, he maintains, is in conflict with the talmudic principle of *kol pesuka dela paskeih Moshe anan la paskinan* (We may not end a verse at any place where Moses did not do so).[8] He interprets this prohibition to include the dividing up of a verse and the utilization of just one part of it. After stating the difficulties, he contents himself with the uncharacteristic admission: "I know not how to resolve all this."[9] It was resolved in a most straightforward way, however, by Isaac Luria and his school, by simply omitting the five words of the part-verse.[10]

R. Isaac Elijah Landau quotes an oral communication of R. Hayim of Volozhin which sets out to resolve the problem of the tautology created by the added part-verse. R. Hayim avers that, following on from the verse *vezot haTorah asher sam Moshe lifnei Benei Yisrael*, we should say, *al pi Adonai yaḥanu ve'al pi Adonai yisa'u, et mishmeret Adonai shamaru al pi Adonai beyad Moshe*, which is a complete verse in *Parashat Beha'alotekha* (Num. 9:23).[11] Not only does his suggestion leave the other problems unresolved, but we also have no evidence of that verse ever having been adopted into any official liturgical tradition or printed siddur.

The explanation I have offered elsewhere was that the added part-verse arose as a means of reassurance for those about to be called up to the Torah, who

7. See *Arukh HaShulḥan* (Tel Aviv, n. d.), vol. i, sec. 134:3, p. 233.
8. Berakhot 13b.
9. See *Barukh SheAmar* (Tel Aviv: Am Olam, 1979), 190.
10. See Isaac Elijah Landau's *Dover Shalom* commentary, published in *Siddur Otzar HaTefillot* (New York: Hebraica Press, 1966), 416; R. Samuel Vital (1598–1677), *Siddur Ḥemdat Yisrael* ("According to the intentions of the Arizal and edited by the *mekubbal* Rabbi Samuel Vital"), publ. Rabbi Hayim Eleazar Shapira (Mukacevo, 1901). See also sources quoted in *Tefillat Ḥayim*, ed. D. Reimer (Jerusalem: Tzeror HaHayim Publications, 2004), 107–8.
11. See *Siddur Otzar HaTefillot* (New York: Hebraica Press, 1966), 416.

might have been fearful of the *ayin hara* (evil eye) effect of being designated as one of a specific number of people called up to the Torah. It is not improbable that the more superstitious might well have viewed that head-count by the gabbai as partaking of the nature of a mini-census. I argued that the method devised to 'reassure' them of the permissibility of that exercise was to add a phrase from a context which describes how the Levitical families of Gershon, Kehat, and Merari were 'numbered' and 'selected' to undertake specific tasks in the Sanctuary, *al pi Adonai beyad Moshe.* The contextual message of the latter part-verse was that, if the counting and designation of people takes place in the Sanctuary – and, by extension, the synagogue – then there was no prohibition, and no danger of *ayin hara.*

But if that composite verse presents problems, the origin and purpose of the *hagbaha* ritual itself is even more problematic, especially within the Ashkenazi rite, which prescribes that it be performed after the reading of the Law has been completed. Having already spent so much time on the reading, with the various *keru'im* (those called up) having already affirmed, through their blessings, that this was the same Torah which God gave to His people, what further purpose could be served by the addition of that *post facto vezot haTorah* affirmation?

Surprisingly, neither Ismar Elbogen, who can be relied upon generally to provide an authoritative analysis of the sources and the stages of development of liturgical texts and rituals, nor the more popular writer, A. Z. Idelsohn, make any reference to the origin of *hagbaha* and the problems of the "*VeZot HaTorah*" verses.[12]

As mentioned, the first direct reference to the *hagbaha* ritual is found in the late talmudic Tractate Soferim (eighth century CE), compiled well before the Masoretic period when a concerted attempt was made to render the text of Torah scrolls uniform. The latter exercise reached its final stage of development in the tenth century with the publication of the respective codices of Aaron ben Asher in Tiberias and Ben Naphtali in Babylon, with the former generally regarded as the more authoritative tradition. We may assume that the description of *hagbaha* found in Soferim reflects the practices of Eretz Yisrael going back centuries.

In the period before Masoretic standardisation not only did copyists' inadvertent errors abound, but there was also much scope for conscious

12. See I. Elbogen, *HaTefilla BeYisrael* (transl. of the German original, *Der Jüdische Gottesdienst in Seiner Geschichtlichen Entwicklung*, Leipzig, 1913) (Tel Aviv: Dvir, 1972, 1988), 148; A. Z. Idelsohn, *Jewish Liturgy and its Development* (New York: Schocken Books, 1960 (1932)), 115.

tampering with the text by the various groups of sectarian dissidents who lived, cheek-by-jowl, together with the Jews and who were fixated on disseminating their theology among worshippers in the mainstream Judaean synagogues and academies.

The two primary sources of liturgical composition and inspiration during the first few centuries of the Common Era were the synagogues (*battei knesset*) and the academies of higher talmudic studies (*battei midrash*). The scholars would generally have prayed where they studied, in the *beit hamidrash.* There they created extempore prayers and praises of God and the Torah, to be recited both before and after offering their expositions. These were frequently related to the themes of their discourses.[13] We may assume that only members of the academy would have been invited to lead services there, so the fear of sectarian influence in that institution would have been minimal. The situation in the general public's institution of the *beit knesset,* on the other hand, would have been quite different. There it would not have been difficult for crypto-sectarians, posing as visiting scholars, to have infiltrated, and, when asked to lead a service or deliver a *derasha,* to have introduced their own dissident formulae, a situation to which the talmudic sages were particularly sensitive.

That early period was, as expected, characterized by a wide variation of liturgy from town to town and even from synagogue to synagogue. Unlike our contemporary situation, wherein most synagogues have full- or part-time rabbis or rabbis who are regular worshippers and who can be called upon for guidance on, or maintenance of, halakhic and liturgical propriety, the situation in the early period of the synagogue, when liturgical as well as halakhic principles were still being developed, was that many synagogues would have been founded, attended, and led by those who were fairly ignorant of such principles or even of the formulae of the basic prayers and biblical passages in general usage. It is in this way that we may understand the mishnaic denunciation of *battei knnesiyot shel ammei haaretz,* synagogues of the ignorant.[14]

---

13. See J. Heineman, *HaTefillah BiTkufat HaTanna'im VeHaAmora'im* (Jerusalem: Magnes Press, 1964), ch. 10.
14. Mishna Avot 3:14. This reference to *battei knesiyot shel ammei haaretz* has clearly mystified some of the classical commentators of the Mishna, who studiously avoid the literal translation, "synagogues of the ignorant", and understand it rather in the sense of "social gatherings of ignorant people". Hence *Tiferet Yisrael's* rather tortuous and unconvincing explanation that the phrase is a metaphor for a place of social relaxation and conversation. He explains that those who involve themselves in serious study need such relaxation for their minds in the same way that the body requires sleep or relaxation from its physical labours. Such social retreats are appropriate, he

Such a chaotic liturgical situation is also reflected in the incredible account of R. Eleazar Hisma (first–second centuries CE), who, when visiting another town, found himself unable to lead a service in its synagogue when called upon to do so:

> R. Eleazar visited a place. They invited him to lead the congregation in the recitation of the *Shema*, to which he replied, "I'm not competent." They then invited him to lead the recitation of the *Amida*, to which he gave the same reply. Worshippers then started to shout insults: "Is this really the R. Eleazar who is so widely acclaimed? He misrepresents himself as a Rabbi!" Deeply humiliated, he went to R. Akiva and related to him the experience. The latter asked, "Would you like me to teach it to you?" to which he responded, "Yes". So Akiva taught it to him.[15]

It is significant that the passage refers here to a rabbi who had gained a significant reputation as a scholar, with free access to the great master, Rabbi Akiva. The latter personally taught the relevant *nusaḥ* to him, and did not delegate such an apparently straightforward aspect of synagogue service to a young colleague cognizant with liturgical matters. This clearly reflects a situation wherein very few scholars could keep abreast of the variety of *nusḥaot* that existed at that time.

"According to a recent analysis by M. D. Swartz, mystics and non-mystics in the talmudic period had their own forms of prayer but did not shrink from borrowing elements of content and structure from each other",[16] and it is against that background that we may appreciate how difficult it was for uneducated worshippers – the majority – to identify any variation as a heretical intrusion. In such a climate we also understand why the sages of the period were so concerned about the gullibility of the masses; and hence

asserts, "for distinguished people from whose everyday conversation wise counsel may be derived (see Sukka 21b). However, in places where ignorant people gather socially [i.e. *battei knesiyot shel ammei haaretz*], to speak ill of others and to indulge in unseemly conversation – with neither God-fearing content nor ethical or moral sensibility – no relaxation of the mind is attained." It is clear that *Tiferet Yisrael* has ignored the literal sense of the term *battei knesiyot* (synagogues) and construed it as if it had stated, simply, *knesiyot*: social gatherings, assemblies, meetings. Rabbi Obadiah MiBartenura leaves his understanding of the phrase vague, commenting, merely, "where they assemble and idly chatter", which might or might not be a reference to synagogues.

15. Leviticus Rabba 23:4.
16. See S. C. Reif, *Judaism and Hebrew Prayer* (Cambridge University Press, 1993), 105.

the many talmudic references to the dangers of religious infiltration by sectarians (Sadducees, Essenes, etc.) and adherents of other faiths (Christians, Zoroastrians, Samaritans, etc.), and to the various measures that were taken to counter such infiltration.

The broad term to describe the objective of those polemical enactments was *lehotzi miyedei tzedukim*, "to frustrate the Sadducees". As this group constituted Judaism's first dissident movement, accounting for a most important and influential segment of the Judaean population, the name became synonymous with heresy of any kind.

Examples of the many prescriptions to deter the dissidents from praying with the community of the faithful included (a) the removal of the Decalogue from daily prayer in order to rebut the early Christian belief that it alone is invested with higher authority, having been revealed directly by God at Sinai, with the rest of the Torah being possessed of lesser authority on account of it having been mediated by human hand;[17] (b) the bold substitution of the biblical phrase *uvore ra* (who creates evil; Isaiah 45:7) with the liturgical version, *uvore et hakol* (who creates all things), in order to thwart the attempt of adherents of Persian dualism to find any support in Jewish prayer for their concept of two divine forces, one of good and the other of evil;[18] (c) the anti-Karaite introduction of Mishna "*Bameh Madlikin*" into the Friday eve service, as well as the prescription of a special blessing over the Sabbath lights in the geonic period;[19] (d) the several medieval synagogue hymns, such as "*Yigdal*", "*Elohai Neshama*", and "*Ein Keloheinu*", which, in polemical vein, overemphasize affirmations of the Jewish credo, with the clear objective of offering a rejection of the dualistic, Sadducean, Christian, or Karaite theologies.[20]

The New Testament widely chronicles the attempts of the early disciples to convert Jews, and the persuasiveness of such charismatic missionaries as Paul. The sages' denial of a place in the hereafter to those reading 'external

17. See Y Berakhot 1, fo. 3c.
18. Berakhot 11b. One may wonder why the dualists were not more than content with the 'proof' for their theology ostensibly offered by the biblical version itself, surely a far more authoritative citation than any liturgical quotation from it!
19. See N. Wieder, "*Berakha bilti yadua al keriat perek 'Bameh Madlikin'*", *Sinai*, 82 (Shevat – Adar 5738–1978), 218–21.
20. On prayer as a vehicle of polemic, see Jeffrey M. Cohen, *Blessed Are You* (New York: Jason Aronson, 1993), 46–8.

literature'[21] betrays the widespread dissemination of these works and the extent to which they had won such a very large readership. We may take it for granted, therefore, that those same authorities would have been equally concerned at the inevitable smuggling into synagogues of copies of deviant religious tracts. These would have taken the form of Torah sections and prophetic texts doctored by new-Christian *minim* (heretics, dissidents) and containing their Christological and/or messianic interpolations, and left for the unwary to read or study.

These crypto-sectarians, who, when asked to lead a service, had no qualms at weaving into their prayers heretical sentiments, on the evidence of the Mishna and Talmud, would most certainly have resorted to smuggling such texts into the synagogues. This explains the early interdiction against committing oral traditions,[22] including blessings and prayers,[23] to writing, out of fear of the infiltration of sectarian/Christian ideas.[24] This would also account for the rise of the Masoretic movement and the collation of laws relating to the writing of sacred scrolls, which culminated in the publication of Tractate Soferim.

In the light of the above I find it probable that the practice of raising the scroll aloft to display the text to the entire congregation originated already in the first few centuries CE, with the intention of enabling all worshippers to scan the text and satisfy themselves that an authentic version was about to be read to them,

---

21. See Mishna Sanhedrin 10:1. While the scope of the term 'external literature' is difficult to determine precisely, it is generally defined as "works written by heretics". These are explained as "works of Aristotle and his colleagues, and also includes the chronicles of the lives of idolatrous kings and songs of love and passion that contain no wisdom or benefit, but merely wastage of time" (Commentary of Obadiah MiBartenura ad loc.). What interests me particularly is the extent of the dissemination of such works in Judaea, thus providing a perspective for viewing the climate in which the ritual of raising aloft the Torah arose.
22. See Temura 14b; Gittin 60b; Y Megilla 4:1. These sources are supported by the fact that there is not a single reference anywhere in the Talmud to the existence in the academies of a written version of the Mishna. Where any doubt is raised as to a textual reading, the student is advised to consult a *tanna*. The prodigious memory of the latter professional enabled him to quote by heart from anywhere in the Bible, as well as any opinion aired or decision given in the *beit hamidrash*.
23. Shabbat 115b.
24. Precisely how long that prohibition against committing oral material to writing remained operative is a matter of scholarly debate, with the suggested *terminus ad quem* ranging from the period of the *savora'im* (early sixth century) to the eighth century, and with some scholars (such as S. C. Reif in private communication) arguing that it remained in force as late as the period of Sherira Gaon (tenth century).

and that no tampering with it had taken place. This was clearly in the spirit of the requirement of Tractate Soferim:

> After raising it aloft, the *magbia* must display the text, first to those standing on his right and his left side before turning it to show it to those in front and those behind him; for it is incumbent upon every worshipper, male and female, *that they see the wording*, bow and make the affirmation, *vezot haTorah asher sam Moshe lifnei Benei Yisrael...* or the verse *Torat Hashem temima meshivat nefesh* (Ps. 19:8).[25]

Significantly both these verses convey the key sentiment that the Torah being displayed is the traditional one (*asher sam Moshe*), and that it is *temima*, an accurate, unchanged version. It is also significant, and most rare, that women are specifically included in this ritualistic obligation – which underscores my theory that the objective of this ritual is a precaution against sectarian infiltration, a situation from which women would also require protection. I believe that Moses Naḥmanides (1194–1270), in his commentary on the verse "Cursed be he who does not confirm [*asher lo yakim*] the words of this law" (Deut. 27:26), provides support for this view:

> This verse is thus a summons to acknowledge the *mitzvot* in our hearts, to perceive them as true in our eyes and to believe that one who fulfils them will gain reward, and one who transgresses will be punished. Therefore, if one denies [the validity] of any single law, or if it appears to him as valueless, he is "accursed". However, if his transgression – such as the eating of pig or other detestable thing – was as a result of his inability to resist his passion, or if he did not make a Sukka or take a lulav purely as a result of laziness, he does not fall under this [accursed] denunciation. For the Torah does not state, *asher lo ya'ase* (He who does not *observe*), but, rather, *asher lo yakim*, "who does not confirm" (literally, raise up), in the sense of 'not upholding,' 'not affirming the truth and binding nature of, the Torah'. And this refers to *one who rebels through denial.*[26]

So the nuance of the term, and the symbolism of the act of, "raising up the words of the Torah", for Naḥmanides, suggests a public demonstration of the truth of

25. *Masekhet Soferim*, ed. M. Higger (New York: Debei-Rabbanan, 1937), 14:8 (p. 261). Emphasis mine.

26. My translation.

the Torah in the face of its detractors and deniers. This, in turn, leads him to elucidate an abstruse talmudic passage which he views as the underlying rationale of our ritual of *hagbaha*:

> In the Talmud Yerushalmi, Tractate Sota (7:4), I have seen the following comment on the verse "Cursed be he who does not 'raise up' the words of this Torah": Is there such a thing as a fallen Torah? R. Simeon b. Yakim [*sic!*] says, "This curse refers to a *ḥazan* who stands and carries aloft the scroll but does not hold it sufficiently firmly, with the result that it falls."[27] It appears to me, however, that it refers to a *ḥazan* who does not lift up the scroll to show its script to the congregation, as is expressly stated in Tractate Soferim. This is so that the text may be exhibited to the people standing to his right and left, before turning around to show it to those in front of and behind him; for it is incumbent upon all men and women to see the script and to bend and recite *vezot haTorah asher sam Moshe*, etc., *and that is our practice.*[28]

We have here clear evidence that, according to Naḥmanides, the *hagbaha* practice arose as an anti-heretical gesture. While his view, that it was a general measure of defiance to detractors and an affirmation of the Torah's 'elevated' truth, is not specifically in line with the thesis I have proposed, and does not explain why the Torah is displayed with the text exposed, and why the written text, rather than just the scroll, has to be seen by all around, it does confirm my basic theory and establishes the rationale of the ritual as a polemical gesture.

Rabbi Yaakov Lorberbaum of Lissa (1760–1832) observes that from the wording of the Soferim passage it is clear that the original practice was to do the *hagbaha* and *gelila* before the reading of the Torah, and he offers that as the reason why Joseph Karo, in his *Shulḥan Arukh*, places the section on *hagbaha* (*Oraḥ Ḥayim* 134) before that of *keri'at haTorah*.[29] This also supports my explanation of the objective of this *hagbaha* ritual; for there would be little purpose in people

27. See *Naḥlat Yaakov* commentary on Tractate Soferim, ad loc.
28. See *Perush HaRamban al HaTorah* (Jerusalem: Mosad Harav Kook, 1960) on Deut. 27:26. Emphasis mine.
29. Rabbi Shem Tov Gaguine (*Keter Shem Tov*, vols. i–ii, Jerusalem: Makhon Jak, 1998 (1934), p. 275) ingeniously, if unconvincingly, interprets this talmudic statement, that "there is a curse on a *ḥazan* who does not lift up the Torah", as proof for the authenticity of the Sephardi way of reading from the Torah, with the scroll in an upright position, as opposed to the Ashkenazi practice of having it horizontal on the reading desk. Had earlier Ashkenazi authorities entertained

checking to ascertain that they had an authentic version once they had already made their blessings and read from it. Surely, to remove any apprehension that they might be about to make a blessing over, and read from, an unacceptable text, it would have had to be exhibited and checked beforehand.

Rabbi Hayim Joseph David Azulai (1724–1806) makes the surprising assertion in his *Birkei Yosef* that the recitation of "*VeZot HaTorah*" is akin to a *davar shebikdusha* (the most sacred of liturgical genres, to which "*Barekhu*", *Kaddish*, and *Kedusha* belong, and which affirms God's paramount sanctity), and may be recited, therefore, even by one who is in the middle of the *Shema* section of the service.[30] Rabbi Jacob Emden (eighteenth century), in his *Siddur Beit Yaakov*, concurs, stating that "even if one is about to recite the *Amida*, *yafsik* – he should interrupt to view closely the Torah text."[31] While his view does not enjoy much halakhic support, it does serve to indicate the great importance attributed to this ritual, lending credence to my view that its theological significance goes to the very heart of the fight to assert the inviolability of the traditional text against the inroads of sectarianism.

Since, on the evidence of Tractate Soferim, the original custom was to perform *hagbaha* and to recite the "*VeZot HaTorah*" verse before the reading from the Torah, we need to explain why Ashkenazi tradition moved it to the end. We may speculate that, following the establishment of a standard Torah text, by the Ben Asher and Ben Naphtali schools of Masoretic activity, and the total separation of mainstream Jewry from its sectarian offshoots, there was no longer any need to perform that close examination of the text in advance of it being read. The result was that the "*VeZot HaTorah*" affirmation lost its immediacy and could therefore be moved to the end of the reading, where it served the purpose of acting as a kind of *hadran*, or farewell tribute, to the Torah. On Sabbaths and festivals, when a *haftara* was read, it would also serve as a demarcation, creating a transition from the most holy section of the Pentateuch to the less sacred and authoritative words of the prophets.

---

any thought that the statement could yield such an interpretation, however, they would hardly have risked such a curse!

30. See Hayim Joseph David Azulai, *Birkei Yosef*, sec. 67, n. 3, quoted in *Shaare Teshuva* on *Shulḥan Arukh, Oraḥ Ḥayim* 134:2, n. 6. Azulai refers to a situation where a latecomer is praying in an adjoining chamber of the synagogue, and is in the middle of the "*Emet Veyatziv*" blessing of the *Shema* when he observes *hagbaha* being performed in the synagogue. Azulai states that the man must interrupt that blessing in order to recite the "*VeZot HaTorah*" verse. See also *Entziklopedya Talmudit*, viii. 171.

31. See *Siddur Beit Yaakov* (Lemberg: D. Balaban Publ., 1904), 84 (sec. 21, end).

The now diminished significance of "*VeZot HaTorah*" explains why R. David Avudraham (fourteenth century), in his detailed section on the reading of the Law,[32] makes no reference to the recitation of the "*VeZot HaTorah*" verse or to the exhibiting of the Torah to those all around, stating merely that "the scroll is taken out, and, standing before the Ark, the *ḥazan* recites in a loud voice the verse '*Gadlu*' [Ps. 34:4] and raises the scroll upwards in his hands." This omission is put into context by a contemporary halakhist, R. Aaron HaKohen of Lunel, author of the *Orḥot Ḥayim*, who states categorically that many communities in his day no longer performed *hagbaha*.[33] The very weak and dubious rationale offered for this situation was that it was in order not to burden the community with having to stand up, or out of fear that the upraised Scroll might fall. Notwithstanding the latter authorities, and perhaps because of the weakness of the rationale offered for abandoning the ritual, it stubbornly retained its appeal. Thus, R. Jacob ben Samuel Hagiz reports that the Sephardi practice in Jerusalem at his time (mid-seventeenth century) was to take the open-wide scroll around the whole synagogue, to enable everyone to look at the text.[34]

I incline rather to the view that Avudraḥam's omission was in recognition of the fact that the threat of sectarianism had now passed and there was consequently no necessity for any such close examination of the text in order to detect scribal tampering.

It is conceivable that the silence on the part of the redactors of Tractate Soferim, as well as authorities and commentators down the ages, regarding the origin and objective of the *hagbaha* ritual, may have been occasioned not necessarily by their ignorance of its origin, but by a conscious and effective attempt at its suppression. For we would hardly have expected the creators of the ritual to have wished to publicize the fact that the authenticity or accuracy of their synagogue Torah texts was in doubt! Perhaps this explains why, at a later time, in Ashkenazi communities, it became the practice to perform *hagbaha* with the

32. *Umagbia hasefer beyado lemaala*. See *Avudraḥam HaShalem*, ed. S. Wertheimer (Jerusalem, 1963), 127.

33. See *Orḥot Ḥayim, Hilkhot Sheni VeḤamishi*, sec. 8. That Ashkenazi authorities should have been prepared to abandon a ritual specifically described in Tractate Soferim should not surprise us. This particular tractate, although included among the minor tractates of the Babylonian Talmud, was written in Eretz Yisrael and reflects its halakhic and liturgical traditions. It was never quoted by the Babylonian *geonim*, and, according to M. Higger, was unknown by them. See *Masekhet Soferim*, ed. M. Higger (New York: Debei-Rabbanan, 1937), 58.

34. See J. Hagiz, *Halakhot Ketanot*, sec. 255.

text facing towards the *magbia*, the one lifting it up, rather than, as originally, with that side exhibited to the worshippers to aid their examination of the text for any traces of sectarian tampering.

The main proponents of this new way of performing *hagbaha*, such as R. Joseph Colon (Maharik, d. 1480), claimed that it was more respectful to the text for the *magbia* to be facing towards it, a view strongly supported by the authoritative halakhist, R. Joel Sirkis. In his *Bayit Ḥadash* commentary on the *Tur* he states: "This is now the practice in far-flung Jewish communities, *ve'ein leshanot* – and we should not do otherwise."[35] The fact that he found it necessary to add this last caution suggests that there was still a measure of resistance to the innovation. Sirkis lived from 1561 to 1640, so we may conjecture that our present-day Ashkenazi way of holding the Torah, with the text facing the *magbia*, made its appearance around 1450 (the period of Maharik's authority), but did not become entrenched as the universally practised Ashkenazi method until at least the end of the life of Sirkis, namely, the latter decades of the seventeenth century.

Ruth Langer notes that, although the earliest preserved manuscripts of the Ashkenazi rite do refer, sporadically, to the recitation of the accompanying verses of the *hagbaha* ritual – "*VaYehi BiNeso'a*", "*Ki MiTsiyon*", "*Gadlu*", and "*Romemu*" – yet it took until the mid-sixteenth century for the printed prayer books to include the other attendant verse, "*Lekha Adonai HaGedula*", as well as the specific Tractate Soferim instructions that the Torah be lifted up and "*VeZot HaTorah*" be recited.[36] She views the addition of the latter verses in Ashkenazi tradition as part of an attempt during that century to dramatize the ritual of taking out the Torah and its ceremonious procession to the *bima* so that it came to represent and recreate the experience of standing at Sinai and receiving the Torah.

35. See *Baḥ* on *Tur* 147, s.v. *hagolel*.

36. Ruth Langer, "Sinai, Zion, and God in the Synagogue: Celebrating Torah in Ashkenaz", in ead. and Steven Fine (eds.), *Liturgy in the Life of the Synagogue: Studies in the History of Jewish Prayer* (Winona Lake, Ind.: Eisenbrauns, 2005), 139 n. 44. My thanks to Professor Reif for directing me to Ruth Langer's article.

A Talmudic Discourse on *Kevod Habriyot*

Rabbi Dr Alan Kimche

One of Lord Sacks' best-received works was entitled the 'Dignity of Difference.' In it, Rabbi Sacks explores the notion that all human beings are created in the image of God and are therefore worthy of respect; this idea has long been considered by *Ḥazal* to be of crucial importance in Jewish thought. In honour of Lord Sacks' retirement, I present a brief outline of their attitude to this fascinating concept.

This essay is a study of two conflicting *sugyot* – Berakhot 19b and Shevuot 30b – on the theme of *kavod habriyot*. I will show that the resolution of that conflict will yield a deeper understanding of the halakhic alternatives.

FIRST *SUGYA*: THE FORBIDDEN GARMENT

There is a biblical prohibition against wearing any item of clothing that contains a mixture of wool and linen fibres called *kilayim*, a generic biblical name given to several forms of forbidden mixtures, such as plant grafting, or *shatnez*, a unique word meaning fabric of wool and linen interwoven.[1] No reason for this prohibition is given in the biblical text, but in the event of a person realizing that an item of clothing does contain such a mixture, it must be removed without delay.

1. See Lev. 19:19 and Deut. 22:9–11.

Clearly the removal of clothing in public will cause embarrassment, and for the halakha to require it is seen as an infringement of human dignity; nevertheless, a ruling is given in the Talmud by the great *amora* Rav that this *kilayim* prohibition is of such halakhic severity that it is mandatory to comply with it despite personal embarrassment.[2] Rav's ruling is the focal point of our *sugya*.

The *sugya* opens as follows:

> R. Judah said in the name of Rav: a person who finds *kilayim* in an item of his clothing must remove it [immediately] even if he is in public [and disrobing in public will cause him embarrassment].
>
> What is the reason [that we will subject him to this embarrassment in order to fulfil the requirement of avoiding *kilayim* without delay]? "There is no wisdom, no understanding, and no counsel [which will prevail] against [the honour of] God."[3] Wherever there is [a situation which will create] a *ḥillul Hashem* [a desecration of God's honour] we give no respect [to human beings, even] to a scholar.

The Talmud has accepted that dignity is violated by requiring a person to disrobe in public, and this would ordinarily be inappropriate behaviour. There does exist a Torah idea which the Talmud will later label as *kevod habriyot* (human dignity) and which creates a halakhic consideration for the shame experienced by the person who is required to disrobe. However, when dignity comes into conflict with the biblical injunction against wearing forbidden cloth, *kevod habriyot* is of secondary importance. If we generalize this specific ruling, Rav states that halakhic obligations override loss of human dignity.

The rest of the *sugya* is dedicated to a talmudic debate that examines and analyses the scope of the halakhic principle of *kevod habriyot*, in order to find if there are other cases where it will have the weight to override halakha, as well as to define its scope and applicability.

Understanding the Strategy of the *Sugya*

Our passage in Berakhot 19a is a classic talmudic *sugya*, in which various earlier rulings are cited that appear to conflict with Rav's ruling. In each of the rulings presented, the *kevod habriyot* principle is attributed sufficient halakhic weight that it is able to override other halakhic requirements. Thus each ostensibly poses

2. Berakhot 19b.
3. Prov. 21:30.

a challenge to Rav. In the first three challenges, the Talmud finds solutions by adjustments within Rav's position; that *kevod habriyot* only overrides laws of rabbinic origin, and that the right to *kevod habriyot* can be waived where there is no actual loss of human dignity.

The fourth challenge: dignity and returning lost property

The simple meaning of the verses in Deuteronomy 22:1–3 is that there is a halakhic obligation placed on an individual to take responsibility for returning lost items to their owners. However, the Talmud presents a close analysis of the biblical text and derives from it that there are some exceptions to this rule, such as on the grounds of *kevod habriyot*:

> We have learnt [regarding the verse "You shall not see your brother's ox or his sheep lost"] "and ignore them". [In the biblical requirement to return lost property this phrase means that one should not ignore items of lost property, rather one should find the owner and return them to him. However, it is written in an elliptical manner to teach that] Sometimes you *are* allowed to ignore them [and not return them], and at other times you are not allowed to ignore them. [The ambiguity or awkwardness of the phrasing lends itself to this interpretation.] How is this [distinction applied]?

Three examples of situations in which it is permissible to ignore items of lost property are then given:

> If he is a kohen and he sees the lost property in a graveyard.
> If he is an elder of the community [and the item of lost property is of the kind which he is not accustomed to taking with him in public, a lost animal for example] and it is below his dignity to go in public carrying this item of lost property.
> If his time [spent on returning it] is more valuable than the value of the lost item. [Since the halakha requires the owner to compensate the finder for his time spent on returning the item, he would cause the owner to lose out financially.]

From the second of these examples emerges a principle that the biblical legislation to return lost items is waived because of the personal dignity of the elder. If it can be universalized, this constitutes a challenge to Rav.

The answer given thrice earlier, that we are only dealing with a rabbinic law, fails to resolve this problem, for the rule of lost property is unquestionably of biblical status. Eventually, the *sugya* redefines the scope of Rav's ruling, in turn emphasizing a new and important distinction within the categories of biblical law and the halakhic system:

> This [case of returning lost property] is an issue of monetary law [pertaining to loss and recovery of items of value], and we cannot deduce from it [a principle that would apply also in a different category of biblical law, which includes] matters that are ritually forbidden [such as the *shatnez* clothing mentioned by Rav].

With this new categorization the *sugya* has now significantly revised Rav's ruling. Initially we understood Rav to be saying that no single biblical law will be trumped by *kevod habriyot*, but now the Talmud has decided that his rule will not apply to biblical laws pertaining to monetary matters; rather, it is restricted exclusively to matters of ritual prohibitions.

Why differentiate between monetary and ritual law? This distinction is not explained in the Talmud itself, and it is left to post-talmudic commentators to suggest reasons for it. *Tosafot* writes that it is based on the following argument, reduced to seven steps:[4]

1. The biblical requirement to return lost property is predicated on the assumption that there is an owner who is asserting his ownership of this item, and there is a mitzva to restore it to him.
2. It is only the rights of the owner which are being protected by the biblical obligation to return the lost item. Should the object be ownerless, the obligation disappears.
3. In matters of material ownership the owner always has the option of waiving his proprietary rights (*meḥila*). In this case it means that he could render the lost item ownerless.
4. It follows that the biblical law which requires a person to return lost property can be neutralized by the owner relinquishing his rights to the object in

4. *Tosafot,* Shevuot 30b, s.v. *aval issura ein hokhma,* that monetary matters are more lenient than ritual issues since the owner can be *moḥel,* i.e. he can waive his ownership. R. Moses Sofer, *Responsa Ḥatam Sofer, Oraḥ Ḥayim* 37, suggests that the biblical law in lost property is that the Torah requires the owner to waive his ownership rather than cause a loss of *kevod habriyot.*

question. Indeed, elsewhere the Talmud has a lengthy discussion regarding cases where a lost item need not be returned since we assume the owner has reached a mental stage of *ye'ush* – that is, he has given up any hope of finding the item; these cases are therefore legally equivalent to those of *meḥila*.[5]

5. If the owner has not relinquished his ownership, a rabbinical court has the mandate to exercise the waiver mechanism on behalf of the owner when they deem it necessary.[6]
6. Where the returning of a lost item will cause the finder a loss of dignity, the *kevod habriyot* principle is sufficient for the rabbinical authorities acting in their legislative capacity to utilize these powers and declare the lost item ownerless, thereby neutralizing the biblical obligation.
7. Thus, when we find that the law about lost property is overridden by *kevod habriyot*, it is not really an example of one law overriding another, but rather of the power of the rabbinic court to withdraw all ownership rights from the lost item, and it is this that renders the biblical law inoperative in our case.

An alternative explanation for this differentiation between monetary and ritual law is found in the commentary of Meiri, where the argument runs like this:[7]

1. The Talmud rules that if a person has to choose between recovering his own lost property or that of another person, even if it is his father's or his teacher's, he is allowed to give priority to his own.
2. It follows that no one is required to lose his own property in order to save the property of another person.
3. We have no greater regard for a person's money than for a person's dignity.
4. It follows that no one is required to lose his dignity in order to save the material belongings of another person.[8]

We could at this point in the *sugya* restate Rav's ruling as follows: *kevod habriyot* cannot override biblical law, but it will override (a) all rabbinic law, and also (b) all biblical requirements in monetary matters.

The *sugya* now offers a final challenge to Rav.

---

5. See Bava Metzia 23a.
6. Generally referred to as *hefker bet din hefker*, which is based on the prerogative of a rabbinic court to confiscate property when it sees fit to do so.
7. R. Menaḥem Meiri, *Beit HaBeḥira*, commentary on Berakhot 19b.
8. R. Jacob Joshua Falk, *Penei Yehoshua*, commentary on Berakhot 19b.

The fifth challenge: the met mitzva

The *sugya* here assumes that all matters connected to the treatment and burial of a corpse fall under the halakhic category of *kevod habriyot*. The text cited by the narrator of the *sugya* considers a case where the person is en route to perform a biblical command and comes upon a *met mitzva*. If he stops to attend to its burial he will lose the opportunity to fulfil the biblical command, and the question arises as to which takes precedence.

The final stage of the *sugya* attempts to refute Rav by applying the following line of thought: If it is true that the *met mitzva* is an instance of the *kevod habriyot* principle to preserve the dignity of the corpse, and the obligation to attend to the *met mitzva* overrides the other biblical obligation that he is now not going to be able to perform, then it follows that we have a ruling which states that *kevod habriyot* does have the power to override biblical law – a counterexample to Rav's position.

Hence important biblical requirements, such as circumcision of one's son on the eighth day or bringing the paschal lamb on the day before Passover, are overridden by the *kevod habriyot* requirement to bury the dead:

> Why is this so [i.e. that the abandoned corpse is given priority over a biblical requirement on account of human dignity considerations]? Surely [according to the ruling of Rav] we should apply the principle that "there is no wisdom or understanding or counsel [which will prevail] against [the honour of] God" [and give priority to biblical law over *kevod habriyot*]?

The *sugya* once more finds a conceptual distinction which will defend Rav but in the process will further limit his position:

> These [the cases of neglecting the paschal sacrifice or the circumcision, in order to bury the dead] are instances of passive violation of a biblical law, and we cannot deduce from them a principle [regarding the halakhic 'weight' of *kevod habriyot*] that would apply in matters that require an active violation of biblical law [such as the wearing of mixed wool and linen in Rav's original case].

The Talmud has further diminished the scope of Rav's ruling by introducing a categorization of talmudic law which is new to this *sugya*, but appears in several other places in the Talmud. The general rule is that active violations of the halakha are of significantly greater severity than passive non-observance. The final version of Rav's ruling would therefore read:

Kevod habriyot will override
(a) all rabbinical law;
(b) all biblical laws in monetary matters; and
(c) all other cases where ritual biblical law is violated passively.

THE SECOND *SUGYA*: THE TESTIMONY OF A SCHOLAR

Jewish law rules that a witness who has information that could assist in a court case is obligated to come forward and give that testimony.[9] When the Talmud discusses these laws in the fourth chapter of Tractate Shevuot, it looks at various cases that may be exceptions to this law. In this context the following ruling is given:

> Rabba bar R. Huna said:[10] If a Torah scholar is aware of testimony [which could assist a litigant in his court case] but it is demeaning for him to go to a court [and stand before judges] who are less [prestigious and knowledgeable] than him and testify before them, he need not go[11] [considerations of *kevod habriyot* would exempt him from this requirement, as it would not be fitting for his honour to do so].[12]

The conditions of this case are such that a person is halakhically required to do something which in itself is not a demeaning or embarrassing act; it is only a blow to the person's dignity given his particular social relationship to others.

The narrator of the Talmud then qualifies our initial ruling, limiting the exemption of the senior scholar to only some types of cases:

> This [principle giving priority to the value of the scholar's dignity over his obligation to testify] applies in [only a court case considering] monetary matters, but in matters of prohibition [i.e. a court case deciding whether an item or a person is subject to any laws of halakhic prohibition] "there is no wisdom or understanding or counsel against God" [and he

9. Lev. 5:1, Bava Kamma 55b, *Mishne Torah, Hil. Edut* 1:1.
10. Babylonian *amora* of the third century CE, son of R. Huna, and head of the academy in Sura.
11. R. Yom Tov Ishbili (Ritba, Spain, fourteenth century) rules that he must not go, even if he is willing to do so, because it undermines the honour of the Torah (*levazzot torato*). However, Maimonides rules (*MT Hil. Gezelah* 11:17) that the scholar is allowed to waive his honour and return the lost item if he wishes to go beyond the letter of the law, and presumably would rule likewise here.
12. Shevuot 30b.

> must testify to prevent the court from permitting something prohibited, because] wherever there is [a potential] desecration of God's name, we do not give respect to a scholar.

This conclusion leaves us with the ruling that indeed the scholar is not exempted from testifying in cases which have a bearing on items of halakhic restriction and prohibition. In those cases he must swallow his pride and present himself to the junior court.

However, when this ruling in Shevuot is compared to our first *sugya* analysing the ruling of Rav,[13] an important contradiction becomes apparent.

The Point of Conflict between Berakhot and Shevuot

As the fifth and final challenge to Rav's ruling, the Talmud in our first *sugya* cited a *baraita* in Tractate Nazir that discussed the case of a person who was on his way to perform an essential mitzva, either to perform the biblical commandment of the paschal lamb or to arrange for the circumcision of his son. These are both positive *mitzvot* of the highest order, with severe penalties for one who fails to perform them.[14] Nevertheless the Talmud assigns priority to the burial of a human corpse one encounters because it is a violation of human dignity to leave it unburied.

The text concludes that this is because they are both cases where *kevod habriyot* permits a person to fail to perform an obligatory commandment, as opposed to someone who is committing a forbidden act. Therefore our first *sugya* concludes that *kevod habriyot* will override only a *passive* violation of a biblical law, that is, failing to do a biblical requirement, but not an *active* one, such as the wearing of *shatnez* in Rav's ruling.

Turning now to our second *sugya*, we find that the Talmud requires the senior scholar in question to compromise his dignity and give testimony in a junior court. This is mandated in order not to violate the prohibition of failing to testify in a case where one has information for the court, which *kevod habriyot* cannot override.

But why is that? Surely this scholar would only be in passive violation of biblical law if he failed to testify, and according to the first *sugya*, the *kevod habriyot* principle should be sufficient reason to override his obligation to testify.

---

13. Berakhot 19b.
14. Rashi on ibid. highlights the status of both these obligations, the failure to perform them being punishable by *karet* (excision).

The answer to this question would seem to have numerous practical ramifications in halakhic rulings. Much of Judaism requires the fulfilment of commandments that require positive action, such as prayer, tallit and tefillin, the matza of Passover and the sukka of Sukkot, the shofar of Rosh Hashana, care for the elderly or for one's parents, and the like. None of these constitute *issurim*, where an action or an item is forbidden; therefore, violation of these *mitzvot* will generally be of a passive non-performance type. If circumstances are such that the performance of any of these *mitzvot* will require a person to behave in a way which compromises his dignity by being embarrassed or humiliated in some way, is one permitted to ignore the commandment and preserve one's dignity? The first sugya will answer in the affirmative, but the second will require one to go ahead with the mitzva irrespective of personal honour.

RESOLVING THE DISPUTE BETWEEN THE TWO *SUGYOT*

Tosafot

Tosafot suggests two solutions to our problem: (1) The Talmud differentiates between degrees of loss of dignity. A major loss of dignity is the subject of the first *sugya* and includes gross instances of shame such as having to disrobe in public, as well as leaving a corpse unburied. In such cases of extreme loss of dignity, *kevod habriyot* will override (passively) even biblical violations. But in the Shevuot case (our second *sugya*), having to testify in front of a lesser court is loss of dignity of a lesser magnitude and considered a minor loss, and insufficient grounds for biblical law to be waived even in a passive mode. (2) In the second *sugya*, if the scholar fails to testify it may well cause someone else to actively violate a prohibition, on account of the court giving an incorrect ruling. This is a more severe violation than an ordinary passive breach of halakha, since his failure to testify will be a direct cause of another person's active violation.[15]

The first solution offered by *Tosafot* draws on the intuitively obvious idea that infringements of personal dignity should not be seen as one monolithic category. Some situations are only a minor embarrassment, 'soft' cases of loss of dignity, which could be absorbed by most people as part of their general life experience. In other cases, however, of 'hard' violation of *kevod habriyot*, the humiliation will be of such deep consequences that it could create a trauma for the person concerned. The first *sugya* deals with the latter type when it states that *kevod habriyot* can override passive biblical violations, while the second deals with the former when it says that *kevod habriyot* does not override any biblical laws, and therefore there is no contradiction.

15. Shevuot 30b, s.v. *aval issura ein hokhma*.

In the second solution, however, this is not so obvious. *Tosafot* accepts the talmudic distinction between passive and active violations of halakha as stated in our first *sugya*, but a new area of scope is added to the active–passive distinction. *Tosafot* here states that before we can categorize any act as being truly passive and subject to being trumped by the *kevod habriyot* principle, we need to look beyond the act itself and assess its consequences for others. If we can find a causal connection between a passive omission by person A and an active violation of halakha by person B, then A can no longer be considered merely passive. Therefore, if we can identify an active violation taking place even vicariously by a third party, it will be sufficient for the principle of *kevod habriyot* to lose its power to override the biblical law.[16]

For purposes of illustration, using the scenario of the second *sugya* as an example, consider the case of a court that is hearing evidence regarding the personal status of a woman.[17] The court must determine if she is a widow and therefore allowed to remarry, or if her husband is still alive elsewhere and she is still married and thus forbidden to marry another man. On the basis of evidence available the court is set to decide that the husband died aboard a ship that sank, and that consequently she is now marriageable. A senior scholar, however, has evidence indicating that the husband survived the accident and is alive elsewhere – but in the case in question it is below his dignity to testify and be cross-examined by a junior court.

If we allow this scholar to avoid appearing before the court, it is true that he will only be passively violating the biblical requirement to testify, and if we follow the rule that *kevod habriyot* allows passive violations of this kind, we must conclude that he need not testify. But consider the consequences. Without his evidence the court will permit a married woman to 'remarry', and his failure to testify will cause her to be in active violation of the adultery prohibition, albeit unintentionally. In the second solution, *Tosafot* suggests that it is this causal link to the consequences of one's passivity that makes the difference.

16. *Noda BiYehuda, Oraḥ Ḥayim* 35 (quoted and analysed by R. Jacob Kanievsky (Steipler Gaon), *Kehillot Yaakov, Shevuot* ch. 26), connects this idea of vicarious activity to the dispute between Maimonides and Asheri regarding the removal of *shatnez* from another person even though it causes a loss of dignity. Maimonides' view would follow the thesis of the second solution proposed by *Tosafot*, and he rules that even the active violation of another person is sufficient to trump *kevod habriyot*. Rosh/Asheri, on the other hand, state that if the other person is unaware, the principle of *kevod habriyot* will override the requirement to tell him, since it is only passive on the part of the one person and the active element is only vicarious.
17. This is Rashi's illustration, ibid., s.v. *aval kulhu*.

An analysis of this line of argument requires a description of the basic talmudic concept of collective responsibility, *arevut*.[18] This principle establishes that any individual who could prevent another person from any misdeed and fails to do so is personally liable as an accomplice to the misdeed that was committed. The Talmud states:

> Rav and R. Hanina and R. Johanan said: Anyone who could protest against [the behaviour of] a member of his household [to prevent them from violating the halakha] and fails to do so is implicated in their sin. Similarly one who could protest against the [behaviour of] the people of his city [such as a leader or a king who is feared and obeyed[19]] or the entire world [and could prevent them all from sin, is implicated in all their misdeeds].[20]

This statement of collective liability is seen as an application of the more general notion of national interconnectedness expressed in the dictum *kol Yisrael arevim zeh bezeh*,[21] all of Israel are morally connected to each other.[22]

Rabbenu Ḥananel

An alternative way to resolve these two conflicting statements of the Talmud is presented by the *Arukh*,[23] in the name of Rabbenu Ḥananel.[24] This approach gives a different analysis of our first *sugya*. According to this view, the only reason that the Talmud gave priority to *kevod habriyot* over the requirement to bring the paschal lamb or circumcise one's son is that these are *mitzvot* of a particular type.

---

18. R. Elḥanan Wasserman (20th-c. Lithuania), *Kovets He'arot* 48:10 and 69:30. See also his *Kuntres Divrei Soferim* 3:28 and *Kovets Shiurim*, Gittin 26.
19. Rashi ad loc.
20. Shabbat 54b.
21. Shevuot 39a.
22. Wasserman, *Kovets He'arot* 48:10 and 69:30. Also see R. Judah Loew (Maharal of Prague, 16th c.), *Netivot Olam, Netiv Tokhaha* ch. 2, who connects the collective liability principle to the principle of national interconnectedness. In the *mussar* ethical literature see R. Jonah Gerondi, *Shaarei Teshuva* no. 195, and the anonymous *Orḥot Tzaddikim* 24:6, who explain that *kol Yisrael arevim* dictates a collective responsibility for the misdeeds of others.
23. Halakhic compilation/dictionary by R. Nathan ben Yeḥiel (11th-c. Italy).
24. Rabbenu Ḥananel b. Ḥushiel (d. 1053, Kairouan, Tunisia, probably of Italian origin) was considered the *resh rabbanan*, head of the leading rabbinical academy of Oriental Judaism (a term originally restricted to the heads of the Babylonian academies). A disciple by correspondence of Ḥai Gaon, whom he often cites, Ḥananel's commentary on the Talmud is seen as one of the most important sources of the views of the Babylonian *geonim*. R. Isaac Alfasi (Rif) incorporates much material from him in his *Sefer HaHalakhot*, one of the main pillars of normative halakha.

In both cases there is a set time in which to fulfil the mitzva and by attending to the burial the person involved will miss the correct time. However, in both cases, if one fails to comply within the correct time the mitzva can still be performed – albeit not in its ideal manner – at a later date. Therefore our first *sugya* rules that only in these cases does *kevod habriyot* have priority; in all other types of commandments, which cannot be done at a later point, one cannot use *kevod habriyot* to override a biblical requirement at all, and that is consistent with both *sugyot*.

This analysis contributes a new definition to the halakha. Even if we follow a view which is more restrictive of *kevod habriyot*, the power of the principle is still sufficient to allow for the passive postponement of the fulfilment of a biblical law, but not for its cancellation.

SUMMARY

In the pages above we have looked at the two main talmudic discussions which deal with human dignity and found that

1. both assert that *kevod habriyot* functions as a halakhic principle with wide applicability;
2. in both *sugyot kevod habriyot* overrides rabbinic law, but
3. neither gives the grounding for the principle itself;
4. they differ only in the question of whether *kevod habriyot* can trump a passive violation of a biblical commandment. To this the first *sugya* (Berakhot) answers in the affirmative, and therefore has the stronger version of *kevod habriyot* than the second *sugya* (Shevuot).

Tosafot and Rabbenu Ḥananel both found ways to resolve the disputed *sugyot*, and by doing so they introduced new distinctions into the halakhic system. Moreover, *Tosafot* preserved the conclusion of the first *sugya* as a halakhic principle allowing *kevod habriyot* to trump a biblical commandment passively, but only when there is a major loss of dignity.

Later practical halakhic rulings mainly followed the view of *Tosafot* that human dignity will override even a biblical commandment provided that (a) it is violated only passively, and (b) the violation occurs in order to save a person from a major loss of human dignity, not merely a minor embarrassment.[25] This is of some interest since it forms a significant leniency which will set aside a biblical requirement in specific conditions.

25. R. Abraham Gombiner (seventeenth century, Poland), *Magen Avraham* on *Shulḥan Arukh, Oraḥ Ḥayim* 13:3, n. 8

Should Jews Buy German Products?

Rabbi Mendel Cohen

On Purim 2013 there was fantastic video footage burgeoning on social media, taken from archival Purim clips filmed in Tel Aviv during the 1920s and 1930s. In those years the city hosted an annual Purim '*Adloyada*' street party.[1] It featured then-mayor Meir Dizengoff leading the carnival on a horse, with the Brit Trumpeldor Orchestra playing national tunes. Anyone who owned a piano was asked to play it as close as possible to their balconies, to add to the party atmosphere.

In 1933, during the Nazi threat, signs cried out: "Jews: Reject all German-made merchandise!" as the parade displayed a float of swastika guns threatening world peace. While the world did not heed their chanting at the time, the raw emotions surrounding the question whether one should buy German goods resurfaced in the post-war period.

As a child I befriended a wonderful older gentleman, Mr Katz, who had lost most of his family in the war. He once told me in his strong European accent: "I would never buy a German product." But my mother would only buy a BOSCH

1. A *jeu de mots* on the talmudic dictum (Megilla 7b): "Rabba said: It is the duty of a man to mellow himself [with wine] on Purim, *ad delo yada*, until he cannot tell the difference between 'cursed be Haman' and 'blessed be Mordecai.'"

washing machine (mind you, I can't blame her, with the amount of laundry her ten children produced). My mother's mother had also lost her parents and most of her family in the Holocaust. In this essay I seek to clarify the Torah and halakhic perspective on purchasing German goods,[2] looking specifically at the opinions of the Lubavitcher Rebbe and Rabbi Soloveitchik, two major influences on the thought of the Chief Rabbi, which makes this a fitting piece for a volume honouring Lord Sacks.

CONTRASTING VIEWS

As with so many questions pertaining to Torah and halakha, there is debate and differing views on this matter. By way of introduction two very different rabbinic attitudes may be presented. Rabbi Binyamin Silber takes a highly dismissive position, published in his responsa *Az Nidberu*:

> There is no prohibition or *ḥerem* [ban] against purchasing German-manufactured products more than any other nation's. And to those who suggest tradition states that there was such a ban put on Spain, this would not apply to Germany. To those who say there was definitely such a ban on Spain, the ban was primarily against living there, and that was because of the forced conversions, as many could not withstand the pressure. Heaven forbid, we should not write new Torah laws, suggesting that this is included in the commandment of obliterating Amalek's memory, for until the arrival of Shiloh [Messiah] we are not privy as to who is an authentic Amalekite. So there is no place for such stringency, and those who so claim rely on arguments of 'conscience'.[3]

Rabbi Yohanan Sofer Merloy, on the other hand, formulates a categorical prohibition, comparing Germany to Amalek, the infamous chronic enemy of Israel:

> Our holy Torah writes: "Remember what the Amalekites did to you … how he happened upon you on the way…. You shall not forget!" I think the same commandment can be taught, without a doubt, as a definite obligation to remember what the evil Germans did to the Jews, gathering

2. This essay is based on a lecture by my teacher, Rabbi Chaim Rapaport.
3. Vol. ii, ch. 77 (Benei Berak 5730/1970). Rabbi Silber, a major halakhic authority, passed away in 2008 at age 102. He had authored fourteen volumes of responsa, entitled *Az Nidberu*, and a number of books on halakha.

> Jews in all European countries where they had taken control.... We are obliged to remember and need to place a *ḥerem* on goods manufactured in Germany, not to purchase or use anything manufactured in Germany".[4]

While the two represent diametrically opposing views – Rabbi Silber sees no place for a ban and the Erlau Rebbe forbids purchase and even use of German products – both, interestingly, make reference to Amalek.

THE COMMANDMENT TO WIPE OUT AMALEK

When the Israelites left Egypt, no nation dared pick a fight with them. Who would take on a people whose God had just crushed the mighty Egypt with ten awesome plagues, and drowned the surviving few in the sea? Only Amalek, driven by profound hatred which defied logic, came to wage battle. God therefore commanded Moses and the Jewish people – twice, in fact[5] – to obliterate their memory. Later King Saul was reprimanded for not killing Amalek.[6] Haman was a descendant of Agag, the king of Amalek.[7] Similarly, all those who have made it their mission to annihilate Israel have been compared to Amalek.

Maimonides, in his *Laws of Kings and their Wars*, clarifies this mitzva: "It is a positive commandment to annihilate the seven nations who dwelled in Eretz Yisrael, as Deuteronomy states: 'You shall utterly destroy them.' Anyone who chances upon one of them and does not kill him violates a negative commandment as (ibid. 16) states: 'Do not allow a soul to live.' Their memory has already been forgotten."[8] Rabbi David Ibn Zimra (Radbaz) explains: "Because Sanḥerib [king of Assyria] came and muddled the world. Therefore we no longer know the true identity of the seven nations. Hence the obligation is no longer effective."[9]

---

4. Rabbi Sofer Merloy is a Holocaust survivor (b. Hungary 1923), the current *rebbe* of the Erlau dynasty, and a descendant of the famed Sofer family. He made the above statement as recently as 12 May 2012.
5. *Beshalaḥ*, *Ki Tetze*.
6. 1 Sam. 15:18–19.
7. In the book of Esther (3:1) his lineage is given when he is called "Haman the son of Hamdata the Agagite".
8. *Mishne Torah, Laws of Kings and Their Wars*, 5:4–5.
9. Based on Mishna Yadayim 4.

However, in the following law, speaking of the commandment to wipe out Amalek, no such qualification is made:

> Similarly, it is a positive commandment to destroy the memory of Amalek, as Deuteronomy states: "Obliterate the memory of Amalek." It is also a positive commandment to constantly remember their evil deeds and their ambush of Israel to arouse our hatred of them, as ibid. 17 states: "Remember what Amalek did to you." The Oral Tradition teaches: "Remember" – with your mouths; "Do not forget" – in your hearts. For it is forbidden to forget our hatred and enmity for them.[10]

The simple question arises why Maimonides makes no mention of Amalek's memory being lost in the confusion associated with Sanḥerib, implying that this commandment is still in force. What would be the difference?[11] If civilization has moved around enough for the seven 'evil' nations to have become unidentifiable, certainly the same would hold for Amalek too?

RABBI SOLOVEITCHIK'S APPROACH

Rabbi Joseph B. Soloveitchik suggests an innovative interpretation: just as the seven nations are no longer identifiable nor is the offspring of Amalek. However, others, non-descendants, can take on the Amalek identity. Rabbi Soloveitchik therefore says that Germany constitutes Amalek, and all directives associated with this commandment must be applied to them as well. According to his reasoning, Amalek is not merely kinfolk and descendants of the original tribe but a status.

Rabbi M. Sorkin, a disciple of Rabbi Soloveitchik, explains: "But I once heard from the mouth of my father my teacher Reb Meir [Soloveitchik], that any nation that pursues the Jewish people with the intention to annihilate them takes on the halakhic character of Amalek."[12] Rabbi Sorkin clarifies:

> With reference to the law of wiping out Amalek: we were commanded two objectives, first to wipe out the memory of Amalek, as it is written

10. *Mishne Torah, Laws of Kings and Their Wars,* 5:4–5.
11. Based on n. 8 above, one might conjecture that when the Messiah comes they would be re-identified.
12. *Harerei Kedem* (Jerusalem 2010), vol. 1, ch. 186, quoting Rabbi Soloveitchik in the name of his father, Rabbi Moshe (son of Rabbi Ḥayim).

> in [*Parashat*] *Ki Tetze*: 'obliterate the remembrance of Amalek'. This is a commandment on each and every one to wipe out every descendant of Amalek. The second [objective] is a war against the nation of Amalek, as it is written in [*Parashat*] *Beshalaḥ*: '[there shall be] a war for the Lord against Amalek from generation to generation', implying that the whole community is obliged to fight with the Amalekites as a nation. And this commandment concerns not solely the descendants of Amalek; rather, against any nation that rises against us to annihilate us we are commanded to wage war, and it is considered a war of mitzva. Whereas the commandment to annihilate Amalek on each individual, as mentioned in Deuteronomy, is solely regarding the offspring of Amalek.

Maimonides' distinction between the seven nations and Amalekites can now be reconciled. Indeed both are obsolete in terms of biological descendants; however, there are new nations that can take on the label 'Amalek' with their determination to annihilate the Jewish people. This is the Brisker innovation of introducing two dimensions to Amalek. Conversely, such an interpretation would also apply to accepting retributions from Germany: "Wipe out the memory of Amalek" would include the rejection of anything originating with that people. *Sefer Nefesh Harav* says just that: "Rabbi Soloveitchik spoke publicly against accepting retributions. He gave two reasons: First, so that they should not feel atoned for their atrocities. Second, they have the status of Amalek, and it is forbidden to take anything from them."[13]

The above approach, then, defines Germans as Amalek, with all its implications, and therefore purchasing goods made in Germany and accepting retribution would be against the halakha.

THE LUBAVITCHER REBBE

The Lubavitcher Rebbe has a more centrist approach. While he also compares Germany to Amalek, to him the question of whether or not to purchase German goods is not one of halakha, rather, one of sensitivity and emotional attitude. He explains his view in a letter from 1970:

> Greeting and Blessing,
>
> I am in receipt of your letter of [date] in which you ask my opinion "as to whether it is a weakness or impropriety" to avoid the purchase of goods

13. Rabbi Tzvi Shechter, *Sefer Nefesh Harav*, p. 87.

> made in Germany. You add that you ask this question as a Jew, in light of Jewish law and custom.
>
> Surely this is more a matter of feeling than a question of Jewish law and custom. Consequently, as in all matters of sentiment, it is difficult to express an opinion that would have universal application.
>
> At any rate, it certainly cannot be categorized as a "weakness". On the contrary, a decision of this kind bespeaks strength of will, all the more so since it entails some inconvenience.
>
> Nor can it be considered an "impropriety", since it is based on a principle which may be considered to come under the category of "Remember what Amalek did unto you". For, as is well known, the inhuman atrocities, etc., against our defenceless and innocent brethren were not perpetrated by a small group, but were carried out with the knowledge, consent, and even co-operation of the vast majority of the German nation.[14]

So on one level we can compare the Germans – or in fact any nation that wishes to annihilate the Jews – to Amalek; as Rambam says, "constantly remember their evil deeds and their ambush of Israel to arouse our hatred of them", and therefore it is in the 'spirit' of the mitzva to refuse to buy German-made products.[15] Yet at the same time, it is not a halakha and is 'more a matter of feeling', and if one is not disturbed by it, its disregard is also acceptable.

The *Sefer HaḤinukh*, while explaining the mitzva of annihilating Amalek,[16] uses a similar idea: "The function of the mitzva of 'remembering what Amalek did' is to take to heart that God hates all those who pursue the Jewish people. And according to his evil and the slyness of his damage will be his downfall, as we find with Amalek." In other words, while the commandment is only regarding Amalek, there is a broader message (albeit not a law or even custom) providing support, in the spirit of the original mitzva, for those who feel uncomfortable purchasing German products.

---

14. *Sparks of Chassidus*, collected from the archives of Rabbi Nissan Mindel, p. 211. Rabbi Mindel served as one of the personal secretaries of the Lubavitcher Rebbe.
15. Rabbi Rapaport has suggested that the term 'spirit of the commandment' could be applied in this instance.
16. "*Shoresh HaMitzvot*", mitzva 603, source of the *mitzvot* of Amalek. Generally the approach of "*Shoresh HaMitzvot*" is to accentuate ideas that are not in the commandment but similar to it – 'in its spirit', as it were.

In the following letter the Lubavitcher Rebbe embraces the same principle when it comes to retribution and explains why he recommends accepting German funds: "Times have completely changed now from the way they were at the initial stages of debate as to whether to accept retribution or not, since it has been prolonged a few years with much publicity. It is self-understood that no one individual can change the general impact (of the Germans).... In my opinion, she should do all in her means to claim the maximum amount due to them."[17] Again following the principle that Germans are not Amalek, the Rebbe takes a pragmatic stance making it permissible to accept retributions.

To sum up, while Rabbi Soloveitchik prohibits any German products or retribution, as Germans, too, are Amalek, the Lubavitcher Rebbe, on the one hand, embraces the analogy but on the other states that "a decision [not to purchase goods] of this kind bespeaks strength of will", that is, it is not a halakhic matter. And since it is not law, when it comes to retribution, people should do everything possible to make the maximum claim.

GERMANY OF TODAY

The Lubavitcher Rebbe writes in his letter from 1970: "Moreover, I do not think that anyone seriously believes that the Germany of today is entirely different from the Germany of two decades ago", implying that Germany had not yet left the state of 'the spirit of Amalek'. Clearly, Germany of today is different, and one of Europe's staunchest supporters of Israel. In light of this, the challenge to Rabbi Soloveitchik's approach would be: if one generation of Germans earned the title of Amalek, how many generations would it take to remove that identity? Clearly it is not a commandment on the offspring, unless they haven't changed their ways. Clearly if one is still disturbed, or if one is a first- or second-generation survivor like the Erlau Rebbe, then, "as in all matters of sentiment, it is difficult to express an opinion... it certainly cannot be categorized as a 'weakness'", but those who are not concerned by it have no reason to be.

THE JEWISH APPROACH

In the years that followed the Holocaust, Jews wanted to return to their normal lives, get married, find employment, have children, and focus on the future, whether or not they personally condemned the purchase of German goods. The struggles and challenges as a people have continued but we are as alive as ever. Rather than focusing on whether or not we can purchase German goods,

17. *Shaarei Halakha Uminhag*, iv. 207, in response to women asking whether to accept retribution.

we should take steps to strengthen ourselves as Jews. As the Lubavitcher Rebbe states in his letter of 1970, "Each and every one must do everything possible to counteract the tide of assimilation by positive and dedicated action to strengthen the eternal Jewish values and Torah-true institutions in his community and environment." As for a solution to the dilemma of claiming retribution, he proposed in his letter from 1952 that "The woman should donate a fifth [of the retribution funds] to *tzedaka* [charity]". *Tziyon bemishpat tipadeh ushaveh bitzdaka,* Zion shall be redeemed through justice and her penitent through righteousness. May we be redeemed of this exile and returned to Zion through our collective acts of study of Torah and performance of *mitzvot.*

Parallel Thinking: Science, Torah, and Cognitive Dissonance

Rabbi Moshe Freedman

Driven by hunger, a fox tried to reach some grapes hanging high on the vine but was unable to, although he leaped with all his strength. As he went away, the fox remarked, "Oh, you aren't even ripe yet! I don't need any sour grapes."
AESOP'S FABLES

PARALLEL THINKING

The American Jazz age author F. Scott Fitzgerald famously wrote that "the test of a first-rate intelligence is the ability to hold two opposed ideas in mind at the same time and still retain the ability to function."[1] Twenty-six years later, the social psychologist Leon Festinger proposed the theory of cognitive dissonance, suggesting that the human mind has an inner drive to harmonize all personal beliefs, philosophies, and modes of behaviour when confronted with the cold truth of external, independent, and objectively verifiable evidence. Festinger's theory is that the psychological pain of cognitive dissonance compels us to seek

1. *The Crack-Up*, ed. Edmund Wilson (New Directions, 1945), 69.

ways of restoring the balance in our minds while maintaining the integrity of our belief system or justifying our behaviour. The theory has become an accepted part of normative psychology, but in the light of modern scientific discovery it is particularly germane to those groups who continue to profess religious beliefs.

Indeed, Festinger's original work focused on monitoring the beliefs of members of an eschatological cult called 'the Seekers'. Chicago housewife and group leader Dorothy Martin claimed to have received messages in her home from alien beings from the planet Clarion via psychographic writing and claimed that a UFO landing was imminent. Only believers would be saved from the destruction of the world.[2] Many followers gave up their jobs and sold their possessions in preparation for the impending doom.

When Martin's predicted day of reckoning failed to materialize, she claimed that the world had been spared because her followers had spread the "force of good and light" throughout the world.[3] Instead of abandoning their discredited beliefs, cult members strengthened them and began an even more aggressive campaign of proselytizing. Such behaviour highlights the fact that when reality hits hard, believers are often unwilling to surrender their tightly held convictions. They would prefer to dogmatically advance the most absurd doctrines in order to buttress their beliefs, rather than entertain the possibility of simply being wrong.

Nevertheless, cognitive dissonance is not only reserved for radical cults and lunatics. Part of being human is to have a set of morals, convictions, and beliefs which are open to scrutiny and dispute. Yet simply forgoing the ideals by which one lives in the light of a challenge to them leaves each of us vulnerable to never having a fixed set of principles or philosophies to guide us. How are we to function if we are constantly questioning ourselves or waiting for incontrovertible proof of everything we consciously accept as true? This is especially germane to religious beliefs as worldwide more than eight in ten people identify with a religious group.[4]

While some would delight in seeing religious adherents abandoning their faith in favour of a more rational, scientific explanation of the world, the healthiest approach to challenges against one's beliefs is not abandonment of them, but to keep an open mind and begin a journey of rigorously honest, impartial, and unprejudiced enquiry.

---

2. Leon Festinger et al., *When Prophecy Fails* (1956).
3. Ibid. 169.
4. Pew Research Religion and Public Life Project, "The Global Religious Landscape" (18 Dec. 2012), http://www.pewforum.org/2012/12/18/global-religious-landscape-exec/.

At first, all options must be open. The internal struggle between conflicting ideas then evolves into an adventure of scrutinizing premises, hypotheses, and suppositions in order to determine the truth. It is as much the process of investigation, together with the conclusions drawn, which ultimately yields a better understanding and appreciation of both sides of the debate.

Perhaps this is what F. Scott Fitzgerald meant; a first-rate intelligence would look to hold on to opposing ideas in parallel while making an unbiased and honest evaluation of that which is plausible and that which is patently not. This is the basis for 'parallel thinking'.

THE NATURE OF FAITH

It has been reported that the dogmatic reinforcement of religious beliefs plays a central role in strengthening those convictions when confronted with scientific scrutiny.[5] For observant Jews, belief in God and the divine origin of the Torah forms an axiomatic and incontrovertible part of their being. Notwithstanding the obvious differences between established religion and New Age cults, when it comes to faith there appear to be few qualitative differences between Dorothy Martin's followers and an observant Jew. Do members of organized and established religions not appear to non-believers to have the same cultish adherence to faith as Martin's UFO cult? On the contrary, the only difference between established religions and more recent cults appears to be of age rather than quality.

Three hundred and fifty years after the beginning of the Enlightenment, the triumph of rational, evidence-based scientific investigation in explaining the physical world should not be underestimated. Scientists have been successful in drawing back the veil from reality, revealing the most remarkable secrets from the intricate inner workings of matter to the mechanics of the cosmos. In this time, our understanding of the world has accelerated at an astonishing rate.

By implication, such success suggests that beliefs which seemingly contradict the scientific view of the world, and in addition require faith due to a lack of evidence, or because there can be no evidence, should be consigned to the dustbin of a pre-Enlightenment age of archaic, obsolete convictions together with geocentricism, flat Earth theory, and fairies at the bottom of the garden. To a scientist engaged in evidence-based research, an abstract, nebulous concept such as 'faith' appears to be in complete opposition to the philosophy of science with its rigorous demands for proof. If so, it is understandable that scientists would

5. Azim F. Shariff et al., "The Devil's Advocate: Secular Arguments Diminish both Implicit and Explicit Religious Belief", *Journal of Cognition and Culture*, 8 (2008), 417–23.

discount even the possibility of the existence of God or that the Torah is divine before any analysis of a potential conflict between science and religion has even begun. Disappointingly, whenever scientists indulge in entering the debate, they seem compelled to strictly adhere to the premise that God could not possibly exist[6] or that God and religion must have been invented to explain the world.[7]

If we are to endeavour to fulfil F. Scott Fitzgerald's ideal of a first-rate intelligence and hold two opposing ideas at the same time, we must initially assume that both positions, in this case the scientific and biblical accounts of reality, are equally valid until we find evidence to the contrary. This may be a difficult step for a scientist to take, but failing to do so is probably triggered by erroneously subscribing to an intractable dogma of reductionist materialism, a philosophy which appears to pervade all current scientific thinking.[8]

To accomplish this point, whereby both sides of the debate begin on an equal footing, is indeed a momentous achievement in itself. It is the prerequisite of true dialogue. However, it is only half the battle. It sounds simple, but before we can engage in any sort of debate or even begin to ask the right questions about the conflict between science and Torah, we must make sure that we properly understand both the scientific position and the depth and intricacy of what the Torah is teaching mankind.[9] If we fail to grasp the complexity of either side, or worse, still prejudge either position through ignorance, misinformation, or our erroneously predetermined assumptions, we will inevitably poison the exchange of ideas with falsehood, thus ruining the opportunity for greater understanding. Those who claim fidelity to the truth must be prepared to accept it in humility and recognize that it may be larger than their own minds.

In contrast, those who enter the debate soaked in their own prejudice may attain personal satisfaction at verifying their preconceived position but their offerings will contribute nothing to a greater understanding of the issues at hand. This is what our sages meant when they stated that an argument for the sake of Heaven will endure and bring us towards the truth, whereas an argument that is not for the sake of Heaven will not.[10] Much of the current discussion around

6. Martin Rees, *Just Six Numbers: The Deep Forces that Shape the Universe* (Phoenix, 2001), 166.
7. Richard Dawkins, *The God Delusion* (Black Swan, 2007), 57.
8. John N. Gray, "The Limits of Materialism", broadcast on BBC Radio 4, "Points of View", on 5 May 2013.
9. This principle was pointed out by Rabbi Shaya Karlinsky, Dean of Darche Noam Institutions (Shapell College of Jewish Studies/Yeshivat Darche Noam).
10. Mishna, Pirkei Avot 5:17; cf. commentary by Rabbi Ovadiah of Bartenura ad loc.

science and Torah falls into the latter category, with both sides being guilty of corrupting the debate.

EVOLUTION AND THE AGE OF THE UNIVERSE

The two most contentious issues between science and Torah are Darwin's theory of evolution with its modern upgrade known as Neo-Darwinism, together with the scientific view that the universe is approximately 13.75 billion years old with the Earth forming around 4.5 billion years ago. Both would seemingly contradict the biblical account of creation; evolution explains the origin and diversity of life on the planet, which has developed without the need for a guiding Creator. Life developed over billions of years, not the six days spoken about in Genesis and, in addition, according to an analysis of the generations listed in the Torah and books of the prophets, there have only been around 6,000 years since the beginning of time.

Such stark differences highlight the fact that to attempt to live with both science and Torah and accept the veracity of both appears to be fraught with the greatest cognitive dissonance of all. Most would understandably react by shunning either science or religion in favour of the other; for every scientist who derides the idea of faith, there are dozens of religious devotees who attain cognitive bliss by questioning the basis for scientific propositions such as the theory of evolution or the age of the universe. Yet such behaviour creates the false dichotomy we have had to endure which has forced many to take sides unnecessarily. Such an approach is anti-intellectual and demeaning to the more enlightened among us who sense a greater complexity to the world.

Many religious adherents do not understand science sufficiently to realize that it cannot be rebuffed with the usual mantras of "evolution is just a theory" or "scientists change their mind all the time". Both of these claims require a response, not only because they should be addressed, but because doing so will give us a greater understanding of the nature of science.

In a scientific context the word 'theory' does not imply uncertainty but rather "a supposition or a system of ideas intended to explain something, especially one based on general principles independent of the thing to be explained".[11] Then there is the question of 'proof'. Those engaged in arguments between science and religion often fail to recognize the many types and levels of evidence, verification, and substantiation which are all given the label of 'proof'.

The only type of scientific proof which is absolute is a mathematical proof. For example, Pythagoras' theory states that for a right-angle triangle,

11. *Oxford English Dictionary.*

the square of the hypotenuse is equal to the sum of the square of the other two sides. There are a variety of irrefutable proofs that clearly show this to be an incontrovertible fact. It is quite simply the truth. When one moves into the realm of experimental science, proof takes on a statistical character. The efficacy of a drug must be tested against a control group given a placebo. Since it is impossible to test the entire human population, a sample group must be taken. Analysis of the results will determine with some degree of certainty whether the drug works or not. This is what I call scientific proof. It is not the same in nature as a mathematical proof, but is backed by repeatable results, which are the hallmark of good science.

Evolution is a complex set of ideas, many of which are directly observable, provable, and repeatable in the laboratory. Some aspects of evolution cannot be observed directly as they are historical or happen over long periods of time. They can nevertheless be reasonably inferred from the evidence at hand.[12] This evidence is not the same as proof in a mathematical sense but it certainly forms the basis for a reasonable and rational position. Coupled with the fact that evolution is applied practically in many areas of scientific research and development, it cannot be dismissed as being "just a theory". Similarly, in a court of law the prosecution is not required to prove the guilt of a suspect without doubt, but beyond reasonable doubt.

Other attacks against science claim that since scientific theories change when new evidence comes to light, they are unreliable;[13] only religion, which is based on the ageless, unchanging word of God, can claim to be true.[14] Unlike religion, science is by definition not dogmatic and welcomes change in light of new evidence. This does not mean that every scientific concept remains in a state of flux. The nature of evidence-based analysis is that when the evidence begins to stack up and results can be repeated and verified, it is reasonable to say that the theory holds true.

---

12. For example, it is impossible to look back in time and observe speciation, but it may be inferred from homologous similarities between species (such as bone structure), the fossil record, vestigial structures, and embryology.
13. The example most often given is that of the shift from steady state theory, which stated that the universe had always existed, to the big bang. Steady state theory was held by most scientists until the evidence came to light of an expanding universe (through Edwin Hubble's observation of red shift), leading to the big bang theory, which implied to many religious adherents the confirmation of the idea that the universe was created.
14. Rabbi Menachem Mendel Schneersohn, *Mind Over Matter: The Lubavitcher Rebbe on Science, Technology and Medicine* (Shamir, 2004), 13.

Nevertheless, in the interests of being even-handed, it would be remiss to neglect the glaring mistakes made by scientists when they venture into the debate tightly grasping the premise that religion has it wrong. Many famous science writers are also vehement secularists and lobby for a range of atheist philosophies in the arenas of education, politics, and society at large. Most are not trained in theology or philosophy and are often ill equipped to tackle to subtleties of either.[15]

When I was a young child I used to believe that thunder was caused by rainclouds bumping into one another. I also believed that Rice Krispies were responsible for causing freckles. Thankfully, my knowledge of science has developed and I am now enlightened enough to know that thunder is caused by the rapid expansion of air following a lightning strike and that freckles are caused by concentrations of melanin, not breakfast cereal.

No one would be content to trust in their child-like explanations of scientific phenomena, so why are so many people satisfied to believe their child-like comprehension of the Bible?

Understandably, those who read of six days of creation and stories of Adam and Eve in the Garden of Eden, who ate from a forbidden tree after being duped by a talking snake, would assume that this book is an absurd set of peculiar fairy tales made by bronze-age man to try and explain the world around him. Those who have read the Bible but have failed to engage in a thorough analysis of the original text will miss the subtle messages it seeks to teach, which are rarely, if ever, of a scientific nature. Over the course of Jewish history, our sages and commentators have understood the Torah's account of creation in a far less infantile way and many of them have not been motivated by a need to reconcile the Torah's account of creation with science. While some might cry foul at these attempts at apologetics, it is important to note that many were often writing well before modern scientific understanding.

---

15. Steve Jones, *The Serpent's Promise* (Little, Brown, 2013). Professor Jones predicates his book on a range of erroneous biblical assertions. One specific example is that, while mentioning the medieval biblical commentator Rashi as a biological ancestor to a vast number of Jews today (p. 28), he assumes, like many, that the first chapter of Genesis gives a chronological account of creation (see p. 84, where he writes that "Genesis has a different view for the Lord commanded 'Let the earth bring forth grass' even before he created the Sun"). He fails to note that Rashi himself asserts that the Torah was not making any such assertion (see Rashi on Gen. 1:1, s.v. *bereshit bara*; cf. n. 22 below; see also Mary Midgley, *The Solitary Self: Darwin and the Selfish Gene* (Heretics, 2010), where she points out the philosophical flaws in Richard Dawkins's *magnum opus, The Selfish Gene.*

The creation process itself is not seen by our commentators as a series of new creations, but rather as a natural process which is divinely driven. Indeed, all natural processes are considered to be driven by God.[16] Even the idea of common ancestry is not necessarily anathema to the Torah's account of creation as understood by our commentaries. Similarity between the species was recognized by Jewish philosophers as early as the eleventh century.[17] Others noted that the creation process was gradual,[18] while, even more astonishingly, the idea that man evolved from animals was understood from the text of the Torah as early as the sixteenth century.[19] Both man and animals were created from "the ground", implying that we share the same physical matter.[20] Only man was given a God-like soul, which is understood to reflect our ability to have free choice through a higher level of consciousness than that of the animals.[21] Yet other commentators who predate modern science note that the creation story cannot be relating a chronological or scientific account of the formation of the world and the creatures and plants on it because the order does not make sense.[22] For those literalists

16. Ps. 104; Midrash Rabba, Gen. 10:6; Rabbi Samson Rafael Hirsch, "The Educational Value of Judaism", in *Collected Writings*, vii. 261–2; Maimonides, *Guide of the Perplexed* 2:48.
17. Rabbenu Baḥya ben Joseph ibn Pakuda, *Ḥovot HaLevavot, Shaar HaYiḥud* 1:7.
18. Rabbi Meir Leibush ben Yeḥiel Mikhel Wisser (known as Malbim), commentary on Gen. 1:20.
19. Rabbi Obadiah ben Jacob Sforno on Gen. 1:26.
20. Compare Gen. 2:7 with 2:19.
21. Gen. 2:7. The significance of God breathing into Adam a *nishmat ḥayim* (living soul) is that it gave Adam a uniquely human quality. Humans appear to be physically similar to other animals and have the same animalistic tendencies that all animals possess, such as the drive to eat, reproduce, and survive. Nevertheless, the Torah teaches us that we were given a unique connection to God which transforms the paradigmatic human (Adam) from being mere animal hominid to being a *nefesh ḥaya* (a living being). This is translated by Onkelos into Aramaic as *ruaḥ memallela* (a speaking spirit). This does not imply that Adam was the first human to speak, but rather relates to a much deeper function. In Jewish thought the human soul contains three components: the *nefesh, ruaḥ,* and *neshama.* The *nefesh* is the lowest part found in all animals and is associated with the animalistic urges mentioned earlier. The *neshama* (related to the *nishmat ḥayim,* living soul, in the verse) is the highest part and may be associated with higher consciousness and free will. Free will does not simply mean the ability to choose, but the ability to make moral choices with conscious intent which can override and resist animalistic tendencies. It is this that makes us uniquely human. The *ruaḥ* connects those two parts. Therefore a *ruaḥ memallela* is a *ruaḥ* which acts as a conduit for communication between the higher consciousness (*neshama*) and the lower animal drive (*nefesh*). A corollary of these spiritual components can be found within the structures of the brain. The more ancient structures, known as the reptilian brain, govern the animalistic drives whereas the cortex (and especially the prefrontal cortex) governs the executive functions, which can override the desire to act on impulse.
22. Rashi on Gen. 1:1.

who attempt to understand the six 'days' of creation as twenty-four-hour periods, the sun, together with other celestial bodies, was only created on day four.[23]

Yet there is one sticking point which remains. Even if Jewish commentators have historically explained the Torah in a way that is compatible with science, it may allow us to accept both science and Torah, but still leaves us with a question about the source of the Torah itself. While it is satisfying to be able to reconcile our understanding of the Torah with modern science, it does not automatically imply that it is rational to believe in the divine source of Torah. Taking this to its logical conclusion, *faith in God and the divine origin of the Torah cannot be generated by reconciling science and Torah.*

On the contrary, why should we believe in God and the divinity of the Torah if doing so requires faith? Even if the Torah's true message does not contradict the scientific explanation of reality, the consequence of a lack of direct evidence for God's existence or divine revelation means that faith is still required for those who believe in God. Apparently, given that God cannot be seen or detected through scientific means, His existence and all that is implied by it can never be based on evidence.

Bertrand Russell famously illustrated this point by positing the idea of a cosmic teapot:

> Many orthodox people speak as though it were the business of sceptics to disprove received dogmas rather than of dogmatists to prove them. This is, of course, a mistake. If I were to suggest that between the Earth and Mars there is a china teapot revolving about the sun in an elliptical orbit, nobody would be able to disprove my assertion provided I were careful to add that the teapot is too small to be revealed even by our most powerful telescopes. But if I were to go on to say that, since my assertion cannot be disproved, it is intolerable presumption on the part of human reason to doubt it, I should rightly be thought to be talking nonsense. If, however, the existence of such a teapot were affirmed in ancient books, taught as the sacred truth every Sunday, and instilled into the minds of children at school, hesitation to believe in its existence would become a mark of eccentricity and entitle the doubter to the attentions of the psychiatrist in an enlightened age or of the Inquisitor in an earlier time.[24]

---

23. Gen. 1:14.

24. Bertrand Russell, 'Is There a God?', *Illustrated Magazine*, 1952 (commissioned but never published).

Russell's point seems to be that it is preposterous to claim that since God cannot be disproved as He cannot be seen or detected using scientific methods,[25] His existence is above doubt or scrutiny. Indeed, the burden of proof of God's existence still remains with those who believe in Him. What is more striking, though, is that his point implies *inter alia* that it is equally logical to believe in Russell's cosmic teapot (or any other undetectable fanciful being or object) as it is to believe in God.

One could be excused for thinking that a revelation by God, or any other supernatural being, does not directly contradict the rational, evidence-based scientific explanation of the world. Yet if evidence-based investigation yields far more rational and compelling results, why should we even begin to entertain the premise that God exists any more than a cosmic teapot? Why should the Torah be taken seriously as a divine text which must be reconciled with science for any reason other than to make adherents to its teachings more comfortable about practising their religion, while accepting the truth of science? In essence, an act of divine revelation may not be unscientific, but such extraordinary claims require more than blind faith to be considered rational. Put bluntly, it appears to be no more rational to believe in God than it does to believe in fairies at the bottom of the garden, undetectable cosmic teapots or the Flying Spaghetti Monster.[26]

From the teleological argument (known as the argument from design), made famous by William Paley's watchmaker analogy,[27] to Pascal's

---

25. See Moshe Freedman, 'Will Science Prove God's Existence?' *The Jewish Chronicle*, 18 Aug. 2011, as to why, from a Jewish theological perspective, science cannot detect God or spiritual claims such as prayer or the soul.

26. Following the Kansas State Board of Education decision to permit teaching intelligent design as an alternative to evolution in public school science classes, Bobby Henderson wrote a satirical open letter describing the divine Flying Spaghetti Monster. Henderson satirized creationism by professing his belief that whenever a scientist carbon-dates an object, a supernatural creator that closely resembles spaghetti and meatballs is there 'changing the results with His Noodly Appendage'. The accompanying parody religion, the Church of the Flying Spaghetti Monster otherwise known as Pastafarianism, has thousands of followers around the world keen to expose the flawed logic of the intelligent design movement, while opposing the teaching of creationism in public schools. In 2011, after reading that, according to Austrian law, hats and other such headgear were only allowed in official photographs for religious reasons, Niko Alm, an Austrian Pastafarian, successfully obtained a driving licence while wearing a colander on his head.

27. William Paley's *Natural Theology*, published in 1802: "Suppose I found a watch upon the ground, and it should be inquired how the watch happened to be in that place, I should hardly think… that, for anything I knew, the watch might have always been there. Yet why should not this answer serve for the watch as well as for [a] stone [that happened to be lying on the ground]? For this reason, and for no other; namely, that, if the different parts had been differently shaped from

wager,[28] man has grappled with God's existence, proposing a menagerie of philosophical proofs.

When faced with the question of relying on faith, Jewish philosophers often took a different approach to the classic philosophical proofs. Rabbi Joseph Albo (d. 1444), in fact, entirely dismissed any indication that the fundamentals of Judaism could be based on any sort of deductive reasoning of the mind or physical reality.[29]

Rabbi Moshe Alshikh (d. 1593) also drew attention to the question of why God could not simply reveal the secrets of the universe to mankind. Firstly, with man's finite intellect they would be unfathomable and beyond human comprehension. Secondly, if mankind could understand the deepest questions of the universe it would render him like God, in whom wisdom and will are the same. Alshikh continues and explains the source for Jewish faith:

> God chose a different way, which is superior to the others. It provides a more convincing basis for religion than all the possible intellectual proofs and evidence that can possibly be found. That basis is the direct perception of the senses, which cannot be refuted by intellectual proofs or other types of evidence. Therefore, God chose to provide the generation that received the Torah at Sinai experiences that were totally unique in the history of mankind and which demonstrated all the principles of faith. This was done so that not the slightest doubt remained, so that they had no reason to deviate by the slightest amount from the principles of faith.[30]

In other words, God's reality must be experienced through revelation, not induced through logical thinking. The experience of that revelation is the only reliable basis for faith. That's all well and good for the generation that witnessed God's revelation at Sinai, but over 3,300 years on, we have no direct contact with God.

---

what they are, if a different size from what they are, or placed after any other manner, or in any order than that in which they are placed, either no motion at all would have been carried on in the machine, or none which would have answered the use that is now served by it."

28. Blaise Pascal, in his *Pensées* (1690), argued that if, on balance, the evidence for the existence of God is inconclusive, one is faced with a choice between believing and not believing. If we choose to believe and are right, then eternal bliss awaits us. If we are wrong, we lose very little in the long run. But if we choose not to believe and are right, we gain very little. Yet if we are wrong (God does exist and we have gambled on His non-existence) our loss is enormous. Faced with the possibility of suffering eternal damnation, one would be foolish to discount God.
29. *Book of Foundations: First Discourse*, ch. 17.
30. Commentary on Deut. 5:4.

He does not reveal Himself to us to give us that direct experience and remove "the slightest doubt" of His existence.

Yet while the event of God's revelation may have been thousands of years ago, His message, bound up and encoded in the Written and Oral Torah, was given to the Jewish people together with a process of communicating that message through the future generations. Two elements of that claim can be tested: we can establish whether the message received today has been corrupted from its original transmission, and, in addition, we can test whether the story of God's revelation to the Jewish people is historical or mythical.

If there is one area in which mankind has excelled, it is to communicate with one another through science and technology. If God's revelation was authentic and His message, the Torah, is His communication, it will stand up to the same tests used by scientists and engineers to ensure the integrity of information as it is transferred across the vast expanses of space and time.

RATIONAL JEWISH FAITH: COMMUNICATION AND TORAH

Ever since the dawn of civilization, man has understood the importance of sharing ideas. Communication builds relationships and relationships are the cornerstone of humanity. One of the earliest methods of communicating over large geographical divides was the use of mountain-top signal fires. This form of communication was excellent at rapidly transmitting simple binary messages, such as the onset of war, over large distances. An example of this can be found in the Gemara, where mountain-top fires were lit to signal the onset of the new month.[31] Yet, as a communication system, this method was limited in the complexity of the message it could send; signal fires can convey the result of a simple yes or no question but no more. Nevertheless, it was this concept of using simple yes or no questions to code information that heralded a new era in long-distance communication.

In 1605, the English philosopher and scientist Francis Bacon showed how letters could be encoded using a bilateral cipher. With the invention of the telescope by German-Dutch lens-maker Johann Lippershey in 1608, a raft of inventions capitalized on Bacon's idea. In 1795 the Anglican vicar Lord George Murray invented Britain's first optical telegraph. Messages were coded using six shutters, which transmitted military and naval messages between London and Deal, critical for the impending threat from France and the imminent Napoleonic wars. While electricity had yet to be discovered, the first digital communications system paved the way for the communications boom which continues to this day.

31. Rosh Hashana 23a.

As techniques became more sophisticated, the demand for rapidly transferring ever more complex sets of information over long distances was confronted by a number of engineering problems.

Information Theory

Imagine a makeshift device for speaking to a friend at the other end of a field involving two tin cans, connected at their base with a wire. At one end, one person speaks into their can, which transmits the vibrations of sound along the wire. When they reach the other end, the second can amplifies these vibrations so they can be heard by the listener.

There are two difficulties which challenge the reliability of this system. The first is that over long distances the vibrations will attenuate and the signal will eventually be lost. The second is that the wire is susceptible to interference from extraneous vibrations caused, for example, by the wind. A more common example is the static and hiss heard on a radio caused by electromagnetic interference. If this interference, referred to as 'noise', exceeds a certain limit, it will drown out the signal, rendering the message undecipherable.

The field of information theory attempts to address these problems. The American mathematician, engineer, and cryptographer Claude Elwood Shannon (d. 2001), considered to be the forefather of information theory, described the problem of information transfer over a noisy channel by breaking down each component of any communication system. Shannon's masterstroke was to show that all forms of information can be reduced to a complex set of binary choices, in the same way that the shutters in Lord Murray's optical telegraph only had two states (open or closed). These choices were named by the American mathematician John W. Turkey as binary digits or simply 'bits'.[32] All modern communication, from mobile phones to satellite television, relies on Shannon's theories.

Data Compression and Error Correction

Working with the American engineer Ralph Hartley, Shannon developed the idea that communication could be optimized by maximizing the rate at which data can be transferred and minimizing the effects of noise by detecting and correcting erroneous data.

The two methods used in modern communications to achieve this are data compression and error correction. Data compression methods involve increasing

32. Claude E. Shannon and Warren Weaver, *The Mathematical Theory of Communication* (University of Illinois Press, 1963), 9.

the efficiency of data transfer by removing redundant information. Depending on need, some methods of data compression deliberately compromise on the details of the message in favour of a more concise yet efficient set of data.

Error correction methods involve algorithms which can check the integrity of the data and request that it be retransmitted if received in a corrupted form.

Torah as a Communication from God

The giving of the Torah on Mount Sinai is perhaps the most defining moment in the history of the Jewish people. God communicated His divine wisdom to Moses in the form of the Written and Oral Torah together with the Ten Commandments.[33] In essence, Torah is information and the dissemination of Torah from God to Moses and from Moses to the rest of the Jewish people can be thought of as a system of communication.[34]

It should, therefore, be possible to apply the same concepts found in information theory to both the actual giving of the Torah at Mount Sinai together with the process of its transmission. Theoretically, the same components of Shannon's communication system should be found.

Verification of the Source

The Torah itself describes how the entire nation witnessed the revelation at Sinai.[35] The Torah indicates that this event was like no other in human history: "Did ever a people hear God's voice speaking out of the midst of the fire as you have heard and live?"[36] Significantly, the uniqueness of this national-scale revelation means that the chances of someone fabricating it are vanishingly small. Any individual may claim to have had a personal numinous experience or communication with the Divine. Yet while it is impossible to disprove the claim, it is equally impossible to verify it.[37]

In contrast, it would be challenging, to say the least, for someone to concoct a claim of divine revelation experienced on a national scale. The fact that the story of the Exodus and national revelation at Mount Sinai are stories which are universally accepted by the Jewish people and retold throughout the generations provides a strong and rational indication that these events are historical

33. Lev. 26:46 and *Sifra* on *Parashat Beḥukotai* 2:12.
34. See Mishna Avot 1:1 and Rambam's introduction to the Mishna regarding the unbroken chain of transmission.
35. Ex. 20:14.
36. Deut. 4:33.
37. *Kuzari* 4:11.

fact. While not a 'proof' of the revelation at Sinai as such, the claim of national revelation would have been too exorbitant to fabricate and would have left clear bifurcations in the most fundamental concepts of Jewish thought.[38]

The existence of the Jewish people as a medium for the transmission of Torah, the repetition of the story of the Exodus, and the culture of intergenerational learning are the most profound factors in preserving the authenticity of Torah and its transmission through time.[39] To base one's faith in God revealing

38. See *Permission to Believe: Four Rational Approaches to the Torah's Divine Origin* by Rabbi Lawrence Kelemen (Targum Press, 1990), 63–70.

39. One of the classic challenges to the continual transmission of Torah is the account given of the rediscovery of a Torah scroll by King Josiah (II Kings 20 and II Chron. 34). Following the death of the righteous king Hezekiah (II Kings 20:21), his son Manasseh began to reign over Judah. From the outset Manasseh undid the righteous work of his father and reinstituted every type of forbidden worship, including the sacrifice of his own child (ibid. 21:2–9). He reigned for 55 years, bringing terror and bloodshed to the Land of Israel. His successor was his son Amon, who continued idol worship but was killed by his servants after serving as king for only two years (ibid. 21:23). The next to reign was his son Josiah, who was righteous and sought the help of Ḥilkiya the High Priest to collect funds to rebuild the Temple in Jerusalem (ibid. 22:1–7). During the rebuilding, a Torah scroll is discovered by Ḥilkiya, who brings it to Shafan the scribe, who reads it to Josiah. The king tears his garments and commands Ḥilkiya, together with his other servants, to enquire of God what will happen as a result of the Jewish people's previous idolatrous practices. They ask Ḥulda, a prophetess, who informs them that God will exile the Jewish people as a result of the idol worship practised. Josiah leads a campaign of repentance, which he begins by arranging a public reading from the Torah that they had found in the Temple (ibid. 23:1–3) before removing all of the idols and burning them outside Jerusalem (ibid. 4). When the scroll was discovered, 67 years had passed since the beginning of Manasseh's campaign to banish Jewish practice from Israel and impose idolatry on the nation. The rediscovery of Torah during this episode appears to some as a break in the transmission of Torah. Indeed, many Bible critics use this story to propagate the idea that Deuteronomy was not written by Moses, but much later. It also seems to represent the idea that Torah and Jewish practice had ceased entirely, breaking the chain of transmission from Sinai. Yet the notion that Torah had been forgotten during Manasseh's reign is challenged by both classical and modern commentators. According to tradition, the Torah discovered was the original copy written by Moses himself, which had been hidden during Manasseh's reign. This was to protect it from being destroyed after Aḥaz had burned a Torah scroll (Malbim and Radak ibid. 22:8). In addition, the catalyst for Josiah's fear at finding the scroll was not the discovery of Torah anew, but rather the fact that it unusually opened to the section of the curses in Deuteronomy instead of being rolled to the beginning (Malbim ibid. and Abravanel ibid. 22:15–17). In particular, he saw the verse (Deut. 28:36) "The Lord will lead you and your king whom you will have established over you, to a nation unknown to you or your fathers; and there you will serve other deities [made] of wood and stone" (Rashi on II Kings 22:8). Later commentaries also show that Torah and Jewish practice had not been broken completely during the time of Manasseh. Rabbi Zvi Hirsch Schlez (ninteenth century) makes a number of points. Firstly, the gap between the reign of the righteous

Himself to the entire nation at Mount Sinai is therefore qualitatively different to the sort of blind faith which is often espoused by religious adherents. It is evidence-based faith, both rational and logical, and while it may not necessarily be an incontrovertible proof of God's existence, it demonstrates a level of reasonable evidence equal to many scientific concepts.

Accuracy of the Written Torah

There are many laws which attempt to ensure that the text of the Written Torah remains unadulterated. God explicitly commands that the Torah should remain unchanged,[40] even if later prophets who commune with God intimate that a particular law is no longer valid, or attempt to innovate something themselves.[41] Just as any signal may be corrupted by noise, the writing of new Torah scrolls is threatened by scribal errors.

Shortly before Moses died, he wrote thirteen Torah scrolls; one for each of the twelve tribes and one to be kept in the Ark of the Covenant.[42] The third-century CE Rabbi Yannai explained that the purpose of the Torah scroll kept in the Ark was so that it would act as the standard to which other later copies could be compared.

Hezekiah and that of Josiah was only 57 years. It is fair to say that there were people alive during Josiah's discovery who had been alive during the reign of Hezekiah. Indeed, even Manasseh repented towards the end of his life (II Chron. 33:16). Since Amon only reigned for two years, it seems far-fetched to say that the knowledge and observance of Torah would have been entirely lost to Jews at the time of Josiah. In addition, according to the account in the book of Chronicles, Josiah was righteous from the start, long before the discovery of the Torah scroll: "And he did that which was right in the eyes of the Lord, and he walked in the ways of David his father, and turned aside neither to the right nor to the left. And in the eighth year when he became king, when he was still a youth, he started to purge Judah and Jerusalem of the high places, the *asherim*, the graven images, and the molten images" (II Chron. 34:2–3). Rabbi Schlez notes that this would have been impossible had the Torah been forgotten entirely. Therefore it should not be assumed that the episode with Josiah indicates a break in the chain of transmission. On the contrary, it shows how strong that chain is when placed under decades of strain by the scourge of idol worship and the evil tyrants who deliberately tried to eradicate Jewish practice and Torah learning (see *Niflaot MiTorat HaShem Yitbarakh, Even Pina*, Introduction, 23–4). Sid Z. Leiman also points out that a break in tradition is not compatible with the text. He writes in *The Canonization of Hebrew Scripture: The Talmudic and Midrashic Evidence* (pp. 143–4 n. 77), "As the narrative unfolds in 2K 22:8 ff. it assumes the existence of a pre-Josianic Torah. Moreover, the people could hardly have been made accountable for violating a law code which neither they nor their forefathers had ever seen." See also J. H. Hertz, *Pentateuch and Haftorahs*, pp. 937–9.

40. Deut. 4:2.

41. Shabbat 104a (cf. Lev. 27:34).

42. Deuteronomy Rabba 9:9 (cf. Deut 31:9).

In addition, there are a variety of laws which are designed to minimize scribal errors. In writing a new Torah scroll, the scribe must copy from an existing text. For example, if even one letter has been written by heart, it is disqualified.[43] A Torah scroll is further disqualified if even a single letter is omitted or added,[44] and each letter must be surrounded by blank parchment to ensure that letters do not touch one another, forming new letters.[45] For the same reason, each letter has to be formed properly.[46] This set of laws (together with many others) provides the safety mechanisms comparable to an inbuilt automated repeat request error correction method. However, since after the destruction of the First Temple the Ark of the Covenant was lost together with the Torah of Moses, Jewish scribes no longer had the original Torah against which to check their copies. Coupled with national dispersion and separation, small differences began to occur in the Torah texts. Nevertheless, after all of the trials and tribulations, displacements and dispersions, pogroms and persecutions over the last two thousand years, very few scribal mistakes have been made.

Rabbi Professor Mordechai Breuer (d. 2007) analysed different Torah scrolls for differences and errors. While it was a complex study, in conclusion only twelve irreconcilable differences were found, all of which regard the spelling of different words but in no way change their meaning.[47] Nevertheless, if we consider these differences as noise, we can calculate the signal-to-noise ratio of the Written Torah in the same way that a telecommunications signal is assessed for its transmission. In modern internet wireless systems, a typical signal-to-noise ratio of 40 to 50 dB is considered excellent. By taking the number of letters in the Torah and the twelve differences, the error rate is 0.004%. This is equivalent to a signal-to-noise ratio of over 80dB.

Written Torah, Oral Torah, and the Ten Commandments

The Talmud[48] discusses the meaning of the following verse: "And the Lord said to Moses, 'Come up to Me to the mountain and remain there, and I will give you the stone tablets, the Law and the commandments, which I have written to instruct them.'"[49] The Talmud concludes that not only were the Ten Commandments and

43. *Shulḥan Arukh, Yoreh De'a* 274:2.

44. Ibid. 275:6.

45. Ibid. 274:4.

46. Ibid. 274:5.

47. One example can be found in Gen. 4:13, where the word מִנְּשֹׂא can also be spelt מִנְּשׂוֹא.

48. Berakhot 5a.

49. Ex. 24:12.

the Written Torah given at Sinai, the entire gamut of Oral Torah was also given at that time. Rabbi Moses Ḥayim Luzzatto (Ramḥal) writes that God did not want to give man a Torah that could be understood without explanation.[50] On the contrary, the Written Torah contains many vague, indeterminate, and undefined concepts such as the prohibition of *melakha* (creative activity) on Shabbat,[51] or the precise description of a mezuza or tefillin.[52]

Nevertheless, while the Torah details the giving of the Ten Commandments, it is clear that these are a subset of commandments already contained within the Torah. This then begs the question as to what the purpose was of giving Moses and the Jewish people two tablets containing a mere fraction of the total information. If they do not add anything new to the Torah they would appear to be superfluous.

Rashi[53] quotes Saadya Gaon, who wrote poems extolling the 613 commandments. Saadya does not merely list all the commandments; he links them to each of the Ten Commandments. In other words, the Ten Commandments contain the whole of Torah in some condensed form. Clearly, much of the detail of the Torah is lost, but their concise nature means that it is easier to transmit and remember them.

Noise in the Transmission of Torah

Just as every system of communication is affected by noise, God's divine will is also open to distortion from two primary sources. The first is deliberate fabrication or filtering of the information. God Himself makes the distinction between Moses and other prophets.[54] The Midrash[55] describes how the prophecy of Moses was different to that of all other prophets. While other prophets witnessed God's message through an unclear lens, Moses spoke to God directly, without distorting the message. This is what the Torah means when it says that God spoke to Moses face to face,[56] mouth to mouth.[57]

Yet the dissemination of Torah is equally (and in some circles primarily) focused on the process of teaching the Oral Torah. This has become associated

50. Rabbi Moshe Ḥayim Luzzatto (known as Ramḥal, d. 1746), *Essay on Fundamentals.*
51. Ex. 31:15.
52. Deut. 6:9.
53. Rashi on Ex. 24:12.
54. Num. 12:6, 12.
55. Leviticus Rabba 1:14; cf. Ramḥal, *Derekh HaShem* III:5:1, 4.
56. Deut. 5:4.
57. Num. 12:8.

with the teachings of the tannaic sages, whose discussions and debates were redacted by Rabbi Judah HaNasi around the year 200 CE into the Mishna. Around three hundred years later, Ravina and Rav Ashi compiled the Gemara, which contains the wisdom of the later amoraic sages, who analysed and scrutinized the words of their tannaic predecessors. Together with a plethora of other ancient texts, later commentators and scholars were able to crystallize Jewish law and apply it to every contemporary challenge.

Nevertheless, even a cursory glance at the Talmud (the compilation of the Mishna and Gemara) reveals a range of views in almost every area of Jewish law and thought. Although it seems that God originally transmitted one message to Moses, it wasn't long before noise entered the system causing disparity and a divergence in opinion. Doubts and uncertainties morphed into disagreements and disputes and the very integrity of God's message seemed to be under threat.

The Talmud readily accepts that laws were forgotten when unpractised.[58] Yet the system by which Jewish law is applied to everyday life contains its own checks and balances to try to derive the correct approach; ultimately, if Jewish law is to be useable, there must be some way to decide which path of many should be followed.

Indeed, there are many examples in the Talmud where different sages will reach different conclusions in their analysis. Nevertheless, the Gemara will try to reconstruct the original law.[59] Sometimes students will misunderstand the words of their teachers, who often spoke in terse language.[60] There are even examples of two students giving conflicting reports about the teachings of their teacher. In each case, the Talmud will attempt to reconcile the disagreement and test each position until a final conclusion is reached.[61]

On occasions, the matter will be left unresolved, such as in the question of which type of *shofar* note should be blown between the *tekiot* (long blasts) on Rosh Hashana.[62] This is why we must sometimes resort to compromise in order to fulfil God's Will.[63]

58. Berakhot 33a; cf. *Tosafot* on Berakhot, s.v. "Let us see then what Ezra did ordain".

59. Temura 15a–16a.

60. Based on the dictum in Pesaḥim 3b, לעולם ישנה לתלמידיו דרך קצרה – "One must always teach one's students in a succinct way". This resonates again with the concept of data compression; condensing the message facilitates its transmission. Yet there are examples where students have misunderstood their teacher.

61. Bava Metzia 46b–47a; ibid. 66a and 101a.

62. Rosh Hashana 33b.

63. Maimonides, *Mishne Torah, Laws of Shofar, Sukka, and Lulav* 3:2.

There are however, many other occasions when differences in opinion are not examples of noise but of two (or more) legitimate expressions of the original message. This is what the Gemara means when it says *elu ve'elu divrei Elokim ḥayim hen* – these and those are the words of the Living God.[64] It means that both conflicting opinions are part of the system of Jewish law; even if only one of the positions can be ruled part of Jewish practice, the other opinion is still a legitimate expression of Torah even if it was never accepted into Jewish practice.

Feedback

During the Second World War, the American author and academic Wilbur Schramm (d. 1987) joined the Office of War Information to investigate the nature of propaganda. During his time he developed new models of communication, building on the original work of Shannon and Weaver. He later became the founding director and research professor of the Institute for Communications Research at the University of Illinois at Urbana-Champaign.

Schramm developed Shannon's original linear model of information transfer by adding one extra feature: the concept of feedback. He writes that communication is "a relationship built around the exchange of information".[65] In our Torah model this reflects the idea that Torah learning should not be an academic subject but must change us in some way.[66] Those differences in behaviour, those small acts which allow us to grow stronger in our connection to God, have effects which, according to Jewish mysticism, reverberate back into the heavens.[67]

DISSEMINATION OF TORAH: THE JEWISH PEOPLE ARE THE MEDIUM

Shannon and Hartley wrote a theorem which states that the amount of information that can be reliably transmitted over a communications channel of a specified bandwidth[68] in the presence of noise (known as channel capacity) is directly related to increasing the bandwidth of the medium over which the information

64. Eruvin 13b.

65. "The Unique Perspective of Communication: A Retrospective View", *Journal of Communication* (Summer 1983), 15.

66. Ramḥal, *Derekh HaShem* IV:2:2.

67. Ibid. I:4:9,10 and I:5:4.

68. The rate at which information can be transmitted.

is being transferred and reducing the signal-to-noise ratio through error correction and noise reduction techniques.[69]

The Written Torah is replete with commands for parents and grandparents to pass on Jewish teachings and heritage to the next generation.[70] God praises Abraham because he "commands his children and household after him".[71] In the *Shema*, which draws on three sections from the Torah, we repeat twice a day the commandment to educate our children.[72] God warns us about forgetting our heritage and exhorts us to pass on the stories and teachings of our ancestors to our children and grandchildren.[73]

Hebrew has two words for tradition: *kabbala* and *mesora*. The word *kabbala* comes from the root *k-b-l* meaning receive, and *mesora* comes from the root *m-s-r* meaning to pass on. Tradition, therefore, in a Jewish sense, means to receive Jewish knowledge and teachings from the previous generation and to pass them on to the next.

In terms of Shannon's concept of information transfer, the Jewish people represent both the receiver of the message and the medium by which its transmission continues. We must learn Torah to understand God's will but also teach it to others so that His message is perpetuated. The ultimate destination of this message is represented by our children and grandchildren, the next generations, who wait expectantly to be inspired by their parents, grandparents, and teachers.

Every parent and every teacher, every child and every student represents the medium through which God's message is transmitted. Whenever a parent inspires in their child a love of Judaism or whenever a teacher or rabbi imparts their knowledge to others, the bandwidth of Jewish learning and experience widens, thus strengthening our collective connection to God.

In our time, Lord Sacks has led our community with an unrivalled passion for Judaism and the Jewish people. Coupled with his profound scholarship, his uniquely thoughtful and insightful reflections have provided a Jewish perspective on every subject, from politics to science, economics to sociology, morality to faith. He has consequently widened the bandwidth of Jewish learning and experience, inspiring a generation of Jews from all backgrounds to thirst for a

69. R. V. L. Hartley, "Transmission of Information", *Bell System Technical Journal* (July 1928), and C. E. Shannon, "Communication in the presence of noise", *Proceedings of the Institute of Radio Engineers*, 37 (1) (Jan. 1949), 10–21.

70. Gen. 18:19 and Rashi ad loc.; Ex. 13:8, Deut. 6:7, and Deut. 4:9–10.

71. Gen. 18:19.

72. Deut. 6:7.

73. Deut. 4:9–10; cf. Ex. 13:8.

stronger connection to the lessons and experiences of our forefathers at Sinai while making them relevant to modern life. His contribution to public life and the esteem in which he is held outside of Anglo-Jewry has engendered a deep sense of pride within our community. He has ensured that our tradition is seen as an important voice in wider public affairs, relevant far beyond our synagogues, study halls, and homes. In essence, he has been a champion of faith within a society which has all but lost its faith.

IMPLICATIONS FOR FAITH

To sceptics, faith is the process which seeks to bypass rational thought in order to alleviate the pain of cognitive dissonance. Science is provable and evidence-based, whereas religious ideas such as God are, by definition, not. For some, when science challenges belief, faith takes effect to sooth the psychological distress. This is the faith that any rationalist would rile against, prompting the eminent evolutionary scientist Richard Dawkins to write that "Faith is the great cop-out, the great excuse to evade the need to think and evaluate evidence. Faith is belief in spite of, even perhaps because of, the lack of evidence."[74]

But Jewish faith was never meant to be blind, it was meant to be as evidence-based as science.[75] We do not believe in God because we have bamboozled ourselves into doing so. Nor do we believe because it makes us feel better about the world or because that is what our parents taught us to do, as their parents taught before them and so on, *ad nauseum*. We believe in God and the divinity of the Torah because we have a *mesora* – a chain of transmission which contains all of the necessary features of any modern communication system needed to ensure a proper transmission from source to receiver.

74. "Inheriting Religion", *The Nullifidian*, Nov. 1994.

75. Maimonides, *Moreh Nevukhim* (*Guide to the Perplexed* 3:51). Maimonides also writes:

> One should not believe something to be true unless it belongs to one of three categories. (1) Something that can be validated by clear proof based upon human reasoning or empirically, e.g. arithmetic, geometry, or astronomy. (2) Something that can be perceived directly by one of the five senses. For example, if he sees something is red or black, or he tastes something is bitter or sweet or he can feel that something is hot or cold… (3) Something which he has received as a tradition from the prophets and righteous people. A sensible person needs to classify everything he believes into that which is based on rational proof, that which he directly perceives with his senses, and that which he believes because of valid tradition. Anyone who believes something outside these three categories is described by the verse (Prov. 14:15), "A fool believes in everything." (*Letter on Astrology*)

See also Rabbi Samson Rafael Hirsch, *Collected Writings*, i. 97 ff.; Rabbi Simḥa Zissel Ziv Broida (known as the Alter of Kelm, d. 1898), *Ḥokhma and Mussar* 2:62.

This teaches us two things. Firstly, that our knowledge of God comes from His national revelation to our people, collectively experienced by our forefathers and universally passed down from generation to generation in an unadulterated form.[76] Secondly, the text of the Torah He gave them can be shown beyond reasonable doubt to be the same as the one we have today.

We do not believe in God "in spite of, even perhaps because of, the lack of evidence" but see our faith as rational and evidence-based. Malbim expressed it as follows:[77] "Knowledge is something which is perceived directly with the senses or is understood through such a clear proof that it is impossible to doubt it at all. *Emuna,* on the other hand, is something which is not comprehended in an irrefutable manner but is accepted from highly reliable sources and is believed based on their say-so."

In truth, the Hebrew word *emuna* does not really translate as faith, but rather as a steady faithfulness or nurturing process based on something which is known from investigation.[78]

Jewish faith requires parallel thinking. The greatest rewards come to those who have the intellectual courage to evaluate the world without prejudice. By accepting F. Scott Fitzgerald's challenge to gain a first-rate intelligence by functioning with two opposing ideas in mind, we learn to maintain our cognitive integrity and harmony while engaging in the most exciting adventure to the heart of the truth. Once there, the most supreme cognitive emancipation comes when parallel thinking gives rise to integrated thinking, allowing us to skip between two previously conflicting worlds. Our efforts yield a higher truth, where science and Torah reveal different but equally valid perspectives on reality.[79] Reconciliation without the dregs of dishonesty or prejudice provides the greatest gift in satisfying our complex human minds while giving us the most solid foundation on which to lead the most fulfilled, engaged and integrated lives.

---

76. Rabbi Moses Sofer (known as Ḥatam Sofer, d. 1839), on *Yoreh De'a* 2:340, where he asserts that "Parents don't [deliberately] teach lies to their children."

77. Malbim, commentary on Hosea 2:21.

78. Ex. 17:12: וַיְהִי יָדָיו אֱמוּנָה עַד בֹּא הַשָּׁמֶשׁ , "Moses' hands were held *steady* until the morning"; Esther 2:7: וַיְהִי אֹמֵן אֶת הֲדַסָּה, "And he had *raised* Hadassa". The word "amen" derives from the same root. Hosea (2:22) implies that *emuna* is designed to lead to knowledge of God. See *Metzudat David* ad loc.

79. See Chief Rabbi Jonathan Sacks, *The Great Partnership* (Hodder and Stoughton, 2011).

'Married to an Angel': The Halakhic Conundrum Concerning Elijah and Other Transcendent Spouses

Rabbi Jonathan Hughes

Rabbi Sacks was in the process of retiring from his position as Chief Rabbi when I joined the rabbinate in the United Kingdom. During that brief overlap, we not only shared several engaging conversations, but even a pulpit during Sukkot at Hendon United Synagogue (Raleigh Close). In his sermon, Rabbi Sacks delivered inspirational words of blessing to me in anticipation of my impending move to become rabbi at Richmond United Synagogue. Those sentiments have stayed with me to this day and I shall never forget his warm encouragement and indomitable effervescence. Thank you, Rabbi Sacks.

According to Torah tradition, there have been two individuals who transcended the normal limitations of the human condition and attained a type of immortality. The first is Elijah, who was one of the greatest prophets of Jewish history. As well as stalwartly defending ethical monotheism against the burgeoning idolatry of his time, Elijah performed spectacular miracles, including resurrecting the dead and bringing fire down from the sky. II Kings 2:11 informs us that while the mercurial

Elijah was still alive, he ascended to Heaven in a whirlwind, accompanied by a chariot and horses of flames. He is now known as the 'Angel of the *Brit*' and is said to be present at each *brit mila* ceremony, when a newly born Jewish soul is sealed into the covenant of Abraham. In the book of Malachi, Elijah's return is prophesied as a harbinger of the Messiah.

In Ketubot 77b the Talmud tells us about the *amora* Rabbi Joshua ben Levi, who hoodwinked the Angel of Death and entered the supernal world while he was still alive. The Gemara explains that Rabbi Joshua ben Levi was so prodigious that when he was on his deathbed, the heavenly court instructed the Angel of Death to go to him and fulfil anything that the sage desired. Rabbi Joshua ben Levi requested to see his ultimate resting place in Gan Eden and, when shown his eternal abode, he, like Elijah, leapt into the spiritual realm and was permitted by God to remain there.

However, back on earth, a problem surfaces. Both Elijah and Rabbi Joshua ben Levi left behind a wife and, before their ascendancy, the following Torah verses applied to their marriages:

> If a man is found lying with a married woman, they shall both be put to death – the man who was lying with the woman and the woman – and you shall eradicate the evil from Israel.... And you shall take them both out to the gate of that city and you shall stone them and they shall be put to death, the maiden because she did not scream in the city and the man because he afflicted the wife of his friend; and you shall eradicate the evil from within your midst. (Deut. 22:22, 24)

These sources raise a perplexing halakhic conundrum: would Elijah's wife have been permitted to remarry after her husband had become a supernatural being? On the one hand, she had been hitherto an *eshet ish* – a married woman, forbidden by the Torah from having relations with any other man. Thus, since her husband technically never died and they never divorced, what exactly changed that would have allowed her to remarry under Jewish law? Perhaps these Torah verses dictate that she would never have been allowed to remarry and that her relations with another man would be considered adulterous. She would simply have been left for the remainder of her days as an irremediable *aguna* – a woman chained to a non-functioning marriage, barred from the opportunity of ever remarrying and ensnared in the permanent marital grip of her departed, but not deceased, spouse. (A similar concept exists in an extreme form in Hinduism, whereby according to the Sati rite, a widow is not only prohibited to remarry, but she is enjoined to be cremated alive along with her dead husband!)

Nevertheless, since Elijah had, to all practical intents and purposes, shuffled off this mortal coil, perhaps this alone could determine that his wife would no longer be considered married to him. If so, she would be free to remarry. The problem is how would such liberation be achieved halakhically without the conventional means of death or divorce? In his opus *Kovetz Shiurim*, Rabbi Elḥanan Wasserman (d. 1941) uses his profound analytical verve to dissect this fascinating issue, revealing some truly remarkable insights.[1]

Rabbi Wasserman begins his examination by citing a responsum by Rabbi Israel Isserlin ben Petachia (Mahari): "The wife of Elijah and the wife of Rabbi Joshua ben Levi are permitted [to remarry] because it is written [in Scripture], 'the wife of his friend' [Deut. 22:24] – and not 'the wife of an angel'; and they [Elijah and Rabbi Joshua ben Levi] are completely spiritual and not physical."[2] Mahari's view is that the prohibition of *eshet ish* applies specifically to *eshet re'ehu* – the 'wife of his friend', the phrase stated by the Torah in Deuteronomy 22:24. According to Mahari, this phrase acts as a condition, implicitly excluding a woman who is married to an 'angel' from the injunction against *eshet ish*. Thus, since these two men metamorphosed from mere mortals into angelic beings, their wives ceased to qualify as the wives of another man's 'friend'. It would seem that, for Mahari, the ambit of the halakhic connotation of the Torah's term 'friend' only embraces the relationship between beings that share the same sphere of reality. A heavenly creature is too aloof to be described as a 'friend'.

However, Rabbi Wasserman argues that Mahari's ruling is problematic. Indeed, the Gemara in Kiddushin 13b asks for the Torah source that a husband's death enables his widow to remarry. After considering several options, the Gemara concludes that the source lies in the following verse: "and should the latter husband hate her, he shall write her a bill of divorce, and give it in her hand, and send her out of his house; or if the latter husband who took her as a wife should die" (Deut. 24:3).

Here, the Torah juxtaposes the concept of a *get* – a bill of divorce – to the death of a husband. This comparison is called a *hekesh*, which dictates that if two matters are placed in the same verse in the Torah, this can constitute a divine instruction to apply the rules of one to the other. In this instance the *hekesh* indicates that just as a *get* is an entity that releases a wife from the bonds of marriage, death is also to be considered a process that possesses the ability to emancipate a woman from the nuptial union and the status of *eshet ish*.

1. Vol. ii, Section 28.
2. Mahari was born in 1390 in the Duchy of Styria and died in 1460 in Lower Austria. He was a Talmudist and halakhist, best known for his famous work *Terumat HaDeshen*.

Rabbi Wasserman comments that, according to Mahari's theory, a wife such as Elijah's does not qualify as the 'wife of his friend'. This is because another man cannot be a 'friend' of the deceased in any real sense as they do not share the same plane of existence. Therefore, the Gemara should have cited this exclusion clause as the source for the law that a widow may remarry. However, the Gemara makes no mention of this verse whatsoever and instead concludes its discussion by adducing the *hekesh* as the source that a widow may remarry. Rabbi Wasserman deduces from this omission that the Gemara must have understood that, based on simple reason alone, even if a wife ceases to qualify as the 'wife of his friend', the prohibition of *eshet ish* remains nonetheless. Once established, this injunction remains forever until a positive and destructive halakhic force removes it. It just so happens that the Torah reveals through the *hekesh* that death, like divorce, has the potency to dissolve the prohibition of *eshet ish*. According to Rabbi Wasserman, the Gemara appears to hold that a change in status from 'friend' to 'non-friend/angel' is by itself insufficient to expunge the prohibition of *eshet ish*.

Consequently, the Gemara would seem to rule out the possibility that the clause of the 'wife of his friend' is the source that Elijah's wife would have been permitted to remarry. If the husband's becoming a non-friend by dying does not in and of itself allow a widow to remarry, it is unlikely that a husband turning into an angel is any different. Thus, the Gemara, which is a binding authority, would seem to seriously undermine Mahari's suggestion.

The remaining question is whether human transcendence can be considered a form of death and thereby be directly included in the *hekesh*. To this end, Rabbi Wasserman cites the following *baraita* in *Seder Olam*,[3] cited in Bava Batra 121b: "Seven people encompassed the entire world and they are: Adam, Methuselah, Shem, Jacob, Amram, Aḥaya HaShiloni, and Elijah – and he is still in existence". This *baraita* means to say that seven people's lives form an unbroken chain from Creation until the present day and beyond. These are: Adam HaRishon (1–930), who was seen by Methuselah (687–1656), who was seen by Shem (1558–2158), who was seen by Jacob (2108–2255). Jacob was seen by Amram, who was born to his grandson Kehat in Egypt during the last seventeen years of Jacob's life. Aḥaya HaShiloni, who prophesied in the days of King Jeroboam, was born in Egypt during Amram's lifetime. Elijah saw Aḥaya and he never died. As Rabbi Samuel Eidels (Maharsha) explains, this teaches that the world constantly

3. *Seder Olam*, meaning 'Order of the World', is a chronology that details the dates of events that appear in Tanakh from Creation to Alexander the Great's conquest of Persia. It was written in approximately 160 CE by Rabbi Jose ben Ḥalafta.

requires a righteous person of the stature of these seven in order to merit continued existence. At any rate, this *baraita* clearly states that Elijah is not considered to have died and, therefore, his wife could not have been deemed a widow and could not remarry on that basis.

In addition, Rabbi Wasserman adduces the Gemara in Bava Metzia 114b, which records the episode when the *amora* Rabba bar Avuha came across Elijah in a non-Jewish cemetery. Rabba asked Elijah, "Are you not a *kohen*? Why then do you stand in a cemetery?" According to tradition, Elijah is a reincarnation of Pinḥas, who was the grandson of Aaron the *kohen*, both of whom were of the priestly caste. It is a well-known halakha that a *kohen* may not expose himself to the contraction of *tuma* (ritual impurity) which is prevalent in a cemetery in which Jewish people are interred. Elijah responded that because this was a non-Jewish cemetery, no such impurity existed.

Rabbi Wasserman analyses this Gemara by citing a verse in Psalms, which states: "liberated among the dead like the slain that lie in the grave, whom You remember no more" (Ps. 88:6). This verse is expounded to teach that when a person dies, he becomes liberated from the commandments forever, even after he is eventually resurrected. Rabbi Wasserman deduces that if Rabba bar Avuha was concerned about Elijah violating the prohibition against a *kohen* exposing himself to *tuma*, his understanding must have been that the prophet had never died and was, therefore, bound to observe the Torah's dictates. Consequently, his wife would not be considered free to remarry on account of being a widow because she had never actually been widowed! Without a Talmud-endorsed source to teach that an immortal 'angel's' wife may remarry, perhaps one may have to conclude that Elijah's wife would not have been permitted to do so.

Rabbi Wasserman furthermore contends that even Mahari himself could not have considered Elijah to have died since if he had, he could have quite easily relied on the *hekesh* that determines that a widow may remarry. As a result, Mahari was understandably forced to find an alternative source to permit Elijah's wife to remarry. However, Rabbi Wasserman has proved, based on the Gemara in Kiddushin, that the phrase 'wife of his friend' cannot be the scriptural basis of such a permit, as explained. Thus Mahari's verdict seems to be unsustainable from every angle. Nevertheless, Rabbi Wasserman assumes the responsibility to defend him. He begins his defence by reference to Gittin 39b, which discusses a case involving a convert to Judaism who dies with no children and no heirs. The Gemara teaches that, as the proselyte has no Jewish relatives, all of his property is considered ownerless, including his slaves, who, in this instance, are under the age of 13. The *amora* Samuel states, however, that a slave only goes free when there is no dominion of a master over him (which remains extant in this case) and this determines that these underage slaves cannot be emancipated.

In the *Tur, Yoreh De'a*, Section 267, Rabbi Moses Isserles (Rema) explains that Samuel does not mean that a slave is liberated when he has no actual owner. Rather, his point is that a slave is liberated when there is no one else who can potentially assert ownership over him. Therefore, for Samuel, if the slave is an adult at the moment when the convert owner dies, and there is no one else who currently has dominion over him, he acquires himself and is freed. In contrast, a slave who is a minor (under 13) cannot take ownership of himself because the Torah dictates that he is legally incapable of independently effecting an acquisition due to his lack of mental maturity. Thus, when his convert owner dies, an obligation to serve a master remains upon him; it is just that there is currently no master for him to serve. Indeed, at the moment the convert owner dies, it is possible for someone else to acquire the minor slave. Without a document of emancipation, this minor slave finds himself in limbo, with no available remedy to achieve emancipation. According to Rema, even when the slave reaches halakhic adulthood, this obligation to serve a master remains.

Rabbi Wasserman explains that Rema's interpretation is based on a source in the Torah that dictates that a master's death emancipates his slave. This source is comprised of two verses. The first pertains to the laws governing a special genre of maidservant, which is representative of slaves generally: "And if a man should lie carnally with a woman, and she is a slave-woman who has been designated to a man, and she was not redeemed, nor was freedom given *to her*; there shall be an inquisition; they shall not be put to death because she had not been freed" (Lev. 19:20; emphasis mine). The second verse relates to the legal effects of a bill of divorce: "When a man will take a wife, and have relations with her, and it shall be that if she does not find favour in his eyes, because he found some unseemly thing in her, that he shall write *to her* a bill of divorce, and give it in her hand, and send her out of his house, and she shall leave his house, and go and become another man's wife" (Deut. 24:1–2; emphasis mine).

In both verses the Hebrew term *lah*, meaning 'to her', is used. As Rashi explains in Gittin 39a, the sages expounded these verses using what is known as *gezera shava*. This is one of the Oral Tradition's methods of talmudic exegesis, whereby the use of the same word in two separate passages in the Torah indicates a legal parallelism between the halakhot that relate to these two contexts. The *gezera shava*, or 'equivalent decree', determines that a law or laws in one context are transferred to the other. In this instance, there is an established law in the context of marriage that there is a prohibition, entitled *eshet ish*, against the wife engaging in relations with any man other than her husband. While the husband is still alive, the only thing that can liberate the wife and allow her to remarry is for the husband to give her a *get*, a bill of divorce. However, a husband's death allows his widow to remarry even without a *get*. Using the aforementioned *hekesh*, the Torah here indicates that a husband's death is equivalent to a *get* in the sense that it instantaneously cuts the cords of marriage, removing the prohibition of *eshet ish*. This concept is transferred, via the *gezera shava*, to the context of slaves and dictates that a slave only requires a bill of emancipation while his master is alive and that the death of a master emancipates his slave in lieu of such a document.

According to Rabbi Wasserman, Rema understood that the *gezera shava* rigidly governs the modus operandi of the slave's emancipation following his master's death. Indeed, Rema holds that the giving of a *get*, or the death of a husband, sever the marital bonds only at the moment when they initially occur. The ensuing liberation of the ex-wife or widow is entirely founded upon that original severance. When this pattern is imported by the *gezera shava* into the context of the laws concerning slaves, it asserts that the master's death specifically emancipates a slave at that specific time and the slave is only free afterwards on account of the 'act' of death. Since in this case the slaves are minors and cannot be emancipated automatically when their master dies, the master's death no longer serves to emancipate them when they come of age. This is because its liberating potency is lost the moment after its inception.

Rabbi Joseph Karo (*Beit Yosef*) disputes Rema's ruling. He holds that when these slaves reach adulthood, they are automatically emancipated. Rabbi Wasserman presents two hypotheses to explain *Beit Yosef*'s opinion. Initially, he contends that Rabbi Karo may have held that the liberation of a widow is not caused solely by the 'act' of the husband's death itself. Rather, it is produced and re-produced by the ongoing reality that her late husband is deceased. Therefore, even beyond the moment of the husband's death, the reality of his continuing death remains a potent trigger for his widow's liberation. Consequently, the *gezera shava* dictates that when the minor slaves reach adulthood and are capable of acquiring themselves, the fact that their master is dead serves as a real and present legal impetus to emancipate them. Though it has been delayed, it now takes full effect.

Rabbi Wasserman then proposes an alternative understanding of *Beit Yosef*'s position. He purports that, according to Rabbi Karo, it could in fact be that a widow is liberated simply because she does not have a husband. Thus, the Torah teaches that a widow is only prohibited to a man other than her husband at a time when she has a husband who is connected to her in a real sense. According to this hypothesis, the focus is not on the husband's status, on whether he is around; rather, it is on the wife's situation. The main concern of the Torah, then, is whether the wife practically has a husband or not. Consequently, this pattern transfers, via the *gezera shava*, to the laws governing slaves: when they reach adulthood, we focus on the fact that *they themselves* now do not have a master and they therefore go free as a widow would.

Rabbi Wasserman does not discuss whether *Beit Yosef* would apply either of these hypotheses to the workings of a *get*, which is the source from where we learn that a widow may remarry. One could also argue that a woman is liberated after divorce because she is currently divorced. Alternatively, it could be that a *get* only operates at the time of its being given and the husband's death is an inherently distinct process.

Rabbi Wasserman uses this alternative hypothesis, that a widow is liberated simply because she does not have a husband, to defend Mahari's explanation of the status of Elijah's wife. To recap, Mahari ruled that she would have been permitted to remarry after her husband's ascension on account of the verse that instructs that only the 'wife of his friend' is forbidden to marry another man, as opposed to the wife of an angel. However, Rabbi Wasserman exposed two problems with this. First, the Gemara implies that this verse is not the source and that a husband becoming a 'non-friend' does not in fact remove the prohibition of *eshet ish*. Second, the Talmud explicitly confirms that Elijah did not die and, therefore, his wife could not be considered a widow and would not be permitted to remarry on that basis.

Rabbi Wasserman suggests that Mahari's ruling may have been based upon the same thinking that underpins *Beit Yosef*'s understanding of how a husband's death liberates his widow. This is that a wife is permitted to remarry because she currently has no husband. This requirement is also fulfilled in the case of Elijah's wife: once he had ascended to Heaven, she could no longer be deemed to have a husband in her life. Nevertheless, because he did not actually die, the *hekesh* governing a husband's death cannot be applied directly to him. Therefore, the clause of the'wife of his friend' is required and can function as an independent and specific scriptural basis to essentially extend the law of liberation applying to a widow to the wife of an angel.

Indeed, one could suggest that a *hekesh* is an exposition that can not only transfer a law to another context, but can also transform its underpinning. In this instance the *hekesh* may have taken the law that a *get* removes the prohibition of *eshet ish* and not only exported it to the context of a husband's death, but altered the way the liberation works. In its new 'home' (the death of a husband), the focus now becomes the wife's status and situation, rather than what the husband does or where he goes to. The *hekesh* has the power to teach the novel understanding that the crucial factor now is whether the wife has a husband, not the actual death of the husband (which is similar to a one-off act of giving a *get*). It would appear tenable to suggest that only after this revelation is it possible to then interpret the simple reading, or *peshat*, of the phrase 'the wife of his friend' as an actual exclusion clause, ousting an angel's wife from the prohibition of *eshet ish*. Consequently, Rabbi Wasserman maintains, 'the wife of his friend' could serve as the Torah's extension of the dynamics of the emancipation of a widow, dictating that Elijah's wife would have been permitted to remarry, enabling us to refute the counter-argument that her husband never really died.

Rabbi Wasserman's analysis was cited a generation later by Dayan Aryeh Leib Grosnass of the London Beth Din (d. 1996) in a responsum about a bizarre case in which a married man underwent transgender change.[4] The newly created 'woman' went on to marry a man under English law. The question was whether the wife, who was for all intents and purposes left without a husband, nevertheless required a *get* in order to remarry. The essence of the enquiry was how the mechanics of the permission for a widow to remarry work. If it is based on the fact that she no longer has a husband, then it would stand to reason that since this husband had become a woman, it is comparable to a husband's death and she would be permitted to remarry without a *get*. However, if it is specifically the action of the husband's dying that releases the wife from the nuptial bonds, since here the husband merely altered his gender and did not die, she would still be considered married to him and would require a *get* in order to remarry.

Indeed, Dayan Grosnass adduces Rabbi Wasserman's insight that it is specifically because Elijah became an angel that his wife would have been allowed to remarry without a *get*. Since he no longer existed in this realm, it could be likened to a kind of death. However, Dayan Grosnass questions whether the case of a man who succeeds in comprehensively changing his gender could be compared to some form of death (at least as a husband), given that this person continues to live in the world. This question remains unresolved.

4. *Lev Arye*, vol. ii, no. 49.

A Brief Study of Responsa Literature

Rabbi Geoffrey Hyman

It is an honour to contribute to this volume for Lord Sacks upon his retirement after twenty-two years of service as Chief Rabbi to Anglo-Jewry. Our relationship goes back a long time. When I graduated from Jews' College in 1979, Jonathan received his ordination (*semikha*), and when I received mine in 1982, he gained his doctorate. Already whilst I was studying for my first degree, he had been appointed lecturer in Jewish philosophy and I was privileged to study under him for a year. Later, he took over as teacher of homiletics and mentored me for several years. Over the thirty-seven years I have known him his words have been a constant inspiration to me. He is a rarity in that he is gifted both as a master of oratory and a brilliant, prolific writer. We arrived at Jews' College from different worlds, I from that of the traditional yeshivas, Gateshead and Chaye Olam, London; and he from the world of academia in Cambridge. But it was our great mentor, Rabbi Dr Nachum Rabinovitch, then principal of Jews' College, who unified the variant strands of our pasts and inspired us with a global view of Judaism and a faith that challenged the world. I knew from the Rav that Jonathan was destined to reach great horizons. During his tenure as Chief Rabbi his stature has grown beyond any prediction and his achievements have been outstanding. The wide impact his writings have made globally is beyond belief.

The essay I present here is a brief introduction to responsa literature, with which I have had a love affair since my yeshiva days, when I used to browse through such works on a Shabbat afternoon in the library of Gateshead. I was spellbound by the expanse of subject matter together with the historically interesting questions that were put to these great rabbis. For me it brought the halakha alive and illustrated its timeless nature as it tackled everyday issues, whether sociological or technological. Under the guidance of Rabbi Rabinovitch we learnt that a rabbi had an absolute obligation to seek the halakhic truth when answering a *she'ela* (halakhic question), nor was it simply enough to rely on someone else's view; rather, one had to turn to the primary sources and comprehend the *ta'amei halakha* – the conceptual principles behind the source material. The Rav of course was a master of this method and already as a young rabbi he was writing *teshuvot* (responsa) on the most complex of issues.[1]

THE ANTIQUITY OF THE *SHE'ELA*

Asking a *she'ela* as to what the halakha should be in a given case is as old as the Torah. In Numbers 9:6–14 the laws of Pesaḥ Sheni are given in response to the question put to Moses by several people who had become *tamei* (impure), and were therefore excluded from offering the paschal lamb. Moses responded with the words, "Stay and I will listen to what God will command you". Rashi notes: "Just like a disciple who knows that his master will give him the answer". God does indeed respond and presents Moses with the laws of Pesaḥ Sheni, enabling those affected to bring the paschal sacrifice at the later date. Similarly, in Numbers 27:1–11 the daughters of Zelophehad asked Moses why they, as their father's only heirs, should be excluded from inheriting his portion in the Promised Land. Again, Moses asks the Almighty and a revision of the law is given.[2] Both these biblical cases illustrate the concept of the '*she'ela* and *teshuva*' concerning a specific legal problem, and in both of them the answer results in a modification of the earlier legislation.

It is important to note that whilst the Torah was being revealed to Moses, he could pose a question directly to God, but post-Revelation a response from heaven has no relevance, for then the halakha is subject to the rule based on the

1. He was, in fact, the first to write on the subject matter of microwaves in halakha; see *Siaḥ Naḥum* (Jerusalem, 2007), 151, which was originally penned in 1961, when domestic microwaves were only being introduced. His responsum won the approval of the well-known halakhic decisor Rabbi Joseph Elijah Henkin.
2. According to Sanhedrin 8a, it was not a new law but had been previously given and forgotten.

verse "It is not in heaven",[3] and the decision must be reached by human endeavour alone.

Some of the rabbinic debates recorded in the Talmud reflect the continuing development of the halakha as it was applied over a five-hundred-year period. The Talmud records numerous questions asked by rabbis and students alike. There are even *she'elot*[4] that appear in the Talmud that are purely hypothetical, such as in the case of the "the flying tower",[5] upon which, the Talmud notes, the rabbis expounded three hundred laws.

THE RISE OF RESPONSA LITERATURE

After the close of the talmudic period, the continued asking and answering of *she'elot* led to the production of independent works of responsa. The earliest extant collection of these is *Halakhot Pesukot min HaGeonim* from the geonic period, circa 589 CE, which was first published in Constantinople.[6] Early responsa have also been discovered among the fragments of the Cairo Geniza. Of course, other collections could have existed but failed to survive.

Following the geonic period, the medieval rabbis known as *rishonim*[7] produced numerous collections, such as those of the well-known Talmudists: Alfasi (Rif), Rashi, Rabbenu Tam, Maimonides, Naḥmanides, Meir of Rothenburg, Solomon ben Aderet (Rashba), Asher ben Jehiel (Rosh), Nissim ben Reuben (Ran), and later Isaac ben Sheshet (Rivash). This period was followed by that of the *aḥaronim*,[8] which started from around the sixteenth century and includes works right up to the present time. To list the greatest of these works of the last five hundred years would be well beyond the limitations of this brief essay. It is estimated that since the sixteenth century, over 100,000 collections have been

3. Deut. 30:12. See Bava Metzia 59b, the dispute over the oven of Akhnai, which became a frenzied debate between R. Joshua and R. Eliezer B. Hyrkanus. R. Eliezer invoked heavenly intervention, but R. Joshua, quoting Deut. 30:12, stated: *lo bashamayim hi* ("it is not in heaven"). This was interpreted by R. Jeremiah as: "The Torah has already been given at Sinai", therefore even the heavenly voice, which sided with R. Eliezer, had to be ignored, as the Torah itself stated that law must be decided by majority opinion (see Deut. 23:2).
4. Plural of *she'ela*.
5. Ḥagiga 15b.
6. See the entry "She'elot U-Teshubot" in the *Jewish Encyclopedia* (New York, 1905–6), and "Responsa" in the *Encyclopaedia Judaica* (Jerusalem, 1971). Also suggested there is that, already during the talmudic period, singular responsa existed in a written form; see Yevamot 105a and Ḥullin 95b.
7. Lit. the early ones.
8. Lit. the later rabbis.

produced so far. The era of the *aḥaronim* has also seen a change in the organization of the material: following the writing of the *Shulḥan Arukh* in 1563 by Rabbi Joseph Karo,[9] who based his literary structure on that of the earlier *Arba'a Turim* by Rabbi Jacob ben Asher,[10] the hitherto random material within these collections of *shut*[11] was now collated according to the order of the four sections of the *Shulḥan Arukh*, permitting easier access to subject matter.

Traditionally, following the period of the *rishonim*, the later rabbis could not contradict the earlier authority of the *rishonim* in formulating their decisions, just as the *amora'im*[12] could not override the views of the earlier *tanna'im*.[13] Therefore in the post-sixteenth-century responsa, apart from relying on talmudic sources to reach a decision, the writers also cite source material from the *rishonim*.

Two distinct types of responsa emerged during the nineteenth century: in the first, the author prioritizes and focuses on talmudic sources if available. He will also present the *taamei halakha* and may also refer to relevant material from the *rishonim* and early *aḥaronim* but with little reference to the later *aḥaronim* or his contemporaries. In the second, the author readily quotes material from other halakhic authorities, whether contemporary or older, to build up his case and reach his decision. Often the material is presented without regard to the historical chronology of the sources.

A comparison between the *teshuvot* of Rabbi Moshe Feinstein and those of Rabbi Isaac Jacob Weiss will suffice to illustrate these two distinct methodologies.[14] In working through a response to a *she'ela*, *Iggerot Moshe* will immediately quote a talmudic source if available as the basis of his analysis, whereas *Minḥat Yitzḥak* will often start his discussion by quoting profusely from other major authorities and then may reflect back on a relevant talmudic passage. This difference of approach can also be traced back to earlier halakhic decisors.

THE RANGE OF SUBJECT MATTER

The study of responsa literature is not only essential to the halakhist but relevant to the historian as well, as numerous responsa reflect the social and cultural background of our people as they lived and moved from place to place during the last

9. 1488–1575.
10. Died *c.*1343.
11. Abbreviation for *she'elot uteshuvot*.
12. The scholars named in the Gemara who lived after the close of the mishnaic period.
13. The scholars named in the Mishna.
14. Moshe Feinstein, *Iggerot Moshe* (New York, 1958–1985); Isaac Jacob Weiss, *Minḥat Yitzḥak* (Jerusalem, 1978).

thousand years.[15] Responsa also record the technological and medical advances of each generation, from the early use of watermills in the production of flour for matza-baking to the latest advances in medicine, such as organ transplantation and neurological definitions of death.

Once in a while, one even comes across *teshuvot* which are hypothetical and esoteric. A remarkable example of this is the responsum of the Ḥakham Tzvi,[16] who analysed the question of whether or not a golem[17] could be counted as part of the required quorum for a *minyan*. Further light is shed upon this unusual problem when one reads the responsum by the Ḥakham's son, Rabbi Jacob Emden.[18] In his collection of responsa, Rabbi Emden reveals a family tradition according to which the Ḥakham Tzvi's grandfather, the Baal Shem of Chelm,[19] had actually produced such a being.[20] He even records his father's account of the events that led to the golem's destruction: apparently the golem became too powerful and so the Baal Shem decided to destroy it by removing the written formula from its forehead. But as he was doing so, the creature scratched his face and he was left with a lasting scar.

In the perusal of responsa literature one is left with an indelible impression of the authors' incredible mastery of the source material. These experts of halakha possessed an encyclopaedic knowledge not just of the Talmud but of the later works as well, and they often wrote their responses whilst burning the midnight oil or in the midst of physical illness. Sometimes they preface their response with an apology for being so severely limited by time but then proceed to respond with a flowing pen, expressing their knowledge freely and showing their true genius. To have the ability to pinpoint one singular talmudic reference which will in one swipe answer a difficult *she'ela* requires extraordinary talmudic knowledge. One such impressive example was Rabbi Moshe Feinstein's *teshuva* on the question posed to him about the permissibility of a blind man taking his

15. Whilst I was a student at Jews' College, Rabbi Rabinovitch gave me a printout of references from the Bar-Ilan computer collection of *teshuvot*, and I was set the task to write a report to Professor Carlebach, head of sociology at Sussex University, who was researching the status of the Jewish maidservant in the Middle Ages. My search resulted (if my memory serves me correctly) in about five relevant *teshuvot* out of a total of about 300 references.
16. Rabbi Tzevi Hirsch Ashkenazi (1656–1718), *She'elot UTeshuvot Hakham Tzevi*, no. 93.
17. An 'automaton' created from clay and animated by the insertion of a mystical formula as described in *Sefer Yetzira*.
18. Lived 1697–1776.
19. Elijah, Baal Shem of Chelm, d. 1583.
20. *She'elot UTeshuvot Yaavetz*, vol. ii, no. 82; see also his *Megillat Sefer*, ch. 1 (p. 30 in the English edn., trans. Rabbi S. B. Leperer and Rabbi M. H. Wise, publ. Maryland by Publishyoursefer.com).

guide dog into the synagogue.[21] Rabbi Feinstein answered in the affirmative, citing a passage from the Jerusalem Talmud, where reference is made to permitting access to the house of learning for a man together with his donkey.[22]

MODERN ACCESS TO RESPONSA MATERIAL

Advances in technology made over the past several decades have revolutionized the study of responsa literature, granting access to a wider readership than ever before. During the mid-1970s Bar-Ilan University pioneered a dial-up access to the vast collection of responsa that they had stored on a main-frame computer. The university later developed a CD version for easier access on a personal computer. Now the material is available via their website by paying a subscription.[23] Other suppliers still offer their collections in CD format, whilst in recent years another provider, Otzerot Hashut, has produced a collection on a portable hard-disc drive.

Unfortunately, whilst the wealth of material is readily available to the researcher proficient in Hebrew, there still remains a relative scarcity of sources for those unversed in the language. True, there are many individual articles both in print and online, with more and more books written in English on halakhic issues, using the vast material from responsa collections. However, there still remains a shortage of specialist books written on the subject, whether containing collections translated into other languages, studies written on the history of responsa literature, or analysis of the material. Perhaps this hindrance is due to the huge volume of material of over 100,000 collections, some of which are multi-volumed. Is it humanly possible to become a master of such a large amount of data? But as Rabbi Tarfon stated in the Ethics of the Fathers: "The day is short, the task is great, the labourers are lazy.... It is not for you to complete the task, but neither are you free to stand aside from it."[24]

21. *Oraḥ Ḥayim*, vol. i, no. 45.

22. Megilla 3:3.

23. www.biu.ac.il/JH/Responsa/contact.htm.

24. Avot 2:20–1. Translation taken from the *Authorised Daily Prayer Book*, trans. Chief Rabbi Lord Sacks (London, 2007).

The Blessings over the Torah: Their Meaning and Some Practical Applications

Rabbi Michael Laitner

"Just as the Torah is central to Jewish life, so the reading of the Torah is central to the synagogue service."

(JONATHAN SACKS, *AUTHORISED DAILY PRAYER BOOK*)

During my years in the United Synagogue rabbinate, I have benefited greatly from Chief Rabbi Lord Sacks' creative *shiurim* and writings about prayer which uncover the profound spiritual and religious messages in the siddur.

These *shiurim* were not delivered in isolation. Lord Sacks also asked us to reveal the siddur to our communities, to share these messages with them. To that end, I have been privileged to teach the Shabbat morning explanatory service at Finchley United Synagogue (Kinloss) and in so doing, have immeasurably enriched my own understanding of the siddur, for which I am extremely grateful both to Lord Sacks and the participants in our service.

In that spirit, this article presents some brief thoughts on the topic of the blessings recited by the person who is called up to the Torah, as well as addressing a fundamental and practical question relating to this central part of the synagogue service.[1]

I also thank another former principal of Jews' College and colleague of Lord Sacks, Rabbi Dr Irving Jacobs, for having opened my eyes to this and so many other topics, as well as for the study method which both the Chief Rabbi and Rabbi Dr Jacobs have taught me.

The book of Nehemiah records the lowly spiritual state of the Jews in Jerusalem in his time (approximately 450 BCE). One famous Rosh Hashana morning, Ezra assembled the people at the Temple's Water Gate and began to teach them the Torah. He did not just read the Torah, though – he also recited blessings over it.[2]

THE MEANING OF THE BLESSINGS

Three times a week, a portion of the Torah is read out to the congregation as part of the synagogue service. A certain number of men are called up (or given an *aliya*) and they are required to recite the following blessings:

The man called up (oleh) *says:* Bless the Lord, the blessed One	העולה אומר: בָּרְכוּ אֶת ה׳ הַמְבוֹרָךְ:
The Congregation responds: Bless the Lord, the blessed One, forever and all time.	והקהל עונין: בָּרוּךְ ה׳ הַמְבוֹרָךְ לְעוֹלָם וָעֶד:
The oleh *continues:* Bless the Lord, the blessed One, forever and all time.	והעולה חוזר: בָּרוּךְ ה׳ הַמְבוֹרָךְ לְעוֹלָם וָעֶד:

1. For further reading please refer to the following sources, in addition to those cited below, all of which have been of assistance in the preparation of this article: *Aspaklaria* (Tel Aviv: Sifriyati, 1978), vol. iv; *Entziklopedya Talmudit* (Jerusalem: Talmudic Encyclopaedic Publications Limited, 1956), vol. iv; Macy Nulman, *The Encyclopaedia of Jewish Prayer* (London and New Jersey: Aronson, 1993) (all referring to *birkat haTorah*); *Siddur Rabbenu Shelomo ben Rabbenu Shimshon Migarmiza* (Jerusalem: Chemed, 1972); Y. Yaakovson, *Netiv Bina* (Tel Aviv: Sinai, 1991); J. Hertz, *Commentary on the Siddur* (New York: Bloch, 1948); Ismar Elbogen, *Jewish Liturgy: A Comprehensive History*, trans. Raymond P. Scheindlin (Jewish Publication Society, 1993).
2. Neh. 8:7.

Blessed are You, Lord our God, King of the Universe, who has chosen us from all peoples and has given us His Torah. Blessed are You, Lord, Giver of the Torah. [The Torah is now read]	בָּרוּךְ אַתָּה ה׳ אֱלֹהֵינוּ מֶלֶךְ הָעוֹלָם. אֲשֶׁר בָּחַר בָּנוּ מִכָּל הָעַמִּים. וְנָתַן לָנוּ אֶת תּוֹרָתוֹ. בָּרוּךְ אַתָּה ה׳, נוֹתֵן הַתּוֹרָה:
After the reading, the oleh says: Blessed are You, Lord our God, King of the Universe, who has given us the Torah of truth, planting everlasting life in our midst. Blessed are You, Lord, Giver of the Torah.[3]	ואחר קריאת הפרשה: בָּרוּךְ אַתָּה ה׳ אֱלֹהֵינוּ מֶלֶךְ הָעוֹלָם. אֲשֶׁר נָתַן לָנוּ תּוֹרַת אֱמֶת וְחַיֵּי עוֹלָם נָטַע בְּתוֹכֵנוּ. בָּרוּךְ אַתָּה ה׳, נוֹתֵן הַתּוֹרָה:[4]

The first of the two blessings that the *oleh* (the person called up to the Torah) recites refers to the covenantal relationship between God and the Jewish people, which was reaffirmed at Mount Sinai through the giving of the Torah.[5] In this blessing we bless God for having chosen to give it to us.[6]

The second blessing mentions *Torat Emet* (the Torah of truth) – in the traditional explanation this is a reference to the Written Torah. The phrase *ḥayei olam* – 'everlasting life' – on the other hand represents/stands for the Oral Torah, since, we may suggest, it is the legal framework and consequential dynamism provided by the latter which have helped the Torah flourish through being applied to changing circumstances by rabbinic decisors throughout the ages. The phrase *nata betokhenu* has the gematria of 613, corresponding to the number of *mitzvot* in the Torah.[7]

These blessings, and the context in which we say them, clearly express our belief in the Revelation at Sinai. Indeed, we stand and hold the Torah at the time of making these blessings, showing that we too are receiving and holding onto it from Sinai, part of the unbreakable chain.[8]

3. Chief Rabbi Lord Sacks, translation to the *Authorised Daily Prayer Book*, 4th edn. (London, 2006), 125.
4. Hebrew text from http://www.onlinesiddur.com/shac/. Our text as an 'authorized' version goes back at least as far as the ninth-century *Seder Rav Amram Gaon*, the most influential of early siddurim.
5. Following Ps. 119:142. Also see *Tur, Oraḥ Ḥayim* 47.
6. See Avoda Zara 2b for the famous *midrash* about God offering the Torah to various peoples before the Jews accepted; see also *Masekhet Soferim* 14:6.
7. *Siddur Beit Yaakov* of Rabbi Jacob Emden (Lemberg edn. 1903, 84b).
8. Rabbi Mordecai Yaffe, *Levush*, ch. 139.

At certain times in Jewish history, the emphasis on faith as reflected in these blessings needed to be even clearer. *Masekhet Soferim*,[9] a collection including some material from both talmudic and post-talmudic times, notes an alternative text for the final blessing of the *oleh*: *asher natan lanu Torah min hashamayim* (who has given us Torah from Heaven).[10]

It would seem, on the basis of what we have seen so far, that it would be very difficult to justify calling an irreligious Jew to the Torah to recite these blessings, since his own attitudes to mitzva observance or Jewish faith do not reflect the values of faith implicit in them. Yet centrist Orthodox communities have members, and welcome visitors, whose attitude towards observance or belief in Torah from Heaven (or other fundamentals of Jewish faith) may not be at one with the affirmation of faith proclaimed by these blessings.

How such congregants may be called up to the Torah and recite its blessings is a critical question for communal rabbis, who would be expected to call up a male congregant for a special family occasion or a *yahrzeit* regardless of their level of religiosity. Can such call-ups be justified? And if so, how can the resulting blessings represent true statements of faith?

CONTEMPORARY RABBINIC ATTITUDES TO CALLING UP A NON-BELIEVER

Rabbi Ovadia Yosef was asked,[11] *inter alia,* about whether a Jewish man who shaves with a razor (in a way which is in contravention of halakha) can be called up to the Torah. In his customary encyclopaedic way, Rabbi Yosef initially quotes numerous sources in outlining why it is inappropriate to call up such a Jew (or indeed any Jew whose lack of observance would disqualify him from being a witness), before providing another wide range of sources which apply more lenient halakhic principles allowing such a person to have an *aliya.*[12]

---

9. *Soferim* 13:8. This tractate may have been finalized in Israel around the eighth century.

10. Elbogen (p. 141) suggests that this version was meant for home rather than public use and feels that the 'faulty' text of *Masekhet Soferim* means that we cannot settle this question. Rabbi Dr Irving Jacobs, in response to a question from the present writer, suggests that this shows that the Babylonian Talmud's version of these blessings was not adopted in the Land of Israel. He also suggests that the phrase *Torah min hashamayim* as used here was directed against the Pauline calumny that God was not the author of the whole Torah and that He only gave the Ten Commandments. We may suggest that this reasoning would date this particular version of the blessing to pre-mishnaic times.

11. *Yeḥave Daat* 2:16.

12. For example, Rabbi Yosef also notes that the Talmud in Megilla 23a rules that *hakol olin leminyan shiva,* that anybody can be called up to the seven *aliyot* on Shabbat – hence the interpretation that our sages did not exclude anybody on the basis of their level of observance.

After extensive analysis, Rabbi Yosef's conclusion is that it is permitted in essence to call up a non-observant Jew, but that it is preferable to do so via a *hosafa* (extra call-up) rather than as one of the obligatory number of *aliyot* for that day. In this response, Rabbi Yosef emphasizes the importance of providing opportunities for bringing people closer to Jewish observance, in as pleasant a way as possible.[13]

Conversely, in a responsum written in 1950, Rabbi Moshe Feinstein (d. 1986) addresses the question of giving an honour in a synagogue service to a man whose work benefitted the community greatly and who was a person of great kindness, but who had married out and had left Orthodoxy for Reform.[14] Focusing his discussion on the prohibition of *ḥanifa*, inappropriate flattery, Rabbi Feinstein rules that we may show respect to such a person and offer him an honour such as the opening of the ark, as long as it is clear that we are not endorsing the negative elements of his behaviour. Right at the end of his comments, Rabbi Feinstein specifically says that such a person should not be called to the Torah.

CONCLUSION

I am privileged to work in a United Synagogue and United Hebrew Congregations rabbinate that, led by Chief Rabbi Lord Sacks for so many years, teaches aspirational Judaism, accepting with love all Jews that we encounter, regardless of religious level. Furthermore, by joining an Orthodox community, which practises authentic Judaism, our members show affiliation to the aspirations of Judaism, however far they may feel from them personally.[15] This applies to both the most observant and the least observant Jew – who sit together in the same synagogue – for religious life is like an escalator on which one cannot stand still; one must choose to go forward or, otherwise, one slides backwards.

---

13. See also Responsa *Bemareh HaBazak* 1:2 (Jerusalem: Eretz Ḥemdah Kollel, 1999), which also ruled permissively in response to a query from an Israeli rabbi serving in a diaspora community where there were very few observant Jews.

    The late Rabbi Ḥayim David HaLevi (d. 1998), the former Chief Rabbi of Tel Aviv, was also lenient in response to a question from a rabbi whose synagogue was hosting the bar mitzva of a non-religious family. This rabbi was concerned lest the family go to a Reform synagogue, should the Orthodox one not allow the bar mitzva. Rabbi HaLevi instructed the rabbi to accept the bar mitzva request, and reach out to the family with warmth, showing them the pleasantness of Torah and *mitzvot*.

14. *Responsa Iggerot Moshe, Oraḥ Ḥayim*, 2:51.

15. See Jonathan Sacks, *Community of Faith* (London, 1995) for an extensive treatment of this subject.

Therefore, whenever we hear a Jew make the blessings on being called up to the Torah, we should be inspired by the words of faith which he states and the honour which he gives to the Torah by saying them, however true to his words his actions may be. These blessings join him and every one of us to the chain of Judaism from Sinai.

Unfair to Teraḥ?

Rabbi Zorach Meir Salasnik

The father of our first patriarch is perceived in a strongly negative light in Jewish tradition. The most familiar event in his life can be sourced from a *midrash* that relates how Teraḥ owned a shop selling idols, and one day, leaving his son Abram in charge, he returned to find the idols broken.[1] Abram subsequently explained that a fight had occurred and the idols had smashed each other. To Teraḥ's response that idols are only wood and stone and could not possibly have instigated a riot, Abram reasoned with him that if they were so impassive, perhaps he should not worship them.

The first identification of Teraḥ as an idolater is in the book of Joshua (24:2), which states that he was the father of Abraham and Naḥor, and they worshipped idols. Who are meant by 'they'? The traditional explanation is Teraḥ and Naḥor. However, linguistically, it could be all three: Teraḥ, Abram, and Naḥor. Any or all of those three could have become, subsequently, believers in God.

Rashi, too, seems to adopt an unsympathetic view of Teraḥ. Explaining why his death in Ḥaran is recorded in the Torah prior to Abram leaving for Canaan, even though Teraḥ was to live for a further sixty years, Rashi quotes a midrashic aphorism that "the wicked are called dead even in their lifetime."[2]

1. Genesis Rabba 38:13.
2. Rashi on Gen. 11:32.

Ostensibly, then, this is the only possible view of Teraḥ – an idolator, 'wicked' even. Yet the written text of the Torah presents him in a neutral light – as a man who, after the death of one of his sons, Haran, led the remaining members of his family towards Canaan, perhaps to remove them from oppression or from unhappy memories, perhaps for economic benefit, maybe even for the spiritual advantages that his son Abram would ultimately find in the Holy Land. But that journey was never completed, at least not by Teraḥ. He stayed in Ḥaran, a few hundred miles short of his desired destination, whilst it was Abram who reached Canaan. In so doing, was Abram attempting to move away from Teraḥ's lifestyle, or was he actually completing his father's mission?

To try and answer this question, we must examine how Abraham himself perceived the qualities of his immediate family. When dispatching Eliezer to find a wife for Isaac, he specified that a girl from a Canaanite family must not be chosen. However, if his sole motive had been merely to avoid Isaac marrying a Canaanite, there would have been no need to specify that Eliezer should go "to my native land and my birthplace."[3] The servant could have looked among the more distant relatives of the descendants of Shem or of Japheth. Clearly, Abraham recognized that the appropriate matriarch could only be from Teraḥ's family.

Indeed, all our matriarchs are descended from Teraḥ. Sarah, according to the Midrash, was the daughter of Haran, son of Teraḥ.[4] Rebecca was the daughter of Betuel, son of Naḥor, son of Teraḥ. Rachel and Leah were daughters of Laban, son of Betuel. Although it is possible that, apart from Sarah, the other three were all born after Teraḥ's death, genetic qualities or the memory of him that his family would have passed on seemingly inspired the attributes that enabled them to be appropriate matriarchs of the Jewish people.

Moving forward in time, we can continue to see this dichotomy within Teraḥ's descendants. In Tractate Avoda Zara 2b, we read that God offered the Torah to every nation, but was declined when one of the commandments was found to be contrary to their nature or heritage. This is based on Deuteronomy 33:2, which relates God venturing from Sinai, where the Torah was given, to Seir, the home of Esau, and to Paran, the place of Ishmael. In *Sifrei* 343, however, only four nations are specified as declining the Torah: Esau, Ammon, Moab, and Ishmael. The *Torah Temima* on the above verse explains the distinction between Esau and Ishmael, whose approach by God is hinted at in the verse, and the other

3. Gen. 24:3-4.
4. Megilla 14a.

nations, for whom it is the Talmud that details their having declined the offer.[5] As descendants of Abraham, Esau and Ishmael had more connection with the Torah. I would go further and suggest that the *Sifrei's* choice in including Ammon and Moab's response, but not that of other nations, is that descendants of Teraḥ also had more connection with the Torah than the rest of the world (albeit not as much as Abraham's direct descendants).

While these nations did not rise to the challenge presented from Sinai, it is noteworthy that the exemplars of Torah acceptance and subsequent conversion in the Bible are often the offspring of Teraḥ. Jethro, the very first non-Israelite to embrace the Torah, was descended from Midian;[6] Ruth from Moab;[7] and Naama, Solomon's wife, from Ammon.[8] Yet most descendants of Teraḥ failed to take the opportunity provided by the giving of the Torah. They could have risen to the challenge as offspring of Abraham, the personification of *ḥesed* (kindness), or even of the Teraḥ who ultimately repented.[9] Instead, they related to Esau's penchant for killing, Ishmael's for stealing, and Lot and his daughters' incest.

To conclude where we began, examining the man Teraḥ based simply on what we are told in the text: looking at the initial verses of *Parashat Lekh Lekha* in the context of those last verses of *Parashat Noaḥ* in which Teraḥ travelled towards Canaan but did not complete his journey, Chief Rabbi Emeritus Lord Sacks writes:

> These are the generations of Teraḥ. Teraḥ fathered Abram, Naḥor, and Haran; and Haran fathered Lot.... Teraḥ took Abram his son and Lot the son of Haran, his grandson, and Sarai his daughter-in-law, his son Abram's wife, and they went forth together from Ur of the Chaldeans to go into the land of Canaan, but when they came to Ḥaran, they settled there. The days of Teraḥ were 205 years, and Teraḥ died in Ḥaran.[10]
>
> The implication seems to be that far from breaking with his father, Abraham was continuing a journey Teraḥ had already begun.
>
> How are we to reconcile these two passages? The simplest way, taken by most commentators, is that they are not in chronological sequence. The call to Abraham (in Gen. 12) happened first. Abraham heard the divine summons, and communicated it to his father. The family set

5. I am indebted to Rabbi Nisson Wilson for drawing this to my attention.
6. Ex. 18:1.
7. Ruth 1:4.
8. 1 Kings 14:21.
9. Rashi on Gen. 15:15.
10. Gen 11:31.

> out together, but Teraḥ stopped halfway, in Ḥaran. The passage recording Teraḥ's death is placed before Abraham's call, though it happened later, to guard Abraham from the accusation that he failed to honour his father by leaving him in his old age (Rashi, Midrash).
>
> Yet there is another obvious possibility. Abraham's spiritual insight did not come from nowhere. Teraḥ had already made the first tentative move toward monotheism. Children complete what their parents begin.[11]

It is possible that in his positive view of the Teraḥ–Abram relationship, Lord Sacks is thinking of the encouragement given to him by his own father. Often the Chief Rabbi Emeritus mentioned how he would ask him a question to which, not knowing the answer, his father would reply that he had not had the benefit of education, but his hope was that his children would learn and eventually be able to respond. The father encouraged the son to achieve in the next generation what he could only wish for himself. Like Abraham, Lord Sacks finished the journey that his father had encouraged him to begin.

11. *Covenant and Conversation, Lekh Lekha* (27 Oct. 2012/11 Cheshvan 5773).

Until Elijah Comes: Two Views of the Messianic Era

Rabbi Rashi Simon

It is a pleasure to dedicate this essay in honour of Chief Rabbi Jonathan Sacks on the occasion of his retirement from office after more than two decades of dedicated and fecund service to the Jewish community and indeed British society as a whole.

As I write these lines, Erev Pesaḥ 5773, my thoughts turn to the expected arrival of the Prophet Elijah, harbinger of the redemption. The lines that follow are an attempt to trace the two broad views in our tradition as to the nature of the messianic era.

In Leviticus 26:3–6 the Torah describes the prosperity and security which will follow "if you walk in My decrees and observe My commandments and perform them":

> I will provide you with rain at the right time, and the land will give its produce and the tree of the fields will give its fruit… you will eat your bread to satiety and you will dwell securely in your land. I will provide peace in the land, and you will lie down with none to frighten you. I will rid the land of dangerous animals and a sword will not cross your land.

The Torah develops this theme until verse 12: "I will walk among you… and you will be a nation [dedicated] to Me." Concerning this verse Naḥmanides (Ramban) writes:

> והנה הוזכר כאן גן עדן והעולם הבא ליודעיו, ואלה הברכות בתשלומיהן לא תהיינה רק בהיות כל ישראל עושין רצון אביהם... ודע כי לא השיגו ישראל מעולם לברכות האלה בשלימותן לא הרבים ולא היחידים מהם, שלא עלתה זכותם לכך... ועל כן תמצא לרבותינו ז״ל שיזכירו בפסוקים האלה לעתיד לבוא: מלמד שתינוק מישראל עתיד להיות מושיט וכו׳, עתיד הקב״ה לטייל עם הצדיקים לעתיד לבוא, כי לא נתקיים, אבל יתקיים עמנו בזמן השלימות.
>
> We have here a reference to Gan Eden and the World to Come to those who understand it. These blessings in their entirety will apply only when all of Israel perform the will of their Father [in Heaven]…. Be aware that Israel never achieved the complete fulfilment of these blessings, in numbers great or small, as their merit did not suffice…. Therefore you will find that the sages apply these verses to the future: "'A child of Israel will extend his hand [to the eye of a viper]': In the future the Holy One blessed be He will stroll with the righteous", for it has not yet been fulfilled, but it will be realized in the time of completeness.[1]

If, as Ramban teaches, this passage refers to the messianic era, a close reading may reveal an insight into the nature of that epoch. Indeed, Ramban himself does this for us, specifically in interpreting the phrase in verse 6, והשבתי חיה רעה מן הארץ:

> על דעת ר׳ יהודה שאמר מעבירן מן העולם, הוא כפשוטו שלא יבואו חיות רעות בארצם, כי בהיות השבע וברכות הטובה והיות הערים מלאות אדם לא תבאנה חיות בישוב, ועל דעת רבי שמעון שאמר משביתן שלא יזיקו, יאמר והשבתי רעת החיות מן הארץ, והוא הנכון, כי תהיה ארץ ישראל בעת קיום המצוות כאשר היה העולם מתחילתו קודם חטאו של אדם הראשון... והנה בבריאתו של עולם נאמר בחיות שנתן להם העשב לאכלה...
>
> ובהיות ארץ ישראל על השלימות תשבות רעת מנהגם ויעמדו על הטבע הראשון אשר הושם בהם בעת יצירתם.
>
> "I will rid the land of dangerous animals": In the view of Rabbi Judah, the intent is to remove them from the world [i.e. your environs], and this is the simple meaning, that menacing animals will not enter your land. For when there is plenty and the cities are full of people, the animals will not enter the inhabited places.

1. Naḥmanides, *Commentary on the Torah,* Lev. 26:12.

> But in the opinion of Rabbi Simon, the meaning is that Hashem will rid the animals of their ferocious nature, that is, I will remove the *ferocity of the animals* from the Land. And this [in my view] is correct, as the Land of Israel at the time of the fulfilment of the *mitzvot* will be as the world was at its inception, prior to the sin of Adam…. At the time of Creation the animals were given the grass of the field to eat [Gen. 1:30]…. When the Land of Israel is in its state of perfection, the violent [and carnivorous] nature of the animals will be expunged and they will be restored to the original nature that was implanted within them at the time of their creation.

In other words, Rabbi Judah maintains that the blessing will take the form of a natural state of prosperity and peace, as a result of which ferocious animals will hunt their prey, as is their nature, in the forests, away from human habitation, and will not menace society. Rabbi Simon, on the other hand, is of the view that God will remove the *ferociousness of the animals* entirely. They will no longer maul and kill one another, even for food, but they will become herbivorous, as was the Divine intent at the dawn of Creation.

Ramban endorses the latter view, and notes that these blessings have never (yet) been fulfilled in their entirety. The *Sifra*, evidently Ramban's source, records this tannaitic dispute and adds, expressing a belief in the miraculous nature of the transformation of the world,

> And so it says [in the famous vision of Isaiah 11:6–8], "The wolf will live with the sheep and the leopard will lie down with the kid; and the calf and the young lion and a fatling together, and a young child will lead them. A cow and bear will graze and their young will lie down together; and a lion, like cattle, will eat hay. A suckling will play by a viper's hole; and a newly weaned child will stretch his hand toward an adder's lair."[2]

Isaiah concludes this famous passage with the stirring words, "They will neither injure nor destroy in all of My sacred mountain; the earth will be as filled with knowledge of God as the waters cover the sea."

Of course the passage from Isaiah is only one of a great many prophecies which foretell of an idyllic, utopian future for Israel in the messianic era. What is Rabbi Judah to make of this and similar prophecies? It would seem that he must

2. *Torat Kohanim, Beḥukotai* 2:1.

understand it as a metaphor only. This suggestion is explicit in the writings of the Rambam, as we shall see.[3]

The tannaitic dispute is echoed in the Talmud in a well-known passage. Berakhot 34b records the view of Rabbi Ḥiya bar Abba in the name of Rabbi Yoḥanan: All the prophets prophesied only about the messianic era, but as for the World to Come, "No eye except yours, O God, has seen" (Isaiah 64:3).[4] The Gemara continues: "And he [Rabbi Yoḥanan] disagrees with [the *amora*] Samuel, who said, 'The sole difference between the present and the messianic days is delivery from servitude to foreign powers,' as the Torah says, 'for the destitute people will not cease from the land' [Deut. 15:17]."

In contrast to Ramban's endorsement of the "transformed world" vision of Rabbi Simon, Maimonides (Rambam) emphatically follows the view of Samuel as he writes in *Hilkhot Melakhim*, 12:1–2:

> Let no one think that in the days of the Messiah any of the laws of nature will be set aside, or any innovation be introduced into creation.[5] The world will follow its normal course. The words of Isaiah, "And the wolf shall dwell with the lamb, and the leopard shall lie down with the kid", are to be understood figuratively, meaning that Israel will live securely among the wicked of the heathens, who are likened to wolves and leopards, as it is written: "the wolf of the deserts despoils them, the leopard stalks their cities" [Jer. 5:6]... All similar expressions used in connection with the messianic era are metaphorical... Said the rabbis [i.e. Samuel, as above], "The sole difference between the present and the messianic days is delivery from servitude to foreign powers."[6]

3. *Mishne Torah, Hilkhot Melakhim* 12:1, also "*Ma'amar Teḥiyat HaMetim*", in *Iggerot HaRambam* (Jerusalem: Mossad HaRav Kook, 1981), 370.
4. See also Sanhedrin 91b; Shabbat 151b.
5. In his *Animadversions* (*Hasagot*) Rabad disputes this assertion by citing our verse in Lev. 26:6: "I will remove the ferocious animals from the Land." Rabad clearly understands this verse as Rabbi Simon (and Ramban). Of course the same allegorical approach of Rambam (see further) to the verses in Isaiah and Jeremiah may be applied here. Radvaz says exactly this, before attempting to partially reconcile the two views. See also following note.
6. I. Twersky, *A Maimonides Reader* (New York, 1972), 234. Similarly, *Hilkhot Teshuva* 9:2. The Gra (Vilna Gaon), in an extended gloss (to *Melakhim* 12:2), seeks to reconcile this unequivocal statement with *Teshuva* 8:7, where Rambam cites approvingly the opposing epigram of R. Hiya bar Abba, through recourse to the concept of the Messiah from the house of Joseph as a preliminary to the Messiah from the house of David. See also *Leḥem Mishne* on *Teshuva* 8:7.

We have here a classic instance of the divergent views of the rationalists, represented by Rambam, and the mystics (*mekubbalim*), represented by Ramban (who was among the first to introduce the kabbalistic tradition to a wider readership through his popular and influential Torah commentary[7]).[8] It has been suggested[9] that with the lengthy and arduous exile, and particularly the trauma of the Spanish Expulsion, the supernatural, "transformed world" messianic vision of Ramban and the mystics gradually gained ascendancy, for example through the writings of Rabbi Judah Loew (Maharal),[10] Rabbi Moses Ḥayim Luzzatto (Ramḥal),[11] the Vilna Gaon,[12] and the hasidic masters over the rational but more quotidian view of Rambam and the philosophers.[13]

---

7. For more on Ramban's role in disseminating and popularizing the esoteric tradition, see R. Meir ibn Gabbai, *Avodat HaKodesh*, ch. 13, quoted in R. Joseph Irgas, *Shomer Emunin: HaPetaḥ VeHaMavo LeḤokhmat HaKabala*, Introduction 2, Principle 2 (p. 11 in Ahavat Shalom edn.: Jerusalem, 5770). Also quoted in C. D. Chavel (ed.), *Ramban al HaTorah*, 1:542 (*Hashmatot uMiluim*).
8. To be sure, the dispute predates Rambam and Ramban: In *Maamar Teḥiyat HaMetim* (above, n. 1), Rambam specifically cites eleventh-century Spanish exegetes, "R. Moses ibn Gikatilla and [R. Judah] ibn Balaam and other commentators [such as R. Abraham ibn Ezra on Isaiah 11:6] who preceded me" in arguing for a metaphorical interpretation of Isaiah's vision. Cf. Radak ad loc., who limits the phenomenon to the Land of Israel (here described as "My holy mountain").

   Isadore Twersky, in *Introduction to the Code of Maimonides*, p. 451 n. 231, suggests that the target of Rambam's polemic may be R. Hai Gaon's "detailed apocalyptic forecast" cited in *Arugat HaBosem*, ed. Ephraim Urbach, 1:256 ff. Professor Twersky continues:

   > Clearly, in these chapters on Messianism, Maimonides is bold and vigorous, striking a major blow for the antiapocalyptic conception. It should be noted, however, that relying on a single Talmudic statement while ignoring a host of other statements is consonant with his approach of subordinating details to one overriding, formative principle… Maimonides' approach to the problems of messianic theory – his polemic with predecessors and the criticism, in turn, directed against him – is paradigmatic for the entire history of messianic thought which may be seen as a history of conflicting interpretations (literal versus metaphorical) of key scriptural verses.
9. Most notably in the academic world by Gershom Scholem in his seminal work *Shabatai Zevi* (see I: Background of the Sabbatian Movement), although I first heard it from Rabbi Berel Wein of Monsey, now Jerusalem.
10. See *Kitvei Maharal MiPrag*, ed. Avraham Kariv (Jerusalem: Mossad HaRav Kook, 1972)), 1:108–77, esp. 167–9.
11. e.g. *Derekh Hashem*, 2:4:8 and 4:7:2.
12. As above, n. 6.
13. There is a hint of the sympathy for the supernatural messianic era in the comments of Radvaz referred to above, n. 5. This is even more striking in the comments of the Gra, as above, n. 6. See also the comments of Professor Twersky above, n. 8.

I would like, however, to consider also Rambam's evocative comments immediately preceding these remarks at the end of *Hilkhot Melakhim* 11:[14]

> But if he does not meet with full success, or is slain, it is obvious that he is not the Messiah promised in the Torah. He is to be regarded like all the other wholehearted and worthy kings of the House of David who died and whom the Holy One, blessed be He, raised up to test the multitude, as it is written, "And some of the wise men will stumble in clarifying [these words], and in elucidating and interpreting when the End will be, for it is not yet the appointed time" [Dan. 11:35].
>
> Even of Jesus of Nazareth, who imagined that he was the Messiah, but was put to death by the court, Daniel had prophesied, as it is written, "And the sons of the corrupt among your people will exalt themselves to establish a vision, but they will stumble" [Dan. 11:14]. For has there ever been a greater stumbling than this? All the prophets foretold that the Messiah would redeem the Jews, help them, gather in the exiles, and support their observance of the *mitzvot*. But he caused Israel to be put to the sword, their remnant to be dispersed and humiliated. He was instrumental in changing the Torah and causing the world to err and serve another besides God.
>
> But it is beyond the human mind to fathom the designs of the Creator; for our ways are not His ways, neither are our thoughts His thoughts. All these matters relating to Jesus of Nazareth and the Ishmaelite [Mohammed] who came after him only served to clear the way for King Messiah, to prepare the whole world to worship God with one accord, as it is written, "For then I will turn to the peoples a pure language, that they may all call upon the name of the Lord to serve Him with one consent" [Zeph. 3:9].[15] Thus the messianic hope, the Torah, and the commandments have become familiar topics – topics of conversation [among the inhabitants] of the far isles and many peoples, uncircumcised of heart and flesh. They are discussing these matters and the commandments of the Torah. Some say, "Those commandments were true, but have lost their validity and are no longer binding"; others declare that they had an esoteric meaning and were not intended to be taken literally; that the Messiah has already come

14. His remarks are absent in many standard editions; see n. 16 below.

15. In *Kuzari* 4:21 R. Judah HaLevi writes essentially the same idea (approximately 150 years earlier). Whether Rambam was familiar with the *Kuzari* is uncertain.

> and revealed their occult significance. But when the true King Messiah will appear and succeed, be exalted and lifted up, they will forthwith recant and realize that they have inherited naught but lies from their fathers, that their prophets and forebears led them astray. [16]

Looking, for the moment, beyond the candid characterization of Christianity and Islam as standing in contrast to the Torah, we see here also the perspective that, over the centuries, mankind has indeed progressed towards better times.

It is easy to despair of improvement in the human condition when considering the violence, godlessness, and moral turpitude all around, to say nothing of the shocking retrogression of the twentieth century in so many ways, including the Holocaust, the carnage of two world wars, and the millions of victims of Stalin and Mao Zedong. Yet here we see another view. Perhaps the non-Torah content of Christianity and Islam are nevertheless, ironically, part of the divine plan to spread the teachings of the Torah throughout the world.

I had exactly this thought in the summer of 1992, when, on a visit to Gibraltar, my wife and I found ourselves waiting for a bus in Andalucia. I was approached by an affable and well-presented man of my age (then), who, noticing my *kippa*, asked me if I was from Israel. When I told him that I was from the USA, and I lived in Britain, he was surprised, as he thought that all *kippa*-wearers are from Israel. After dispelling that misconception, we got to talking, and I asked him where he was from, as it was obvious from his accent that he was not Spanish. He informed me that he was from the Fiji Islands, and that he was with his country's delegation at the Expo in Seville, which was ongoing that summer. In reply to my question, he told me that the natives of Fiji are predominantly Christian. I probed a little further, and, feigning naivety, I asked if they have 'always' been Christian, or if there was a native religion which predated Christianity.

"Oh, definitely," he said. For thousands of years, the Fijians had been pagans and idolaters, practising a primitive religion in which human sacrifice predominated. Cannibalism had been common and had in fact been a characteristic feature of Fijian culture. This was the case until Christian missionaries arrived in the eighteenth and nineteenth centuries.

---

16. *Hilkhot Melakhim* 11:4. The passage has been censored in the standard contemporary editions, but is found in the Rome 1475 and Amsterdam 1703 editions. It has been restored in the new Frankel edition (Jerusalem 5766). (It also appears in English in Twersky, *A Maimonides Reader* [Springfield, NJ, 1972], 226–7, from where this translation is taken.)

I nonchalantly asked him how long ago cannibalism was to be found in Fiji. He informed me that even in his grandparents' time (that is, mid-twentieth century) cannibalism was not uncommon. It was the influence of the missionaries (and, latterly, the British) which gradually expunged it. I thought to myself: as a Jew, I have many criticisms of Christianity – theological, philosophical, historical, and political. But Christianity has undeniably made a profound contribution to human civilization. (The same can be said for Islam, of course.) The Rambam needs no endorsement – certainly not from me – but here is a resounding example of the teachings of the Torah, albeit presented through the prism of a different religion reaching "the far isles" of the South Pacific.

In sum, whether we follow the view of Ramban and the *mekubbalim* or that of Rambam and the rationalists, there is undoubtedly abundant room for improvement, in the status of Israel and of all mankind. Nevertheless, the divine plan for Man continues towards its successful and much-anticipated dénouement. May the Redeemer come speedily, and תשבי יתרץ קושיות ובעיות.[17]

17. This well-known epigram is found in *Tosefot Yom Tov*, end of Eduyot.

"For Zion's Sake I Shall Not Remain Silent": May We Publicly Criticize the State of Israel?

Rabbi Gideon D. Sylvester

I am delighted to present this essay in honour of my beloved and revered teacher Rabbi Sacks, whose Torah is a constant source of inspiration.

INTRODUCTION

Public attacks on Israel are often associated with deep hatred of the Jewish people and its right to a homeland. With the increasing vehemence of this "new anti-Semitism", our communities have become ever more defensive, treating all public criticism of Israel with grave suspicion.[1]

---

1. See Anthony Julius, *Trials of the Diaspora: A History of Anti-Semitism in England* (paperback edn., Oxford, 2012), 441–2, where he explains that the "new anti-Semitism" may be recognized by its "indifference to the complexity of the historical record, and its one-eyed refusal to find fault with any party other than Israel". I am most grateful to Anthony for his generous help and support with this project.

Concurrently, however, some Diaspora Jews have been arguing that if they are called upon to give financial and political assistance to Israel, redress the increasing disaffection of young Jews, and shield Israel from ongoing criticism, then they are entitled to speak out when they perceive things to be wrong. They wish to end the tradition of unconditional public support for Israel, especially when they feel that the Israeli government's policies pose an existential, moral, or physical danger to the country.[2]

The State of Israel now houses approximately half of the world's Jews and it is the Jewish people's largest undertaking in thousands of years. Allegiance to our people is central to our faith. Maimonides makes it a condition of life in the World to Come: "Someone who withdraws from communal ways, even if he didn't commit any sins, but differentiates himself from the congregation of Israel and does not fulfil any communal commandments or fast any of the communal fasts, but goes in his own way like one of the gentile nations as if he isn't a Jew, does not have a share in the World To Come."[3]

2. See e.g. the website of J Street, which quotes former Israeli Prime Minister Ariel Sharon, "Israel is not only an Israeli project. Israel is a Jewish, worldwide project." Followed by the remark that Israelis have priority in deciding the fate of their nation, it continues: "However, as conscientious Americans committed to Israel's future, we have a civic duty to be involved in the US policy-making process. As members of the Jewish people, we have a right and obligation to be honest about the circumstances in which Israel now finds itself. J Street is continuing in that proud tradition. Israelis have to make their own choices; as friends and family, we are offering our perspective and our advice out of love." http://jstreet.org/what-right.

   The J Street website also makes reference to a poll conducted by the Begin-Sadat Center for Strategic Studies (BESA Center), the Bar-Ilan University Center for International Communication (CIC), and the Anti-Defamation League (ADL) in 2012, which showed that 61% of Israelis say that American Jews have a right to freely and publicly criticize Israel and Israeli policies under some or all circumstances, while 36% said they do not. http://www.adl.org/press-center/press-releases/israel-middle-east/poll-of-israeli-public-shows-overwhelming-appreciation-for-the-us.html.

   J Street's British sister organization Yachad, while declaring its loyalty to Israel and opposition to Israel's detractors, says that it opposes the occupation: "Now is the moment for diaspora Jews to play their part, to draw on the most enduring Jewish values and do all they can in the search for peace. As a growing consensus across the diaspora now agrees, we have both the right and the responsibility to step up."

3. Maimonides, *Hilkhot Teshuva* 3:11. See also Yevamot 47a: the first question addressed to a potential convert regards his or her willingness to join and associate with a persecuted people. This element of Jewish responsibility is discussed in Rabbi J. B. Soloveitchik's essay "*Kol Dodi Dofek*", translated into English in Bernhard H. Rosenberg and Fred Heuman (eds.), *Theological and Halakhic Reflections on the Holocaust* (Hoboken: Ktav, 1992).

How we express our fidelity to Israel is more complex. For some, it means that the government of Israel is entitled to our unconditional support. Israel, they argue, has enough enemies; when Jews demonstrate against the policies of the Jewish State, it sows doubts in the minds of the world's leaders, creating dissonance amongst those whom we call upon to support and defend Israel.[4]

This belief that Jews should give total support to Israel has been given new theological underpinning by Religious Zionists who speak of the State of Israel as "the beginning of the flowering of messianic redemption". They have bestowed mystical significance on the organs of government so that, according to one commentator, the state and its institutions are now "regarded as endowed with a divine imperator", and "army uniforms became the new priestly garments". This turned criticism of Israel into something bordering on heresy.[5]

Others argue that if the government's mistaken policies are morally flawed, then the country is best served by critical friends who can persuade it to change course, restoring its moral standing, reputation, and credibility around the world. Willingness to criticize Israel, they maintain, is an important element of contemporary Zionism.[6]

While the importance of rabbis and educators acting as ambassadors for the Jewish State is widely acknowledged, little has been said about how we should respond when they criticize the State of Israel. Is it religiously sanctioned?[7]

SPEAKING BADLY OF THE JEWISH PEOPLE

Criticism of the Jewish people, however well justified, was never loved by the rabbis. A *midrash* relates how Resh Lakish and Rabbi Abahu once visited the city of Caesarea, a place of mixed reputation. Rabbi Abahu clearly felt uncomfortable

4. See e.g. Rabbi Yosef Blau, "Did American Orthodox Jews Forsake their Israeli Brothers? A Rejoinder", in *Jewish Action Magazine* (Winter 5766/2005), 41, and Benjamin Kerstein, "All Criticism of Israel is Anti-Semitic", *Jerusalem Post*, 20 July 2012.
5. Moshe Koppel, "The Demise of Self-Negating Religious Zionism", in Chaim I. Waxman (ed.), *Religious Zionism Post Disengagement, Future Directions* (New York, Yeshiva University Press, 2008), 123.
6. See e.g. Rabbi Emanuel Feldman, who bitterly criticizes the Modern Orthodox community in America for failing to protest the disengagement from Gaza: "not only did this American Orthodox community not growl angrily; it did not even offer a protesting meow"; "Modern Orthodoxy and the Failure of Nerve", *Jewish Action Magazine* (Winter 5766/2005), 38.
7. The idea that diaspora rabbis might act as political ambassadors for Israel was raised by Israeli Government Minister Yuli Edelstein, who approached the Israeli Chief Rabbinate about training rabbis to act as spokespeople for the Israeli government. www.haaretz.com/jewish-world/2.209/experts-warn-against-israeli-plan-to-use-european-rabbi-for-pr-1.265070.

there; "Why are we going to this city of cursers?" he asked. Infuriated by the question, Resh Lakish promptly dismounted from his donkey, shovelled up some sand, and stuffed it into the mouth of his fellow scholar. When Rabbi Abahu recovered from this assault, he asked his companion why he had acted so savagely. "God does not want you to slander the Jewish people!" Resh Lakish replied.[8]

The *Malshin*

The idea of relying on non-Jews to act as our referee is also frowned upon by our sources. Jewish law commands us to settle our disputes within our own Jewish communities. Even where a non-Jewish court would give an identical ruling to a *beit din*, we should resolve our arguments in Jewish courts.[9]

Since turning to the non-Jewish courts is forbidden, there was no character more detested in Jewish lore than the *malshin* (informer), a person who handed his fellow Jew over to the non-Jewish authorities.[10] Maimonides defines the crime and the severity of its punishment: "There are two types of informer: One who informs on his fellow Jew to gentiles such that he will be killed or beaten; and one who informs on his fellow Jew such that his money will fall into the hands of gentiles or into the hands of a brigand. Both of these types of informer do not have a share in the World to Come."[11]

Our sages went to tremendous lengths to avoid handing over fellow Jews to the Roman authorities, even at the price of enormous personal suffering.[12]

As contemporary enemies of the Jewish State call its legitimacy into question, campaigning for boycott, divestment, and sanctions (BDS), the laws prohibiting handing our people or their property to non-Jews take on renewed significance. The scale of this transgression may be magnified by the potentially dire consequences for the huge number of Israelis who may be affected by it.

---

8. Pesaḥim 87a; Midrash Shir Hashirim Rabba 1:6. The Midrash also criticizes Moses, Elijah, and Isaiah for failing to defend the Jewish people. See also Pesaḥim 87a, where the Talmud suggests that the prophet Hosea was commanded to marry an unfaithful woman because of his own lack of faith in the Jewish people.
9. Maimonides, *Hilkhot Sanhedrin*, 26: 7.
10. For a full discussion of the development of the laws of the informer, see Michael J. Broyde, "Informing on Fellow Jews who Commit Crimes, Mesira in Modern Times", available at www.come-and-hear.com/editor/moser-broyde.
11. Maimonides, *Hilkhot Teshuva* 3:12.
12. See e.g. Gittin 7a, which relates how one scholar, Mar Ukva, had the misfortune to live in a neighbourhood where he was constantly troubled by thugs who made his life unbearable. He repeatedly asked his teacher whether he could hand them over to the authorities, but was told to wait for divine intervention.

Is this a reason to keep quiet about perceived wrongdoing? The talmudic sages were sometimes torn between their reluctance to turn over fellow Jews to the authorities, their ethical duties, and their responsibilities to protect the rest of the community. Such dilemmas were faced by Rabbi Elazar, who joined the Roman police force to help track down Jewish criminals. In a story which may parallel current debates over public criticism of wrongdoing in Israel, the Talmud describes his heartache as he tried to navigate his way between crime prevention and treachery to his people. Some of his fellow rabbis accused him of "delivering up God's people for slaughter". Rabbi Elazar responded that he was only "weeding out thorns from the vineyard" – doing God's work in clearing out criminals from the land. But his colleagues were not impressed, and retorted, "Let the owner of the vineyard [God] Himself come and weed out the thorns."[13]

Reflecting the complexity of both sides of the argument, in his commentary on the *Shulḥan Arukh*, Rabbi Moses Isserles codifies the position that some crimes may be reported to the secular authorities.[14]

The watershed came at the very end of the nineteenth century in a ruling by Rabbi Yeḥiel Mikhel Epstein (1829–1908), who stated that the law of the informant applied at times and in places where the judicial system was unjust and discriminatory against Jews, but in enlightened countries, where justice would be done, there was no reason to withhold due process. This decision formed the basis of subsequent rulings permitting people to inform the police when Jews commit offences. For those who feel that Israel will receive a fair hearing from other governments around the world, this could form the basis for public criticism of Israel's government.[15]

If religious Jews appear indifferent to the moral failings of their people or the State of Israel, it would constitute a desecration of God's name; causing people to think less of God and His people.[16] Such a violation of our faith is one of the most serious offences in Jewish Law. Rabbi Yehuda Amital (1924–2010), *rosh yeshiva* of Yeshivat Har Etzion, constantly cited it as the motivating factor

13. Bava Metzia 83b. See also Nidda 61a for Rabbi Tarfon's dilemma over whether to shield suspected criminals from the Roman authorities.
14. Commentary of Rabbi Moses Isserles on the *Shulḥan Arukh, Ḥoshen Mishpat* 388:7.
15. Rabbi Yeḥiel Mikhel Epstein, *Arukh Hashulḥan, Ḥoshen Mishpat,* note to 388:7.
16. See Yoma 86a, which says: "But in the case of one who is guilty of the desecration of [God's] name, repentance does not suspend, Yom Kippur does not atone, and afflictions do not cleanse. Rather they all suspend, and death cleanses – 'And it was revealed in my ears, by the Lord of hosts; Surely this iniquity shall not be forgiven you till you die'" (Isa. 22:14). See also Maimonides, *Hilkhot Yesode HaTorah* 5: 11.

behind his outspoken criticism of the Israeli government. His attacks came from the dual perspectives of the head of a West Bank yeshiva and sensitivity to the suffering of Israel's minorities.

When censured by students for being too condemnatory of the government, Rabbi Amital responded with the talmudic principle that when God's name is desecrated, one responds without even deferring to the honour of the scholars:[17]

> So long as I feel that I am able to say something that will be to the benefit of the Torah, to the benefit of *Am Yisrael* or of *Eretz Yisrael,* I will not refrain from speaking out. So long as I believe that I am able to diminish the desecration of God's name, to increase the glory of heaven to bring individuals closer, to save Jews from bloodshed or to save something of *Eretz Yisrael,* I have not refrained from speaking out.[18]

Laws of *Lashon Hara* (Forbidden Speech)

Assuming that there are times when speaking out against moral failings of Israel is appropriate, there remains the religious prohibition against slander.[19] While most of these laws were written in the context of someone who slanders an individual, in his compendium of the laws of forbidden speech, Ḥafetz Ḥayim (1838–1933) rules that gossiping about a large group (such as a family or community, and by extension a government or nation) would be a far more serious transgression, since it would be impossible to trace all the victims for the purposes of apologizing and making amends. In our day, as social media and news reports can reach millions of people almost instantaneously, the power of speech is magnified as is the need to choose our words carefully.[20]

Ironically, the speed of modern communications may also create a degree of leniency. Ḥafetz Ḥayim reluctantly ruled that once a story is in the public domain it may qualify for the leniency of "a story has been told in front of three

---

17. Berakhot 19b.
18. Rabbi Yehuda Amital, *Commitment and Complexity: Jewish Wisdom in an Age of Upheaval* (New Jersey: KTAV Publishing House, 2008), 132.
19. Ḥafetz Ḥayim suggested that a gossiper could potentially transgress thirty-one biblical commandments, the most fundamental being "You shall not go out as a talebearer among your people" (Lev. 19: 16). See introduction to Rabbi Yisrael Meir HaKohen, *Sefer Ḥafetz Ḥayim* (Jerusalem: Merkaz Hasefer, 1984), 22–52.
20. Ibid. 4:12, pp. 111–12. See also 8:12, where he rules that speaking *lashon hara* to non-Jews is forbidden.

people" (*be'apei telata*) and therefore widely enough known that repeating it does not constitute a new sin.[21] Another leniency in the laws of *lashon hara* allows one to pass on and discuss derogatory information to prevent further suffering. This might allow us to publicize and discuss news stories concerning actions of the Israeli government to shield part of the population from its policies. Ḥafetz Ḥayim, however, lists several conditions that must be met before one may engage in such speech.

First, the person criticizing should have seen the act for himself, and not rely on what he has heard from others. He should examine the information carefully to be sure that it has been substantiated. This is particularly applicable in our context, where there is so much misreporting and deliberate distortion.[22] The second condition is that before publicizing the criticism, one must try to rebuke the perpetrator, since he may repent of what he has done and rectify the damage, obviating the need for a public critique. In the context of modern Israel, this might mean communicating one's criticism and questions to the Israeli government or its ambassadors, giving them a fair opportunity to respond before publicly castigating them.

We must examine our own motives to ensure that there is no social or personal benefit from our criticism. This may be particularly apposite to Jews working for human rights organizations, the media, or community frameworks where there are expectations of and financial compensation for criticism of the Israeli government's policies.

Finally, Ḥafetz Ḥayim demands that the consequences of publicizing our complaints must be proportionate, meaning that the perpetrator should not receive a greater punishment than a properly constituted Jewish court would have imposed. This is hard to quantify, since the effects of criticism are cumulative and each component cannot be measured. We cannot establish how much damage might be afflicted on Israel's good name, its alliances, or its security as a

21. Ibid. 2:3, pp. 69–84.

22. Most famously, in April 2002 world media reported on a massacre committed by Israeli soldiers against Palestinians in Jenin. The story, which ran for several days, turned out to be a fabrication. For an account of the press reports see Anthony Julius, *Trials of the Diaspora* (n. 1 above), 471–2. There is also a danger that anti-Zionists will distort the words of loyal Zionists who offer criticism of Israel. London Mayor Ken Livingstone, for example, claimed that he was merely echoing the words of Chief Rabbi Jakobovits when he said it would have been better if Israel had not been created: www.jpost.com/International/London-mayor-misquotes-former-chief-rabbi-on-Israel. For a full discussion of how anti-Zionists distort speech in order to make their case, see Julius ibid. 494–9.

result of a particular protest. This is certainly a further reason for caution in the way that we address issues.

Professor Gerald Steinberg's NGO Monitor has dedicated the last decade to tracking and reporting on the political advocacy of human rights organizations that direct their criticism against Israel. He takes issue with them for failing to check their evidence, receiving financial benefit from foreign governments, and taking their criticisms to foreign audiences when he maintains there are enough mechanisms to deal with the issues. This critique precisely parallels Ḥafetz Ḥayim's ruling.[23]

ARGUMENTS FOR THE SAKE OF HEAVEN

While Judaism frowns upon gratuitous criticism of our people and forbids gossip, it does make room for alternative views within the Jewish community. According to tradition, the holiest book of Jewish mysticism emerged out of a discussion among the rabbis about the failures of the Roman government.[24] Deeply valued by our culture is the concept of the "argument for the sake of heaven", which seeks to reach the truth, rather than an argument that aims to achieve a personal victory.[25]

Rabbi Sacks points out that for a community to flourish, it is essential that there is room for such dissent. He quotes the research of Harvard economic historian A. O. Hirschman, who argued that allowing people to feel that their complaints can be expressed and will be listened to is essential to maintaining group loyalty.[26] Rabbi Sacks terms this "the dignity of dissent" and he suggests that it is perfectly normal for it to be applied in the Israeli context.

> Often the sharpest criticism of Israel's policies comes from within, from its writers and intellectuals, academics and journalists. That is what makes Israel the free society that it is. Israel is not perfect. No nation or

23. Gerald Steinberg, "Breaking what silence?", *The Jerusalem Post*, 11 September 2012: http://www.jpost.com/Opinion/Op-Ed-Contributors/Breaking-what-silence.
24. Shabbat 33b.
25. See e.g. Eruvin 13b, which describes how Beit Hillel and Beit Shammai argued for three years over existential questions until a heavenly voice declared that each were speaking the words of the living God. See also Ḥagiga 3b, which describes groups of scholars sitting together offering contradictory rulings about whether matters are pure or impure, permitted or forbidden, kosher or not.
26. Jonathan Sacks, *Future Tense* (London: Hodder and Stoughton, 2009), 199–200.

> government is. Therefore, criticism of it is legitimate. If justified it should be heeded; if unjustified it should be argued against.[27]

This view has been echoed by contemporary commentators who argue that by brooking no criticism of Israel, the American Zionist establishment prevents freedom of expression and alienates large numbers of Jewish students, who no longer feel they have a place in the organized Jewish community.[28]

While Jewish institutions in Britain traditionally professed total loyalty to the policies of the government of Israel, there have always been dissenters. One of Britain's most influential rabbis and a former president of the British Mizrachi Organisation, Rabbi Kopul Rosen (1913–62), argued that this policy was a dereliction of moral duty which had been cynically created by fund-raisers who needed an emotionally laden story of a perfect Jewish State.[29]

Rabbi Joseph Soloveitchik (1903–93), the leader of American Modern Orthodoxy, also fiercely guarded the idea that the rabbinate should be independent and able to state their opinions free from political interference. When David Ben Gurion signalled that he could secure for him the position of Chief Rabbi of Israel, Rabbi Soloveitchik retorted that it was "precisely Ben Gurion's ability to ensure who was elected Chief Rabbi of the State of Israel that kept him from accepting the office".[30]

Perhaps the most outspoken critic of some of Israel's policies was former British Chief Rabbi Lord Jakobovits (1921–99). He was a passionate Zionist, deeply concerned for the security of Jews everywhere as well as for the moral stature of the State of Israel. He described his dilemmas of whether to speak out against Israel's policies as amongst the hardest he had ever faced. He resolved them with reference to a talmudic passage stating that a scholar who has been ordained must issue appropriate rulings and may not withhold Torah from the public: "Teachers who refrain from teaching must bear responsibility for the casualties of ignorance by their silence, and rabbis may be indicted before the bar of Heaven and of History for Jewish national aberrations compounded by their

27. Ibid. 98.
28. This seems to be borne out by the recent Pew Report, which shows that while more than half of Jews aged 65 and older say caring about Israel is essential to their Jewish identity (53%), only 32% of Jewish adults under the age of 30 say caring about Israel is central to what being Jewish means to them: www.pewforum.org/2013/10/01/chapter-5-connection-with-and-attitudes-towards-israel/.
29. Ibid.
30. Gerald J. Blidstein, "Rabbi Joseph B. Soloveitchik's Letters on Public Affairs", *The Torah U-Madda Journal*, 15 (2008–9), available at www.yutorah.org/lectures/lecture.cfm/745797.

silence."[31] He felt that while Diaspora Jews could not impose their views on Israel or participate in Israel's decision-making process, they had the right to express their views and that sometimes these would have the benefit of perspective that comes with distance, especially on security matters.[32]

He condemned in the harshest terms those who attempted to gag Israel's critics:

> The attempts to silence dissent and constructive criticism also sit particularly ill with a people which cannot forget the awesome price paid for silence in the face of suffering and injustice not long ago.
>
> Are we of all people again to become the "Generation of Silence" responsible for aberrations or missed opportunities by default? Rather should we heed the Prophet's cry, "For the sake of Zion, I will not remain mute and for the sake of Jerusalem I will not be silent".[33]

Addressing the phenomenon of Palestinian terrorism, Rabbi Jakobovits criticized the Jewish community for failing to speak up for the legitimate rights of Palestinians:

> Even if we could do little or nothing to solve the problem, surely as Jews – faithful to our ethical heritage of marked sensitivity to the sufferings of the stranger and the homeless – we should not have left it to gangs of murderous terrorists to draw the world's attention to this stain on humanity. Had we cried out in protest against the intolerable degradation of hundreds of thousands of human beings inhumanly condemned to rot in wretched camps for a generation, had we aroused the world's conscience over a tragedy of such magnitude, we might have prevented the growth of a monster organization which has already destroyed so many innocent lives.[34]

---

31. Rabbi Immanuel Jakobovits, *If Only My People* (London: George Weidenfeld and Nicolson Ltd, 1984), 175. The reference is to Sota 22a.
32. Ibid. 80–1. For a description and analysis of Rabbi Jakobovits' interventions regarding Israel, see Miri Freud-Kandel, "Immanuel Jakobovits: A Coherent Theology of Apparent Contradiction", *Modern Judaism*, 30:2 (May 2010), 127–52.
33. Chief Rabbi Jakobovits' response to an article in *JC*, 23 June 1978, quoted in Meir Persoff, *Immanuel Jakobovits: A Prophet in Israel* (London: Vallentine Mitchell, 2002), 184. The quotation is from Isaiah 62:1.
34. Immanuel Jakobovits, "A Reassessment of Israel's Role in the Contemporary Jewish Condition", 289. Quoted in Miri Freud-Kandel, "Immanuel Jakobovits" (above, n. 32).

He was haunted by the feeling that he could have better used his extraordinary influence with Prime Minister Margaret Thatcher and in the House of Lords to speak out for Palestinian rights and thereby reduce the anger which led to terrorism.[35]

Not everyone appreciated all of Rabbi Jakobovits' interventions. Chief Rabbi Goren of Israel was quoted on the front page of the London *Times* saying, "I call upon the rabbis in the world and the Jews of Great Britain who hold the holy city of Jerusalem and the Land of Israel sacred to spew this dangerous man from our midst."[36]

Rabbi Goren's disagreement with Rabbi Jakobovits was about the substance of what he said, not about his right to speak, as demonstrated by the fact that one of their arguments occurred when Rabbi Jakobovits rejected an invitation from Rabbi Goren to sign a petition addressed to the government of Israel protesting the evacuation of Yamit as part of the peace agreement with Egypt.

AMERICAN ORTHODOX CRITICISM OF ISRAEL

In America, a major shift has also taken place. Traditionally the American Orthodox community supported the policies of Israeli governments. Rabbi Yosef Blau attributes this to the towering weight of Rabbi Joseph B. Soloveitchik, who argued that Israel was the source of security for Jews, entitling its governments to make whatever decisions they felt were necessary for the security of the state.[37]

Yet even amongst these right-wing Religious Zionists a major break took place after the withdrawal from Gaza and subsequent dismantling of the settlement at Amona, which this community saw as a betrayal of Israel's role as the harbinger of redemption. The decline in faith in the Israeli government was accelerated by the failings revealed by the Second Lebanon War and increasing allegations of corruption amongst Israeli politicians.[38]

The change was confirmed at the biennial convention of the Orthodox Union in Jerusalem, which voted to set aside the existing policy of never publicly criticizing Israel.[39]

---

35. I. Jakobovits, *If Only* (above, n. 31), 175.
36. Ibid. 91. See also Chaim Bermant, *Lord Jakobovits, the Authorised Biography of the Chief Rabbi* (London: Weidenfeld and Nicolson, 1990), 145–60, for a discussion of these events.
37. Rabbi Y. Blau, "Did American Orthodox Jews Forsake their Israeli Brothers?" (above, n. 4).
38. This analysis is based on Chaim I. Waxman, "If I forget thee, O Jerusalem", in id. (ed.), *Religious Zionism* (above, n. 5), 426–9.
39. "OU Adopts Resolutions at Jerusalem Convention", at www.ou.org/ou/print_this/8961.

CONCLUSION: MAKING A POSITIVE CONTRIBUTION

While it is hoped that the State of Israel will always act in accordance with the highest ethical standards, no country is perfect and a secular state at war may sometimes struggle to attain the highest moral and religious standards. Orthodox leaders from across the political spectrum have felt the need to speak out. Indeed, for Rabbi Jakobovits it was particularly important that the moral protests were not the sole province of secular Jews; they needed to come from an Orthodox rabbi demonstrating the centrality of the highest ethical standards to our religion.[40]

Jewish law requires that if we wish to make such protests we must first establish the validity of the claims to ensure that they have not been duped by anti-Israel propaganda. If we are clear that there is a genuine problem, then we should direct our protests to the internal channels of Israeli democracy. If that fails, and it seems that protest is appropriate, then it must be done from the purest motivations in measured and appropriate tones and limited to the specific policy under question, without lending support to those who question the very legitimacy of the Jewish State.

While protest may at times be unavoidable, there are many other ways to make our views known and to have a positive influence on the Jewish homeland. By working in and supporting the fields of education, law, and human rights, we can advance the Jewish values of justice, loving-kindness, and democracy, bringing credit to our nation and peace and security and prosperity to our land.

40. Chaim Bermant, *Lord Jakobovits* (above, n. 36), 160. For an example of what Rabbi Jakobovits was trying to avoid, see Yossi Klein Halevi, *Like Dreamers* (New York: Harper Collins, 2013), 123–6, where he describes how the religious Zionists were incapable of understanding the moral dilemmas faced by secular soldiers in the Six Day War: "Religious Zionists who proclaimed their belief in chosenness were, in effect, insisting on the right of the Jews to behave as any other nation while secular Zionists who rejected chosenness were insisting that Jews be held to a higher standard."

Ein Mazal LeYisrael: Randomness and Providence in Jewish Destiny

Rabbi Nissan Wilson

Rabbi Sacks has often drawn our attention to the distinction between power and influence, and those of us privileged to serve in his rabbinate have enjoyed a two-decade long master class in the art of influence-through-teaching. Rabbi Sacks is a model teacher because he is at once a brilliant scholar who knows his subject and an insightful leader who understands his listener. He has been able to deeply influence a generation of students and followers of all faiths in his twenty-two years as Chief Rabbi. It is my hope and prayer that Lord Sacks is blessed with continued good health and strength to fulfil his dream of influencing a generation of leaders.

The Amalek/Haman world-view is commonly understood as being one which considers all events as being random or happenstance. This notion is based on the talmudic sages quoted by Rashi on the *Parasha* of Amalek in Deuteronomy,[1] where a number of explanations are cited for the words *asher korkha baderekh* – "who

1. Deut. 25:17.

met you on the way". The key word *korkha* shares the same root as the word *mikre*, which is often translated as 'coincidence' or 'happenstance'.

In understanding this observation of the talmudic sages it has been suggested that the Amalek world-view sees no plan or order to anything that happens in the world, but rather a random sequence of unrelated events. Thus Amalek attacks *baderekh* – on the way – confident that they can cut short the journey of the Israelites to Har HaElokim and the final destination of the Promised Land.

This explanation provides a reasonable point of departure for understanding the Amalek/Haman philosophy, but, as I will demonstrate, it is an oversimplification that is challenged by a number of key points in the narrative of the book of Esther and its midrashic commentaries.

HAMAN'S *GORAL*

To establish a suitable date for the annihilation of the Jews, Haman drew *goralot* (lots), which fell on the month of Adar. Mindful that Adar was the month in which Moses had died, Haman was buoyed by this result, believing that he was more likely to succeed in what was known to be an 'unlucky' month for the Jews.

Far from suggesting a belief in total randomness and happenstance, Haman's actions actually imply belief in a kind of fate or destiny. Indeed, had he considered there to be no underlying order, he would have done just as well to pick out a date at random.[2] Haman was not using the lottery simply as a device for selecting an arbitrary date, but rather to establish the month that was most auspicious for the Jews' destruction.

The Vilna Gaon's commentary on this part of the narrative further supports this point.[3] He cites the well-known talmudic dictum that *ein mazal leyisrael* (lit. "there is no fortune for the Jews", but typically rendered as "the Jews are not dependent on luck"). Offering an explanation that is more faithful to the literal reading than many other explanations, Rabbi Elijah suggests that, whereas each of the other nations has an archangel or a 'star' (a *mazal*) that assumes responsibility for that nation, Israel does not have such a *mazal* but is subsumed within the more general *mazal* that determines the natural order of events. Of course, the

2. See Rabbi Judah Loew on *hipil pur* (*Or Ḥadash*, p. 136), who explains that Haman engaged a third party to draw the lots in order to avoid his own subconscious impacting on the result. Only by using a neutral third party could he be sure that the date drawn was indeed the destined one.
3. *Perush HaGra LeMegillat Ester* 3:7. See also 9:26.

Jewish people are able to raise themselves above this system of *mazal* and merit a higher form of Divine providence, as will be explained further in this essay.

Haman, however, sees only the lower *mazal* system and thus seeks to determine the moment at which his own *mazal* will be ascendant as the most auspicious time for him to succeed in his crusade against the Jews.[4] Indeed, his world-view appears to be more one of determinism than of pure randomness. To be sure, Haman's philosophy cannot be reduced to fatalism, for he believes that his own efforts can help determine the outcome. But he does have faith in some underlying order and prospective destiny, and he seeks to ascertain that order so that he can shape events to suit his own aspirations.

MIRACLE OR *MIKRE*

Such a worldview would be markedly stretched by apparently miraculous occurrences that seem not to fit with the predetermined natural order. Haman's approach to such occurrences is displayed in his reaction to the sudden turn of events which sees his nemesis, Mordecai, elevated to the highest honour as Haman himself is dishonoured and demeaned.

Haman returns home and tells his family *et kol asher karahu* – everything that had occurred. In again using the keyword *kara,* suggests the Vilna Gaon,[5] the verse reveals Haman's attempt to explain these events as being *mikre* – happenstance or random coincidence, and not a part of the underlying order as he understands it. The response of his wife Zeresh and his advisors is telling as they explain to him that in fact destiny clearly now favours Mordecai and the Jews. In light of this fact they advise him to surrender his scheme to destroy the Jews and dismantle the gallows he had constructed for hanging Mordecai.

Yet Haman refuses their advice as he is unable to see these events as constituting a coherent order. Although recognizing that this sudden turn of events was never in the script, he is unable to abandon the original script and accept a different narrative or a new order. He is thus forced to label events that others would call miracles as random coincidence, which can have no bearing on the predetermined natural order.

4. See also Rabbi Judah Loew, *Or Ḥadash*, p. 133. Although he differs from the Vilna Gaon by explaining the lottery in terms of determining the inauspicious time for the Jews, his commentary nonetheless highlights Haman's desire to tap into a destined outcome that was part of the natural order.
5. *Perush HaGra LeMegillat Ester* 6:13.

MORDECAI AND *MIKRE*

The word *mikre* appears to have more than one connotation, as Mordecai's communication to Esther in chapter 4 verse 7 is described with exactly the same words used to describe Haman's recounting of events to his family.

Hearing of the decree of annihilation issued against the Jews, Mordecai sends a message to Esther to apprise her of the plight of her people and ask her to intercede on their behalf. Mordecai sends this message to tell her *et kol asher karahu* – everything that had occurred. Far from suggesting coincidence, Mordecai's message to Esther is surely intended to convey a belief that every event is by divine decree and that providence has placed her in a position to play a role in her people's salvation. Why would Mordecai use words that could be construed as implying that such events are mere happenstance?[6]

Rabbi Judah Loew (Maharal) suggests a number of explanations for Mordecai's choice of words, with the common theme being the notion that *mikre* implies an event or an entity that does not fit with an intelligently designed framework or plan.[7] Following this line, we may suggest that Mordecai's turn of phrase is intended as a statement that the threatened annihilation of the Jews must be seen as *mikre* as it is patently irreconcilable with God's six-thousand-year plan for the created world. Thus, when Esther conveys her reticence to intervene on behalf of her people, Mordecai admonishes her with the following words: "If you indeed remain silent at this moment, relief and deliverance will come to the Jews from elsewhere, while you and your father's house will perish."[8]

Mordecai is warning Esther against hedging. As the threat of annihilation is *mikre*, it will – one way or another – undoubtedly pass and the Jews will prevail. Esther should not conceive of her decision as one that will affect the directional flow or ultimate destiny of the Jewish people, but rather as something that will determine how her own name (and that of her family – "her father's house") will be etched into Jewish history.

There is a higher order, a divinely ordained plan for creation, according to which total annihilation can never occur.[9] Although events that do not fit with

---

6. Although Midrash Rabba (Est. 8:5) explains that these words were used to hint at Haman/Amalek's involvement in this terrible decree, a *peshat* reading of the verse would nonetheless imply that Mordecai is actually describing the decree and the events surrounding it as *mikre*.
7. *Or Ḥadash*, 4:7.
8. Est. 4:14.
9. According to Rabbi Moshe Ḥayim Luzzatto in *Daat Tevunot* (*siman* 168, Friedlander), the term *mazal* is used sometimes to describe the form of providence that guides the world to its ultimate purpose or *tikkun*, irrespective of man's deeds. This is distinct from the term *mazal* that is used

this higher order may legitimately be described as *mikre,* that is not to suggest that they are beyond God's control or without His consent,[10] but rather they are exceptional occurrences that deviate from the ultimate plan.[11]

CONCENTRIC CIRCLES

A picture thus starts to emerge of two systems, both of which are essentially deterministic, that run in tandem like concentric circles. Conflicts occur when the two systems appear to suggest divergent outcomes. In Haman's world-view events that are not compatible with the natural order of *mazal* are to be defined as *mikre;* in Mordecai's world-view *mikre* describes events that do not fit with the higher order.

The mystery of how these two parallel systems are able to engage without colliding is beyond the scope of this discussion, but the subtext of the Purim story is the gradual unveiling of the higher system. Where Haman sees a universe with a single, deterministic order – one which indeed does exist – it becomes apparent that there is also a second system that supersedes this lower, natural order. Further, identifying which is the principal system enables a redefinition of which occurrences should be considered *mikre.* Haman's error is evident in his persistently classifying Mordecai's sudden rise as *mikre,* while even his wife and closest advisors had conceded that this astonishing event was evidence of Jewish destiny being rooted in a higher order.

PURIM IN THE PLURAL

Awareness of these two systems enables us to understand why the plural form of the word *pur* (lottery) is used for the name of the festival of Purim. The Megilla

to describe stellar influences on the natural world and may sometimes be referred to as *mazal elyon* (higher *mazal*). The word *mazal,* being etymologically related to *nozel* (flow), is used to describe any form of top-down providence which, rather than responding to man's actions in the form of reward and punishment, represents a decree or diktat that sets the parameters within which man must function.

10. Thus, according to the midrashic teaching that the word *hamelekh* (the king), where unqualified with the name Aḥashverosh, alludes also to God, we find evidence of God's consent to the edict passed by Haman and Aḥashverosh. Probably the most striking example of this is in the words, "And the king removed his signet ring and gave it to Haman son of Hamdata enemy of the Jews" (Est. 3:10).

11. See also Rabbi Judah Loew's repeated use of the word *mikre* throughout his writings, where, in contradistinction to *be'etzem* (meaning 'at its core' or 'in its essence') the word *bemikre* is used to describe events that do not openly reveal God's plan or divine thought. See e.g. *Gevurot Hashem* ch. 12, *Tiferet Yisrael* ch. 2.

simply states that the festival is named Purim (lots) on account of the *pur* which Haman cast.

In early editions of *Perush HaGra,*[12] the Vilna Gaon describes the miracle as one where *hapur nehepakh lepurim* – a transformation from *pur* (singular) to *purim* (plural). A recent edition,[13] though, suggests changing these words to *pur Haman nehepakh lepurenu* – Haman's *pur* was transformed to our *pur* – in line with the text of the "*Asher Heini*" prayer, which is recited after the evening Megilla-reading. However, it would appear that there are variant texts of "*Asher Heini*" itself, with *Sefat Emet*[14] citing *hapur nehepakh lepurim* as an established version.[15] According to *Sefat Emet,* the revelation of a second order and the interplay between the two orders is itself the essence of the miracle and of the festival. This explanation is consistent with the approach of the Vilna Gaon and supports the original unedited text of his commentary.[16]

RANDOMNESS AND HIGHER CAUSALITY

In translating the Persian word *pur* into the Hebrew *goral,* the Megilla gives a wink to the notion that the plural Purim is connected to the "two *goralot*" in Leviticus 16. The plural word *goralot* appears in the Torah in reference to the two rams offered on Yom Kippur.[17] Here, lots are drawn by the kohen to determine which ram should be sent out to the wilderness and which should be offered on the holy altar.

Drawing lots in the Temple itself needs explanation, where, in addition to the lottery of the rams, another lottery, known as the *payis,*[18] is employed to determine the pecking order for the kohanim who are to perform the Temple service. At first glance this lottery appears out of place in the Temple, where we would expect events to emerge as providential rather than arbitrary and random.

When a lottery is employed the result may well appear to be arbitrary and *mikre* as there is nothing in the lower order predetermining the outcome and thus no visible causality. In truth, however, one can learn to view the randomness of

---

12. 3:7.
13. Nubal, Jerusalem, 1992.
14. "Purim, 5631" (Jerusalem, Hotzaot Mir: 1997), ii. 175.
15. See Maharal, *Or Ḥadash,* 7:10 citing the standard version.
16. There appears to be no substantive disagreement between the two versions. The revelation that, beyond the known, lower order, there is a second, higher order is concurrent with the realization that the higher order has been brought to bear in favour of the Jewish people.
17. Lev. 16:8.
18. Mishna Yoma 2.

this lottery as a device for removing human free will to allow space for the providence of the higher order to function unimpeded by man's influence. The Temple lotteries are man's way of asking God to convey His will and steer events in this holiest place in accordance with the higher destiny.[19]

ISRAEL'S *GORAL*

In this context the word *goral* is best translated not as 'lottery' but rather as 'lot', implying a designated portion. In a similar vein *goral* is used in the Yom Kippur liturgy to describe our relationship with God: *Anu naḥalatekha ve'ata goralenu* (We are Your inheritance and You are our destiny).

Far from implying 'chance' or 'the luck of the draw', *goral* here implies a relationship that is meant to be. Perhaps the most powerful and often unspoken message of Yom Kippur is that the very notion of repentance and atonement is predicated on God's undying love for His people. According to the higher order of God's providence, our close relationship endures however far we may have strayed. We may on occasion fall prey to temptation, but our sins and our failures are *mikre*: a brief digression from the main script, a short detour from the real journey.

The full name of the festival as it appears in Scripture is Yom HaKippurim, which may be rendered as *yom* (a day) *kePurim* (like the festival of Purim).[20] Just as the miracle of Purim was rooted in a higher order and a greater destiny which is our *goral* or lot, so too does the wondrous phenomenon of the Yom Kippur atonement stem from God's belief in our ability to reach that higher destiny.

So on Yom Kippur, as we reflect on our relationship with God, this reminder that He is our *goral* gives us the faith to persist in rebuilding a love that may have seemed lost. Although the usual signs of a loving relationship are absent at times, this is not the type of love that one can fall into or out of, but rather a union that is *bashert* – the highest destiny of both partners.

---

19. The extent to which such a method may be employed in regular decision-making is a matter of debate, there being a serious concern of transgressing the biblical prohibition of *niḥush* (necromancy). See Maimonides, *Mishne Torah, Avodat Kokhavim*, 11:4.
20. See *Tikkunei Zohar* 57b.

The Curse of Yoav: The Deadly Challenge of Jewish Education

Rabbi Raphael Zarum

It is a privilege to contribute to this volume in honour of the Emeritus Chief Rabbi, Lord Sacks. He has been a wonderful mentor to me personally, and his profound insight, integrity, and passion have been instrumental in the renaissance of the London School of Jewish Studies (formerly Jews' College) during his tenure as its president.

For his maiden speech in the House of Lords he chose to focus on education. He said: "To defend a country you need an army, but to defend a civilization you need schools."[1] This reflects a fervent concern for Jewish education, upon which he has elaborated in many of his writings. Drawing a parallel between national security and schooling makes a stark point. A nation must invest in education with as much determination and as many resources as it does in its military might. This statement encouraged me to revisit an intriguing story in the Talmud which entwines the worlds of soldiering and schooling. The analysis suggests important lessons about the nature and delivery of Jewish education for practitioners and policymakers alike.

1. http://www.rabbisacks.org/maiden-speech-house-of-lords-26-nov-2009/.

Though no tractate of the Talmud is dedicated exclusively to education, a vast array of insightful statements and stories are spread across its pages, a prominent one appearing in Bava Batra 21a–b. Here we first hear about the innovation of universal Jewish education as well as the eminently practical aspects of schooling such as ideal class sizes and teacher employment structures. One debate focuses on the appropriate pace of the lessons:

> Rava said: If there are two teachers of children: one that teaches at a rapid pace but is not exact, while the other is exact but does not teach at a rapid pace – we should appoint the one that teaches at a rapid pace but is not exact, since the mistakes will correct themselves as a matter of course. Rav Dimi of Nehardea disagreed: We should appoint the teacher that is exact but does not teach at a rapid pace, for once a mistake is implanted, it takes hold.

The disagreement of Rava and Rav Dimi is still deliberated by educationalists today. Should a curriculum be constructed for quantity of knowledge or quality of understanding? Can we risk sacrificing meticulousness for the sake of breadth? Put another way, would we prefer our students to have a surface appreciation of a wide range of topics or a deep comprehension of just a few?

However, our focus here is the dramatic story that Rav Dimi tells to support his position. It centres on a 3000-year-old conversation between King David and the leader of his army, Yoav, the son of Tzeruya. This is how the Talmud relates it:

> It is written, "For Yoav and all [the army of] Israel remained there for six months, until he had destroyed every male [*zakhar*] in Edom" [1 Kgs. 11:16]. When Yoav came before [King] David, the latter said: "Why did you do that [i.e. specifically kill all the males[2]]?" Yoav replied: "Because it is written in the Torah, 'You shall blot out the males [*zakhar*] of Amalek' [Deut. 25:19]." David said: "[Wrong!] We pronounce it like this, '[You shall blot out all] memory [*zekher*] of Amalek' [Deut. 25:19; i.e. males and females]!" Yoav replied: "But I was taught to pronounce the word as *zakhar*!"[3]

---

2. This is Rashi's commentary on David's question.
3. The word in question is made up of three Hebrew letters, *z-kh-r*. Depending on the vowelling, it can be pronounced *zekher*, meaning remembrance, or *zakhar*, meaning male.

> So Yoav went back to his [primary school] teacher and asked him: How did you teach me to pronounce this word? He replied: *z-kh-r*. Thereupon Yoav drew his sword and threatened to kill him. The teacher asked: "Why are you doing this?" He replied: "Because it is written, 'Cursed be the one who does God's work negligently' [Jer. 48:10]." The teacher said to him: "So be satisfied that I am cursed." Yoav responded: "[But the verse continues,] 'and cursed be the one who withholds their sword from shedding blood' [ibid.]." Some say that Yoav then killed him, and some say that he did not kill him.[4]

Suddenly a pedagogical concern confined to the classroom has been propelled to an issue of national security. Yoav's misreading of a single biblical verse led to his failure to fulfil the orders of Israel's king. There is much to analyse in this tantalizing story. Just the visceral image of a fully armed general bursting into a class of infants to confront and threaten his former teacher is enough to highlight the mortal danger that the Sages attach to bad Jewish education. Four questions about this text will enable us to unpack its intricacy and reveal essential educational lessons:

(A) Did Yoav's teacher instruct him correctly or not?
(B) Was Yoav right in his application of the verses from Deuteronomy and Jeremiah?
(C) How does familiarity with the life and character of Yoav deepen our understanding of this story?
(D) Why does this story appear in the second chapter of the talmudic tractate of Bava Batra?

A. TEACHING AND LEARNING

Yoav drew his sword on his former teacher because he was unhappy with his response. But what did the teacher actually say? At first it seems obvious that he said *zakhar* (males), that is, he had taught the verse incorrectly, which led to Yoav's military blunder. Indeed, this is what the Maharsha commentary explains.[5] However, the standard talmudic text itself is unvocalized and it could have equally meant *zekher* (memory), in which case the teacher did teach the correct pronunciation but for some reason Yoav misheard. This could have been due to

4. Bava Batra 21b.
5. Maharsha – Rabbi Samuel Eidels (1555–1631).

his inattentiveness or to the teacher's lack of pedagogical rigour in reiterating, checking, and reinforcing accurate reading. This is the explanation of the commentaries of the *Tosafot*, Rashba,[6] and Ran. [7]

Thus Rav Dimi is citing this story to demonstrate the consequences of teaching at an overly rapid pace. The teacher will not have time to focus on regular student assessment to ensure proper comprehension. In contemporary educational terminology, Rav Dimi is worried that much *teaching* does not necessarily imply an equal amount of *learning*. Some would argue it is the personal responsibility of the students to review their lessons;[8] however, this needs to be accompanied by regular inspection from the teacher; otherwise, as Rav Dimi stated, "once a mistake is implanted, it takes hold".

It is remarkable that the disagreement between King David and Yoav about the correct pronunciation of a word in the Torah is mirrored in the disagreement of the medieval commentators about the correct pronunciation of the same word in the Talmud. Thus the form of the talmudic text itself reflects the lesson it is trying to teach. Indeed, it might also allow us insight into Yoav's frustrations. He is angry with himself either for his lack of diligence when he was a pupil or because it was the teacher who was not diligent in educating him. Either way, Yoav expresses this anger in an act of violence against his teacher and, by association, the institution that failed him.

B. MISAPPLICATION OF SOURCES

The command to eradicate the "memory of Amalek" (Deut. 25:19) was explicitly given to Israel's first king, Saul, when the prophet Samuel told him to "destroy everything that is theirs; do not have mercy on them, but kill every man and woman, child and infant, ox, sheep, camel, and donkey" (1 Sam. 15:3). This command[9] applied to the Amalekites and no other nation because of their unprovoked attack on the Children of Israel after the Exodus from Egypt.[10] So how could Yoav think to apply it – even if only to the males – in the battle with a different nation, namely, Edom? Though Amalek was indeed a descendant

6. Rabbi Solomon ben Aderet (1235–1310).
7. Rabbi Nissim ben Reuven (1320–76).
8. In a shiur in 1988 the noted Tanakh scholar Nechama Leibovitz remarked flippantly, "Any relationship between what I say and what you write down is purely coincidental." Well, that is what I wrote down in my notes.
9. This is one of the 613 commandments and applies for all time (see positive *mitzva* no. 188 in Maimonides' *Sefer HaMitzvot*, and *mitzva* no. 604 in *Sefer HaḤinukh*).
10. Ex. 17:8–16.

of Esau, who was the father of Edom,[11] it had still become a distinct nation. Amalek dwelt apart from Edom[12] and later, when David waged a series of wars to secure his new kingdom, Edom and Amalek were dealt with separately.[13] In extrapolating from Amalek to Edom, we again see Yoav's lack of diligence in applying the Torah.

Another mistake comes in the verse he cites to threaten his teacher. Quoting Jeremiah, Yoav accuses his teacher of negligence and says he will be cursed if he does not strike him down. The only problem is that the context of the verse reveals that it concerns the nation of Moab,[14] and cannot be applied elsewhere.[15] So again, Yoav is misapplying biblical verses and extrapolating commands inappropriately.[16] But what brought him to behave like this? How could he draw his sword on a former teacher?

C. YOAV'S STORY

To fully appreciate the potency of Rav Dimi's story we need to understand Yoav's pivotal role in David's kingdom. He captained the king's army and was involved in the key challenges of his reign, from beginning to end. Yet, as we see from five revealing episodes, he always had his own ideas.

Early in David's career, when he was still trying to establish his rule, he had to contend with Avner son of Ner, the captain of Saul's army. When Avner was defeated, he was chased by Yoav's brother Asahel. Not wanting to harm him or incur Yoav's wrath, he urged Asahel to back off, but had to kill him when he would not relent.[17] Later Avner changed track, making a peace pact with David. However, when Yoav heard this, he berated David and told him that Avner was untrustworthy: "Avner son of Ner came to deceive you and to know all your military movements".[18] Then Yoav tricked Avner into returning and calmly murdered him in revenge for his brother.[19]

---

11. Gen. 36:8, 12.
12. See Naḥmanides' commentary on Gen. 36:12.
13. II Sam. 8.
14. See Jer. 48:1–10. The whole section is a prophecy against Moab.
15. See R. David Kimḥi's (Radak) commentary on Jer. 48:10.
16. You may wonder how Yoav can quote a prophet who lived over 500 years after him. Whether he is prophetic himself or Rav Dimi is putting the words in his mouth, the key point here is that he is *presented* in the Talmud as misquoting the Tanakh.
17. II Sam. 2:12–23.
18. II Sam. 3:25.
19. II Sam. 3:26–7.

In the famous story of David and Bathsheba, it was Yoav whom David entrusted by letter[20] to dispose of her husband in battle.[21] When the deed was done, Yoav informed David in a covert way in order to protect himself and his king.[22]

Later Absalom led a civil war against his father, David. When Absalom lost the battle and was cornered, Yoav fatally wounded him,[23] despite David's express orders not to harm him.[24] Then, when David heard of his son's death and was heartbroken, Yoav fiercely berated him again, this time for his lack of leadership:

> You have shamed all your servants who today have saved your life, and the lives of your sons, daughters, wives, and concubines. By loving those who hate you and hating those who love you, you have today declared that you do not care for your officers and servants; today I see that if Absalom had lived, and we had all died this day, it would be preferable in your eyes! So, now, get up and speak nice to your servants; for by God I swear that if you do not go, you will have no one on your side by tonight![25]

Yoav also tricked and calmly murdered Amasa when David chose him as Yoav's replacement.[26] And when the king was old and weak, Yoav backed the coup of another of David's sons, Adoniya, only to promptly abandon him the moment Solomon, David's son by Bathsheba, was crowned in his place.[27] All these murderous actions – with Avner, Bathsheba's husband, Absalom, Amasa, and Adoniya – led David, on his deathbed, to instruct Solomon to decisively deal with Yoav:

> And you know what Yoav the son of Tzeruya did to me, and what he did to the two captains of the armies of Israel, to Avner the son of Ner, and to Amasa the son of Yeter, whom he killed, and shed the blood of war in

20. In fact, according one *midrash* (Numbers Rabba 23:13), Yoav kept that letter as insurance against being accused of the murder of Uriah, Bathsheba's hapless husband.
21. II Sam. 11:14–15.
22. II Sam. 11:18–25.
23. II Sam. 18:9–15.
24. II Sam. 18:5.
25. II Sam. 19:6–8.
26. II Sam. 20:8–10.
27. I Kgs. 1.

> peace, and put the blood of war upon his girdle around his loins, and in his shoes that were on his feet. So follow your wisdom, and do not let his grey head go down to Sheol in peace.[28]

Yoav spoke improperly to his king, deviously entrapped and cold-bloodedly killed his enemies without licence, and even supported a coup. The Talmud analyses him, debating his motives and the extent of his loyalty to David.[29] In the end it is clear that Yoav was a toughened soldier who exceeded the authority of his office in pursuit of his own agenda, often in devious and immoral ways. He "shed the blood of war in peace", meaning that he was unable to differentiate between military and political situations, preferring to draw his sword rather than draw on diplomacy.

Now it is much clearer why Rav Dimi presented a story about Yoav. He is highlighting the potentially dire results of careless schooling. A good education is meant to promote harmony, not bloodshed; to create peacemakers, not warmongers. "R. Eleazar said in the name of R. Ḥanina: Torah scholars increase peace in the world, as it says, 'And all your children will be taught of God, and great will be the peace of your children' [Isa. 54:13]."[30]

D. EDUCATIONAL RESPONSIBILITIES

Tractate Bava Batra is about the laws of damages, and the second chapter deals with the extent of a person's responsibility for the damage that their actions may have caused to another's property.[31] There is a basic dispute – between the rabbis and Rabbi Jose – that pervades the whole chapter. The rabbis maintain that, in general, the responsibility of damage prevention is with the person who might cause that damage. Rabbi Jose agrees with this when the damage is caused directly, but when it is caused accidentally then he is of the opinion that the injured party should be held responsible for not taking reasonable precautions to avoid such accidental damage. So if a tree from your property accidentally falls into your neighbour's property and causes damage to it, then the rabbis would hold you responsible while Rabbi Jose would expect your neighbour to protect their property from such accidents and to be held responsible if they do not.

Once the theme of this second chapter is appreciated, it is more apparent how the discussion about the responsibility for the proper schooling of children

28. 1 Kgs. 2:5–6.
29. Sanhedrin 49a.
30. Berakhot 64a.
31. Bava Batra 17a–27b.

naturally emerges. Specifically, in the story of Yoav's education, we might view his mispronunciation of the word *z-kh-r* as damage caused to him by his schooling. But who is responsible? If the teacher was inadvertently inattentive when Yoav was practising his reading of that particular verse, then, following the rabbis, the teacher is to blame for his lapse of concentration, whereas following Rabbi Jose, Yoav is responsible for not making sure that his teacher was listening to him. However, all agree that if the teacher was negligent then he is to blame for Yoav's bad education.

This analysis gives a legal framework to responsibilities in the field of education. A child has a right to be taught well and neglect can lead to irrevocable damage. Though Yoav's menacing return to his childhood classroom is reprehensible, the educational system that produced him must take some responsibility for not teaching him effectively.

I have often taught this text to newly qualified teachers as a sober warning to them of the immense responsibility they now have to their pupils. Invariably they ask, "Well, did Yoav kill his teacher or not?" "No one knows," I answer with a knowing smile.

CONCLUSIONS

Though David cursed Yoav,[32] it was Yoav's curse on his childhood teacher, as taught by Rav Dimi of Nehardea, that teaches us that Jewish education is a matter of life and death.

We may sum up the four educational lessons from this text study as (A) the need for careful reading and comprehension,[33] (B) the importance attached to the correct application of sources, (C) the ability to nurture mediation skills rather than aggression, and (D) to engender a deep sense of responsibility before the law.

Not by chance, these lessons have always been the hallmarks of the educational approach of Emeritus Chief Rabbi, Lord Sacks. His meticulous reading of texts, masterful application of sources, ability to reach his audience through skilful communication, and profound reverence for Jewish law have made him a great teacher of Torah. The Jewish people is honoured and enriched by his many talents.

32. II Sam. 3:29.
33. "Military precision" in the classroom might be an apt expression here.

Contributors

Rabbi Dr Harvey Belovski is rabbi of Golders Green Synagogue. A graduate in mathematics from University College, Oxford, he gained *semikha* from Gateshead Yeshiva and subsequently earned a PhD in hermeneutics from Birkbeck, University of London. A sought-after speaker, broadcaster, mediator, and experienced counsellor, he is the principal of Rimon Jewish Primary School, a teaching and research fellow at LSJS, the rabbinic mentor of Chaplaincy, a lecturer at the JLE, the rabbi of PaL, the rabbi of Kisharon, the *rosh* of the Midrasha for women, and a tutor at the Montefiore College *semikha* course. This essay is adapted from a chapter of his PhD dissertation: "Harmonisation as Theological Hermeneutic: The Interpretative Methodology of Rabbi Shemuel Bornstein of Sochaczew".

Dayan Ivan Binstock is the rabbi of the St John's Wood Synagogue. He has been a member of the London Beth Din since 1989. In 1983, he succeeded Jonathan Sacks as rabbi of the Golders Green Synagogue. He is also principal of the Northwest London Jewish Day School and rabbinical advisor to Immanuel College.

Rabbi Shlomo M. Brody, a columnist for *The Jerusalem Post*, teaches at Yeshivat HaKotel and directs the Tikvah Overseas Seminars for Yeshiva and Midrasha Students. He is a presidential graduate fellow at Bar-Ilan University Law School and a junior scholar in the human rights and Judaism project at the Israel Democracy Institute. He has published numerous articles in scholarly and popular publications, and is the author of *A Guide to the Complex: Contemporary Halakhic Debates*.

Rabbi Dr Jeffrey M. Cohen retired in 2006 after having served as senior rabbi of the Stanmore Synagogue. He has also lectured in liturgy and Bible commentaries at Jews' College, London, and at Glasgow University, and has authored over twenty books and two hundred articles in scholarly and popular journals.

Rabbi Mendel Cohen is rabbi at the Saatchi Shul in London.

Rabbi Moshe Freedman was brought up in Kingston, South London, where he attended Tiffin School. He received his bachelor's degree in medical electronics from the University of Liverpool and master's and PhD in Medical Physics from the University of Surrey. Rabbi Freedman then spent five years at David Shapell College of Jewish Studies/Yeshivat Darche Noam in Jerusalem, receiving *semikha* from HaRav Zalman Nechemia Goldberg. Rabbi Freedman joined Northwood United Synagogue shortly before Pesach 2009 and is married with two children.

Rabbi Dr Barry Freundel is the rabbi of Kesher Israel, the Georgetown Synagogue, a Modern Orthodox synagogue in the heart of the US capital. He is associate professor of rabbinics at the Baltimore Hebrew Institute of Towson University and adjunct professor at Georgetown University Law School. He is author of *Contemporary Orthodox Judaism's Response to Modernity and Why We Pray What We Pray: The Remarkable History of Jewish Prayers*, as well as co-editor of the forthcoming *Truth, Debate and Traditional Jewish Thought*.

Rabbi Mordechai Ginsbury has served as a communal rabbi under the aegis of Chief Rabbi Sacks throughout Lord Sacks's term of office, initially as rabbi of the Prestwich Hebrew Congregation in Manchester and, since 1999, as rabbi of the Hendon United Synagogue, Raleigh Close, London. He was a member of Chief Rabbi Sacks's first 'cabinet', with responsibility for outreach and community development. He served as coordinator for the Rabbinical Council of the Provinces In-Service Training Programme from 1987, eventually becoming chairman of the RCP. He was elected chairman of the Rabbinical Council of the United Synagogue in 2005 and was subsequently appointed founding director of P'EIR (Promoting Excellence In Rabbis), the United Synagogue's in-house rabbinic skills and training enhancement programme, of which Lord Sacks is honorary principal.

Rabbi Shmuel Goldin has served as spiritual leader of Congregation Ahavath Torah in Englewood, New Jersey, since 1984. He is an instructor of Bible, philosophy, and Talmud at the Isaac Breuer College and the Mechina Program of Yeshiva University for over twenty years. He is founding director and lecturer at the Eve Flechner Torah Institute, honorary president of the Rabbinical Council of America, and a past president of the Rabbinic Alumni of Yeshiva University. Rabbi Goldin is the author of a series of books on the weekly Torah portion, *Unlocking the Torah Text.*

Rabbi Warren Goldstein has been the chief rabbi of South Africa since January 2005. As a national leader, the chief rabbi drives Torah, humanitarian, and educational initiatives across South Africa. A qualified *dayan,* Rabbi Goldstein's published books include *Sefer Mishpat Tzedek,* on the halakha of business competition, and *Defending the Human Spirit,* which presents the greatness of Torah law in areas of government, morality, and society. His most recent book, *The Legacy,* is co-authored with Rabbi Berel Wein, and presents a moral and strategic vision for the Jewish world today, based on the teachings of the great Lithuanian rabbis. Rabbi Goldstein has a PhD in human rights and constitutional law and is a regular columnist for *The Jerusalem Post.*

Rabbi Jonathan Hughes is rabbi of Richmond Synagogue and is the United Synagogue Living & Learning City Rabbi.

Rabbi Geoffrey Hyman Belfast-born, Rabbi Hyman has been a community rabbi in various London synagogues for over thirty-three years. He is currently rabbi of Ilford United Synagogue, the largest in North-East London. He is a graduate of Jews' College, Chaye Olam Yeshiva, London, and Gateshead Yeshiva.

Rabbi Shlomo Katanka is a fellow of the Kinloss Community Kollel, Finchley United Synagogue, London. He is the author of numerous articles on *minhagim* and the history of Jewish communities.

Rabbi Dr Alan Kimche was born in Melbourne in 1952 and came to London with his parents in 1958. He went on to yeshiva in Jerusalem, where he learned under the guidance of Rabbi Shlomo Zalman Auerbach, who became his lifelong mentor. He continued his studies at the Mir Yeshiva for a further five years under the guidance of Rabbi Hayim Shmulevitz. In 1976, he married Via Evers from Amsterdam, with whom he has seven children. Since 1984 he has been the rabbi of the vibrant community that is Ner Yisrael, London. He received his doctorate from London University in 2005 with a thesis entitled "*Kavod Habriyot*: Human Dignity in Talmudic Law".

Rabbi Anthony Knopf is rabbi of Camps Bay Shul in Cape Town, South Africa. Prior to this he was associate rabbi at Hampstead Garden Suburb Synagogue in London.

Rabbi Michael Laitner is the director of education for United Synagogue Living & Learning, assistant rabbi at Finchley Synagogue (Kinloss) in London, attendant rabbi at its Ashkenazi services, and a qualified solicitor.

Rabbi Dr Aharon Lichtenstein, a disciple of Rabbi Joseph B. Soloveitchik, is a graduate of Yeshiva University and holds a PhD in English literature from Harvard University. He served as a *rosh yeshiva* and *rosh kollel* at Yeshivat Rabbenu Yitzchak Elchanan for several years before joining Rabbi Yehuda Amital in leading Yeshivat Har Etzion in Gush Etzion. He has been co-*rosh yeshiva* of that institute for over forty years.

Rabbi Eugene Newman, MA was the predecessor of Chief Rabbi Sacks at Dunstan Road Synagogue. He was widely recognized as one of the leading historians of the Anglo-Jewish community.

Rabbi Michael Pollak is an educational consultant to a variety of UK Jewish organisations, including the UJIA and PaJes, specializing in the pedagogy of the Jewish classroom. He teaches *daf yomi* and gives various Talmud *shiurim*.

Rabbi Zorach Meir Salasnik has been the rabbi of Bushey United Synagogue since 1979. He is also the Senior Jewish Hospital Chaplain. He is a former chairman of the Rabbinical Council of the United Synagogue and former secretary of the Chief Rabbi's Cabinet.

Rabbi David Shabtai, MD teaches Jewish Perspectives on Bioethics as part of the Straus Center for Torah and Western Thought of Yeshiva University, as well as teaches medical halakha at RIETS and at Lander College for Men. He is the author of *Defining the Moment: Understanding Brain Death in Halakhah*.

Rabbi Rashi Simon, BA, MA, was born in the USA and has been active in adult education and outreach in the UK since 1989. He is the founding director of

Kesher/The Learning Connection and is the coordinator of the Gerut Programme of the London Beth Din.

Rabbi Joseph B. Soloveitchik (1903-1993) was not only one of the outstanding Talmudists and rabbinic leaders of the twentieth century, but also one of its most creative and seminal Jewish thinkers. Teaching at Yeshiva University for over four decades, he influenced thousands of students and contributed vitally to the dramatic resurgence of Orthodox Judaism in America.

Rabbi Adin Steinsaltz is a teacher and thinker who has devoted his life to making the Talmud accessible to everyone. Originally published in Hebrew, his Steinsaltz Edition of the Talmud has also been translated into English, French, Russian, and Spanish.

Rabbi Gil Student is the publisher and editor-in-chief of the Torah Musings website. He wrote a widely quoted blog on Torah issues and has published across Jewish media.

Rabbi Gideon Sylvester is the United Synagogue's Israel rabbi. He was previously rabbi of Britain's fastest-growing Modern Orthodox community, Radlett United Synagogue. Since making *aliya* he has served as an adviser at the Office of the Prime Minister of Israel and directed the Beit Midrash for Human Rights and Torah at the Hillel House of the Hebrew University of Jerusalem.

Rabbi Dr Akiva Tatz is a South African-born physician, author, and lecturer. He is founder and director of the Jerusalem Medical Ethics Forum, which teaches and promotes knowledge of Jewish medical ethics internationally. He has written a number of books on the subject of Jewish thought and philosophy: *Anatomy of a Search, Living Inspired, Worldmask, The Thinking Jewish Teenager's Guide to Life,* and *Letters to a Buddhist Jew*. His most recent work is *Dangerous Disease and Dangerous Therapy in Jewish Medical Ethics*. He currently teaches at the Jewish Learning Exchange in London and internationally, and recordings of his lectures are widely distributed.

Rabbi Meir Triebitz attended the Juilliard School of Music and holds a degree in mathematical physics from Princeton University. Rabbi Triebitz serves as a second-year Talmud Rebbe at Machon Shlomo, as well as a teacher of philosophy, halakha, and Ḥumash. When not teaching at Machon Shlomo, he runs two different kollels and teaches classes on his ever-popular website, hashkafacircle.com.

Rabbi Nissan Wilson is the rabbi of Clayhall United Synagogue and vice chair of the RCUS. He studied in Gateshead Yeshivah and Heichal HaTorah, Jerusalem. Whilst in Israel, he gained his *semikha* and lectured at Ohr Somayach's Shoresh and Center programmes, before returning to London in 2004. He is currently working on a PhD in education, focusing on intra-religious dialogue and divergent goals in religious education.

Rabbi Dr Raphael Zarum is Dean of the London School of Jewish Studies. He received rabbinic ordination from Chief Rabbi Lord Jonathan Sacks after studying at the Kollel of the Judith Lady Montefiore College. Raphael is the creator of the Torah L'Am crash course and is the author of the Torat Hadracha and Jampacked Bible educational study guides. He is a leading Jewish educator in the UK and teaches at conferences and seminars, synagogues and Jewish community centres across the globe. In 2008 he was ranked 26th in the Jewish Chronicle Power 100 list of the most influential people in UK Jewry.

About Rabbi Jonathan Sacks

Jonathan Sacks became the sixth Chief Rabbi of the United Hebrew Congregations of the Commonwealth in 1991, having previously been Principal of Jews' College, as well as rabbi of the Golders Green and Marble Arch synagogues. After achieving first class honours in Philosophy at Gonville and Caius College, Cambridge, he pursued postgraduate studies in Oxford and London, gaining his doctorate in 1981, and receiving rabbinic ordination from Jews' College and Yeshivat Etz Chaim. He is currently Visiting Professor of Theology at King's College London. He holds 14 honorary degrees, including a Doctor of Divinity conferred to mark his first ten years in office by the Archbishop of Canterbury, Lord Carey.

Rabbi Sacks has received numerous prizes, including the Jerusalem Prize in 1995 for his contribution to diaspora Jewish life, and regularly contributes to the national media, delivering BBC Radio's 'Thought for the Day' and writing for the 'Credo' column in *The Times*. He has written more than two dozen books, several of which have won awards, including the Grawemeyer Prize for Religion for *The Dignity of Difference*, and a National Jewish Book Award for *A Letter in the Scroll*.

Rabbi Sacks was knighted by Her Majesty the Queen in 2005 and made a Life Peer, taking his seat in the House of Lords in October 2009 as Baron Sacks of Aldgate in the City of London.

Born in 1948 in London, he has been married to Elaine since 1970. They have three children and six grandchildren.

Dedicated in loving memory of Rosalind Beckman *z"l*
by her husband, Brian and her sons, Jonathan, Daniel, and Joshua
in tribute to Rabbi Jonathan Sacks who married us and
who has been a friend and an inspiration.

Wishing the Chief Rabbi a happy and healthy retirement.
Best wishes, Charlotte & Elliot Benjamin

Lord Sacks is a world renowned and respected inspirational,
moral, and religious leader. His publications changed social
and moral thinking and challenged us to look deeply at our
prejudices and preconceptions. Esther & Simon Bentley

לזכר נשמות רבקה בת משה ניסן ז״ל וישראל יצחק בן מיכאל הכהן ז״ל

With grateful thanks to Lord Jonathan Sacks. A brilliant
Chief Rabbi, leader, writer, and orator.
In loving memory of my father Joel C Breslauer *z"l*.
Keith & Lauren Breslauer and Family

In honour of my Mother, Dr Susan Lees, on her 70th birthday.
May Hashem bless you with many happy and healthy
years and nachas from your children.
Noah Bulkin

To Lord Sacks. A wise wonderful irreplaceable man. We are so proud to
be a small part of this tribute. Gillian and Irving Carter and family

In honour of the Bar Mitzva of Elie Elmalem.
Thiery and Catherine Elmalem

In honour of the ninety-first birthday of Ralph Emanuel

In cherished memory of Judge Israel Finestein and his wife Marion

Dedicated by Evelyn & Ronnie Gorney in memory of:
Cecil Joshua Israel (יהושע בן אהרן שלמה הלוי ז״ל)
Helga and Kurt Gorney
Yekutiel ben Chaim *z"l*
Chana ben Eliyahu Refael

We are delighted to be associated with this publication
in honour of such a great *Talmid Chacham.*
Karen & Jonathan Hodes

In memory of Clara Hunter, daily missed by her family, and in whose blessed memory, her sons read Kaddish daily with the Chief Rabbi – who provided support, guidance and friendship.

Honoured to be associate with this tribute, in memory of
Berry and Phyllis Page

In loving memory of our beloved grandfather
Cyril E Lee, Reb Yisrael Menachem Ben Reb Shlomo Dov HaLevi.
From Debbie & Joshua Krasner & Family

In loving memory of
our father and grandfather, Rabbi Maurice Landy
הרב מרדכי בן שמחה הלוי, who would have loved this book
our mother and grandmother, Rachel רחל בת אהרן זאב
and my brother Arnold Woolf Landy אהרן זאב

With grateful thanks to Lord Jonathan Sacks.
In loving memory of William Lobel Ze'ev ben Chaim HaLevi
and Richard Lobel Raphael ben Ze'ev Halevi. Lobel Family

With grateful thanks to Lord Jonathan Sacks. A brilliant
Chief Rabbi, leader, writer, and orator.
In loving memory of our dear parents Jascha and Helga Lossos
Chaim and Deborah Steinfeld

הרה״ח כתריאל בלומנפלד הי״ד
נתבקש לשמיים בירושלים בח׳ אדר א׳ תשל״ח

With grateful appreciation for helping in the creation of the Ner Yisrael Community
Pam & Jerry Shatzkes

For Micky B, Binyamin Shlomo, Rina, Doniel Moshe, Ariella Sara, Jacob Aaron
and any more grandchildren to come
Havi and Jonathan Stewart

לעילוי נשמת
R. Yonah Avraham ben Shmuel Storfer *z'l* and
R. Shabsai ben Menachem Mendel Blinder *z'l*

Dedicated in memory of Margit Tenenblat and her
children Julia aged 16 Henrich aged 12.
Perished in the Holocaust Budapest 2nd July 1944.

Dedicated to the memories of Minne Trent and Jack Steuer.
By Jeremy & Monica Trent

In the name of Joseph and Devorah Wineman.
By their chidren Bernard, Hadassah, Vivian, & David

In memory of Joe & Marjorie Feigenbaum

In memory of the unforgettable Myrtle Lovat
Lawrence Lovat and family

לעלוי נשמת
שלמה בן אברהם קאלמן
From Debbie and Avram and Children

In Memory of רחל בת אשר and יצחק בן שמואל
The Rogoff Family

The fonts used in this book are from the Arno family

Maggid Books
The best of contemporary Jewish thought from
Koren Publishers Jerusalem Ltd.